# The Great War at Sea
## A Naval History of the First World War

This is a major new naval history of the First World War, which reveals the decisive contribution of the war at sea to Allied victory. In a truly global account, Lawrence Sondhaus traces the course of the campaigns in the North Sea, Black Sea, Atlantic, Adriatic, Baltic, and Mediterranean, and examines the role of critical innovations in the design and performance of ships, wireless communication, and firepower. He charts how Allied supremacy led the Central Powers to attempt to revolutionize naval warfare by pursuing unrestricted submarine warfare, ultimately prompting the United States to enter the war. Victory against the submarine challenge, following their earlier success in sweeping the seas of German cruisers and other surface raiders, left the Allies free to use the world's sea lanes to transport supplies and troops to Europe from overseas territories, and eventually from the United States, which proved a decisive factor in their ultimate victory.

**Lawrence Sondhaus** is Professor of History at the University of Indianapolis, where he is Director of the Institute for the Study of War and Diplomacy. His previous publications include *Naval Warfare, 1815–1914* (2001), *Strategic Culture and Ways of War* (2006), and *World War One: The Global Revolution* (2011).

# The Great War at Sea

A Naval History of the First World War

Lawrence Sondhaus

CAMBRIDGE UNIVERSITY PRESS

# CAMBRIDGE
UNIVERSITY PRESS

University Printing House, Cambridge CB2 8BS, United Kingdom

Cambridge University Press is part of the University of Cambridge.

It furthers the University's mission by disseminating knowledge in the pursuit of education, learning and research at the highest international levels of excellence.

www.cambridge.org
Information on this title: www.cambridge.org/9781107036901

© Lawrence Sondhaus 2014

This publication is in copyright. Subject to statutory exception and to the provisions of relevant collective licensing agreements, no reproduction of any part may take place without the written permission of Cambridge University Press.

First published 2014

Printed in the United Kingdom by Clays, St Ives plc

*A catalogue record for this publication is available from the British Library*

ISBN 978-1-107-03690-1 Hardback

Cambridge University Press has no responsibility for the persistence or accuracy of URLs for external or third-party Internet websites referred to in this publication, and does not guarantee that any content on such websites is, or will remain, accurate or appropriate.

# CONTENTS

*List of figures*  vii
*List of maps*  ix
*Acknowledgments*  x

Introduction  1

1  Ambition, ideology, and arms races  8

2  Preparing for war  30

3  Global prelude  62

4  European waters, 1914–15  94

5  Submarine warfare: the great experiment, 1915  136

6  Combined operations, 1915  171

7  The year of Jutland: Germany's fleet sorties, 1916  204

8  Submarine warfare: the great gamble, 1917–18  241

9  War and Revolution, 1917  278

10  Final operations   309

Conclusion: peace and naval disarmament   352

*Bibliography*   371
*Index*   381

# FIGURES

| | | |
|---|---|---|
| 1.1 | Admiral Alfred von Tirpitz (source: Bundesarchiv, Bild 134-B2595) | page 12 |
| 1.2 | HMS *Dreadnought* (source: Naval Historical Foundation) | 16 |
| 1.3 | Austro-Hungarian dreadnought *Tegetthoff* (source: Bundesarchiv, Bild 134-B1653) | 23 |
| 2.1 | Guglielmo Marconi (source: Alamy, BA7P3N) | 33 |
| 2.2 | Admiral Sir John Fisher (source: Getty Images, 184255304) | 50 |
| 2.3 | British Grand Fleet at sea (source: Getty Images, 90769469) | 56 |
| 3.1 | Vice Admiral Maximilian von Spee (source: Bundesarchiv, Bild 134-B2899) | 65 |
| 3.2 | The *Scharnhorst* at Valparaiso, with *Gneisenau* in background (source: Bundesarchiv, Bild 183-R36018) | 77 |
| 3.3 | Battle cruiser HMS *Inflexible* (source: Bundesarchiv, Bild 134-B2517) | 83 |
| 4.1 | Admiral Anton Haus (source: public domain image) | 100 |
| 4.2 | Vice Admiral Augustin Boué de Lapeyrère (source: Amazon) | 105 |
| 4.3 | Admiral Sir David Beatty (source: Getty Images, 53371024) | 115 |
| 4.4 | Admiral Franz von Hipper (source: Bundesarchiv, Bild 183-R10665) | 126 |

| | | |
|---|---|---|
| 5.1 | U 53 surfaced with crew (source: Getty Images, 3249687) | 144 |
| 5.2 | Admiral Duke of the Abruzzi (source: Getty Images, 134573278) | 166 |
| 5.3 | Admiral Sir Reginald Bacon (source: Alamy, CF95TG) | 169 |
| 6.1 | French battleship *Bouvet* (source: Getty Images, 184249074) | 177 |
| 6.2 | Gallipoli landing, 1915 (source: Alamy, B4101D) | 180 |
| 6.3 | William II meeting Enver Pasha aboard *Goeben* (source: Imperial War Museum) | 188 |
| 6.4 | Captain (later Admiral) Aleksandr Kolchak (source: Getty Images, 170980972) | 200 |
| 7.1 | Vice Admiral Reinhard Scheer (source: Bundesarchiv, Bild 134-B2958) | 206 |
| 7.2 | German dreadnought *Friedrich der Grosse* (source: Bundesarchiv, Bild 134-B0747) | 209 |
| 7.3 | Admiral Sir John Jellicoe (source: Getty Images, 3287236) | 215 |
| 7.4 | The badly damaged *Seydlitz* after Jutland (source: Imperial War Museum) | 224 |
| 7.5 | Vice Admiral Souchon with staff (source: Alamy, BBWCX5) | 236 |
| 8.1 | Admiral William S. Sims (source: Getty Images, 78957428) | 253 |
| 8.2 | Captain (later Rear Admiral) Miklós Horthy (source: Alamy, CPMPPH) | 267 |
| 8.3 | Captain Lothar von Arnauld de la Perière (source: Bundesarchiv Bild, 134-B2604) | 274 |
| 9.1 | Pavel Dybenko (source: Alamy, B9PN6K) | 282 |
| 9.2 | Horse scow as landing craft (source: Bundesarchiv, Bild 146-1977-101-42) | 293 |
| 9.3 | Wreck of the *Slava*, following the Battle of Moon Sound (source: public domain image) | 301 |
| 10.1 | Sinking of the *Szent István* (source: Bundesarchiv, Bild 134-C1133) | 317 |
| 10.2 | Aircraft carrier HMS *Argus* (source: Naval Historical Foundation) | 334 |
| 11.1 | Vice Admiral Ludwig von Reuter (source: Alamy, CP1PEE) | 355 |

# MAPS

| | | |
|---|---|---|
| 1.1 | The North Sea | *page* 4 |
| 1.2 | The Baltic Sea | 4 |
| 1.3 | The Black Sea | 5 |
| 1.4 | The Adriatic and Ionian seas | 6 |
| 1.5 | The North Atlantic Ocean | 7 |
| 3.1 | German East Asian Squadron | 71 |
| 4.1 | Mediterranean Sea showing the flight of the *Goeben* | 103 |
| 6.1 | Gallipoli and the Dardanelles | 183 |
| 7.1 | Battle of Jutland | 220 |
| 9.1 | The Gulf of Riga | 295 |

# ACKNOWLEDGMENTS

I would like to thank my editor at Cambridge University Press, Michael Watson, for giving me the opportunity to write this book. I am grateful for the thoughtful suggestions of the reviewers of my initial proposal, one of whom eventually read the full manuscript and, along with my editor, provided detailed comments which were very helpful in shaping the finished product. Finally, I would like to acknowledge family and friends, colleagues and students for their support and patience during the year in which this project dominated my life.

# INTRODUCTION

In the Great War of 1914–18, a conflict distinctive first and foremost for its unprecedented bloodshed, less than 1 percent of the 8.5 million combatant deaths were naval personnel lost at sea. Such a disproportionate distribution of the human sacrifice might lead one to conclude that the Great War at sea had, at best, a peripheral significance to the final outcome, and yet no serious scholar has ever made such an argument. Prior to 1914, in history's most expensive arms race to date, Britain defied the expectations of Germany in making the financial sacrifice necessary to maintain its naval superiority. Largely because of this superiority, the Allies were able to keep the fleets of the Central Powers contained in the North Sea, Baltic, and Adriatic, and to impose blockades on Germany and Austria-Hungary that, by 1916, contributed to serious food shortages in both countries. Faced with an insurmountable Allied supremacy in surface warships, the Central Powers attempted to revolutionize naval warfare by giving a central, offensive role to the submarine, a vessel originally conceived for a peripheral, defensive role (primarily as a harbor defender, against enemy blockade). In refocusing their efforts on undersea warfare, they created the issues that prompted the United States to intervene in a war in Europe, an unprecedented and, ultimately, decisive development. The focus on submarine warfare also caused the Central Powers to leave their capital ships rusting at anchor for much of the war, with dire consequences for the morale of most of their seamen. In 1917–18, Germany and Austria-Hungary (along with Russia, whose Baltic and Black Sea fleets had been similarly idled) experienced serious naval mutinies, and revolutionary movements in all three countries attracted significant numbers of sailors. By the end of the war, the victory of the Allies against the submarine challenge, following on their earlier success in sweeping the seas of German cruisers and other surface raiders, left them free to use the world's sea lanes to transport supplies and troops to Europe from their overseas territories, and eventually from the United States, without which their ultimate victory could not have been accomplished. Thus, while the overwhelming majority of the effort, and the casualties, came on land, the action at sea was undeniably decisive to the outcome of the war.

Each of the following chapters is framed to explain why the naval war mattered in the course of the Great War. For example, in Chapter 3, discussion of the early Allied victory in the naval war beyond Europe (1914–15) emphasizes the significance of this triumph for the subsequent free movement of food, fuel, and other materials essential to the Allied war effort, and, of course, for the exploitation of the manpower of the British dominions and India, the French colonies, and the United States, millions of troops whose deployment facilitated Allied victories on land in Africa, the Middle East, and, later in the war, in Europe. Chapter 4 discusses the role of naval considerations in prompting the Ottoman Empire to join the Central Powers and Italy to join the Allies, and the sequence of events that allowed the Allies to secure the Mediterranean in a way they would not in the Second World War, at least until 1943–45. Chapters 5 and 8, which deal primarily with German submarine warfare and the Allied response to it, address the complexities of the wartime Anglo-American relationship, both before and after the entry of the United States into the war in April 1917, and the impact of the Allied blockade of the Central Powers in determining the overall outcome of the war. Finally, the Anglo-American relationship at the peace conference and into the early postwar era will dominate the Conclusion, which will address the naval consequences of the emergence of the United States as the world's leading economic power and net creditor, and Britain's unaccustomed role as debtor, factors which provided the context for the Washington Naval Treaty (1922) and the interwar regime of naval disarmament.

Each chapter also highlights how the naval dimension of the Great War mattered in the evolution of warfare at sea. For example, Chapters 1 and 2 include discussion of the pre-1914 quest of navies to secure a prominent strategic role, as well as their efforts to adjust to dramatic improvements in the speed and firepower of warships. Chapter 2 highlights the role of wireless communication in the global naval campaign of 1914–15, foreshadowing its significance during the rest of the war and in the Second World War. Chapter 5 focuses on the introduction of unrestricted submarine warfare and the Allied countermeasures against it, such as Q-ships (armed merchantmen with concealed guns) and the antisubmarine barrages at the Straits of Dover and Otranto. Chapter 6 uses the Allied failure at Gallipoli as a case study of unsuccessful combined (navy–army) operations, and compares it with the failure of the German combined operations at Riga the same year, discussing the lessons learned that influenced future combined operations. In Chapter 7, analysis of the Battle of Jutland compares the British and German navies in a variety of areas: command, control, and communications; tactical and operational cooperation across ship types; design, durability, and performance of ship types; firepower and fire control. Chapter 8, on the resumption of unrestricted submarine warfare and the entry of the United States into the war, discusses the political and practical challenges that had to be overcome in order to develop an effective inter-Allied system of convoys. Chapter 9, encompassing the final operations involving Russia, includes the second, successful German combined operation at Riga, and discusses its impact on the future of amphibious warfare. In general, the comprehensive approach recognizes the war's place in naval history as the last in which every country considered a Great Power – eight in this case – possessed truly significant naval power. The conclusion highlights the role of the postwar disarmament talks, coming in the wake of the demise of the navies of the Central Powers, as a step in the broader process of reducing the number of great naval powers to the three of the Second World War, two of the Cold War, and one in the twenty-first century.

As in my general study of the war,[1] the chapters presented here reflect a synthesis of the best scholarship on the subject, and also benefit from my own expertise on Germany and Austria-Hungary. In comparison with other general English-language accounts of the topic, this account of the naval war places greater emphasis on the strategies and operations of the Central Powers, reflecting my broader conclusion that at sea, as well as on land, the Great War may be conceptualized as a series of Allied reactions to the actions of Germany and Austria-Hungary, and my conviction that understanding their actions is key to understanding the war as a whole.

---

[1] Lawrence Sondhaus, *World War I: The Global Revolution* (Cambridge University Press, 2011).

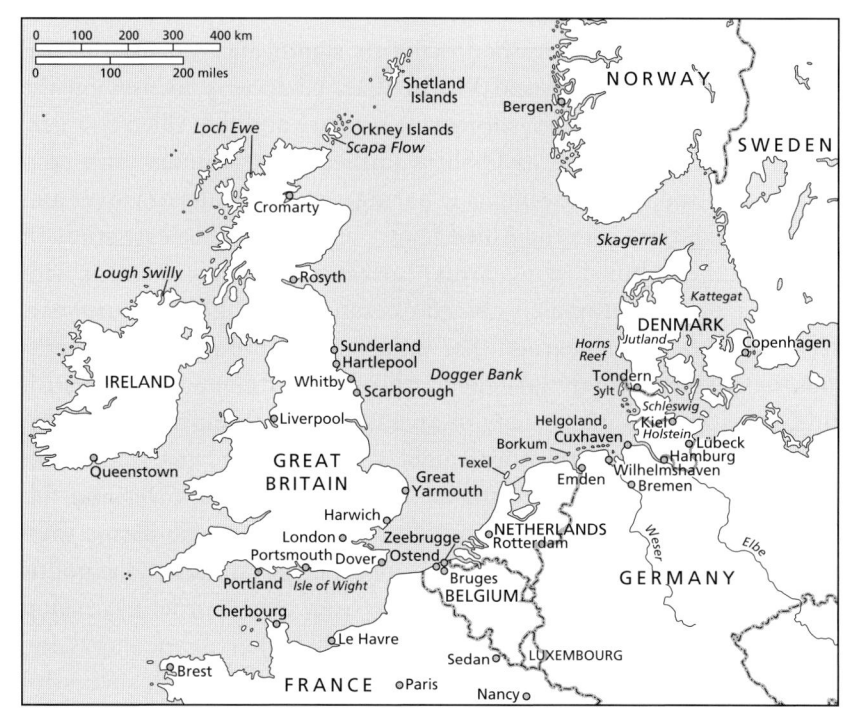

**Map 1.1** The North Sea

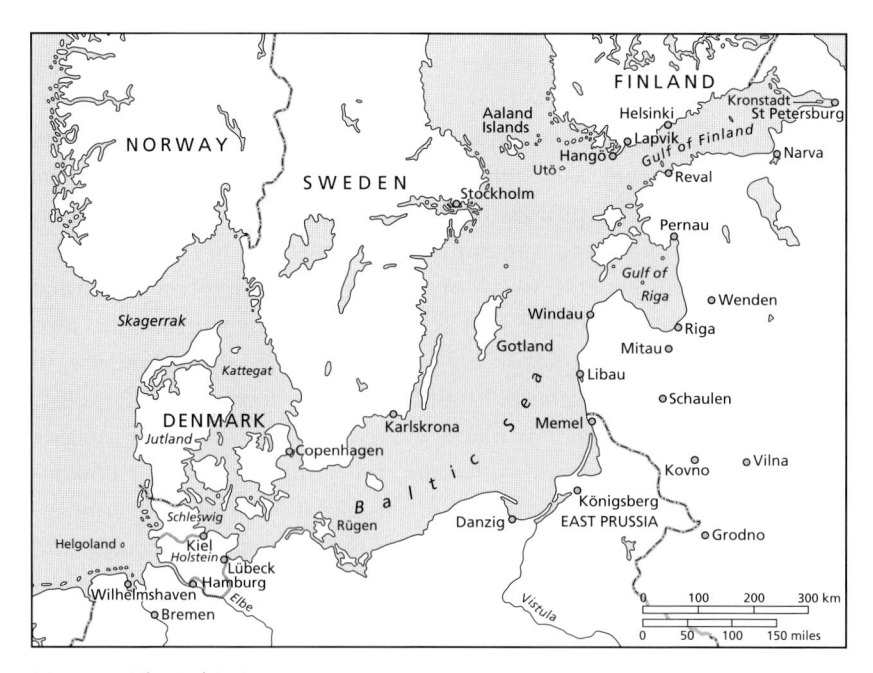

**Map 1.2** The Baltic Sea

Map 1.3  The Black Sea

Map 1.4 The Adriatic and Ionian seas

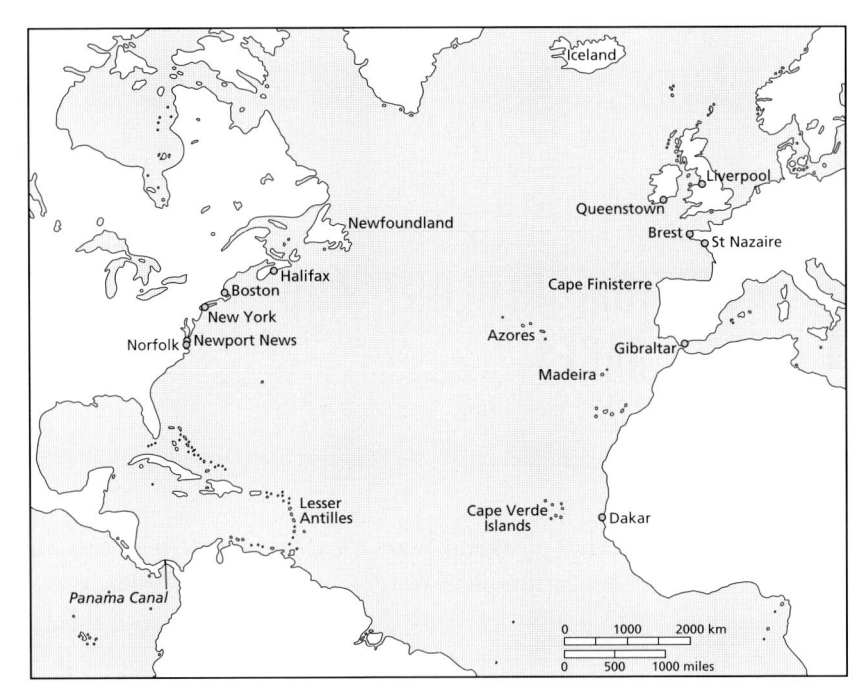

Map 1.5  The North Atlantic Ocean

# 1 AMBITION, IDEOLOGY, AND ARMS RACES

During the Franco-Prussian War (1870–71), while the Prussian army recorded a series of triumphs from Sedan to the gates of Paris, the modest north German fleet languished at anchor. Alfred Tirpitz, then a twenty-one-year-old *Unterleutnant*, spent most of the war at Wilhelmshaven aboard the *König Wilhelm*, one of three armored frigates in a German navy that was far too weak to take on a French fleet that featured seventeen ships of the same type. "We youngsters were ... indignant at not being let loose on the enemy," Tirpitz recalled later, but material inferiority dictated a passive posture. Thus, afterward, "the campaign which had been so glorious for the army lay heavy on the navy."[1] Admiral Prince Adalbert, cousin of King William I, and, since 1848, the greatest champion of Prussian sea power, underscored the navy's irrelevance by spending the war with the army. Owing to the inconsequential role played by the navy, it was allowed a representation of just twenty-two officers and seamen in the massive postwar victory parade held in Berlin in June 1871. In a time of great national triumph, the younger generation of German sea officers had difficulty dealing with such humbling experiences. Within a year, more naval officers transferred to the army than had done so in the previous decade.

Over the past century countless historians have stressed the significance of Prussia's triumph over France in 1871 in establishing the conditions that eventually led to the First World War. After the

---

[1] Alfred von Tirpitz, *My Memoirs*, 2 vols. (New York: Dodd, Mead, 1919), vol. 1, pp. 9–11.

decisive victory by Prussia and its German allies, Chancellor Otto von Bismarck's decision to proclaim William I as German emperor at the Palace of Versailles further humiliated the French. Thereafter, Bismarck's insistence that France cede Alsace-Lorraine to the new German empire (Second Reich) made it impossible for the two countries to live in harmony and difficult for others to have close relations with both of them, thus providing the catalyst for a Europe of competing alliance systems. Finally, the requirement that France should pay a substantial indemnity to the victors set the precedent for the reparations that France would expect Germany to pay when the outcome was reversed in 1918. In addition to these political and diplomatic consequences, 1871 also confirmed the newly unified Germany as Europe's foremost military power, displacing France. The cult of the offensive that affected all European armies by the turn of the century had its roots in the Prussian–German way of war. Karl von Clausewitz's *On War* was translated and studied throughout Europe, often with a Darwinian preface, and the German military – its strategy, tactics, organization, and armaments – became a model for the rest of the world. But the Franco-Prussian War had equally fateful naval consequences. For Tirpitz, the humiliation of 1870–71 helped to form his belief that Germany must have a navy strong enough to engage any other fleet.[2] The quest to erase that humiliation ultimately placed Germany's navy and naval ambitions at the center of a reordering of European alliances, an arms race of unprecedented cost, and the development of new tactics and technologies, all of which shaped the character of the Great War at sea.

## The German navy from unification to the Tirpitz plan

After 1871 the Imperial German navy grew considerably, but not to a coherent grand design. Over the next dozen years, the three armored frigates and two smaller ironclads on hand during the war against France were joined by a hodgepodge of eleven additional armored warships of various types. As early as 1883 Germany at least briefly had the

---

[2] On the effects of 1870 on Tirpitz, see Volker R. Berghahn, *Der Tirpitz-Plan: Genesis und Verfall einer innenpolitischen Krisenstrategie unter Wilhelm II* (Düsseldorf: Droste, 1971), pp. 58–59.

third largest armored fleet behind Britain and France, and the following year the Second Reich belatedly entered the scramble for colonial possessions, claiming territories in Africa and the Pacific. But the country only slowly developed a self-sufficient naval–industrial complex. Some German warships were built in British shipyards, and almost all of the rest had British armor plate or other components imported from Britain; the *Oldenburg*, commissioned in 1886, was the first battleship in the fleet constructed entirely of German steel. Meanwhile, during the 1870s and 1880s, a "Prussian school" of naval thought slowly evolved. Rooted in the military thought of Clausewitz, the "Prussian school" promoted an offensive posture, ironically for a navy materially incapable of assuming it.[3] In 1888, the accession of William II, a naval enthusiast who viewed Britain as Germany's role model and principal rival, ushered in an era of increased warship construction, coinciding with the emergence of Krupp (already world-renowned for its artillery) as the world leader in armor production. Yet throughout the first decade of the new reign, naval expansion continued to follow no particular plan; Germany's largest new battleships, the four units of the 10,000-ton *Brandenburg* class, were dwarfed by their British contemporaries of the 14,150-ton *Royal Sovereign* class, and the most replicated new battleship design, the eight 3,500-ton coastal defenders of the *Siegfried* class, were too small to have much fighting value.

In 1890, an American naval officer, Alfred Thayer Mahan, published *The Influence of Sea Power upon History, 1660–1763*, the first of a series of books in which he provided battle-fleet proponents with historical arguments to support their cause. Drawing his examples from the early modern competition for empire between Britain and France, Mahan promoted the notion that "command of the sea" had been won or lost in decisive engagements between concentrated fleets of ships of the line, the battleships of the wood-and-sail era. His lively narratives of a bygone era of naval warfare deliberately played down the significance of cruising ships such as frigates, which the leading naval powers had traditionally dispersed worldwide to patrol the sea lanes and to protect their colonies. Mahan's works were especially influential in Germany,

---

[3] On the "Prussian school," see Rolf Hobson, *Imperialism at Sea: Naval Strategic Thought, the Ideology of Sea Power, and the Tirpitz Plan, 1875–1914* (Boston, MA: Brill, 2002), ch. 3.

where his followers included William II and Tirpitz, neither of whom had been enthusiastic advocates of the battleship. During the 1880s, Tirpitz had embraced the concepts of the French *Jeune École*, which emphasized torpedo boats and cruisers; he rose to become head of the navy's torpedo service before reading Mahan and turning to the battleship in 1891. William II, meanwhile, had advocated the cruiser as the warship type best suited to support his dream of a global German colonial and commercial presence, and only slowly came round to the battleship even after his first reading of Mahan. As early as 1893, when Tirpitz was still a captain, serving as chief of staff in the High Command in Berlin, a critique of the navy's annual maneuvers encouraged officers to remedy their deficient education in "tactics and strategy" through the "study of naval history," especially "the works of Captain Mahan."[4]

Because Mahan shared many strategic assumptions with Clausewitz, the earlier work of the navy's own "Prussian school" accelerated the reception of his ideas in Germany; for example, both Mahan and the "Prussian school" emphasized the Napoleonic–Nelsonian faith in the offensive and the quest for the decisive battle. But, because the "Prussian school" reflected the continental focus of Clausewitz, Tirpitz needed the underpinning of Mahan to formulate a strategic vision for Germany in which the navy would have a central role. Starting with his *Dienstschrift IX* of June 1894, he advocated a battleship-centered fleet concentrated in home waters. Tirpitz appreciated the need to translate his vision into specific material goals, as reflected in his initial appeal for a 4:3 standard of superiority over either the French Northern Fleet or Russian Baltic Fleet (whichever was larger).[5] Subsequently, in his famous "risk theory," first disclosed publicly in December 1899, he argued that a fleet two-thirds the size of the British navy would have sufficient strategic value to justify the high cost of building it. Tirpitz frequently invoked Mahan during his campaign to expand the fleet. After he became state secretary of the Imperial Navy Office, he distributed several thousand copies of the 1895 German translation of Mahan's

---

[4] "Relation über die Herbstmanöver der Marine im Jahre 1893," Bundesarchiv-Marinearchiv, RM 4/62, pp. 104–184 (especially pp. 160–184); see also Lawrence Sondhaus, *Preparing for Weltpolitik: German Sea Power before the Tirpitz Era* (Annapolis, MD: Naval Institute Press, 1997), p. 196.

[5] Patrick J. Kelly, *Tirpitz and the Imperial German Navy* (Bloomington, IN: Indiana University Press, 2011), p. 96.

Figure 1.1 Admiral Alfred von Tirpitz

first book (its first non-English edition) to support his arguments for the First Navy Law.[6]

In June 1897, shortly after his appointment as state secretary, Tirpitz warned William II that Britain was Germany's "most dangerous enemy... against which we most urgently require a certain measure of naval force as a political power factor."[7] The emperor likewise viewed Britain as the obvious obstacle to Germany's further rise to world power, and eagerly endorsed Tirpitz's plan for a further expansion of the fleet, even though it would bring an end to the generally

---

[6] Hobson, *Imperialism at Sea*, pp. 242–246; Ivo Lambi, *The Navy and German Power Politics, 1862–1914* (Boston, MA: Allen & Unwin, 1984), p. 66.

[7] Tirpitz, quoted in Jonathan Steinberg, *Yesterday's Deterrent: Tirpitz and the Birth of the German Battle Fleet* (New York: Macmillan, 1965), p. 126.

friendly relations the two countries had enjoyed since German unification. Tirpitz also enjoyed the support of foreign secretary (later chancellor) Bernhard von Bülow. Alluding to the boast "the sun never sets on the British Empire," late in 1897 Bülow introduced the bill that the Reichstag soon passed as the First Navy Law with the observation "we now demand our place in the sun."[8] The German Foreign Office's support of naval expansion confirmed just how much things had changed since William II forced Bismarck into retirement in 1890. The old chancellor never considered the British fleet to be a threat to Germany and, as recently as 1889, had lauded British naval power as "the greatest factor for peace in Europe."[9] A Germany satisfied with hegemony over the European mainland had no reason to clash with a Britain focused on dominating the oceans and its colonies.

The Tirpitz plan, developed at a time when Germany was gaining on Britain's leading position in trade and industry, ultimately led Britain to join France and Russia in the Triple Entente, dividing the six Great Powers of Europe into two rival armed camps and making a general war far more likely. Yet Tirpitz's first moves were not considered to be threatening to a Britain still convinced that France and Russia, as the second and third naval powers, were its greatest rivals, not potential allies. Even before the Franco-Russian alliance and military convention (1892–94), the Naval Defence Act of 1889 formally established the heretofore traditional "two-power standard" as the measure of British naval superiority, stipulating that the Royal Navy must be as strong as the second- and third-strongest navies combined. Thanks to the construction program of 1889 and a supplementary program begun in 1894, in direct response to the Franco-Russian alliance, the British fleet of 1898 included twenty-nine battleships and twenty-one first-class cruisers commissioned within the past ten years, far surpassing the combined effort of France (twelve battleships and eight large cruisers) and Russia (eleven battleships and five large cruisers) during the same period.

Compared with navies of such size and strength, Tirpitz's initial proposal seemed modest indeed. His First Navy Law, passed by

---

[8] Bülow, quoted in Terrell D. Gottschall, *By Order of the Kaiser: Otto von Diederichs and the Rise of the Imperial German Navy, 1865–1902* (Annapolis, MD: Naval Institute Press, 2003), p. 226.

[9] Bismarck, quoted in Charles William de la Poer Beresford, *The Memoirs of Admiral Lord Charles Beresford*, 2 vols. (Boston, MA: Little, Brown, 1914), vol. 2, p. 363.

the Reichstag in April 1898, called for Germany to have a fleet that included nineteen high-seas battleships, eight coastal battleships, and twelve large cruisers by 1905, but the totals counted ships commissioned as early as 1878. The battleship number included twelve already built or under construction; the large cruisers included ten already built or under construction; while the coastal battleships comprised the eight 3,500-ton *Siegfried*s already in service. Before passing the First Navy Law, the Reichstag deputies focused their attention on the number of new warships needed to meet its goals – including seven battleships and two large cruisers – largely overlooking Tirpitz's provision for the future automatic replacement of battleships after twenty-five years and large cruisers after twenty years. The international situation soon favored Tirpitz's quest for a much greater commitment to naval expansion. Swept up in the anti-British sentiment prevailing during the Anglo-Boer War in South Africa (1899–1902) and outraged over the Boxer Rebellion in China (1900), where the German ambassador and German missionaries had been among the first foreigners killed, the Reichstag in June 1900 passed the Second Navy Law. Much more than the First Navy Law, the new legislation (raising the authorized strength of the fleet to thirty-eight battleships and fourteen large cruisers) reflected Tirpitz's conviction that a battle fleet in home waters would give Germany leverage in all international conflicts, including those far from home. The newly authorized units included eleven battleships (the eight small *Siegfried*s were now counted as full-sized battleships for replacement purposes), but only two large cruisers. The Second Navy Law solidified Tirpitz's reputation as the Second Reich's most successful politician, after Bismarck. William II showed his gratitude by elevating Tirpitz to the nobility later in 1900 and awarding him a number of other high honors.

    The automatic replacement provision of Tirpitz's navy laws, guaranteeing that a future more left-wing legislature could not undo his master plan, took on greater significance as the years passed and the anti-military Social Democratic Party (SPD) became by far the largest party in the Reichstag, with its share of representatives growing from 14 percent in 1898 to 28 percent in 1912. By 1906, all but one of the authorized thirty-eight battleships and all fourteen large cruisers were either in commission or under construction, and that year Tirpitz secured Reichstag approval for a supplementary law further increasing the number of large cruisers to twenty. With the next large cruiser not due for its twenty-year replacement until 1912, the six new large cruisers filled the gap of 1906–12 and guaranteed that one of the type would be laid down every year indefinitely. At the same time, at least one new battleship (and in some years two or three) would be laid down every year as well, without further approval from the Reichstag. Because it was assumed that replacement ships would have to measure up to the standards of the time in which they were ordered, the Navy Laws allowed Tirpitz to replace smaller old warships with larger new ones. Eventually, the oldest battleships in the fleet of 1898 (the four 7,600-ton *Sachsen*-class battleships, dating from 1878–83) were replaced by four 18,900-ton battleships of the *Nassau* class, while the smallest, the eight 3,500-ton *Siegfried*s, were replaced by units of the 22,800-ton *Helgoland* class and the 24,700-ton *Kaiser* class.[10]

## Dreadnoughts and battle cruisers

During its first years the German naval buildup caused little alarm in Britain. Admiral Sir John Fisher, appointed First Sea Lord in 1904, had entered the Royal Navy at the age of thirteen during the Crimean War. Throughout his fifty years of service, Britain's naval rivals had been France or Russia, or a combination of both, and Fisher initially considered them its most likely future enemies. Fisher had a well-deserved reputation as an innovator. His past accomplishments included the introduction, in the 1890s, of a new ship type, the destroyer (initially called "torpedo boat destroyer"), to counter the torpedo boat threat of the French *Jeune École*. Born in Ceylon (Sri Lanka), the son of an army officer, Fisher's career at sea included four tours of duty beyond European waters; not surprisingly, he viewed the navy's mission in global terms, centered on the defense of the empire and the sea lanes linking British possessions to one another and to the mother country.

To face down the Franco-Russian challenge to these vital interests, he now proposed another new ship type, the battle cruiser: a battleship-sized cruiser, armed with battleship guns, but with some of its armor plating sacrificed for the sake of speed. These features would enable the battle cruiser to outgun any warship that it could not

---

[10] Erich Gröner, *Die deutschen Kriegsschiffe, 1815–1945*, 8 vols. (Coblenz: Bernard & Graefe, 1989), vol. 1, pp. 46–50.

Figure 1.2 HMS *Dreadnought*

outrun, and vice versa. Laying down his first capital ships in 1905–6, Fisher placated battleship proponents with the *Dreadnought*, a ship of 18,110 tons, with ten 12-inch (30.5-cm) guns, armor as thick as 11 inches (28 cm), and a speed of 21 knots, while ordering three battle cruisers of the *Invincible* class, ships of 17,370 tons, with eight 12-inch guns, no more than 6 inches (15.2 cm) of armor, and a speed of 25 knots. The *Dreadnought*, built in just fourteen months (October 1905–December 1906), was intended as a test platform for the unprecedented hull size, all big-gun armament, and turbine engines that would also be featured in the three *Invincible*s. Yet during the brief time the *Dreadnought* was under construction, changes in the international arena determined that battleships of its type, and not battle cruisers, would be the core of the future British fleet. The Anglo-French Entente Cordiale (1904) survived the Moroccan crisis of 1905, and the Russo-Japanese War (1904–5) practically destroyed the Russian navy; meanwhile, the German navy, further strengthened by the supplementary law of 1906, far surpassed the French to emerge as Britain's most likely adversary. Under these circumstances, battleships of the *Dreadnought* design, better suited for warfare in the confined space of the North Sea, appeared more useful than battle cruisers, whose potential global range was no longer as relevant.[11]

Because the size, speed, and firepower of the *Dreadnought* rendered all other battleships obsolete, it became the new model capital ship not just for the British fleet, but for the rest of the world's navies as well. At the same time, the introduction of the battle cruiser brought a worldwide halt to armored cruiser construction. For Britain, Fisher's new designs represented a considerable gamble as well as a new departure. Over the preceding century, the French had been responsible for virtually every breakthrough in warship design (the steam-powered battleship, the armored battleship, the steel cruiser, the torpedo boat, and finally the submarine), in each case hoping to overcome British naval superiority through innovation, only to have Britain use its considerable industrial superiority to build more and better units of each type. Now, Britain was taking the lead as innovator, in the process negating its own considerable advantage over Germany in battleships subsequently classified as "pre-dreadnoughts" (units as old as the *Royal Sovereign*s of 1889 and the *Brandenburg*s of 1890), of which Britain had fifty to Germany's twenty-three, and its even greater advantage in first-class armored cruisers, of which Britain had thirty-five to Germany's eight.

By wiping the slate clean and giving Germany a reasonable chance to catch up, Britain precipitated a naval arms race of unprecedented intensity and cost. The onset of the "dreadnought revolution" raised the stakes by forcing Germany to build much larger (and much more expensive) battleships than had been anticipated in the Navy Laws of 1898 and 1900, but Tirpitz did not shrink from the challenge, indeed, he increased German naval spending still more by insisting that

---

[11] This "revisionist" account of the "dreadnought revolution" is reflected in the works of Jon Tetsuro Sumida, especially *In Defence of Naval Supremacy: Finance, Technology, and British Naval Policy, 1889–1914* (London: Unwin Hyman, 1989), and Nicholas A. Lambert, *Sir John Fisher's Naval Revolution* (Columbia, SC: University of South Carolina Press, 1999). Shawn T. Grimes, *Strategy and War Planning in the British Navy, 1887–1918* (Woodbridge: Boydell Press, 2012), pp. 41–74, dates active planning against the German threat from 1902. Other scholars less convinced of the "accidental" nature of the "dreadnought revolution," include John Brooks, "Dreadnought: Blunder or Stroke of Genius?" *War in History*, 14 (2007): 157–178, and Matthew S. Seligmann, "New Weapons for New Targets: Sir John Fisher, the Threat from Germany, and the Building of HMS *Dreadnought* and HMS *Invincible*, 1902–1907," *International History Review*, 30 (2008): 303–331.

future units in the "large cruiser" category be built as battle cruisers, even though no other European navy copied the design from the British. The type had no particular relevance to the German strategic situation, yet it appealed to Tirpitz because it would allow him to build another twenty battleship-sized vessels under legislation already approved by the Reichstag. These, plus the thirty-eight battleships already approved, would give him a fleet of fifty-eight capital ships (dreadnoughts and battle cruisers), against which Britain would have to build at least ninety in order to maintain better than a 3:2 margin of superiority. Tirpitz's inclusion of battle cruisers in this program gave Fisher an excuse to do likewise in every budget prepared until his retirement, at age sixty-nine, in January 1910. Recent scholarship has revealed Fisher's use of the threat of Germany's world-class ocean liners being armed in wartime as justification for continued battle cruiser construction, and suggests that he may have had this in mind as a mission for them all along.[12]

Tirpitz embraced the changes in capital ship design even though in the short term they caused his fleet to fall farther behind the British. The Germans laid down their last pre-dreadnought battleship, the final unit of the 13,200-ton *Deutschland* class, in August 1905, just two months before the British began work on the *Dreadnought*. They laid down their first dreadnought, the *Nassau*, in June 1907, by which time the British had the *Dreadnought* itself in service and another four dreadnoughts under construction, along with the three battle cruisers of the *Invincible* class. The *Nassau* displaced 18,900 tons, 43 percent more than the *Deutschland* (compared to the *Dreadnought*'s 18,110 tons, just 13 percent more than the last British pre-dreadnoughts of the *Lord Nelson* class), and its construction placed unprecedented demands on the German naval–industrial complex. Rather than delay the *Nassau* and its three sister ships any longer, Tirpitz had them fitted with a primary armament of the same 11-inch (28-cm) guns as previous classes of German battleships, and with triple-expansion engines capable of just 19.5 knots. As long as it took for Germany to gear up for the production of warships as large as the *Dreadnought*, it would have taken longer still to produce its equal in firepower and speed.

---

[12] Matthew S. Seligmann, *The Royal Navy and the German Threat 1901–1914: Admiralty Plans to Protect British Trade in a War Against Germany* (Oxford University Press, 2012), pp. 65–88.

## The prewar naval arms races

In 1908, the Reichstag passed another supplementary law, allowing Tirpitz to accelerate battleship construction. By March 1909, he had laid down Germany's second class of dreadnoughts, the four units of the 22,800-ton *Helgoland* class, still slower than their British counterparts (owing to their triple-expansion engines), but equal in armament, with 12-inch (30.5-cm) guns. Meanwhile, in the "large cruiser" category, Tirpitz followed the 15,800-ton armored cruiser *Blücher* (laid down in 1907) with the 19,400-ton *Von der Tann* (1908) and 23,000-ton *Moltke* (1909), Germany's first battle cruisers and first capital ships with turbine engines. These projects combined allowed Germany almost to pull even with Britain in the naval arms race, because Parliament had funded just two new capital ships (one dreadnought and one battle cruiser) in its budget for 1908–9. By March 1909, Germany had ten dreadnoughts and battle cruisers built or under construction to Britain's twelve, and was on pace to achieve near-parity in capital ships.

Thereafter the British moved decisively to stay ahead in the competition. At the end of March 1909, Parliament approved the naval estimates for 1909–10, including six dreadnoughts and two battle cruisers. Work would start on three dreadnoughts and one battle cruiser by December 1909, with the rest to follow by April 1910 if Germany refused to end the competition. Extremists in Britain called for negotiations based on a "two-German" standard, which Germany was certain to reject. Cooler heads prevailed at the Admiralty, which abandoned the two-power standard in April 1909 in favor of a 60 percent capital ship advantage over Germany. At the time, however, Tirpitz held out for a 4:3 ratio of British superiority. Seeing no chance for a settlement, in July 1909, the House of Commons authorized the remainder of the program for the spring of 1910. The House of Lords held up the measure for months to protest the plan by Britain's Liberal government to finance the so-called "four-plus-four" program by raising taxes on the wealthiest Britons. Nevertheless, by May 1910, Britain had laid down all eight capital ships of its 1909–10 program, and further widened its lead when Australia and New Zealand paid for two battle cruisers, begun in British shipyards in June 1910. They were the last of an astonishing ten capital ships laid down for the British navy within a span of twelve months, demonstrating a resolve to make whatever financial sacrifices were necessary to stay ahead. During the same months, Germany began just three: the first two dreadnoughts of the 24,700-ton *Kaiser* class and the 22,600-ton battle cruiser *Goeben*.

Thus, a year after nearly achieving parity with the British in capital ships built-and-building, Tirpitz faced a 22:13 deficit. He had assumed all along that his naval construction program could push Britain to a breaking point, beyond which it would be unwilling or unable to maintain its superiority. Proven wrong, he became more amenable to negotiations, and in 1911 offered to accept a 3:2 (15:10) British advantage in capital ships, close to Britain's goal of a 60 percent (16:10) advantage, as long as the British included in their total the battle cruisers *Australia* and *New Zealand*, along with any future ships funded by the overseas dominions. At the same time, attempting to use the fleet as the political lever Tirpitz had always claimed it would be, Chancellor Theobald von Bethmann Hollweg insisted that an Anglo-German naval treaty should be part of a broader agreement requiring Britain's explicit recognition of the territorial status quo in Europe, including Germany's possession of Alsace-Lorraine. The British found these conditions unacceptable, and the race continued. In 1910–11 and again in 1911–12, the Germans laid down four capital ships (three dreadnoughts and one battle cruiser) and the British, five (four dreadnoughts and one battle cruiser), narrowing the capital ship ratio slightly, to 32:21. Meanwhile, displacement tonnage and gun calibers increased, while further improvements in turbine design kept speeds at 21 knots for dreadnoughts and 26–27 knots for battle cruisers. Falling short in the quantitative race, the Germans sought a qualitative edge, but here too they had difficulty in keeping up. The new German capital ships of 1911–12 were the first three dreadnoughts of the 25,800-ton *König* class and the 26,600-ton battle cruiser *Derfflinger*, all armed with 12-inch (30.5-cm) guns. Britain responded with four dreadnoughts of the 25,000-ton *Iron Duke* class and the 28,430-ton battle cruiser *Tiger*, all armed with 13.5-inch (34.3-cm) guns.

In February 1912, Britain sent its Secretary of State for War, Lord Haldane, to Berlin in a final attempt to reach a settlement, but Bethmann Hollweg's insistence that any Anglo-German naval treaty must include broader political conditions doomed the negotiations before any discussion of numbers took place. The recently appointed First Lord of the Admiralty, Winston Churchill, subsequently poisoned relations still more by publicly calling the German navy a "luxury" fleet. Tirpitz rejected Churchill's idea of a one-year "naval holiday," and in March persuaded the Reichstag to pass another supplementary navy law adding three more battleships to the authorized strength of the German fleet. It would be his last political victory, as the following year the Reichstag funded a significant expansion of the long-neglected German army. By 1913–14, the navy's share of the German defense outlay fell to just under 25 percent, down dramatically from an all-time high of over 35 percent in 1911–12. The navy budget still included one new battle cruiser per year (the 26,700-ton *Lützow* in 1912–13 and the future *Hindenburg* in 1913–14), but just one new *König*-class dreadnought in 1912–13 and the first two 28,500-ton *Bayern*-class dreadnoughts in 1913–14. Against these five capital ships, Britain over the same two years laid down ten (all dreadnoughts, following Fisher's retirement from the Admiralty): the *Queen Elizabeth* and *Royal Sovereign* classes, giant battleships displacing 27,500–28,000 tons, armed with eight 15-inch (38-cm) guns.

The increasing size, speed, and firepower of warships naturally drove up their cost. The British had built the *Dreadnought* for just under £1.73 million, but the *Queen Elizabeth*, begun seven years later, cost just over £2.68 million. On the German side, the *Nassau* had been built for just under 37 million marks, while the *Hindenburg*, completed eight years later, cost 59 million marks. Yet when politicians and statesmen viewed their country's maritime interests in holistic Mahanian terms, such financial sacrifices appeared reasonable. In 1902, before the introduction of the dreadnought and battle cruiser had escalated naval spending, the future Lord Haldane remarked in the House of Commons that the annual outlay for the British navy, when considered in light of the total value of the country's commerce, was "not an extravagant premium of insurance."[13] Indeed, the value of Britain's surplus of exports over imports alone far exceeded the naval estimates. By 1913, the "premium" had gone up, the naval estimates (£44.4 million) for the first time exceeding 10 percent of the total value of British overseas trade (£434.1 million), but even then Britain's trade surplus (£39.1 million) equaled 88 percent of the year's outlay for the navy, making the "premium" still appear to be reasonable. At the

---

[13] Quoted in Avner Offer, *The First World War: An Agrarian Interpretation* (Oxford: Clarendon Press, 1989), p. 218.

end of July 1914, Britain had twenty-nine capital ships in service and thirteen under construction, while Germany had eighteen in service and eight under construction. The British public paid dearly for this margin of superiority, but the First World War would demonstrate that the financial sacrifice had not been made in vain.

While Tirpitz's program made the German navy the world's second-largest behind the British, it also undermined the Triple Alliance, a cornerstone of German foreign policy dating from Bismarck's time. The pact was already in trouble even before Tirpitz introduced his plan, because, from its birth in 1882, Germany's partners, Italy and Austria-Hungary, were fundamentally incompatible allies. Italians and Austrians had fought each other in five wars since 1815, most recently in 1866, and acquiesced in their mutual friendship only as the price of an alliance with Germany, which Austria-Hungary valued for protection against Russia, and Italy for support against France. But the alignment made sense for Italy only as long as Britain remained a potential enemy of France and on friendly terms with Germany. Italian leaders had hoped the Franco-Russian alliance would pressure the British either to join the Triple Alliance or form a separate Anglo-Italian Mediterranean pact, and were disappointed when neither happened. In December 1900, Italy secretly came to terms with France, agreeing to the future French annexation of Morocco in return for French acceptance of the future Italian annexation of Libya; oblivious to these machinations, in the same month Germany and Austria-Hungary finally agreed to a long-standing Italian demand for a Triple Alliance naval convention, pledging common action in the Mediterranean against France and Russia! Thereafter, Italy considered Austria-Hungary its greatest potential naval adversary, and for Austria-Hungary, less naive than Germany on the question of Italy's trustworthiness, the feeling was mutual.[14] In the years before 1914 Europe's greatest naval race outside the North Sea centered in the Adriatic, pitting the nominal allies against one another.

After embracing cruisers and torpedo boats during the era of the *Jeune École*, in 1893 both Italy and Austria-Hungary resumed their battleship programs. At the onset of the dreadnought revolution Italy

---

[14] Sondhaus, *Preparing for Weltpolitik*, pp. 195, 220; Lawrence Sondhaus, *The Naval Policy of Austria-Hungary: Navalism, Industrial Development, and the Politics of Dualism, 1867–1918* (West Lafayette, IN: Purdue University Press, 1993), pp. 132, 156–157, 210, 236; Christopher Seton-Watson, *Italy: From Liberalism to Fascism, 1870–1925* (London: Methuen, 1967), pp. 181–183, 212.

**Figure 1.3** Austro-Hungarian dreadnought *Tegetthoff*

had eight pre-dreadnought battleships built or under construction to Austria-Hungary's nine, but all the Italian battleships displaced over 10,000 tons, while six of Austria-Hungary's were smaller than that. During the same years, Italy built six armored cruisers to Austria-Hungary's three. Emperor Francis Joseph remained indifferent toward the navy, but his heir, Archduke Francis Ferdinand, embraced its cause and became its leading patron. In a multinational empire suffering serious internal divisions, the fleet grew to enjoy the support of a broad domestic political coalition. The Dual Monarchy had also developed a first-rate naval–industrial complex, and had demonstrated that it could build battleships much faster than Italy, indeed, faster than anyone other than Britain and Germany.[15]

In November 1906, one month before the completion of the *Dreadnought*, Austro-Hungarian legislators authorized the three pre-dreadnoughts of the 14,500-ton *Radetzky* class, the last of which was not laid down until January 1909. During the same period, Italy proceeded with four more armored cruisers, even as Britain and Germany

[15] The source for this paragraph and the next is Sondhaus, *The Naval Policy of Austria-Hungary*, pp. 173, 180–183, 191–198, 203–204, 231–247, 274.

built their first battle cruisers. Italian navy leaders proposed starting a dreadnought program in the 1907–8 fiscal year, but their plans were approved only after the Austro-Hungarian naval commander, Admiral Count Rudolf Montecuccoli, proposed a new fleet plan including four 20,000-ton dreadnoughts. In June 1909, Italy laid down its first dreadnought, the 19,550-ton *Dante Alighieri*, the first battleship designed to carry its heavy guns, twelve of 12-inch (30.5-cm) caliber, in triple-gun turrets, with all four turrets on the centerline. Meanwhile, a constitutional crisis in Hungary paralyzed the Dual Monarchy's legislative process from April 1909 to May 1910, delaying the first of the four Austro-Hungarian dreadnoughts, the *Viribus Unitis*, until July 1910, followed by the *Tegetthoff* (for which the class was named), laid down in September. Like the *Dante Alighieri*, the *Tegetthoff*s were armed with twelve 12-inch (30.5-cm) guns, divided among four centerline triple-gun turrets. Shortly before work began on these ships, the Italian parliament approved the three 22,990-ton dreadnoughts of the *Cavour* class, which were laid down in June, July, and August of 1910. In January 1912, Austria-Hungary laid down its third and fourth dreadnoughts; within two months, Italy responded by starting work on its fifth and sixth. Thanks to its more efficient shipyards, in October 1912 Austria-Hungary became the first European country after Britain and Germany to have a dreadnought in commission, when the *Viribus Unitis* entered service after a building time of just twenty-seven months. The *Dante Alighieri* was commissioned in January 1913, forty-three months after it was laid down. Each navy had three dreadnoughts in commission at the outbreak of the First World War.

During the years from 1911 to 1914, the Ottoman Empire and Greece engaged in a brief naval arms race of their own, accelerated by their involvement in the Balkan Wars of 1912–13, during which the Greeks seized more of the Aegean islands from the Turks. After purchasing two obsolete 10,000-ton *Brandenburg*-class pre-dreadnoughts from Germany in 1910 – the *Kurfürst Friedrich Wilhelm* (renamed *Barbaros Hayreddin*) and *Weißenburg* (renamed *Torgud Reis*) – the Ottoman navy turned to British shipbuilders, contracting Vickers to lay down the 23,000-ton dreadnoughts *Reşadiye* (in August 1911) and *Fatih Sultan Mehmed* (in June 1914), and Armstrong to complete the 27,500-ton dreadnought *Sultan Osman-i Evvel*, initially laid down for Brazil under the name *Rio de Janeiro*. The Greeks countered by ordering one dreadnought from the German shipbuilder Vulcan (the 19,500-ton *Salamis*, begun in July 1913), another from the St. Nazaire shipyard in France (the 23,500-ton *Basileos Konstantinos*, begun in June 1914), and purchasing two pre-dreadnoughts from the United States, the 13,000-ton *Kilkis* (ex-*Mississippi*) and *Limnos* (ex-*Idaho*), in June 1914. Anticipating the Ottoman Empire's alliance with Germany, at the outbreak of war in August 1914 the British seized the *Reşadiye* and *Sultan Osman-i Evvel* for use by the Royal Navy, and broke up the newly laid keel of the *Fatih Sultan Mehmed*. Greece's dreadnought projects fared no better, as Vulcan launched the *Salamis* in November 1914, but never completed it, while St. Nazaire barely started work on the *Basileos Konstantinos* before abandoning the project.

France, like Austria-Hungary, lost valuable time in the dreadnought race by proceeding with the construction of pre-dreadnought battleships already approved at the time the *Dreadnought* entered service, in its case the six 18,320-ton units of the *Danton* class. Europe's largest and most powerful pre-dreadnoughts, the *Danton*s all entered service in 1911, by which time ten countries had dreadnoughts built or under construction (the other five European naval powers plus Spain, the United States, Japan, Argentina, and Brazil) and four had dreadnoughts in commission (Britain, Germany, the United States, and Brazil).[16] The first French dreadnoughts, the four units of the 22,190-ton *Courbet* class, were approved in April 1910 and laid down in 1910–11, followed by the three 23,230-ton *Bretagne*s, begun during 1912, and the five 25,230-ton *Normandie*s, laid down in 1913–14, the latter representing a considerable sacrifice, coinciding with a massive increase in the outlay for the French army. The first of the *Courbet*s entered service in June 1913, the last in August 1914, giving France four dreadnoughts in service and another eight under construction when the war began. Despite its late recovery, France between 1905 and 1914 dropped from second place to a distant third among Europe's naval powers and, beyond Europe, was also passed by the United States and Japan.

Of course, France's alignment with Britain in the Entente Cordiale of 1904 made naval construction a less pressing matter. The same

---

[16] Ray Walser, *France's Search for a Battle Fleet: Naval Policy and Naval Power, 1898–1914* (New York: Garland, 1992), pp. 144–146, 180–196; Paul G. Halpern, *The Mediterranean Naval Situation, 1908–1914* (Cambridge, MA: Harvard University Press, 1971), pp. 54–57.

was true for Russia, whose 1907 rapprochement with Britain completed the third leg of the Triple Entente. At sea as well as on land, the Russian armed forces recovered remarkably quickly from their humiliating defeats at the hands of Japan (1904–5). By 1910, Russia commissioned five pre-dreadnoughts under construction when the Russo-Japanese War ended, which joined the units that had survived destruction in 1905 to give the Russian fleet thirteen battleships and six armored cruisers. The design of the four dreadnoughts of the 23,360-ton *Gangut* class, laid down in June 1909 in St. Petersburg, featured twelve 12-inch (30.5-cm) guns in four centerline triple-gun turrets. All four were launched in 1911 and completed in time to enter service in the Baltic Fleet late in 1914. During 1911, three dreadnoughts of the 22,600-ton *Imperatritsa Maria* class, a design very similar to the *Gangut*s, were laid down at Nikolaiev for the Black Sea Fleet. The cost of the dreadnought program practically tripled Russian naval expenditure, from 87 million rubles in 1908 to 245 million rubles in 1913, over 25 percent of the overall defense outlay, but the money was not well spent. After the shocking losses of 1904–5, the Russian navy maintained an offensive outlook in the Black Sea but not in the Baltic, where the security of the capital, St. Petersburg, dictated a cautious approach that challenged the admirals to make meaningful use of big, expensive battleships.[17]

The emerging non-European powers, Japan and the United States, joined the leading states of Europe in expanding their navies before 1914. The Japanese navy went to war against Russia in 1904 with a fleet that included six pre-dreadnought battleships and eight armored cruisers, of which ten were built in Britain, the rest in other European countries. Two of the battleships were lost to mines during the war, but afterward the Japanese navy incorporated warships the Russians had either surrendered at Tsushima or scuttled at Port Arthur, including eight battleships and one armored cruiser, renovation projects that enabled it to expand rapidly but added little to the fighting strength of the fleet. While Japan's victory over Russia was impressive enough, its dependence on foreign shipyards weakened its claim to first-rate naval power. The trend had continued during the war, when

---

[17] Stephen McLaughlin, "Russia: Rossiiskii imperatorskii flot," in Vincent P. O'Hara, W. David Dickson, and Richard Worth (eds.), *To Crown the Waves: The Great Navies of the First World War* (Annapolis, MD: Naval Institute Press, 2013), pp. 213–256.

the British built two more battleships for Japan (completed 1906). But in the years from 1905 to 1907, the Japanese laid down the first larger warships in their own shipyards: two 13,750-ton armored cruisers of the *Tsukuba* class (completed in 1907–8); two armored cruisers of the *Ibuki* class (completed in 1909–11); and two battleships of the 19,370-ton *Satsuma* class (completed in 1910–11). The *Satsuma*s were the largest pre-dreadnoughts ever built, but they took an inordinately long time to complete (fifty-eight and sixty months) and, like the armored cruisers, had imported guns, armor, and engines. Japan's first dreadnoughts, two units of the 21,440-ton *Settsu* class (completed in 1912), carried twelve 12-inch (30.5-cm) guns imported from Britain, but were built largely with domestic resources, including Krupp armor and Brown–Curtis turbine engines produced under license in Japan. They were also built much faster (thirty-five and forty-two months) than the *Satsuma*s, attesting to the improving efficiency of the shipyards. Japan laid down two dreadnoughts of the 30,600-ton *Fuso* class in 1912–13, which remained under construction when the war began. In 1913, the navy added its first battle cruiser, the 27,500-ton *Kongo*, built in Britain by Vickers; while it was under construction, Japanese shipyards laid down its three sister-ships in 1911–12, one of which was completed in early August 1914, in just thirty-three months. At that stage the Japanese had four dreadnoughts and four battle cruisers built-or-building; counting the four pre-dreadnoughts added since the 1905 war and the four newest armored cruisers (which they rated as battle cruisers), the figures were eight battleships and eight battle cruisers.

This "eight-eight" fleet met a standard the Japanese navy had set in 1910, but it fell short of the goal of a fleet that was 70 percent as strong as the United States Navy, deemed necessary if Japan were to have any chance of defeating the United States in a future war. The United States, like Germany, had made a considerable recent investment in warships that the dreadnought and battle cruiser rendered obsolete: twenty-five pre-dreadnought battleships and twelve armored cruisers (completed between 1893 and 1908), all of which were still on hand when the First World War began, minus the two pre-dreadnoughts sold to Greece. And, like the Germans, the Americans had continued their naval buildup undeterred, viewing the clean slate as a positive rather than as a negative development. Starting with the 16,000-ton *South Carolina* class (completed in 1910), the United States Navy built five pairs of dreadnoughts in the prewar years, ever-larger ships culminating in the 27,000-ton *New York* class (completed in 1914), at which time another four were already on the slips and would be completed during the war, including the 31,400-ton *Pennsylvania* and *Arizona*. These gave the United States fourteen capital ships built or building, more than anyone other than Britain and Germany.

During the prewar arms races the six European powers built all their capital ships in their own shipyards; beyond Europe, the United States and, eventually, Japan did likewise. At a time when dreadnought-type battleships were the largest, most expensive, and most technologically sophisticated weapons systems in existence, it became the mark of true Great Power status to be able to produce one's own entirely from domestic resources, a badge of national greatness analogous to the ability to produce nuclear weapons later in the century. Indeed, the high stakes and high degree of secrecy made the Anglo-German naval race the first truly modern arms race, a competition of a character not to be seen again until the nuclear arms race of the Cold War.

## Conclusion

With the influential works of Mahan providing the ideological backdrop, the decade of the 1890s brought a general consensus that navies should be battleship-centered, and that future naval wars, like the Anglo-French wars for empire in the early modern period, would hinge on decisive encounters between battle fleets. A Europe whose continental conflicts, since the age of Napoleon, had been brief and decisive, readily accepted the notion that wars at sea likewise could be resolved by one or two great battles. In a world in which all great navies were European, the logic that maritime interests worldwide were best defended by a battle fleet based in home waters gained general acceptance, further reinforcing the primacy of the battleship over the cruising vessels traditionally tasked with policing sea lanes and defending overseas colonies. The logic held even after the United States and Japan joined the first rank of naval powers. Within this context, Britain's introduction of new capital ship types, the dreadnought and battle cruiser, further fueled the general competition in battleship-building. The naval race between Britain and Germany far surpassed all others in scope and cost, but concurrent competitions between traditional enemies (Greece and Turkey), ostensible allies (Italy and Austria-Hungary), and future adversaries (Japan and the United States) were no less bitter.

Overall, the extent to which the geopolitical realities of Europe in 1914 had been shaped by the ambitions of Germany, and by the reactions of others to the rise of German power, can hardly be overstated. Tirpitz's quest to make Germany respected at sea as well as on land, endorsed by his emperor and a broad coalition of people, parties, and interests within the Second Reich, had fateful consequences. In the last days of the July Crisis of 1914, Russia's decision to mobilize first brought even the anti-war, anti-navy Social Democrats into the fold in the Reichstag's unanimous vote for war credits. Without a German navy to threaten the security of Britain in the same way as the German army threatened France and Russia, it is difficult to imagine Britain aligning itself with its traditional adversaries, thus creating the context for the German army's violation of Belgium to result in the British standing by the French in the greatest and costliest war yet fought.

# 2 PREPARING FOR WAR

"Your apparatus... would be of use to the service, if the signals could be made over three miles."[1] Captain Henry Jackson thus seemed to set the bar high for Guglielmo Marconi, the twenty-two-year-old Italian inventor who, three months earlier, in June 1896, had secured a British patent for his wireless telegraph. In British naval history, Jackson is best known for his eighteen months as First Sea Lord in 1915–16, served between terms of the legendary Fisher, called out of retirement at the onset of war, and Sir John Jellicoe, promoted out of command of the Grand Fleet after Jutland. But to Jackson himself, the most significant years of his career came two decades earlier, when, as captain aboard the torpedo depot ship *Defiance*, he joined the growing number of scientists and entrepreneurs experimenting with wireless telegraphy. In August 1896, the same month that he met Marconi, he succeeded in sending a signal nearly 55 yards (50 m), the longest working distance available to him aboard the *Defiance*.[2] He soon learned that his Italian counterpart had developed equipment similar, but far superior, to his own. Indeed, the previous summer, in experiments conducted outside his native Bologna, Marconi had transmitted signals 1.5 miles (2.4 km) between two points out of sight of each other. The patriotic inventor had informed Italian authorities of the breakthrough, but they failed to grasp its significance, wished him well, and urged him to make the

---

[1] Jackson to Marconi, September 12, 1896, quoted in Russell W. Burns, *Communications: An International History of the Formative Years* (London: Institution of Electrical Engineers, 2004), p. 294.
[2] Ibid., p. 286.

technology available for public use. Taking advantage of his British connections and ability to speak English (his Irish mother was heiress to the Jameson whiskey fortune), Marconi took his wireless telegraph to Britain, secured his patent, then conducted a series of demonstrations that earned endorsements from experimenters such as Jackson, who had attempted their own wireless transmissions and thus appreciated Marconi's innovations.[3]

In 1896, as in antiquity, men aboard a ship out of sight of land or another ship were completely cut off from the rest of humanity. That isolation was about to end. Within less than two decades, wireless telegraphy would enable navies to command and control ships at sea, over great distances, in a manner heretofore unimaginable. The Great War would be the first in which the action hinged on communication technology, especially during those months of 1914–15 when the conflict remained a true "world war," but even after that, once the conflict was confined, for the most part, to the waters around Europe. In addition to enemy warships and merchant vessels, wireless stations and island stations on undersea cable lines figured prominently on the target lists of the belligerents, confirming the premium everyone placed on reliable telegraph connections. As the war progressed, wireless signals were used not just to maintain contact with one's own ships, but also to determine the location of the enemy. The exploitation of radio waves eventually transformed range-finding and targeting devices as well, but that marriage of technologies would be left to the next generation and the next world war. Thus, coinciding with the prewar naval arms races, Britain, Germany, and the other leading naval powers raced to develop wireless technology, anticipating the significance it would have in a future war at sea, while in a separate and parallel process also competing to develop more effective range-finding technologies and gunnery tactics to exploit the ever-greater capabilities of naval artillery.

## Navies, wireless, and global communication

After attending other demonstrations held by Marconi in Britain over the winter of 1896/7, Jackson achieved a breakthrough of his own in May 1897: using wires fixed in the *Defiance*'s masts in emulation of

[3] *Ibid.*, pp. 288–293.

Marconi's unique grounded vertical antenna towers, he succeeded in telegraphing the gunboat HMS *Scourge* at a distance of 3.1 miles (5 km), thus achieving the first wireless transmission between two ships. Two months later, Marconi returned to Italy, where the navy allowed him to conduct shore-to-ship experiments, resulting in a dramatic breakthrough: successful transmissions from a coastal station at La Spezia to the old armored cruiser *San Martino*, 12 miles (19 km) out to sea. In 1898, the Italian navy equipped other warships with wireless telegraph, and thanks to Jackson's intervention, the British navy tested Marconi's wireless at its summer 1899 maneuvers. Commanding the cruiser *Juno*, Jackson transmitted messages directly to other ships at unprecedented ranges of 60–70 miles (95–110 km) and, using a third ship as a relay station, up to 95 miles (150 km). Afterward, the other leading navies quickly joined the British and Italian fleets in embracing the new invention. Wireless telegraph made its wartime debut in the Anglo-Boer conflict of 1899–1902, more successfully at sea than on land, aboard British cruisers attempting to interdict arms shipments bound for the Boer republics. Meanwhile, in 1897, Marconi incorporated the Wireless Telegraph and Signal Company to exploit his discoveries for commercial purposes, and the team of gifted scientists and engineers he hired accelerated the progress in extending the range of his signals. They passed an early milestone in December 1901 with the first direct transatlantic message, sent from Cornwall to Newfoundland, a distance of 2,100 miles (3,380 km). In the meantime, in April 1900, the Marconi International Marine Communication Company was established to develop shipboard wireless for worldwide use.[4]

German efforts at wireless telegraphy dated from the spring of 1897, when engineering professor Adolf Slaby witnessed a demonstration of Marconi's equipment on a visit to Britain. Germans had experimented with electromagnetic waves long before then; indeed, physicist Heinrich Hertz had been the first to prove their existence, using instruments he devised to send and receive wireless pulses. After his death in 1894, at the age of thirty-six, scientists referred to electromagnetic waves as "Hertzian waves," and eventually the unit of frequency (cycles per second) was named "hertz" in his honor. Marconi later

---

[4] *Ibid.*, pp. 302–303, 345–346; R. W. Simons, "Guglielmo Marconi and Early Systems of Wireless Communication," *GEC Review*, 11 (1996): 48, 50. See also Duncan C. Baker, "Wireless Telegraphy during the Anglo-Boer War of 1899–1902," *Military History Journal*, 11(2) (December 1998), available at: http://samilitaryhistory.org/vol112db.html.

**Figure 2.1** Guglielmo Marconi

claimed that an Italian physicist's obituary of Hertz inspired the experiments that led to his breakthroughs the following year. Slaby's efforts enjoyed the support of William II and the German navy, as well as the backing of the German General Electric Company (AEG) after it failed to secure a German license to produce Marconi's equipment. While Slaby and AEG developed a wireless system for the German navy, physicist Karl Ferdinand Braun and Siemens, Germany's other leading manufacturer of electrical components, did similar work for the German army. In 1903, AEG and Siemens joined forces to form Telefunken, which within a decade became the leading international competitor to Marconi's companies. Telefunken's early foreign customers included the Russian navy, whose poor use of wireless in the Russo-Japanese War of 1904–5, against a Japanese fleet equipped with Marconi sets, hardly inspired confidence in the German alternative. Nevertheless, by the outbreak of the First World War Telefunken boasted a presence in thirty-nine countries, including several in South America. In 1909, its new "quenched spark system" of wireless telegraph became standard equipment on all German warships. That year, Braun and Marconi shared the Nobel Prize in Physics for their contributions to wireless telegraphy.[5]

Britain's domination of the international network of undersea telegraph cables made long-distance wireless especially important to Germany, which assumed that, in wartime, it would not have access to the existing global telegraph grid. In 1911, after two years of experiments, Telefunken sent the first messages to a station at Kamina in Togo, the German colony closest to home, 3,350 miles (5,400 km) from Berlin. By 1914, messages could reach a station at Windhoek in Southwest Africa (Namibia), Germany's most distant African colony, 5,120 miles (8,240 km) from Berlin. Additional wireless stations were built in Germany's other two African colonies, Cameroon and German East Africa (Tanzania), as well as in Germany's east Asian and Pacific colonies, enabling the latter to communicate directly with each other but, owing to the distances involved, not with the African colonies or with Germany. The German government built these colonial stations at a cost of £2 million, but it did not have to subsidize German wireless connections to the United States, which were commercially profitable as well as strategically significant against the anticipated British embargo of German international telegraph communication. In the years from 1911 to 1914, Telefunken and Lorenz AG each established American subsidiaries and developed a capacity for regular transatlantic transmissions. The importance of these efforts became clear in August 1914, as soon as war was declared, when the British cut the five undersea cables linking Germany to its colonies, the United States, and neutral Spain. Germany used its own wireless stations and connections to neutral countries to alert its colonies about the outbreak of war and to warn its merchant marine to steam for the security of German or neutral ports.[6]

---

[5] Michael Friedewald, "The Beginnings of Radio Communication in Germany, 1897–1918," *Journal of Radio Studies*, 7 (2000): 441–463; Sungook Hong, *Wireless: From Marconi's Black-Box to the Audion* (Cambridge, MA: MIT Press, 2001), pp. 2–3, 19; Daniel R. Headrick, *The Invisible Weapon: Telecommunications and International Politics, 1851–1945* (Oxford University Press, 1991), p. 123.
[6] Friedewald, "The Beginnings of Radio Communication in Germany," *passim*; H. E. Hancock, *Wireless at Sea* (New York: Arno Press, [1950] 1974), p. 84.

## The targeting problem: technology and tactics

In the years leading up to 1914, even with national security on the line as never before, countries and companies remained reluctant to change their policies in the area of technology transfer. Indeed, in the heyday of unregulated industrial capitalism, corporate profits mattered more than giving one's own country a monopoly over a technological breakthrough. Just as firms in a number of countries struck agreements with Marconi's company to produce his wireless equipment, most naval powers manufactured their own Whitehead torpedoes, Belleville boilers, and Krupp armor under license. Even in the Anglo-German naval race, British dreadnoughts and battle cruisers had Krupp armor, while their German counterparts eventually were powered by Parsons turbine engines. But as the dramatic increases in the speed and firepower of capital ships made accurate targeting for big guns increasingly problematic, techniques and technology related to range-finding became the first closely guarded secrets.

In the years immediately preceding the First World War, the range-finding system aboard a larger warship had at its core a table-top-sized mechanical analog computer that functioned not unlike an elaborate multidimensional slide rule. Its operators would input the known or estimated variables by setting various knobs, dials, and wheels, to produce a reading on how to aim the ship's guns. In his quest to secure the best range-finder for his own navy and deny it to others, Fisher sought exclusive rights to the devices invented by Arthur Hungerford Pollen and manufactured by Pollen's Argo Company. Under an agreement with the Admiralty concluded in 1906, Pollen promised to cede all his patents, present and future, to the British government, and renounced his right to apply for patents in other countries. But acrimonious negotiations over specific terms delayed a definitive agreement until 1908, and did not bode well for the inventor's future relations with the Admiralty. Pollen was controversial in his own time, and historians remain divided over the trustworthiness of both the man and his inventions. Admiral Sir Arthur Wilson, who became First Sea Lord upon Fisher's retirement, had little faith in Pollen's system and saw to it that the navy continued to purchase competing products, in particular the "tables" designed by British naval officer Frederic Dreyer. The Irish-born son of a noted Danish astronomer, Dreyer was well respected within the service as a gunnery expert and also well connected, serving as Jellicoe's flag captain before and during the First World War, ultimately retiring during the Second World War at admiral's rank. Pollen, in contrast, was a civilian, whom Norman Friedman has characterized as "that typically British creature, a brilliant and very persistent amateur."[7]

Pollen developed a following within the navy in part because so many officers became acquainted with his mechanical computers or "clocks," devices that processed data from a synthetic course plotter to feed to a range-finder. Trials of Pollen's system produced results accurate enough to inspire a number of officers to buy Argo Company stock. After purchasing various iterations of Pollen's Argo Clock and the Dreyer Table for trials, in 1912 the Admiralty let the agreement Fisher had concluded with Pollen lapse, and ordered the Dreyer Table for all dreadnoughts and battle cruisers. The following year, when the Admiralty elected not to buy Pollen's latest computer, the Argo Clock Mark V, Pollen received permission to market it for export. His heretofore secret breakthroughs were publicized in an article in the 1913 *Brassey's Naval Annual* and in an Argo Company marketing brochure circulated that autumn. Pollen had a backlog of orders from foreign countries when the outbreak of the First World War shut down production. Ultimately, a Russian cruiser received the only Argo Clock Mark V ever installed in a warship, but his ideas, once made public, likely influenced similar range-finding devices developed by other navies.

Not surprisingly, the choice of Dreyer over Pollen led to recriminations after the Battle of Jutland confirmed the shortcomings of British fire control, and raised the questions of whether and why the Admiralty had rejected a superior range-finding system. Each inventor had his critics and defenders at the time, and subsequently among historians attempting to explain the outcome of Jutland.[8] For Pollen, the wartime vindication of his concept failed to assuage the pain of his prewar rejection by the Admiralty. He pursued and, in 1925, secured a

---

[7] Norman Friedman, *Naval Firepower: Battleship Guns and Gunnery in the Dreadnought Era* (Barnsley: Seaforth Publishing, 2008), p. 42.
[8] The works of Jon Sumida, especially *In Defence of Naval Supremacy* and "The Quest for Reach: The Development of Long-Range Gunnery in the Royal Navy, 1901–1912," in Stephen D. Chiabotti (ed.), *Tooling for War: Military Transformation in the Industrial Age* (Chicago, IL: Imprint Publications, 1996), pp. 49–96, rank among the strongest recent defenses of Pollen. John Brooks, *Dreadnought Gunnery and the Battle of Jutland: The Question of Fire Control* (London: Routledge, 2005), provides a spirited defense of Dreyer.

settlement of £30,000 after the Royal Commission on Awards to Inventors upheld his claim that the computing mechanism Dreyer incorporated into the Dreyer Table Mark IV "was based upon the same principle as the Argo Clock," though the commission exonerated Dreyer of "any intention or desire to copy" his competitor's invention.[9] The allegation of Dreyer's "plagiarism" of Pollen's invention further embittered the debate, and as late as the 1980s each man's son published a defense of his father's work. While recent scholarship has tended only to rekindle the original controversy, it is more useful to view the work of Dreyer and Pollen in terms of the broader evolution of range-finding techniques and technology. The Dreyer Table represented a culmination of the analytic approach, directly dependent on human observation, whereas range-finding using Pollen's Argo Clock was an early exercise in the synthetic approach, in that it started with a machine-generated estimated or predicted range that could be corrected by measurements derived from observation. As Friedman has pointed out, the synthetic method proved to be superior "because erroneous data are easier to discard" than under the analytic method.[10] After analytic systems, including the British navy's Dreyer Tables, led to such poor results in the First World War, the leading navies all adopted synthetic systems, in the British case based on Pollen's ideas, but older warships often kept their original range-finding systems throughout their service lives. In a tragic postscript, in 1941 the battle cruiser *Hood*, built in the years 1916–20 and still fitted with a Dreyer Table, fell victim to long-range fire from the *Bismarck*, whose guns were directed by a synthetic system.[11]

Success in the next war does not explain the superiority of German range-finding during the First World War, and because (in contrast to the British case) there was no postwar compulsion to explain failures, little has been written on the subject. By 1908, the German navy had settled on a combination of a range differential indicator (*Entfernungsunterschied-Anzeiger*) and a deflection-improvement indicator (*Seitenverbesserung-Anzeiger*) supplemented by a range clock (*Entfernungsuhr*). Thus, at least superficially, the equipment differed little from the components of the British system, but the quality of the components were very likely superior. Imperial Germany was the world's leading manufacturer of precision optical equipment for the

---

[9] RCAI Recommendation of October 30, 1925, text in Brooks, *Dreadnought Gunnery*, p. 290.
[10] Friedman, *Naval Firepower*, p. 41.    [11] Ibid., p. 65.

sciences and also produced the world's best gun sights, for weapons ranging from rifles to the heaviest field artillery. Indeed, prewar Britain imported 60 percent of its optical glass from Germany and Austria, and met just 10 percent of demand through domestic production. Most German capital ships had range-finders produced by Zeiss, featuring superior stereoscopic optics, and fire control systems from Siemens. Superior German optics and data transmission, plus better fire control training methods, may have facilitated a faster reaction to changing ranges, accounting for the relative wartime success of German gunfire over British gunfire.[12]

The quest for a superior range-finding system and the secrecy attending it stemmed from the dramatic increase in gunnery ranges in the twenty years preceding the First World War. In short, the distance a gun could fire increased faster than the ability to aim it with reasonable accuracy, and the decision (ultimately in the dreadnought and battle cruiser types) to arm capital ships with as many of the largest caliber guns as possible only placed a higher premium on finding a solution. For the first thirty years of the ironclad age (1860s–90s), the maximum effective range of the heaviest naval guns did not exceed 2,000 yards (roughly 1,850 m), the same as it had been for the last generation of wooden warships. The experience of the only engagement yet fought between fleets of armored vessels, the Battle of Lissa (1866), influenced tactics and warship design at least through to the 1880s. At Lissa, a numerically and qualitatively inferior Austrian fleet used a line abreast formation and ramming tactics to force a melee against an Italian battle line consisting mostly of larger and more formidable ironclads; afterward, most navies adopted line abreast tactics, most battleships and armored cruisers were fitted with ram bows, and the arrangement of guns aboard many warships reflected the premium placed on massing fire ahead rather than on the traditional broadside. At the Battle of the Yalu (1894) in the Sino-Japanese War, a Chinese fleet, spearheaded by two German-built battleships, deployed in a V-shaped line abreast formation (by then abandoned by all major navies) against a Japanese fleet consisting of a variety of European-built warships, almost all lightly-armored cruisers, deployed in a single line ahead column. The

---

[12] Paul Schmalenbach, *Die Geschichte der deutschen Schiffsartillerie*, 2nd edn. (Herford: Koehlers Verlagsgesellschaft, 1968), pp. 90–92; William A. Paton, *The Economic Position of the United Kingdom, 1912–1918* (Washington, DC: US Government Printing Office, 1919), p. 98.

Chinese opened fire at 5,000 m, the Japanese at 3,900 m, but most of the six-hour battle was fought at a range of just over 2,000 m. The Japanese won the battle, sinking five Chinese cruisers while losing no ships of their own. The battle demonstrated that the line ahead gave commanders a greater degree of tactical control in battle and at least the possibility of coordinated fire, but owing to the primitive state of fire control (the short range notwithstanding, the Japanese scored around 10 percent hits, the Chinese 5 percent) there were also no clear lessons regarding artillery. Most navies considered the successes of the big guns of the Chinese battleships and quick-firing medium-caliber guns of the Japanese cruisers justification for continuing to arm their pre-dreadnoughts with a mixed battery of both types of ordnance, usually four 12-inch (30.5-cm) guns and twelve 6-inch (15.2-cm) quick-firing guns.[13]

The naval battles of the Spanish-American War (1898) appeared to confirm the gunnery lessons of the Sino-Japanese War. Medium-caliber ordnance was responsible for all the hits at Manila Bay (a cruiser engagement where no warship had heavy guns) and most of those at Santiago. In each case, the ranges were similar to the Battle of the Yalu, but the fire control was much worse. At Manila Bay, the American warships scored 141 hits out of some 6,000 shells fired (2.3 percent), against stationary Spanish targets. At Santiago, against Spanish warships in full flight, the American success rate was even lower, at just 122 hits out of 9,433 shells fired (1.3 percent), but the 12-inch (30.5-cm) and 13-inch (33-cm) guns of the American battleships scored 42 of the hits, out of roughly 1,300 shells fired (3.2 percent). It was of some consolation to the US Navy that Spanish fire control had been even worse, reflected in the near total lack of damage incurred by American warships in the two battles.[14]

The miserable performance led to a new focus on improving fire control. When even reasonably well-trained gun crews could hit

---

[13] Charles H. Fairbanks, Jr., "The Origins of the *Dreadnought* Revolution: A Historiographical Essay," *International History Review*, 13 (1991): 261; David C. Evans and Mark R. Peattie, *Kaigun: Strategy, Tactics, and Technology in the Imperial Japanese Navy, 1887–1941* (Annapolis, MD: Naval Institute Press, 1997), pp. 41–47; Lambert, *Sir John Fisher's Naval Revolution*, p. 78; Sumida, "The Quest for Reach," p. 49.

[14] Edward L. Beach, *The United States Navy: 200 Years* (New York: Henry Holt, 1986), p. 394; D. K. Brown, *Warrior to Dreadnought: Warship Development, 1860–1905* (London: Chatham Publishing, 1997), p. 168.

their targets only 1 or 2 percent of the time, all the major navies had to acknowledge the need for better range-finding devices and techniques. The concurrent improvement in the range of self-propelled torpedoes, following the invention of the torpedo gyroscope by Austro-Hungarian naval officer Ludwig Obry, threatened the viability of the large armored warship if long-distance gunnery remained so inaccurate. Torpedo ranges improved from less than 1,000 yards (roughly 900 m) in 1896, at the time of Obry's breakthrough, to 2,000 yards by 1900 and 3,000 yards by 1904, dramatically enhancing the combat potential not just of torpedo boats, but of submarines as well. Britain's Admiral Fisher ranked among those who wondered if torpedo ranges would soon reach 5,000 yards (4,600 m), thus equaling or outstripping the range of battleship guns.[15]

The naval battles of the Russo-Japanese War at least temporarily brought an end to such speculation. In the Battle of the Yellow Sea (1904) Japanese battleships and armored cruisers, equipped with the latest Barr and Stroud range-finders (considered the best British equipment, before the innovations of Dreyer and Pollen), opened fire with their 12-inch (30.5-cm) guns at the unprecedented distance of 11,000 m. Much of the battle was fought at a range of 8,000–9,000 m, at which medium-caliber guns were useless. During the battle Japan's Admiral Heihachiro Togo first tried "crossing the T," a tactic copied from the British, who had introduced it at maneuvers in 1901. Steaming with his line ahead column across the path of the approaching enemy, Togo concentrated the fire of all his ships against the lead ships of the Russian column, forcing it to turn away. After Togo successfully repeated the maneuver, the Russians attempted to break off the action. In the ensuing pursuit, Japanese gunners registered hits on the Russian flagship *Tsesarevich* at 7,000 m, one of which killed Admiral V. K. Vitgeft and most of his staff. The following spring, Togo achieved an even more decisive victory in the Battle of Tsushima (1905), vanquishing Admiral Zinovy Rozhestvensky and a fleet that had steamed all the way from the Baltic to relieve the blockaded and besieged Russian forces at Port Arthur, only to have that stronghold fall while they were still en route. Russian guns scored the first hits of the battle, against the

---

[15] Nicholas A. Lambert, "Admiral Sir John Fisher and the Concept of Flotilla Defence, 1904–1909," *Journal of Military History*, 59 (1995): 647–651; Lambert, *Sir John Fisher's Naval Revolution*, pp. 77–79. On Ludwig Obry, see Sondhaus, *The Naval Policy of Austria-Hungary*, pp. 48, 72 n. 42.

Japanese flagship *Mikasa*, at a range of 7,000 m. The Japanese opened fire at 6,400 m, but even though Tsushima was fought at closer ranges than the Battle of the Yellow Sea, medium-caliber artillery again played little role. After "crossing the T" in the opening phase of the battle, Togo outmaneuvered Rozhestvensky and ultimately blocked his path to Vladivostok, leaving the Russian fleet with nowhere else to go. The large stocks of coal that the Russian warships carried into the battle only hastened their destruction, as widespread fires left many of them unable to defend themselves further as the Japanese closed in to sink them. The last fighting Russian units exchanged fire with their attackers at just 2,500 m, and at such close range medium-caliber artillery finally came into play.[16]

After being so significant in the major battles of the Sino-Japanese and Spanish-American wars, medium-caliber ordnance had little impact at the Battle of the Yellow Sea or at Tsushima, actions in which the big guns of the largest warships had registered hits at ranges then considered extraordinary; furthermore, Togo's success in "crossing the T" of the Russians in both battles demonstrated how capital ships in a line ahead column could maneuver to concentrate fire against an enemy column. It now appeared likely that future naval battles would be fought at unprecedented distances by ships armed with greater numbers of heavier guns. Even before the Russo-Japanese War, the idea of an "all big-gun" warship was already being discussed internationally. Vittorio Cuniberti, the chief engineer of the Italian navy, shortly after the turn of the century had designed an all big-gun battleship which his own navy rejected; in 1903, he published his ideas in an article in *Jane's Fighting Ships* under the title "An ideal battleship for the British navy." By then, the British, American, and Japanese navies all were moving toward a single-caliber battleship design in order to improve fire control, in part because analytic range-finding systems based on splash-spotting could not distinguish between the plumes of water produced by shells as different from those fired from 6-inch (15.2-cm) and 12-inch (30.5-cm) guns. The *Lord Nelson* and *Agamemnon*, the last British capital ships ordered before Fisher took office, would have had an all big-gun armament of 12-inch guns if the sea lords had not overruled the Admiralty's design section; instead, they

---

[16] F. N. Gromov et al., *Tri Veka Rossiiskogo Flota*, 3 vols. (St. Petersburg: Logos, 1996), vol. 1, pp. 379–402; Evans and Peattie, *Kaigun*, pp. 103, 105, 119–124.

were given the standard four 12-inch guns with a very heavy secondary armament of ten 9.2-inch (23.4-cm) guns. As of 1904, however, Fisher's ideal type was not a battleship at all, but the battle cruiser, initially conceived as a large armored cruiser with 9.2-inch guns.[17] To the extent that the major naval battles of the Russo-Japanese War had an influence on Fisher's concept, it was in the abandonment of the 9.2-inch gun as the weapon for his new ships. Thus, the *Dreadnought* and the first battle cruisers of the *Invincible* class featured a primary armament of 12-inch guns and no secondary armament. Like all subsequent "all big-gun" warships they carried smaller guns to ward off torpedo boat attacks – initially twenty-four 3-inch (7.6-cm) guns for the *Dreadnought*, later reduced to ten, and sixteen 4-inch (10.2-cm) guns for the battle cruisers – and also had torpedo tubes, but their primary armament left no ambiguity about how they were to be used.

The British fleet's war game guidelines of 1913 considered 12,000 yards (just under 11,000 m) as the range limit not just for 12-inch (30.5-cm) guns, but also the 13.5-inch (34.3-cm) guns of their newest capital ships. Yet after the prewar navy incorporated its first dreadnoughts and battle cruisers, it usually conducted long-range gunnery exercises at 8,000 yards (just over 7,300 m), only slightly farther than the maximum distance at which 12-inch guns had registered hits in the battles of 1904–5. By the winter of 1912/13, the Germans were conducting some exercises at 11,000–14,000 yards (10,000–12,800 m), but with a success rate of less than 10 percent. Further advances in the range of torpedoes complicated the quest to determine what the realistic big-gun range would or should be in the next war, as all navies considered it too risky for capital ships to fight within torpedo range. By 1914, the German G7 torpedo had a range of 10,000 m, the British Mark II had a range of 10,000 yards (9,100 m), and both navies assumed the other side's capital ships would use their torpedoes effectively in battle. Making the tactical dilemma thornier still, British exercises conducted between 1909 and 1911 led to the conclusion that a dreadnought firing at a range of 10,000 yards would take well over an hour to disable another dreadnought, far too long to linger in waters that might be infested with torpedoes.[18]

---

[17] *Conway's All the World's Fighting Ships, 1906–1921* (London: Conway Maritime Press, 1985), p. 21; Brown, *Warrior to Dreadnought*, p. 182; Fairbanks, "The Origins of the *Dreadnought* Revolution," p. 262.
[18] Friedman, *Naval Firepower*, pp. 84–91.

As vice admiral commanding a squadron of the newest dreadnoughts of the First Fleet, Home Fleet, Jellicoe (with Dreyer as his flag captain) during 1912 came to the conclusion that the focus must shift from extending the range of fire to extending the speed and volume of fire in order to improve the odds that a fleet of capital ships could hit their enemy counterparts before the enemy's torpedoes found their mark. Jon Sumida has concluded that, in December 1912, Jellicoe persuaded Churchill, then First Lord of the Admiralty, and Admiral Prince Louis Battenberg, then First Sea Lord, to have the fleet adopt a "secret tactical system" which called for British capital ships to close well within 10,000 yards, to ranges as close as 7,000–8,000 yards (6,400–7,300 m), then destroy the enemy with no more than 5 minutes of intense gunfire before turning away to evade any torpedoes that may be fired against them. Based on exercises conducted in 1912 and earlier, Jellicoe was confident of a 30 percent hit rate at 7,000–8,000 yards; indeed, in one test a single dreadnought scored thirteen hits out of thirty-nine rounds fired within a period of just 3.5 minutes. Fatefully, this new vision of a battle fleet engagement coincided with, or (as Sumida argues) resulted in the rejection of Pollen's range-finder, which held greater promise for solving the targeting challenges of longer ranges, ranges at which the British navy at least at that stage no longer planned to fight.[19] During the same years the German navy likewise came to the conclusion that future fleet actions would occur at 6,000–8,000 m, roughly the same distances at which big guns had scored hits in the Russo-Japanese War. At least one knowledgeable Russian observer concluded that the British and Germans both were continuing to conduct some long-range gunnery exercises only as a ruse, to obscure the true direction that their tactical thinking had taken.[20]

## Beyond the battle fleets

While preparations for war understandably focused on the capital ships being produced in the prewar arms races, recent technological breakthroughs also enhanced the fighting ability of smaller surface warships and submarines, and facilitated the birth of naval aviation. These

---

[19] See Jon Tetsuro Sumida, "A Matter of Timing: The Royal Navy and the Tactics of Decisive Battle, 1912–1916," *Journal of Military History*, 67 (2003): 85–136.
[20] Friedman, *Naval Firepower*, pp. 90–91.

developments generated considerable debate and creative thought about how smaller vessels and aircraft could be used either to supplement or to substitute for the firepower of big ships with big guns. Thus, strategies and tactics were developed for deploying these assets in battle fleet operations, as well as in contexts where no capital ships would be present.

After dominating strategic and tactical thought during the *Jeune École* of the 1880s, cruisers were increasingly overshadowed by battleships after 1890. Envisaging blue-water forces of battleships engaging other battle fleets in decisive warfare to achieve command of the sea, Mahan minimized the need for cruisers to the point of theorizing that armed merchantmen could easily serve the same purposes.[21] At a time when shipbuilders were constructing steel-hulled merchant ships with watertight compartments, machinery below the waterline, and the structural soundness to mount all but the heaviest artillery, it seemed perfectly reasonable that fast merchantmen could be armed to defend themselves and their slower counterparts.[22] Mahan's lack of appreciation for commerce protection reflected a "militarization" of naval thinking, which, as early as the 1870s, had reached a level where most navies no longer accepted such duties as fundamental to their mission. In the late Victorian British navy, most officers scoffed at the notion that a country with a large merchant marine could build enough cruising warships to actually "protect" its overseas commerce. Such attitudes persisted through the *Jeune École* – a strategy centered on commerce raiding – and into the First World War, when Britain would wait almost three years before adopting a comprehensive convoy system to counter the German submarine threat. The prewar German navy reflected Mahan's thinking in its plans to convert the fast passenger liners of the Hamburg-Amerika Line and North German Lloyd into commerce-raiding cruisers, as did Britain in its belated response of building the *Lusitania* and *Mauretania* to Admiralty specifications, including deck mountings for guns, to counter this threat.[23]

The introduction of Fisher's innovative battle cruisers, though copied only by Germany and, beyond Europe, by Japan, led to a worldwide fifteen-year hiatus in the construction of armored cruisers, versatile

[21] Jon Tetsuro Sumida, *Inventing Grand Strategy and Teaching Command: The Classic Works of Alfred Thayer Mahan Reconsidered* (Baltimore, MD: Johns Hopkins University Press, 1997), pp. 45, 72.
[22] Brown, *Warrior to Dreadnought*, p. 109.
[23] Seligmann, *The Royal Navy and the German Threat*, pp. 10–64.

ships that had seen duty not just in battle fleets, but also on overseas stations, where they usually were the largest units. After work began on the first of Britain's *Invincible*s in 1906, four armored cruisers were laid down in 1906–7 (one each by France, Germany, Italy, and Greece), then none until after the Washington Naval Treaty of 1922 restricted the construction of warships of over 10,000 tons with more than 8-inch (20.3-cm) guns, creating the phenomenon of "treaty cruisers" built to the new tonnage and armament limits. During the same years, navies also stopped building larger unarmored and protected (armored-deck) cruisers, after 1905 constructing these types only as light cruisers of 5,500 tons or less. Even then, few light cruisers were built other than by Britain (which began forty-one in the years from 1905 to 1914) and Germany (which responded with twenty-six). Italy and Japan each laid down six, Austria-Hungary and Russia four, while France and the United States built none at all. The general decline of traditional larger cruiser construction contributed to a remarkable increase in the tonnage differential between capital ships and other new units in the years before the First World War.

Fourteen years before the introduction of the battle cruiser, Fisher introduced the destroyer to counter the torpedo-boat threat of the *Jeune École*. The British navy ordered its first six destroyers in 1892, and thirty-six were included in the construction program approved by Parliament in 1893. The first destroyers were vessels of around 275 tons, capable of 26 or 27 knots, armed with torpedo tubes and light deck guns. Other countries soon copied the type, and by the turn of the century every major navy included destroyers.[24] Flotillas of destroyers typically were attached to battle fleets to protect the capital ships; while Germany used them exclusively in this context, under Fisher's direction Britain deployed destroyer flotillas independently or with cruisers, first in defense of the North Sea coast of England, and eventually in the Channel. By the outbreak of the First World War, the newest destroyers displaced around 1,000 tons and were capable of 35 knots, but older destroyers half as large were still in commission. The British destroyer *Viper* (1899) was the first warship fitted with turbine engines, which revolutionized small-warship capabilities because they weighed hundreds of tons less than reciprocating engines with similar power. After Fisher became First Sea Lord in 1904, all new British destroyers burned oil only. As in the British case, in most other navies destroyers were the

---

[24] Brown, *Warrior to Dreadnought*, pp. 137–141.

first ships with turbine engines and the first fueled by oil rather than by coal.

Thanks to the influence of the *Jeune École*, by the early 1890s most navies had hundreds of torpedo boats on hand and built few, if any, in the years that followed. The French navy alone continued to build large numbers of the type, only because its leadership included a strong minority that continued to advocate torpedo warfare. After the turn of the century, submarines, likewise pioneered by the French, came to occupy the strategic role once filled by torpedo boats. France's 31-ton *Gymnote* (1888) rates as the world's first genuinely successful submarine; it was the first to draw its power from an electric battery and also the first to feature hydroplanes for depth regulation. In twenty years of service it made roughly 2,000 dives without an accident. The 270-ton *Gustave Zédé* (1893), the world's largest submarine for more than a decade after its launch, in 1898 became the first undersea boat to torpedo and sink a target ship while submerged. France went on to commission a total of seventy-six submarines in the years from 1900 to 1914, many of which were modeled after the highly successful 202-ton *Narval* (1900).[25]

Until the conclusion of the Entente Cordiale, Fisher remained concerned about a revival of the *Jeune École* and especially about France's growing submarine force. He was impressed by the power of the submarine not only as an offensive weapon, but as a defender of harbors that would make it impossible for navies of the future to impose close blockades. A posting as British Mediterranean commander (1899–1902) gave Fisher the opportunity to observe the growth of the French undersea force at Toulon, after which an assignment as commander in Portsmouth (1903–4) allowed him to supervise the early growth of Britain's submarine service. The British waited until 1901 to launch their first submarine, designated simply as *No. 1*, built by Vickers after the American Holland design. After this late start, however, Britain commissioned a total of eighty-eight undersea boats by the time war began in 1914, more than any other country. The British traditionally have claimed credit for at least one submarine innovation, the first periscope, introduced to *No. 1* by Captain Reginald Bacon, but other

---

[25] Michael Wilson, "Early Submarines," in Robert Gardiner (ed.), *Steam, Steel, and Shellfire: The Steam Warship, 1815–1905* (Annapolis, MD: Naval Institute Press, 1992), p. 154.

sources contend that the French *Narval* had a periscope from the time it entered service in 1900.[26] Ironically, given what was to come, Germany was slow to embrace the submarine, launching its first *Unterseeboot*, *U 1*, in 1906 and a total of just thirty-six before the war, one less than Russia. Indeed, Fisher envisaged Germany's future employment of the submarine as a commerce raider before the Germans themselves, but his prewar warning that Germany might attempt unrestricted submarine warfare met with universal rejection in Britain. Churchill doubted such a thing "would ever be done by a civilized Power." Julian Corbett, Britain's leading naval strategist, agreed with Churchill, concluding that no country "would incur the odium of sinking merchant ships out of hand."[27]

In the years before the First World War, few navy leaders envisaged just how important aircraft would be in future warfare, or how vulnerable warships of all types would be to attack from the air. In 1908, five years after their first successful flight, the Wright brothers brought their aircraft to Europe for a series of public demonstrations. The French army incorporated airplanes into its annual maneuvers of 1910. The following year, the German navy began experimenting with airplanes but ultimately favored dirigibles, under the influence of Count Ferdinand von Zeppelin and other German airship pioneers. Prewar Italy likewise favored dirigibles, even though Italian pilots were the first to fly airplanes in combat missions in the 1911–12 war against Turkey. In 1912, Britain established separate army and navy air services, and Austria-Hungary established a seaplane station at its main naval base, Pola (Pula). In France, Italy, and Russia, the armies initially monopolized air power and the navies controlled no aircraft. In 1910–11, the US Navy became the first to launch and land airplanes from warships (in each case using temporary deck platforms) and the first to use aircraft for long-range artillery spotting. Early in 1914, the British Admiralty authorized the construction of a seaplane tender, the 7,080-ton *Ark Royal*, built on the hull of an unfinished merchantman. The British remained the clear leader in naval aviation throughout the First World War. No other navy would develop the capability to launch and land wheeled aircraft from a ship, and only the French

[26] Lambert, *Sir John Fisher's Naval Revolution*, pp. 73–86; Wilson, "Early Submarines," pp. 155–157.
[27] Churchill and Corbett, quoted in Offer, *The First World War: An Agrarian Interpretation*, p. 283.

and Russians would join the British in commissioning seaplane tenders. All other navies operated their airplanes or airships from coastal bases.[28]

## Strategy and alliances

The prewar strategic planning of Europe's Great Powers shaped the manner in which the land campaigns of the First World War unfolded, even though neither alliance system had joint war plans. The two powers with the closest relationship, France and Russia, had a military convention that included a timetable for their mutual obligation to mobilize specific numbers of troops in support of each other, but no common plan of attack. Within the Triple Alliance, Austria-Hungary remained ignorant of the specifics of Germany's Schlieffen Plan, even though the general staff chiefs of the two armies, Franz Conrad von Hötzendorf and Helmut von Moltke the Younger, were friends and met frequently, and when it came to war plans both considered it prudent to keep their Italian counterparts in the dark as much as possible.

The conclusion of the Franco-Russian alliance occasioned well-publicized visits by the French fleet to St. Petersburg in 1891 and the Russian fleet to Toulon in 1893, leading Britain (as well as the navies of the Triple Alliance) to assume afterward that a Franco-Russian naval plan existed when it did not. The original Triple Alliance naval convention (1900) assigned the Baltic, the North Sea, and the Atlantic to the German navy, the western Mediterranean to the Italians, the Adriatic to the Austrians, and made the eastern Mediterranean a joint Austro-Italian zone, but the clauses on joint operations were vague. In case of joint action, the allied commander would be the senior officer of the country in whose zone the operations were taking place. The three navies adopted a joint signal code in 1901, but cooperated closely only in the Far East (where, at the time, all the Great Powers maintained larger than usual squadrons because of the Boxer Rebellion). In 1902, the Triple Alliance was renewed for another ten years, but later that year, thanks to the ongoing Franco-Italian rapprochement, the

---

[28] Geoffrey Till, "Adopting the Aircraft Carrier: The British, American, and Japanese Case Studies," in Williamson Murray and Allan R. Millett (eds.), *Military Innovation in the Interwar Period* (Cambridge University Press, 1996), p. 192; Norman Friedman, *British Carrier Aviation: The Evolution of the Ships and their Aircraft* (Annapolis, MD: Naval Institute Press, 1988), pp. 28–30.

Italians stopped sharing intelligence with their allies on the French navy. The Triple Alliance naval convention became a dead letter until the eve of the First World War, when changing conditions in the Mediterranean heightened Italian interest in reviving it.

For Italy, the most important new variable after the turn of the century was Britain's gradual reduction of its traditionally dominant posture in the Mediterranean and, ultimately, the concentration of more of its battle fleet in home waters. The abandonment of the battleship deployments typical of the decades of the *Pax Britannica* began when Britain and Japan concluded an alliance in 1902, inspired by their mutual concern over Russia's ambitions in the Far East. The British had great confidence in the Japanese, who had developed their navy along British lines, using British advisors, in addition to purchasing most of their warships from British shipyards. After Japan's victory in the Russo-Japanese War, Britain recalled all its battleships from the Far East. By then, the conclusion of the Entente Cordiale raised the possibility of further redeployment of British capital ships closer to home. Even before the rising threat from Germany forced Britain's hand, concerns over economy and efficiency dictated some movement. When Fisher became First Sea Lord in October 1904, Britain had eight battleships in the Home Fleet, eight in the Channel, twelve in the Mediterranean Fleet, and five on the China station. After the latter returned home, an enlarged Home Fleet, shifted to the Channel and renamed the Channel Fleet, included fourteen battleships, while the former Channel force, operating out of Gibraltar as the Atlantic Fleet, had nine, and the Mediterranean Fleet nine. Traditionally characterized as a response to a German naval buildup that did not yet warrant such a response, the changes of 1904–5 (which actually reduced the number of home-waters battleships by two) instead reflected Fisher's premium on flexibility and efficiency. The battleships of the Atlantic Fleet could reinforce either the Channel or the Mediterranean, as needed, while three flying squadrons of armored cruisers (eventually to be replaced by battle cruisers), only nominally affiliated with the three fleets, would defend British interests worldwide.[29]

Scholars disagree about when Britain began to view Germany as the primary threat to its security, but recent research indicates serious war planning for a German scenario began as early as 1902. In the first months of his tenure as First Sea Lord, Fisher spoke openly about a

---

[29] Lambert, *Sir John Fisher's Naval Revolution*, pp. 98–115.

Figure 2.2 Admiral Sir John Fisher

"Copenhagen" solution to the construction of the German fleet, evoking the memory of Britain's pre-emptive destruction of the Danish fleet during the Napoleonic Wars, shortly after Denmark allied with France. The prewar decade featured periodic discussion of the navy landing a British force in Schleswig-Holstein, as a means of distracting a number of German troops away from an invasion of France; such plans, which theoretically would help the French without deploying a large British army to France, became a favorite of "anti-continental" army leaders and politicians, but ultimately went nowhere.[30] By the time of the Moroccan crisis of 1905, war plans against Germany reflected Fisher's

[30] Grimes, *Strategy and War Planning*, pp. 41–74 and *passim*; Jonathan Steinberg, "The Copenhagen Complex," *Journal of Contemporary History*, 1(3) (1966): 23–46.

sensibilities in arguing that Britain should use its obvious geographic advantages to strangle German overseas commerce, while employing torpedo flotillas backed by older battleships to defend against the German fleet in the North Sea.[31] Captain Maurice Hankey, an officer in the Royal Marines, served as secretary of a committee Fisher formed late in 1906 to further elaborate plans for an Anglo-German war. Working "under Fisher's immediate inspiration," as Hankey later noted, their efforts soon focused on the economic dimension, emphasizing blockade.[32]

Once Fisher set the tone, from 1908 onward the Admiralty gradually persuaded Prime Minister H. H. Asquith that a campaign of economic warfare must be the centerpiece of war plans against Germany. Since the 1880s the Second Reich had experienced unprecedented population growth, industrialization, and urbanization. By the immediate prewar years, the German agricultural sector accounted for less than a quarter of its net national product, and Germany had become the only continental European power that was a net importer of food, leaving it especially vulnerable to blockade.[33] In light of what is now known about the Admiralty's schemes, it seems clearer than ever that Britain did not act entirely in good faith in negotiating the Declaration of London (February 1909), under which even belligerent powers were obliged to allow food shipments and nonmilitary cargo to pass through a blockade. Parliament never ratified the declaration, the House of Lords finally voting it down in 1911, yet the Foreign Office and Admiralty went into the war at least publicly treating it as part of the body of international law that Britain was bound to respect.[34] But Fisher's attitude toward the declaration – that in wartime it would be disregarded, or that Germany was certain to violate it, thereby freeing Britain from any moral obligation to honor it – reflected the majority view in the Admiralty. Nicholas Lambert's work on the subject depicts a British leadership ultimately fully embracing Fisher's no-holds-barred approach, accepting the violation of Dutch neutrality in much the same way that their German counterparts, under the Schlieffen Plan, accepted the violation of Belgian neutrality, in order to close Rotterdam, a port through which 20 percent of German imports passed. Finally,

---

[31] Lambert, *Sir John Fisher's Naval Revolution*, p. 177.
[32] Quoted in Offer, *The First World War: An Agrarian Interpretation*, p. 235.
[33] Ibid., p. 321.    [34] Ibid., p. 275.

in December 1912, Asquith agreed that during a war against Germany, Britain would limit the overseas trade of Belgium and the Netherlands to what the Chancellor of the Exchequer, David Lloyd George, called "a reasonable margin" beyond "their own consumption," to prevent either from being used by the Germans to circumvent a British blockade of German ports. Thereafter, the cabinet "predelegated" to the Admiralty the authority to wage economic warfare upon the outbreak of war, not just to impose a traditional blockade upon Germany, but to enforce a ban on trade with Germany in any ship flying the British flag (and thus, over half of the world's mercantile tonnage) by giving the Admiralty unprecedented wartime authority over the merchant marine. The Admiralty's plans also called for the use of the London financial market as a weapon of war, but Asquith ultimately sided with the Treasury in rejecting the idea that Britain, via a selective embargo on credit, should precipitate a controlled collapse of the world economy (controlled to limit the damage to the British Empire and its friends) in order to force the economic collapse of Germany.[35]

The growing strength of the German fleet did not affect British peacetime deployments until the end of 1906. By then, Tirpitz had his sixteen newest pre-dreadnought battleships – designated the High Sea Fleet (*Hochseeflotte*) the following year – stationed on the North Sea at Wilhelmshaven. This buildup prompted the British decision to maintain sixteen battleships in the Channel, reducing the Atlantic and Mediterranean fleets to eight apiece. In arguing for the creation of a new Home Fleet over the winter of 1906/7, Fisher initially held to his earlier sentiments regarding home defense, proposing that it include older battleships plus all the destroyers, torpedo boats, and submarines not otherwise assigned, but by the time the new fleet was created in March 1907, it had grown to include the navy's eight best capital ships, stationed on the North Sea at the southeastern English bases of Sheerness and Chatham. As it entered regular service the *Dreadnought* was assigned to the Home Fleet, as were the first battle cruisers and subsequent dreadnoughts.[36]

In the spring of 1909, following the retirement of Fisher's main rival and critic, Admiral Sir Charles Beresford, as head of the Channel

---

[35] Nicholas A. Lambert, *Planning Armageddon: British Economic Warfare and the First World War* (Cambridge, MA: Harvard University Press, 2012), pp. 178–179 and *passim*.

[36] Lambert, *Sir John Fisher's Naval Revolution*, pp. 157–164.

Fleet, that command was absorbed by the Home Fleet. Finally, in the spring of 1912, Churchill withdrew the Atlantic Fleet from Gibraltar to home waters, and moved the battleships of the Mediterranean Fleet from Malta to Gibraltar. Collectively all these units, joined by a thirty-third battleship serving as flagship, were designated First Fleet, Home Fleet, divided into four squadrons of eight, all stationed in home waters except the eight at Gibraltar. The squadron there, like their Atlantic Fleet predecessors, would be in a position to reinforce home waters or return to the Mediterranean (as they did in November 1912, because of the Balkan Wars, remaining for seven months). The redistribution reduced the Mediterranean Fleet at Malta to a division of British battle cruisers backed by older armored cruisers, leaving the French navy as the primary guardian of the Entente's Mediterranean interests. While earlier war plans had called for the fleet operating out of English North Sea bases to impose a close blockade of the German North Sea coast, in April 1912 this was abandoned in favor of a distant blockade, on a line from the Orkneys and Shetlands eastward to the coast of Norway, a strategy definitively adopted in the winter of 1912/13. Operations so far north required bases in Scotland, not England; anticipating this need, the navy five years earlier had begun to improve Rosyth, in the Firth of Forth, as the primary base for a North Sea campaign against Germany, with Scapa Flow, in the Orkneys, identified "as another potential main base."[37]

As the First Fleet, Home Fleet shifted the focus of British North Sea operations farther from the Straits of Dover, new arrangements had to be made for the defense of the Channel against a German sortie, especially since during the same years that Britain deployed all its new dreadnoughts to the North Sea and most of its battle cruisers to the Mediterranean, France sent its last class of pre-dreadnoughts (the six *Danton*s) and first class of dreadnoughts (the four *Courbet*s) to the Mediterranean. The understanding that the British were primarily responsible for the Entente's common defense of the Channel and the French primarily responsible for the Mediterranean finally became official early in 1913 in three separate conventions defining the obligations of the two navies. Under the two Channel conventions, the British had sole responsibility for the seaborne defense of everything east of a line drawn due south from the Isle of Wight, including Le Havre, and

---

[37] Grimes, *Strategy and War Planning*, pp. 103, 176–180.

shared control of the western Channel with the French under a joint command. In each zone the Germans were to be stopped by a combination of cruisers, destroyers, torpedo boats, and submarines, for by that time the British had stripped their Channel ports of battleships except for several older pre-dreadnoughts, while the French, in 1912, redeployed their last pre-dreadnoughts from Brest to Toulon, leaving them with no battleships of any vintage outside the Mediterranean. Meanwhile, the third Anglo-French convention called for the main body of the French fleet, operating out of Toulon and Bizerte (Binzart), to be responsible for engaging the Italian navy in the western Mediterranean, while the British Mediterranean Fleet at Malta had the task of keeping the Austro-Hungarian navy from breaking out of the Adriatic. If the force at Malta proved to be too weak for this task (as British critics of Churchill's redeployments of 1912 feared), it would join the French Mediterranean Fleet; otherwise, it would operate separately.[38]

While the Anglo-French conventions remained secret, the two navies did not attempt to hide their closer relationship. On March 30, 1913, a French squadron arrived at Malta for a four-day visit, which the British Mediterranean Fleet welcomed with "extraordinary enthusiasm," according to the local Austro-Hungarian consul.[39] The two Channel conventions were much more specific than the document pertaining to the Mediterranean, but another Anglo-French convention, signed on August 6, 1914, two days after Britain declared war on Germany, formalized the French role of safeguarding British Mediterranean interests, and gave them the use of Malta and Gibraltar as bases. As late as the July Crisis of 1914 some British politicians and diplomats denied that the Entente obligated their country to come to the aid of France, but as Samuel Williamson has noted, the agreements concluded a year and a half earlier constituted "a virtual Anglo-French naval alliance."[40]

Just as the Italo-Turkish War (1911–12) strained Italy's relations with the Triple Entente and prompted the renewal of the Triple

---

[38] Samuel R. Williamson, Jr., *The Politics of Grand Strategy: Britain and France Prepare for War, 1904–1914* (Cambridge, MA: Harvard University Press, 1969), pp. 320–324.
[39] Haus- Hof- und Staatsarchiv, AR, F 44 – Marinewesen, Carton 13: Kriegsschiffe Frankreich 65, includes detailed reports and press clippings regarding the visit of the French squadron, which lasted from March 30 to April 3. See also Sondhaus, *The Naval Policy of Austria-Hungary*, p. 234.
[40] Williamson, *The Politics of Grand Strategy*, p. 324.

Alliance, the British and French naval deployments during and after that conflict revived Italy's interest in a Triple Alliance naval convention. The French concentration in the western Mediterranean alarmed the Italians, while the diminished British presence in the theater reduced their long-standing fears of steering a course at odds with British interests. The Germans, whose Schlieffen Plan would benefit from an Austro-Italian fleet deploying in the western Mediterranean to disrupt troop convoys from Algeria to France, used their influence to overcome a decade of distrust between Italy and Austria-Hungary and the tensions attending their ongoing Adriatic naval race. The Germans supported an Italian proposal that compensated Austria-Hungary for sending its fleet into the western Mediterranean by Italy deploying "one or more" army corps against France, which would release "one or more" German army corps to help the Austro-Hungarian army hold off the Russians on the Eastern front. The convention was signed in Vienna in June 1913, after Italy offered to designate Admiral Anton Haus (Montecuccoli's successor as Austro-Hungarian naval commander) commander of a battle fleet to include the Italian and Austro-Hungarian dreadnoughts and newest pre-dreadnoughts, joined by any German warships that happened to be in the Mediterranean. In case of war the allied fleet would assemble at Messina, Sicily, then steam westward to engage the French fleet and block the Algerian troop transports.[41]

After the new Triple Alliance naval convention came into effect on November 1, 1913, the allies added an annex listing the ships Haus would command in case war broke out during 1914. The allied force, more than strong enough to defeat the French Mediterranean Fleet, would include Italy's three dreadnoughts, Austria-Hungary's three dreadnoughts, Germany's battle cruiser *Goeben* (flagship of the German Mediterranean Division), four Italian and nine Austro-Hungarian pre-dreadnoughts, backed by seven Italian and two Austro-Hungarian armored cruisers. The annex went on to specify the numbers of light cruisers, destroyers, and torpedo boats each navy was to contribute; in the German case, these would include whatever light cruisers happened to be escorting the *Goeben*. The leaders of the Italian and Austro-Hungarian navies exchanged visits during the winter of 1913/14 and, in March 1914, Rear Admiral Wilhelm Souchon brought the *Goeben* to the upper Adriatic, where it escorted William II and the imperial

---

[41] Sondhaus, *The Naval Policy of Austria-Hungary*, pp. 232–239.

Figure 2.3 British Grand Fleet at sea

yacht *Hohenzollern* on port calls to Trieste and Venice.[42] Such displays of solidarity notwithstanding, a strong mutual suspicion clouded the interactions of the Austro-Hungarian and Italian navies throughout the life of the convention, which became a dead letter on July 31, 1914, when Italy condemned Austria-Hungary's declaration of war against Serbia as an act of aggression.

## Worldwide naval deployments

In 1914, no less than at the present, worldwide naval deployments were constantly changing, with a number of warships underway at any given time. What follows is a country-by-country synopsis of the distribution of the fleets of the world's eight greatest naval powers as of July and August 1914. For the six powers declaring war, the location, strength, and commanders of individual forces reflect the situation after mobilization but before the onset of operations. In most cases specific units accounted for are capital ships (dreadnoughts and battle cruisers), pre-dreadnought battleships, and armored cruisers. All the forces mentioned, of course, also included a variety of light cruisers, destroyers, and other small surface warships, and some included submarines.

[42] *Ibid.*, pp. 239–240.

At the end of July 1914, Britain had twenty dreadnoughts and nine battle cruisers in service, backed by forty pre-dreadnought battleships and thirty-four armored cruisers. At the outbreak of war the British navy abandoned its fleet organization of 1912. The thirty-two units of the First Fleet, Home Fleet (all twenty dreadnoughts, four of the battle cruisers, and eight newer pre-dreadnought battleships of the *King Edward VII* class) now formed the nucleus of the Grand Fleet, based at Scapa Flow, commanded by Admiral Sir John Jellicoe. They were joined by another four pre-dreadnoughts and eleven armored cruisers, which operated with the fleet and on the "Northern Patrol" between the northern islands of Scotland and the Norwegian coast. A revived Channel Fleet, under Vice Admiral Sir Cecil Burney, received twenty older pre-dreadnoughts and one armored cruiser from the Second and Third fleets of the Home Fleet. Forces in southeastern and eastern England, at Dover and on the Humber, included five pre-dreadnoughts and five armored cruisers. Another pre-dreadnought served as guardship at Loch Ewe in northwestern Scotland. Admiral Sir Berkeley Milne's Mediterranean Fleet, stripped of its battleships in 1912, had just three battle cruisers and four armored cruisers. Another eleven armored cruisers were deployed to lead patrols in the Atlantic, including the North American and West Indian station and the West African station; they were joined initially by the battle cruiser *Invincible*, which operated out of Queenstown (today Cobh), on Cork Harbor in southern Ireland, for several days during early August before being withdrawn to the North Sea. The prewar redeployments left few larger warships assigned to more distant bases: one pre-dreadnought and two armored cruisers on the China station, one pre-dreadnought on the East Indies station, and the battle cruiser *Australia* as flagship of the Royal Australian Navy. The battle cruiser *New Zealand*, though paid for by New Zealand and intended for service on the China station, by 1914 had been assigned to the First Fleet. It visited its namesake dominion only on peacetime cruises in 1913 and 1919.

At the time of mobilization Germany counted among its largest active warships fourteen dreadnoughts and four battle cruisers, thirty pre-dreadnought battleships (including eight 3,500-ton *Siegfried*-class coast defenders), and eight armored cruisers. The pre-dreadnoughts included some older reserve units already "replaced" by dreadnoughts under Tirpitz's navy laws, but not yet scrapped. Aside from one battle cruiser (*Goeben*) in the Mediterranean Division and two armored cruisers (*Scharnhorst* and *Gneisenau*) in the East Asiatic Squadron, the initial mobilization assigned all these ships to the High Sea Fleet, based at Wilhelmshaven on the North Sea and commanded by Admiral Friedrich von Ingenohl. The Baltic command at Kiel, under Admiral Prince Henry of Prussia, the emperor's brother, at the start of the war sent everything larger than a light cruiser to the North Sea, but soon received back the oldest pre-dreadnoughts and armored cruisers as its standing force. The Kiel Canal, linking the North Sea to the Baltic across Holstein, enabled the navy to move ships easily between the two commands. Originally opened in 1895, the waterway had to be enlarged to accommodate dreadnoughts, a project not completed until June 24, 1914, four days before the assassination of Archduke Francis Ferdinand at Sarajevo.

France entered the war with four dreadnoughts, twenty-six pre-dreadnought battleships, and twenty-two armored cruisers. Some of the pre-dreadnoughts were over a quarter of a century old, but of the lot, nineteen would see action during the war. The prewar redeployments left all the French navy's dreadnoughts, all active pre-dreadnoughts, and twelve of its armored cruisers assigned to the Mediterranean Fleet (officially the *première armée navale*), based at Toulon and Bizerte, under the command of Vice Admiral Augustin Boué de Lapeyrère. The most significant force outside the Mediterranean, Rear Admiral Albert Rouyer's Second Light Squadron (*deuxième escadre légère*), was assigned to defend the western Channel along with the British navy, but Rouyer's forces and those assigned to patrol the Atlantic were mostly smaller ships, and together included just seven armored cruisers. France's three remaining armored cruisers were stationed in the West Indies, the Far East, and the South Pacific.

When Austria-Hungary declared war on July 28, 1914, its navy included three dreadnoughts, twelve pre-dreadnought battleships, and three armored cruisers, of which the oldest pre-dreadnoughts (three 5,600-ton *Monarch*-class coast defenders) and the oldest armored cruiser were of little use. Admiral Anton Haus served as commander of the Austro-Hungarian fleet, almost all of which was stationed in the Adriatic, either at Pola or at the secondary base at Cattaro (Kotor). Austria-Hungary typically kept one cruiser in the Far East; in 1914, the old protected cruiser *Kaiserin Elisabeth* filled this role. The concentration of Austro-Hungarian forces in the Adriatic underscored the distrust the Dual Monarchy had for its nominal ally, Italy.

Italy's active fleet included three dreadnoughts, of which two had just been completed in May 1914, backed by nine pre-dreadnoughts and ten armored cruisers. Aside from the newest quartet (the *Regina Elena* class) the pre-dreadnoughts were of limited value, as were the three oldest armored cruisers. In home waters, the primary Italian bases were La Spezia on the west coast, Taranto in the south, Brindisi at the mouth of the Adriatic, and Venice. When the rest of Europe went to war, the Italian fleet (commander-in-chief Admiral Prince Luigi of Savoy, Duke of the Abruzzi) had most of its best ships concentrated at Taranto: the three dreadnoughts, the eight newest pre-dreadnoughts, and eight of the nine newest armored cruisers. The old armored cruiser *Marco Polo*, at Shanghai, was the only armored warship based outside the Mediterranean. A number of light cruisers, destroyers, and gunboats patrolled the coasts of Italy's colonial possessions: Libya, the Dodecanese Islands, and Eritrea.

After relegating its oldest pre-dreadnought battleships to training ships on the eve of the war, Russia entered the action with ten pre-dreadnoughts and six armored cruisers in active service. Seven dreadnoughts were under construction, four for the Baltic (to be completed later in 1914) and three for the Black Sea, but until they were in commission, Russia remained the weakest of Europe's naval powers. The Baltic Fleet (Admiral Nikolai Essen), based at Kronstadt near St. Petersburg with forward bases at Helsinki, Reval (Tallinn), and Libau (Liepaja), included four of the pre-dreadnoughts and all of the armored cruisers. The Black Sea Fleet (Vice Admiral Andrei Ebergard), based at Sevastopol in the Crimea, included the remaining six pre-dreadnoughts. After its defeat in the Russo-Japanese War, Russia maintained only limited naval forces in the Far East. As of August 1914, its "Siberian Flotilla," based at Vladivostok, included just the light cruisers *Askold* and *Zhemchug* and other smaller vessels, the Russian navy's only warships based outside European waters.

Japan entered the war with two dreadnoughts and two battle cruisers in service, backed by sixteen pre-dreadnoughts (including the two giant *Satsuma*s, but also two 4,200-ton coast defenders captured from the Russians in 1905). Thirteen armored cruisers included four which the Japanese rated as battle cruisers. The First Fleet (Vice Admiral Yamaya Tamin) and Second Fleet (Admiral Hikonojo Kamimura) were evenly divided in numbers, but the former included most of the newest and best units, while the "battleships" of the latter included the two coast defenders and three other captured Russian pre-dreadnoughts. In the Japanese home islands, the principal naval bases were at Yokosuka, Kure, Sasebo, and Maizuru.

    Finally, the United States had ten dreadnoughts, twenty-three pre-dreadnought battleships, and twelve armored cruisers when war broke out in Europe. The Atlantic Fleet (Rear Admiral Charles Badger), based at Norfolk, but with an important anchorage at Guantanamo Bay, Cuba, was by far the largest US Navy force, including all the dreadnoughts and all the pre-dreadnoughts on active duty. The Pacific Fleet (Vice Admiral Thomas Howard), operating out of San Francisco and Pearl Harbor, Hawaii, included all armored cruisers not deployed on individual missions. The Asiatic Fleet (Rear Admiral Walter Cowles), based at Manila Bay, Philippines, had no armored warships.

## Conclusion

On the eve of the assassination of Archduke Francis Ferdinand at Sarajevo, the state of navies and naval warfare reflected the frenzied pace of change at all levels especially over the preceding decade. Among the naval powers, the British and French were behaving like genuine allies, over the protests of at least some British leaders who continued to insist that the Entente was not an alliance, while the Triple Alliance appeared to be in better shape than it had been in quite some time, with its navies cooperating more than ever before. Yet the disposition of Italy in case of a general war remained the greatest strategic uncertainty, as the Austro-Italian rivalry led to considerable skepticism over whether Italy really would support its alliance partners in a crisis. Aside from the Italians, the Turks ranked as the most significant wild card. Further weakened by the Balkan Wars of 1912–13, the Ottoman Empire was under a new government determined to revitalize the country and restore its relevance internationally, but no one was yet certain what that meant for the Turks or their strategic position in the eastern Mediterranean and Black Sea.

    The prewar assumption that the new capital ship types had rendered their predecessors obsolete would be vindicated as soon as dreadnoughts saw action against pre-dreadnought battleships, and battle cruisers against older armored cruisers. Yet there would be situations throughout the First World War, especially on the side of the

Allies, where warships of the older types were put to good use. On the questions of range and firepower, engagements involving dreadnoughts and battle cruisers would be fought at much greater distances than the leading navies practiced before 1914, with gunnery ranges longer and torpedo ranges shorter than had been assumed. There were surprises in store for the smaller warship types as well. In the North Sea, as well as the Adriatic, late-model light cruisers would be the workhorses of their respective navies, probing, scouting, and patrolling on a daily or weekly basis, while the capital ships spent most of their time in port. Submarines, of course, were to increase dramatically in significance as soon as the war began, assuming an importance few had foreseen. Meanwhile, naval aviation, in its infancy as of 1914, would still not be mature enough to have much of an impact before the war ended, but this likely would have been different if the fighting had gone on for another year or two. All things considered, given the centrality of materiel and technology in naval warfare (compared with the centrality of human factors in the operations of mass armies on land), the navies mobilizing for war in August 1914 should have faced far less uncertainty than the armies, but this was not the case. The Great War at sea, like the conflict on land, would assume a character no one had predicted.

Nevertheless, those most involved in preparing the leading navies for war approached the prospect of it calmly enough. Captain Hankey, at the center of the Admiralty's planning for war with Germany for nearly eight years, later recalled that on the evening of August 4, after Britain issued its ultimatum in response to the German invasion of Belgium, he "went to bed excited but confident." He believed that "in the long run sea power must bring us to victory," and conceded that for him, this conviction "amounted almost to a religion." It was a faith backed by historical precedent. Hankey noted that "the Germans, like Napoleon, might overrun the Continent" and thus "might prolong the war," but "the final issue ... would be determined by economic pressure," the practical application of British naval superiority.[43]

[43] Quoted in Offer, *The First World War: An Agrarian Interpretation*, p. 317.

# 3  GLOBAL PRELUDE

On August 12, 1914, eight days after Britain's declaration of war on Germany completed the initial line-up of European belligerents of the First World War, Vice Admiral Count Maximilian von Spee used wireless telegraphy to coordinate the rendezvous of five warships of his German East Asiatic Squadron with seven supply ships and colliers at Pagan in the Marianas. The western Pacific island, nearly 2,000 miles (3,200 km) southeast of the squadron's home port at Tsingtao (Qingdao), China, would be the last place that this particular constellation of vessels ever assembled. Facing the prospect that Japan, Britain's Far East ally, might soon enter the war, Spee oversaw a frenzied day of activity, as supplies and coal were loaded aboard the warships and personnel exchanged to address various staffing needs. Captain Hans Pochhammer, first officer of the armored cruiser *Gneisenau* (and, six months later, the highest-ranking German survivor of the Battle of the Falklands), remarked that the likelihood of Japanese intervention meant "only one course could now be taken" by the squadron, "to go east through the side that was still open, in order to escape from the pressure of superior forces closing around us, and to seek other hunting grounds." The following day, Spee's warships "disappeared... into the immensity of the Pacific Ocean, without leaving any trace behind us." The burden of secrecy placed demands on every crew member, as all had to be "careful that nothing fell overboard that might betray our passage," and thereby forfeit "our greatest advantage, which was that no one knew precisely where we were."[1]

As soon as the war began, it became clear that the Germans had too few colonies and bases to sustain a worldwide naval campaign. The coaling and supply of overseas cruisers became their Achilles' heel, a weakness they could overcome only through boldness, ingenuity, and effective use of the latest communication technology. It helped their cause that the warship deployment trends of the prewar years, culminating in the decision by the European powers to concentrate their capital ships in European and Mediterranean waters, gave a fighting chance to units caught far from home, in particular the ships of Spee's formidable squadron.

## Spee's odyssey: to Coronel and the Falklands

For over a decade before the outbreak of war, the German naval presence in the Far East had featured two armored cruisers, a role filled since 1911 by the 12,780-ton sister ships *Scharnhorst* and *Gneisenau*, leading a squadron based at the port of Tsingtao on Kiaochow (Jiaozhou) Bay. After acquiring their Chinese colony in 1898, the Germans had transformed it into a congenial home away from home for the colonial officials, soldiers, and sailors stationed there. Economic development had already brought thousands of Germans and other foreigners to the city, creating a European civilian population that seemed destined to grow as commercial opportunities increased. As long as peace prevailed and the Chinese connection to the Trans-Siberian Railway remained open, mail from Germany arrived overland in just two weeks. The manpower of the East Asiatic Squadron served on a staggered two-year rotation, with half being replaced every June. Barring a crisis that would keep the squadron in east Asian waters, shortly after the turnover the commanding admiral (since 1912, Spee) would integrate the newcomers and the veterans by taking his best cruisers on a three-month summer tour of Germany's Pacific possessions, typically steaming as far as Samoa. During the rest of the year, the German squadron and its counterparts from other navies observed traditional peacetime rituals, exchanging port

---

[1] Hans Pochhammer, *Before Jutland: Admiral von Spee's Last Voyage*, trans. H. J. Stenning (London: Jarrolds, 1931), pp. 66–68.

calls at their respective Chinese bases or with the Japanese. Given what was to come, ironies abounded. In February 1913, Spee's squadron called at Hong Kong, where the host ships included the British armored cruiser *Monmouth*, which they would sink less than two years later at the Battle of Coronel. That autumn, the *Gneisenau* enjoyed a six-day visit to Nagasaki, where the following autumn the survivors of the garrison of Tsingtao would return as prisoners of war.

As spring gave way to summer in 1914, the customary annual cycle of activity continued. On June 2, a steamer from Wilhelmshaven brought 1,600 replacements to Tsingtao, and a week later a like number of veterans left for home aboard the same ship. The squadron and its foreign counterparts continued to honor their peacetime rituals right up to the outbreak of the war, exchanging visits and cordial greetings. When the armored cruiser *Minotaur*, Britain's Far East flagship, called at Tsingtao from June 12 to June 16, the program included a variety of athletic activities. Pochhammer recalled the lively competition between two navies soon to be at war. The officers and seamen squared off "in a 1,200 yards race, in polo, in boxing contests, tug-of-war, gymnastics, in high and long jumping, and, of course, in football (soccer)," with the British finding the latter contest "particularly congenial."[2] Four days after the British visitors departed, Spee left Tsingtao with the *Scharnhorst* and *Gneisenau* for the annual three-month summer cruise to Samoa; their itinerary included the islands of Micronesia on the outbound voyage and a southerly course on the return trip, with port calls scheduled in the Bismarck Archipelago and Kaiser-Wilhelmsland (northeastern New Guinea).

Yap in the western Carolines served as Germany's western Pacific communication hub; the island had a powerful wireless station along with direct undersea cable links to China, to Java in the Dutch East Indies, and to Guam on the United States' Manila to San Francisco line. It was from Yap, on June 29, that Spee, cruising in the Marianas at the time, received news of Archduke Francis Ferdinand's assassination at Sarajevo the day before. Because a general war involving Germany did not seem inevitable, or even likely, he proceeded southward and eastward from the Marianas through the Carolines, visiting Saipan and Truk in the days that followed. Spee's squadron initially included just the *Scharnhorst* and *Gneisenau*. The light cruiser

[2] *Ibid.*, p. 20.

Figure 3.1 Vice Admiral Maximilian von Spee

*Nürnberg* had departed Tsingtao two weeks before the armored cruisers, steaming ahead for the Pacific coast of Mexico, where it was to relieve the light cruiser *Leipzig*, deployed earlier by Spee to safeguard German interests threatened by the ongoing Mexican revolution. He left behind at Tsingtao the light cruisers *Emden* and *Cormoran*, four gunboats, one destroyer, and the protected cruiser *Kaiserin Elisabeth*, the only Austro-Hungarian warship stationed outside European waters. On July 17, the *Scharnhorst* and *Gneisenau* reached Ponape (Pohnpei) in the eastern Carolines, where they lingered to await further developments after receiving news that the crisis in Europe had worsened. The days that followed were an idyllic calm before the storm, featuring all-day shore leave and recreational activities. Excursions for the officers included a visit to the 1,000-year-old ruins of Metalanim

(Nan Matol), a sort of miniature Polynesian Venice or Tenochtitlan, built on man-made islands in a lagoon. But increasingly grim news from home forced Spee to turn the squadron's attention to preparing for war, starting on July 28, the day Austria-Hungary commenced hostilities against Serbia.[3]

On July 31, after being informed that war was imminent, Spee ordered that his ships were to be stripped of all nonessential items and fixtures. Almost everything made of wood was considered a fire hazard and had to go. Aboard the *Gneisenau* the officers agreed not to jettison the piano, but after the purge "the sole decoration was the emperor's picture." The discarded materials were simply thrown overboard, to be claimed from the sea by islanders circling the ships in their outriggers. When it came to personal items, Pochhammer remembered the treasured souvenirs officers packed for a mail ship they hoped would reach home, including "Buddhas of every shape and size, bows, arrows, spears, and other curiosities from our colonies."[4] Thus, even before Germany was at war and the squadron officially in harm's way, the ships had been readied for action. Word of Germany's mobilization against Russia and France reached Ponape late on the evening of August 2. The following day, in separate addresses aboard the *Scharnhorst* and *Gneisenau*, Spee "in fiery words exhorted the men to make good their oaths in the service of emperor and empire." In his remarks the admiral noted that "England's attitude is still uncertain, although unfriendly. Consequently we must also regard English ships as enemies."[5] On August 5, Spee received word of Britain's declaration of war on Germany the previous day. On August 6, the light cruiser *Nürnberg* joined the armored cruisers at Ponape, having reversed course at Honolulu rather than proceed as scheduled to relieve the *Leipzig* off the coast of Mexico. In the meantime, back in Tsingtao, the Germans commissioned two auxiliary cruisers. The Russian liner *Riasan*, a German-built vessel plying the Vladivostok–Shanghai route, was captured by the *Emden* on August 3 and brought to Tsingtao, where it received the guns, crew, and name of the much smaller *Cormoran*, while the North German Lloyd liner *Prinz Eitel Friedrich*, commandeered in Shanghai while en route home to Bremen from Yokohama, received the guns and crews of two of the four gunboats Spee had left behind.[6] They promptly put to sea with

---

[3] *Ibid.*, p. 49.   [4] *Ibid.*, pp. 50–51, 54.   [5] *Ibid.*, pp. 52–53.
[6] Otto Brauer, *Die Kreuzerfahrten des "Prinz Eitel-Friedrich"* (Berlin: August Scherl, 1918), pp. 10–12, 17.

the *Emden* in an attempt to catch up with the squadron. Afterward the military governor of Kiaochow Bay, Captain Alfred Meyer-Waldeck, used most of the 3,400 personnel from the remaining ships as reinforcements for the lone battalion of 765 German marines left to defend Tsingtao.

For his rendezvous point with the ships coming out of Tsingtao, Spee chose Pagan in the Marianas, a destination that would require the *Scharnhorst*, *Gneisenau*, and *Nürnberg* to double back to the northwest, nearly 1,200 miles (1,900 km) closer to Japan, a British ally whose intentions were not yet clear. British enthusiasm for the alliance had waned after Japan's decisive victory of 1905 had led a weakened Russia to settle its differences with Britain in the Anglo-Russian entente of 1907. At the same time, the elimination of the Russian Far Eastern threat led Japan to set its sights on a future competition with the United States for hegemony in the Pacific, ambitions Britain had no intention of supporting. Nevertheless, the pact of 1902 remained in effect, and its terms obligated the Japanese to enter the war as soon as the British faced hostilities with two powers. Britain declared war on Germany on August 4, and satisfied the *casus foederis* when it declared war on Austria-Hungary on August 13. But Japan's help was neither needed nor wanted, for Britain's naval forces and the manpower of the dominions of Australia and New Zealand more than sufficed to eliminate the German naval and colonial presence in the Pacific theater. From the onset Britain feared, correctly as it turned out, that Japan's involvement in the war would serve only to allow it eventually to claim many of Germany's east Asian and Pacific colonies at the peace table.

On August 15, Japan sent Germany an ultimatum demanding the disarmament or withdrawal of all German naval vessels in east Asian waters and the cession to Japan of the Kiaochow Bay territory with the base at Tsingtao. Eight days later, after the Germans refused to respond, the Japanese declared war. On August 27, a detachment from Admiral Kamimura's Second Fleet blockaded Kiaochow Bay, and six days later the first of 23,000 troops landed to lay siege to Tsingtao. The British added face-saving contributions – the pre-dreadnought battleship *Triumph*, a destroyer, and 1,500 troops from their Tientsin (Tianjin) garrison – that made it an "Allied" rather than an exclusively Japanese operation. The overmatched defenders withstood shelling by the blockading fleet and air raids launched from the seaplane tender *Wakamiya*, but after eleven weeks Meyer-Waldeck scuttled the remaining warships and surrendered the garrison. Japanese naval losses included the old protected cruiser *Takachiyo*, sunk by a German torpedo boat, along with a destroyer, a torpedo boat, and three minesweepers sunk in various mishaps. The Japanese lost just over 700 men in the blockade and siege, the Germans and Austro-Hungarians 200. The surviving defenders of Tsingtao were the largest body of prisoners taken by the Japanese during the First World War and, in sharp contrast to their counterparts in the Second World War, were reasonably well treated, although the survivors were not ultimately repatriated to Germany and Austria until two years after the war ended.[7]

While the Japanese were still preparing their opening moves, Spee's full-steam sprint northwestward from Ponape allowed his three ships to meet the light cruiser *Emden* and auxiliary cruiser *Prinz Eitel Friedrich* at Pagan on August 12. Along with adding firepower to the squadron, they came laden with supplies to sustain the rest of Spee's cruisers on an extended voyage. Another seven supply ships and colliers participated in the Marianas rendezvous. Of the warships Germany then had at sea in the Pacific, the only ones not present were the *Leipzig*, which had left the coast of Mexico to function as a raider in the eastern Pacific, and the auxiliary cruiser *Cormoran*, which would join the squadron in the Marshalls two weeks later, escorting another two supply ships. The gunboat *Geier*, ordered to the Pacific from German East Africa in June 1914, had reached Singapore when the war began, but Spee could not afford to wait for it. Before conducting further operations, the warships put ashore their Chinese servants (the *Gneisenau* alone had fourteen Chinese laundrymen aboard), while the supply ships and colliers that were to follow the squadron likewise discharged any Chinese or other foreign nationals serving in their crews. Their places were filled by German reservists, many of them pulled from German passenger liners and merchantmen steaming in east Asian waters when the war broke out. For weeks to come Spee would lament the loss of his "good Chinese cooks," writing to his wife that their German replacements, from a North German Lloyd steamer, were "not exactly good."[8]

---

[7] Timothy D. Saxon, "Anglo-Japanese Naval Cooperation, 1914–1918," *Naval War College Review*, 53(1) (Winter 2000): 66–70.

[8] Spee to Countess von Spee, August 18, 1914, and October 1, 1914, in Hermann Kirchhoff (ed.), *Maximilian Graf von Spee, Der Sieger von Coronel: Das Lebensbild und die Erinnerungen eines deutschen Seemans* (Berlin: Marinedank-Verlag, 1915), pp. 19, 21.

During the brief Marianas rendezvous, Spee reassigned officers and skilled personnel from ship to ship as needed. Orientation to new roles and assignments had to occur on the fly, as the situation left no time to spare. After meeting with his captains aboard the *Scharnhorst* on August 13, Spee detached Captain Karl von Müller with the *Emden* to operate as a raider in the East Indies and Indian Ocean, then headed back to the southeast with the rest of his ships. Intent on confusing the Allies as much as possible as to the size and location of his squadron, on August 22, Spee detached the *Nürnberg* for two weeks to go back to Honolulu, show the flag, and also instruct the local German consul to make arrangements for coal and supplies for the squadron in the eastern Pacific.[9] The movements of the German auxiliary cruisers caused further confusion for the Allies, generating countless false reports of the squadron's whereabouts. After meeting Spee's ships in the Marshalls in late August, the *Cormoran* remained in the western Pacific and evaded capture for almost four months before accepting American internment at Guam, while the *Prinz Eitel Friedrich*, operating independently as a raider, crossed the Pacific later than the squadron but on the same general course. Meanwhile, the gunboat *Geier*, coming all the way from East Africa, never caught up with the squadron and, like the *Cormoran*, remained in the western Pacific. Ideally, the decisions Spee made on August 13 would eventually have brought the *Emden* into the Atlantic and home to Germany via the Cape of Good Hope, while the rest of the squadron made its way home by taking the longer route across the Pacific and around Cape Horn. From the start Spee's officers were keenly aware that morale could become a serious problem; Pochhammer recalled later that "these were difficult days... for our men... who naturally had little taste for following this route."[10]

From the start of their uncertain venture, Spee's own fatalism often proved to be difficult to hide. One of the few Catholics in the mainly Protestant German naval officer corps, the admiral had the local bishop in Ponape hear his confession – and those of his sons Heinrich, a lieutenant aboard the *Gneisenau*, and Otto, an ensign aboard the *Nürnberg* – and had a priest visit the ships to hear the confessions of Catholic sailors, all out of concern for whether or when they would again have access to the sacrament. After the ships were cleared for action and underway, it helped matters that Spee "did not like too

[9] Headrick, *The Invisible Weapon*, p. 161.   [10] Pochhammer, *Before Jutland*, p. 73.

many formalities,"[11] and did what he could to lessen the inequities which, later in the war, would spawn revolutionary activity aboard the larger warships of the German fleet. At a stroke he eliminated a social barrier that the Imperial navy as a whole never was able to resolve, combining the mess of the officers with that of the deck officers (*Deckoffiziere*). The latter, unique to the German navy, fulfilled tasks assigned to senior petty officers (NCOs) and engineering officers in other navies, and had always chafed at their second-rate status. As they cruised across the Pacific, the ships conducted strenuous drills. The *Scharnhorst* and *Gneisenau* simulated attacks against each other, and at times against their colliers and supply ships, and conducted gunnery practice against a target towed by one of their supply ships. The crews needed little encouragement to take the drills seriously, for everyone knew that at any moment the squadron might have to fight, or flee from, a superior Allied force. This same reality prompted Spee to coal his ships more frequently than normal, topping off their bunkers whenever coal was available and conditions allowed it. To avoid dirtying their uniforms beyond hope of cleaning, the men coaled their ships wearing "old clothes that could not be used for any other purpose," and "to put everyone in good humor" many sailors turned the occasion into a competition for the "most comical" or "fantastic costume."[12]

Aside from these occasions, the gravity of the squadron's situation permitted little levity, but on September 10, when the ships crossed the Equator, they staged the ceremonies customary in many navies, with crew members dressed as Neptune and Triton "baptizing" all aboard who were experiencing the crossing for the first time. Afterward the drills resumed, in preparation for the battle Spee intended to seek with the enemy off Samoa, which had fallen to the Allies in late August. It was a risky decision, since the battle cruiser *Australia* – much larger, faster, and more powerful than the *Scharnhorst* or *Gneisenau* – could have been anchored there. The bold stroke brought a frustrating standoff, as Spee found that "the nest was empty" of Allied warships, while ashore, the colony was occupied by a force of New Zealanders too numerous to dislodge with a landing party.[13] Spee opted not to shell the colonial capital, Apia, "for fear of hurting innocent people"

---

[11] Ibid., p. 194.   [12] Ibid., pp. 76, 83.
[13] Spee to Countess von Spee, September 14, 1914, in Kirchhoff, *Maximilian Graf von Spee*, p. 20.

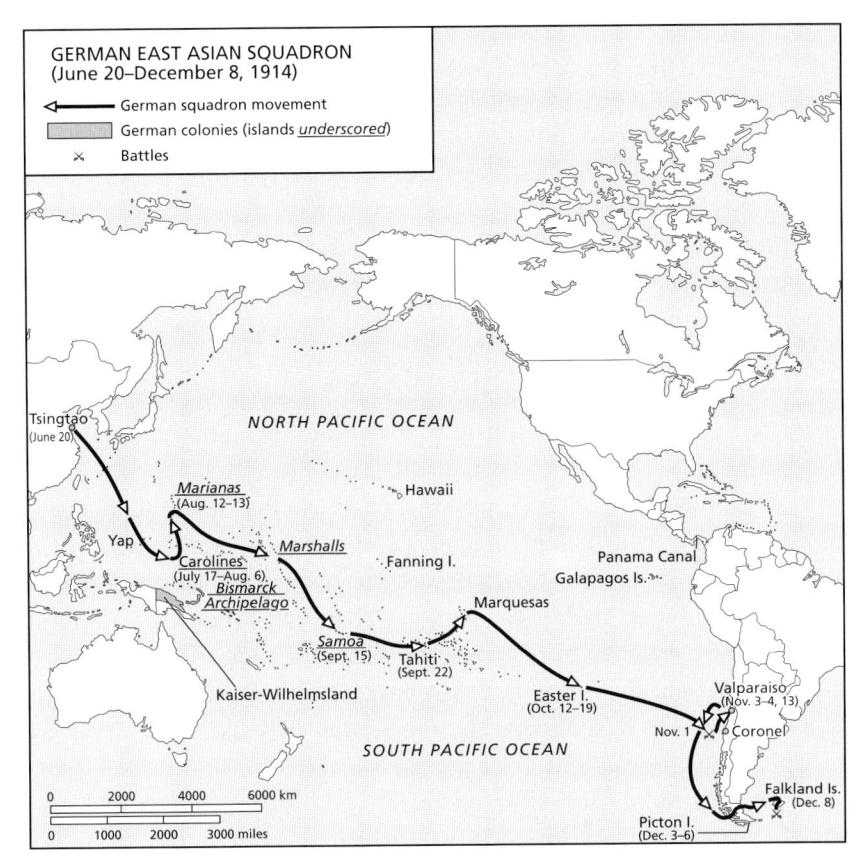

Map 3.1 German East Asian Squadron (June 20–December 8, 1914)

or "damag[ing] German property."[14] Having revealed the squadron's location for no gain, he did not linger off Samoa. When his cruisers next made landfall on September 22 at Tahiti, where the people and property were French, he had no reservations about shelling the town of Papeete. Gunfire from the armored cruisers leveled two blocks of homes and businesses, sank the French gunboat *Zélée* and a German prize it had taken, and panicked local officials into igniting a 40,000-ton coal depot to prevent it from falling into Spee's hands.[15]

Throughout Spee's campaign and the Allied effort to hunt him down, wireless telegraphy played a central role, at times supplemented by sporadic exchanges delivered via undersea cable from various island

[14] Pochhammer, *Before Jutland*, p. 106.
[15] "Saw Papeete Razed by German Shells," *New York Times*, October 8, 1914.

outposts and neutral ports.[16] In the targeting of communications, early casualties included the German wireless station on Yap in the western Carolines, destroyed by shellfire from the British armored cruiser *Minotaur* on August 12, and the British cable station on Fanning Island (Tabuaeran), whose destruction by a landing party from the *Nürnberg* in early September cut Canada's direct link to Australia and New Zealand for two weeks. Less spectacular, but far more significant to Spee, wireless enabled the German East Asiatic Squadron to coordinate a regular resupply of coal, critical to its attempt to cross the world's largest ocean with no secure bases along the way. Thanks to the wireless, Spee orchestrated timely appearances by his own colliers and others contracted via the German consul in Honolulu, but unfortunately for the officers and crews of the squadron, access to other supplies came on a hit-or-miss basis. Three months after leaving Tsingtao and six weeks removed from being replenished in the Marianas rendezvous, they began to experience shortages of the most basic items. According to Pochhammer, by late September "soap had become scarce, and henceforth we scoured ourselves with sand and soda." Smokers who had nursed along their supplies of tobacco had been less careful with their stock of matches; aboard the *Gneisenau* they averted a crisis by fabricating an electric lighter for the mess room.[17]

Yet the demeanor of the admiral and his officers revealed that while circumstances on board were increasingly spartan, they were far from desperate. The Germans continued to pay or barter for fresh meat, fruit, and vegetables from island natives, and when they requisitioned money or stores belonging to an enemy government – such as in France's Marquesas Islands, their next stop after Tahiti – they conscientiously left behind a written receipt. Their brief sojourn in the undefended Marquesas also brought the crews the luxury of "a slight relaxation," and for most of them, their first contact with dry land since Ponape two months earlier. Pochhammer later recalled that the warships took on a Noah's Ark appearance after foraging expeditions ashore. "Pigeons were already flying around, hens were clucking on coal baskets, and the little black pigs had a small [coal] bunker all to themselves."[18] Describing the same scene in a letter home, the *Gneisenau*'s Lieutenant

---

[16] John Keegan, *Intelligence in War* (New York: Alfred A. Knopf, 2003), uses this campaign as a case study of the state of the art of wireless communication during the First World War.

[17] Pochhammer, *Before Jutland*, p. 114.  [18] Ibid., pp. 119–120.

Heinrich von Spee informed his mother that "the living conditions are quite primitive and cramped, but that won't hurt."[19] Unfortunately, the food and water of the Marquesas did not agree with all of the men. After being "practically free of any serious illness" up to that point, the crews of the ships succumbed to "a slight epidemic of dysentery" once the squadron was underway to its next stop, Easter Island. The affliction turned serious in some of the men, and two of them died.[20]

At Easter Island the *Scharnhorst*, *Gneisenau*, and *Nürnberg* met up for the first time with the light cruisers *Leipzig* and *Dresden*, which most recently had been cruising off the west and east coasts, respectively, of South America. Once again, Spee used wireless to orchestrate a concentration of ships that otherwise would have been impossible, contacting the *Leipzig* and *Dresden* at a distance of roughly 3,000 miles (4,800 km), when each of the vessels and the ships of Spee's squadron were 1,500 miles (2,400 km) away from the island. Colliers and supply ships laden with fuel and provisions came from Valparaiso in neutral Chile to join the rendezvous. Like the meeting in the Marianas a week after the war began, Spee's Easter Island rendezvous brought together a total of five warships and seven supply ships or colliers; all were present from October 12 to October 14, and the armored cruisers stayed on until October 19. The Germans found that the inhabitants of the isolated island, a Chilean possession, knew little of the war. The only other foreign visitors were a British expedition studying the island's mysterious stone statues, and Spee had no difficulty purchasing cattle and sheep from a local rancher of British origin, who even accepted a check as payment for the livestock. Unfortunately for the Germans, heavy seas lasting the entire week complicated the effort to replenish the warships. "Of all our so-called periods of rest, our stay at Easter Island... was by far the most disagreeable," recalled Pochhammer, because the "long southwesterly swell made us roll day and night, hurling the ships against each other, and impeding the coaling, the launching and hoisting of boats, as well as our communications with the land."[21] A number of men sustained injuries during these operations, including a lieutenant from the *Dresden* who broke his leg. He and the other worst cases, along with those men who had yet to shake

---

[19] Heinrich von Spee to Countess von Spee, October 10, 1914, in Kirchhoff, *Maximilian Graf von Spee*, p. 56.
[20] Pochhammer, *Before Jutland*, pp. 122–123.   [21] *Ibid.*, pp. 124–125.

off the dysentery contracted in the Marquesas, at this stage were judged unable to continue with the squadron. Lieutenant Heinrich Schneider of the *Dresden* later noted the irony that these forty "seriously ill" men, sent to Valparaiso aboard the supply ship *Yorck*, were pitied at the time by their shipmates.[22] Destined for hospital and convalescence in Chile, they proved to be the lucky ones when, two months later, so few of their comrades survived the Battle of the Falklands.

From Easter Island, Spee's replenished warships steamed 1,860 miles (3,000 km) eastward to the Juan Fernandez Islands, around 400 miles (650 km) off the coast of Chile, where they encountered the *Prinz Eitel Friedrich* for the first time since August. Low on coal and supplies, the auxiliary cruiser was ordered by Spee to proceed to Valparaiso. Under international law, any belligerent warship calling in a neutral port could stay for twenty-four hours without requesting internment for the duration of the war. The *Prinz Eitel Friedrich* availed itself of what the law would allow, but when it returned, restocked, to the islands, the squadron was gone, having steamed for the port of Coronel upon receiving word that the British light cruiser *Glasgow* had called there on October 31.[23] In the waters off Coronel, on the evening of November 1, Spee's cruisers encountered the *Glasgow* and three other ships from the British navy's Fourth Cruiser Squadron, under the command of Rear Admiral Sir Christopher Cradock.[24]

Tasked with keeping open Britain's trade with the ports of the Americas, Cradock began the war in command of a large force of cruisers dispersed from the coast of Canada to Brazil, but faced just two German light cruisers functioning as commerce raiders: the *Karlsruhe*, eventually bottled up in the Caribbean; and the *Dresden*, which Cradock's own flagship *Good Hope* and its escorts pursued through the South Atlantic until it disappeared around Cape Horn into the Pacific, en route to join Spee at Easter Island. Cradock spent most of October at Port Stanley in the Falkland Islands, awaiting the arrival of the *Canopus*, a pre-dreadnought battleship dispatched from the Channel Fleet to boost his firepower in case he encountered Spee, but Cradock

---

[22] Heinrich Schneider, *Die letzte Fahrt des kleinen Kreuzers "Dresden"* (Leipzig: K. F. Koehler, 1926), p. 63.
[23] Brauer, *Die Kreuzerfahrten*, p. 49.
[24] Unless otherwise noted, sources on the Battle of Coronel are Geoffrey Bennett, *Coronel and the Falklands* (London: Batsford, 1962), and John Irving, *Coronel and the Falklands* (London: A. M. Philpot, 1927).

considered the new addition practically worthless, as it was far slower than his cruisers (and Spee's cruisers, too, for that matter). Cradock left for the Pacific on October 22, and steamed for Coronel after an intercepted wireless message indicated that the *Leipzig* had called there. Unaware that Spee was deliberately sending all his transmissions via the *Leipzig*'s wireless in an attempt to mask the size and location of his force, Cradock expected to encounter only that lone light cruiser. Though the Admiralty warned him that it was likely that Spee was headed his way, he convinced himself that the German squadron might be in the vicinity of the Galapagos Islands, 2,800 miles (4,500 km) to the north, en route to the recently opened Panama Canal, the fastest route home to Germany – and one Spee never considered taking.[25]

Cradock arrived off Coronel with two armored cruisers, the 14,150-ton flagship *Good Hope* and the 9,800-ton *Monmouth*, both somewhat older than the *Scharnhorst* and *Gneisenau*. Aside from the *Glasgow*, which came out of Coronel to rejoin him, his only other ship was the armed merchant cruiser *Otranto*. The *Canopus*, needing engine repairs after the long voyage from Britain, left Port Stanley later and trailed Cradock's cruisers at a distance of some 250 miles (400 km), escorting his colliers. Off Coronel, Cradock was shocked to find not only the *Leipzig*, but Spee's entire squadron aside from the *Nürnberg*, which arrived during the ensuing action. He did not consider waiting for the *Canopus* and instead engaged Spee despite the unfavorable odds. Shortly after 18:00, in heavy seas and with the southern springtime dusk approaching, the two columns of warships began to close 20 miles (32 km) offshore. The Germans took a southerly course east of the British line, leaving Cradock's ships silhouetted against the setting sun. The 8.2-inch (21-cm) guns of Spee's *Scharnhorst* recorded their first hits on Cradock's *Good Hope* at 18:39, at a range of over 11,000 yards (10,000 m); the *Gneisenau*, next in the German line, hit the *Monmouth* at 13,000 yards (11,900 m). British return fire remained ineffective even as the columns closed their distance to a mere 5,300 yards (4,850 m). Spee estimated thirty-five hits against the *Good Hope* alone, which at 19:50 finally succumbed to a fatal explosion amidships. The *Monmouth*, meanwhile, did not return fire after 19:20 but remained afloat, a crippled hulk, until dispatched by shells from the *Nürnberg* at 20:58. The darkness and stormy seas made rescue efforts impossible, and both

---

[25] Keegan, *Intelligence in War*, p. 123.

British armored cruisers sank with all hands. The *Otranto* and *Glasgow* escaped to return to Port Stanley, en route warning the *Canopus* and the colliers to turn back. In contrast to the British losses – Cradock and 1,569 of his officers and seamen – the only German casualties were two "slightly wounded" men aboard the *Gneisenau*, which was struck by four British shells. The *Scharnhorst* sustained two hits, while Spee's light cruisers came through completely unscathed.[26] For the Germans it was a complete triumph, achieved at negligible cost, inspiring the devout Spee to acknowledge the Almighty in the post-battle message he wired to the other ships of the squadron: "With God's help a beautiful victory, for which I express my recognition and best wishes to the crews."[27]

After the victory, Spee had the squadron visit the port of Valparaiso in order "to exploit our victory on the spot," as Pochhammer later explained, to "show to the whole world that we were still in perfect health, in fact without the slightest damage and quite prepared for new fights."[28] Thus, Spee exposed as fabrications the British reports first denying that the battle had even occurred, then claiming that some of the German cruisers had been sunk or severely damaged. In addition to the twenty-four hour restriction, international law did not allow a belligerent navy to send more than three warships at a time to call in a neutral port. In order to comply with the rules, Spee anchored at Valparaiso on November 3–4 with just the *Scharnhorst*, *Gneisenau*, and *Nürnberg*. The *Leipzig* and *Dresden* followed on November 13.

Like the *Prinz Eitel Friedrich* the day before the battle, the ships of Spee's squadron received an enthusiastic reception from the local community of some 3,000 Germans. The victory off Coronel made a difference, however, in the demeanor of Chilean officials and the general public; suddenly less circumspect about what the British might think, they greeted the Germans as heroes. On November 3, following a formal reception including the Chilean naval leadership, local government officials, and diplomats from some of the consulates, Spee and most of his officers attended a dinner at the German Club

---

[26] Spee's report of the battle, dated Coronel, November 2, 1914, is reproduced at wwi.lib.byu.edu/index.php/Graf_von_Spee%27s_Report. German accounts of the battle give all times as one hour earlier than British accounts.
[27] Quoted in Hans Pochhammer, *Graf Spees letzter Fahrt: Erinnerungen an das Kreuzergeschwader* (Berlin: Täglichen Rundschau, 1918), p. 158.
[28] Pochhammer, *Before Jutland*, pp. 156–159.

Figure 3.2 The *Scharnhorst* at Valparaiso, with *Gneisenau* in background

of Valparaiso. The local Germans "naturally wanted to celebrate," but Spee "absolutely rejected" the idea, insisting upon a more restrained affair and limiting his own participation to 90 minutes.[29] Speaking to a former German naval surgeon who had emigrated to Chile, the admiral struck a fatalistic tone even in the afterglow of victory: "You must not forget that I am quite homeless. I cannot reach Germany. We possess no other secure harbor anywhere in the world. I must fight my way through the seas of the world doing as much mischief as I can, until my ammunition is exhausted, or a foe far superior in power succeeds in catching me. But it will cost the wretches dearly before they take me down."[30] Notwithstanding Spee's relative gloom, his ships were swamped with enthusiastic visitors from the shore, many of them German expatriates. They also processed hundreds of applicants for enlistment, from among the expatriates as well as the crews of the dozens of German merchantmen trapped by the war in Valparaiso harbor. As first officer, Pochhammer served as judge of all applicants for the *Gneisenau*, many of whom were "unsuitable for service on a warship." The most valuable additions included engineers and stokers

[29] Spee to Countess von Spee, November 3, 1914, in Kirchhoff, *Maximilian Graf von Spee*, p. 40.
[30] Quoted in Kirchhoff, *Maximilian Graf von Spee*, p. 73.

to reinforce the engine room, but he also enlisted "ship's carpenters" and "a few bakers and artisans."[31]

These scenes were repeated when the *Dresden* and *Leipzig* visited Valparaiso. Aboard the *Dresden*, Schneider reported that "children and women distributed cigarettes, tobacco, chocolate, and other delicacies" so generously that the crew were left with bulging pockets. "We could have eaten ourselves sick on the grapes and other fruits that could not take a long voyage."[32] He found the whole experience emotionally overwhelming. The gifts to the squadron included Christmas presents that, Pochhammer noted, were stored with great care aboard the supply ships, "to be given the men on Christmas Eve." Later in the month, farther down the coast of Chile, a shore party even cut and stowed several evergreen trees to ensure that the men of the squadron would have Christmas trees when the time came. "Who could say where we should be at Christmas?"[33] Most of them would be dead.

While ashore in Valparaiso, Spee received a telegram from Berlin ordering him to "break through for home."[34] Having conceded that he could not reach Germany, the admiral was in no hurry to give it a try. His armored cruisers finally rounded Cape Horn on December 2, the light cruisers on December 4, after becoming separated in stormy weather. The *Gneisenau*, which steamed close to the tip of the continent, and the *Dresden*, which strayed well south into the Drake Passage, both encountered formidable icebergs en route, Schneider reporting that the *Dresden* "nearly collided with one of them."[35] Spee had the armored cruisers anchor off Picton Island in the Beagle Channel from December 3 to December 6, to take on coal from a captured British merchantman and to allow the straggling light cruisers to catch up. Pochhammer recalled that, during the respite, "the sportsmen shouldered their guns and plunged into the thickets which fringed the shores of the island."[36] The officers exchanged visits from ship to ship, and Spee came to the *Gneisenau* one evening for a game of bridge. At midday on December 6 the squadron raised steam, and as soon as they were underway the commanders of the ships told their officers and crews that they would be attacking the Falkland Islands, roughly 400 miles (650 km) to the northeast, to destroy the wireless station and coal stocks there. Spee

[31] Pochhammer, *Before Jutland*, p. 167.   [32] Schneider, *Die letzte Fahrt*, pp. 84–85.
[33] Pochhammer, *Before Jutland*, p. 186.
[34] Quoted in Keegan, *Intelligence in War*, p. 133.
[35] Schneider, *Die letzte Fahrt*, p. 93.   [36] Pochhammer, *Before Jutland*, p. 193.

arrived off Port Stanley on the morning of December 8, only to find a British force much larger than his own, including two battle cruisers, anchored there.[37]

In London, the Admiralty had responded to the lopsided defeat at Coronel – the first suffered by a British naval squadron since the Napoleonic Wars – by dispatching Vice Admiral Sir Doveton Sturdee to the South Atlantic with the battle cruisers *Invincible* and *Inflexible*, to intercept Spee after he rounded Cape Horn. At the same time, the battle cruiser *Princess Royal* was ordered to the West Indies, and the battle cruiser *Australia*, then at Fiji, to the Pacific coast of Central America, in case Spee decided to steam for the Panama Canal. These were the types of missions Fisher had envisaged for his fast battleship-sized cruisers, and it would be the only time during the Great War that any vessel of the type was used for such a task. On November 19, the British received confirmation that Spee would indeed be rounding Cape Horn, when analysts in the Admiralty Intelligence Division's "Room 40" decoded a German wireless message intercepted days earlier. Sturdee reached the Falklands on December 7, and took stock of the forces at his disposal to hunt Spee down. After the debacle at Coronel, the *Canopus* had been grounded as a guardship and the *Glasgow* reinforced by the armored cruisers *Carnarvon* and *Kent*, the light cruisers *Bristol* and *Cornwall*, and the armed merchant cruiser *Macedonia*, the latter replacing the departed *Otranto*. After crossing the Equator into the South Atlantic, Sturdee had used the cruiser *Vindictive* at Ascension Island to relay his wireless messages. Closer to the Falklands, these duties fell to the light cruisers *Bristol* and *Glasgow*. Thus, the British concealed their buildup by keeping their battle cruisers and armored cruisers off the airwaves.

The German plan for the attack on Port Stanley called for the *Scharnhorst*, *Leipzig*, and *Dresden* to provide long-range covering fire, while the *Gneisenau* and *Nürnberg* steamed into the harbor to provide close-fire support for landing parties sent ashore to destroy the wireless station and other naval facilities. Like Cradock before Coronel, Spee interpreted the limited enemy wireless traffic to mean a limited enemy presence in the area. He expected to find Port Stanley harbor either empty or guarded by ships he could easily subdue; on his approach he

[37] The following paragraphs are based upon Bennett, *Coronel and the Falklands*, passim, and Irving, *Coronel and the Falklands*, passim. See also Headrick, *The Invisible Weapon*, p. 161; Friedman, *Naval Firepower*, pp. 106–107; Brooks, *Dreadnought Gunnery*, pp. 217–218; Keegan, *Intelligence at War*, pp. 133–140.

recognized that this was not the case, canceled his plans, and had the squadron reform at sea, covered by the *Scharnhorst*, which exchanged fire with the *Canopus* from a range of 14,000 yards (12,800 m). Facing the prospect of fighting a superior enemy force, Spee opted to flee rather than to fight. The British ships were coaling when the Germans arrived, giving Spee some hope that his squadron could escape before they raised steam. Sturdee was soon in hot pursuit, leading the way in his flagship *Invincible*, leaving behind only the immobilized *Canopus* to protect Port Stanley. Boasting a top speed of 25½ knots, the British battle cruisers were faster than any ship in Spee's squadron and a full 2 knots faster than his armored cruisers. The combination of broad daylight, clear skies, and calm seas further favored the pursuers, and they gradually closed the gap as the Germans fled southeastward from the Falklands.

Around 13:00 the big guns of the battle cruisers began to fire, missing badly from 16,500 yards (15,000 m), but soon their shells were splashing close enough for Spee to order his squadron to disperse. He steamed toward the northeast with the *Scharnhorst* and *Gneisenau* in order to lure the *Invincible* and *Inflexible* away from the light cruisers, which could continue to operate on their own as commerce raiders. As Spee had presumed, Sturdee chased the two armored cruisers with his battle cruisers, their 12-inch (30.5-cm) guns continuing to rain shells in the general direction of their prey. Both battle cruises had an earlier version of the Argo Clock rather than a Dreyer Table, which gave few valid ranges, but even after the change in course westerly winds continued to leave the pursuers partially blinded by their own funnel smoke, making range-finding problematic regardless of the equipment. Spee's zigzagging further foiled British attempts to target his ships, but this tactic also enabled them to close faster. In any event, Spee had no choice but to shorten the range in order to give his own 8.2-inch (21-cm) guns a chance to hit the enemy ships, accuracy being at a premium because the two armored cruisers had already spent nearly half of their stock of shells at the Battle of Coronel. But the decision to close with a superior foe also increased the damage to his own ships and hastened their demise. The *Scharnhorst* was the first casualty, succumbing at 16:17 to gunfire from a distance of almost 11,000 yards (10,000 m). Observing from the deck of the *Gneisenau*, Pochhammer praised Spee's final maneuver, turning into the approaching enemy. "Just as he had previously sacrificed his armored cruisers to save his light cruisers," he now chose "to sacrifice the *Scharnhorst* to save the *Gneisenau*."[38] The admiral went down with his ship, which sank with all hands (860 dead).

The *Gneisenau* fought on for nearly two hours after the *Scharnhorst* was sunk, refusing to surrender even after coming under fire from the *Invincible*, the *Inflexible*, and the armored cruiser *Carnarvon* at a range of 7,000–10,000 yards (6,400–9,100 m). In his long and graphic account of the demise of the *Gneisenau*, Pochhammer emphasized the calm order and professionalism that prevailed as the ship lost half its crew and, ultimately, its ability to fight any longer. "Our ship's capacity was slowly diminishing... Debris and corpses were accumulating, icy water dripped in one place and in another gushed in streams through panels and shell-holes, extinguishing fires and drenching the men to the bone. Whenever it was possible to do so, efforts were made to man guns," and "ammunition was passed from hand to hand when wagons were lacking." Finally "the *Gneisenau*, whose damaged engines were no longer capable of much speed, began to turn slowly over on her starboard." The armored cruiser withstood a remarkable fifty hits from the 12-inch shells of the *Invincible* and the *Inflexible* before finally sinking. When the time came to abandon ship, "the men left their stations in perfect order and the wounded comrades were carried above. Hardly any staircases and ladders were left, but the sheet-iron crumpled up in numerous places offered a support sufficient for climbing on deck through the breaches."[39]

Because of the enrollment of the additional reservists and volunteers at Valparaiso, the *Gneisenau* went into the battle with more than its standard complement of 764; roughly 800 were aboard, of whom 400, according to Pochhammer's estimate, made it into the icy waters. After the *Gneisenau* sank at 18:02, its battle flags still flying, the British closed quickly, dispatched boats, and pulled 187 survivors from the sea, including Pochhammer and sixteen other officers. Meanwhile, the light cruisers *Nürnberg*, *Leipzig*, and *Dresden* had scattered, chased, respectively, by the *Kent*, *Glasgow*, and *Cornwall*. Like the German armored cruisers, the *Leipzig* and *Nürnberg* refused to strike their flags even when hopelessly damaged. The *Kent* sank the *Nürnberg* at 19:27, and the *Glasgow* sank the *Leipzig* at 21:23. Only the *Dresden* – the newest of the German cruisers and the only one with turbine engines – mustered enough speed to escape destruction. As for the remaining ships,

[38] Pochhammer, *Before Jutland*, p. 212.  [39] *Ibid.*, pp. 214–215.

the *Macedonia* and *Bristol* captured and scuttled Spee's two colliers, and a third German support vessel that had functioned as a supply and hospital ship escaped to give itself up for internment in Argentina.

December 8, 1914, was an especially tragic day for the Spee family, as the Battle of the Falklands claimed not just the admiral, but also his two sons, Heinrich going down with the *Gneisenau*, Otto with the *Nürnberg*. For the British, the victory was even more decisive than the German triumph at Coronel. Sturdee lost no ships and just ten men, while the Germans lost four of their five cruisers and 1,870 men. In addition to the 187 men rescued from the *Gneisenau*, eighteen survived the sinking of the *Leipzig* and ten survived the *Nürnberg*. Back at Port Stanley after the battle, Sturdee considered himself fortunate to have destroyed the German squadron in a single action. Because his battle cruisers had scored hits at rates of between 5 and 10 percent, they nearly exhausted their stocks of 12-inch shells (the *Inflexible* firing a total of 661 during the battle, the *Invincible* 513) in order to sink the *Scharnhorst* and *Gneisenau*. Their light casualties notwithstanding, Sturdee's ships also had not come through entirely unscathed. The two German armored cruisers fired at an impressive rate and with impressive accuracy, initially straddling (though not hitting) their pursuers at a range of 15,000 yards (13,700 m), and ultimately scoring a number of hits at shorter range, including twenty-two on the *Invincible*. Sturdee would not be the last British admiral to praise the sturdy construction of German warships, or the range and rate of their fire, but in the afterglow of victory he did not have the luxury of lingering in the Falklands to ponder lessons learned. Just three days after the battle, the Admiralty ordered the *Invincible* and the *Inflexible* to steam for home. Prepared to spend months in the South Atlantic searching for the German East Asiatic Squadron, Sturdee had to marvel at his good fortune that Spee obligingly came to him the day after his arrival.

Between their departure from Tsingtao in June 1914, a week before the assassination at Sarajevo, and their destruction nearly six months later, Spee's ships had steamed almost exactly half-way around the world, on a 15,000-mile (24,000 km) odyssey crossing the Pacific from west to east and finally rounding Cape Horn, before meeting their end off the Falklands. Their voyage was unique in modern warfare, as no body of warships in the age of steam had traveled so far and for so long under such hostile conditions. Of the 2,500 men aboard the five warships ultimately attached to the squadron, barely 500 ever saw

**Figure 3.3** Battle cruiser HMS *Inflexible*

Germany again. Of these, some 300 escaped the Battle of the Falklands aboard the *Dresden*, only to be hunted down by British cruisers in the Pacific three months later.

## In Spee's wake: the Allied conquest of Germany's Pacific colonies

Just as the German East Asiatic Squadron would have benefited from a more extensive German colonial empire to support it, the modest empire Germany did have would have benefited from a more robust naval presence to defend it. As it turned out, during the flight of Spee's squadron eastward across the Pacific, the Allies seized German colonies in his wake, the Japanese taking possession of everything north of the Equator, the Australians and New Zealanders everything south of it. In only one case – Samoa, Germany's undefended easternmost Pacific colony – did Allied forces strike before Spee's arrival, 1,400 New Zealanders taking the island on August 29, 1914, complete with its coal depot and wireless station, without firing a shot.[40]

[40] Sondhaus, *World War I*, p. 109.

Two weeks later, on September 11, the Australians entered the fray, putting ashore 2,000 troops at Rabaul in the Bismarck Archipelago, where they captured another German coal depot and panicked the local garrison into destroying the wireless station at nearby Bita Paka. On September 17, after a series of firefights, the Germans surrendered the rest of the Bismarck Archipelago. A week later, Australian troops took Madang, the largest German settlement in Kaiser-Wilhelmsland, and over the next two months they subdued the remaining German outposts in that colony. The Allies, still uncertain about the location and course of Spee's squadron, provided each of these operations with a strong naval escort, consisting mostly of units of the Royal Australian Navy (the battle cruiser *Australia*, escorted by three light cruisers and three destroyers).[41]

Meanwhile, elements of Vice Admiral Tamin's Japanese First Fleet, deployed under the guise of hunting for Spee's squadron, left their bases much too late to overtake the fleeing Germans. They concentrated on occupying the three German Micronesian archipelagos that were now left undefended: the Marianas, the Carolines, and the Marshalls. In the process, Tamin, flying his flag in the armored cruiser *Kurama*, went through the motions of following the German squadron's earlier course as far as Eniwetok Atoll in the Marshalls, but did not arrive there until September 29, over a month after Spee left. After occupying Jaluit on October 3, Tamin no longer maintained the fiction that he was pursuing Spee, steaming west to seize the most important German outposts in the Carolines, Ponape (October 7) and Truk (October 12). By then, a second squadron led by Rear Admiral Tatsuo Matsumura in the pre-dreadnought *Satsuma* had left Japan, and landed troops on Yap and Palau in the western Carolines (October 7) and on Saipan in the Marianas (October 14). Unlike the Australians and New Zealanders, who (at least after Samoa) encountered some German resistance everywhere they attacked, the Japanese occupied all these islands without sustaining or inflicting any casualties.[42]

In early October, after an Australian expedition arrived to occupy Yap only to find that the Japanese had just landed there, Britain and Japan recognized the need for an agreement to prevent their forces from colliding in the rush to seize German colonies. Thus, the Equator became the dividing line between the Japanese and the British (Australia–New Zealand) zones of occupation, a "temporary wartime

[41] *Ibid.*   [42] *Ibid.*, pp. 109–110.

measure" according to the British, but not as far as the Japanese were concerned. As early as December 1, 1914, the Japanese foreign ministry informed the British Foreign Office that "the Japanese nation would naturally insist on the permanent retention of all German islands north of the Equator," and expected Britain to support this position at the postwar peace conference.[43] By the time the Treaty of Versailles made it official four and a half years later, Japan was already treating the Carolines, the Marianas (minus US-owned Guam), and the Marshalls as Japanese colonies. From west to east their newly acquired Micronesian empire stretched for some 2,600 miles (4,200 km), securing Japan's domination of the western Pacific between the US possessions of Hawaii and the Philippines. Of all the victors of the First World War, none gained so much at so little cost as Japan. Indeed, the 700 men who died in the accidental loss of the dreadnought *Kawachi* to a magazine explosion later in the war (July 1918) accounted for most of the Japanese navy's wartime fatalities.

After all the German colonies had been occupied, Allied forces in the Pacific finally, belatedly got serious about cooperating to track down Spee's squadron. The gunboat *Geier*, pursued by superior Japanese forces, never came close to a rendezvous with Spee; after putting in at Honolulu on October 17, the *Geier*'s captain chose internment over battle with the pre-dreadnought *Hizen* and armored cruiser *Asama*, waiting just outside the three-mile limit. Those ships then headed for the west coast of the Americas where, by late November, the battle cruiser *Australia* and armored cruiser *Izumo* headed an Anglo-Japanese squadron forming off the coast of Mexico. Sweeping the seas methodically in the general direction of Chile, they had only reached the waters off Panama when word arrived that Spee had been defeated at the Falklands.[44] The *Australia* (like Sturdee's *Invincible* and *Inflexible*) then proceeded to the North Sea to join the Grand Fleet, as there was no longer a German threat significant enough to justify deploying a capital ship anywhere else.

Japan's naval operations between August and December 1914, ultimately extending not just to Hawaii, but all the way to the coast of Mexico, further strained its already tense relationship with the

[43] Quoted in Mark R. Peattie, *Nan'yo: The Rise and Fall of the Japanese in Micronesia, 1885–1945* (Honolulu, HI: University of Hawaii Press, 1988), p. 45.
[44] Saxon, "Anglo-Japanese Naval Cooperation," p. 71; David Stevens, "1914–1918: World War I," in David Stevens (ed.), *The Royal Australian Navy* (Melbourne: Oxford University Press, 2001), pp. 36–37.

United States. The Japanese acquisition of so many islands astride the route between Hawaii and the Philippines only made matters worse, laying the groundwork for the Pacific theater of the next great war. The behavior of the Japanese in China after 1914 likewise stands as a milepost on the road to the Second World War. Their infamous "Twenty-One Demands" of January 1915 were aimed at reducing the fragile Chinese Republic (established three years earlier) to little more than a Japanese protectorate. Provisions included the solidification of Japan's control over the port of Tsingtao, Kiaochow Bay, and adjacent territories in the province of Shantung (Shandong) seized from the Germans in November 1914, as well as Port Arthur and the sphere of influence in Manchuria taken from the Russians in 1905.[45]

The conquest of Germany's African colonies, accomplished almost entirely by ground forces, lies beyond the purview of a naval history, though in each of the four cases (Togo, Cameroon, German Southwest Africa, and German East Africa) British cruisers provided some support for troops ashore. Concerns that Spee might successfully round Cape Horn and break out into the South Atlantic also influenced Allied actions in Africa. In September 1914, at Swakopmund and Lüderitz Bay, British and South African forces destroyed German wireless stations that would have been valuable assets to Spee had his squadron survived. Later the same month, following up on their easy conquest of Togo, the Allies landed a force that took the port of Douala in Cameroon, but waited nearly three months before allowing it to advance inland, until after word arrived of Spee's defeat at the Falklands.[46]

## The Allies secure the seas, 1914–15

While the operational history of the German East Asiatic Squadron had been brief enough, the German warships not under Spee's command that attempted to function beyond European waters fared even worse, as all were either sunk or blockaded by the time of the Battle of the

[45] Japan's Twenty-One Demands (January 18, 1915; revised text April 26, 1915), Japanese Ultimatum to China (May 7, 1915), Chinese Reply to Japanese Ultimatum (May 8, 1915), texts reproduced at: www.firstworldwar.com/source/21demands.htm.

[46] See Sondhaus, *World War I*, p. 113.

Falklands. The light cruiser *Königsberg*, on the German East African station when the war began, destroyed just one enemy merchantman before engaging the British protected cruiser *Pegasus* off Zanzibar on September 20. The *Königsberg* won the battle, sinking the *Pegasus*, but afterward sought refuge in the Rufiji River to make repairs. British warships soon blockaded it there, where it remained a focal point of local Allied attention until it was finally sunk ten months later. The light cruiser *Karlsruhe*, assigned to represent Germany at the opening ceremonies of the Panama Canal in August 1914, went on to sink sixteen merchantmen (72,800 tons) in the Caribbean, successfully evading ships detached from Cradock's Fourth Cruiser Squadron, before being lost to an accidental explosion on November 4, off the Lesser Antilles. The light cruiser *Emden*, detached by Spee to function as a raider in the East Indies and Indian Ocean, likewise sank sixteen Allied ships (70,800 tons), but registered its greatest success against a target ashore: an oil depot at Madras, where it destroyed 346,000 tons of fuel in a 10-minute bombardment on September 22, coincidentally, the same day that Spee shelled Tahiti. Because of the threat it posed to Allied troop convoys en route to the Suez Canal from French Indochina, Australia, and New Zealand, the *Emden* earned the distinction of the most-pursued German raider. Having stripped most of their own warships from the region, Britain and France accepted Japan's offer to help escort their Indian Ocean convoys. The Japanese assigned mostly light cruisers to these duties, but in mid-October the armored cruiser *Ibuki* deployed to Wellington to join a convoy of New Zealanders it would escort all the way to Aden.[47] The Russians also made a nominal contribution, sending the *Zhemchug*, one of their two Vladivostok cruisers, only to have the *Emden* sink it in a raid on Penang, Malaya, on October 28, shortly after it arrived. The *Emden*'s career ended in the Cocos Islands on November 9, when it lost an artillery duel with the Australian cruiser *Sydney* after its captain, Müller, made the mistake of lingering too long to destroy a wireless station and cut the undersea cable linking British India to Australia. The approach of the *Sydney* forced Müller to raise steam and abandon ashore a fifty-three-man demolition team, the fate of which became the greatest naval survival story of the war. The shore party's commander, *Kapitänleutnant* Hellmuth von Mücke, first commandeered a schooner to sail from the Cocos to Sumatra, then

---

[47] Saxon, "Anglo-Japanese Naval Cooperation," p. 71.

a steamer to cross the Indian Ocean to Yemen, then an Arab dhow to ascend the Red Sea to a point where his men gained access to the Hejaz Railway. They suffered just three casualties en route, killed in a shootout with Bedouins near Medina. They arrived in Constantinople six months after their odyssey began, and were welcomed as heroes upon their return to Germany.[48]

The loss of the *Königsberg*, *Karlsruhe*, and *Emden*, plus the four cruisers sunk at the Falklands, left the only German survivor of that battle, the 3,660-ton light cruiser *Dresden*, as the lone German warship (armed civilian ships excepted) still operating outside European waters at the end of 1914. The *Dresden*'s commander, Captain Fritz Lüdecke, wanted the ship to raid Allied shipping in the Pacific and, ultimately, the Indian Ocean, but its engines were not equal to the task. After coaling at the Chilean port of Punta Arenas, the world's southernmost city, the *Dresden* cruised off the coast of Chile early in the new year, capturing just one Allied merchantman before having to flee from the British armored cruiser *Kent* on March 8–9, 1915. The *Dresden* escaped and made for the Juan Fernandez Islands, in the process spending the rest of its coal and damaging its own engines irreparably. Local Chilean authorities granted Lüdecke provisional internment, but the *Kent* soon arrived to challenge it. The British rejected the interned status of the *Dresden* on the grounds that Spee earlier had followed the rules governing belligerent visits to neutral ports only on the mainland of Chile, not its offshore possessions of Easter Island and the Juan Fernandez Islands. On March 14, the light cruiser *Glasgow* arrived and joined the *Kent* in opening fire. Lüdecke raised a white flag and sent Lieutenant Wilhelm Canaris, fluent in English, to stall while his crew set scuttling charges and abandoned ship. Afterward the British allowed Lüdecke and his officers and crew, numbering over 300 in all, to spend the war interned in Chile. Canaris, also fluent in Spanish, was among the few to escape, across the Andes to Argentina, then on to Germany. He ended the war as a U-boat commander and later rose to admiral's rank in the navy of Nazi Germany, serving as Hitler's intelligence chief before being executed late in the Second World War for his role in the anti-Nazi resistance. Most of his shipmates did not see Germany again until the winter of 1919/20.[49]

[48] See Hellmuth von Mücke, *The Emden–Ayesha Adventure: German Raiders in the South Seas and Beyond, 1914* (Annapolis, MD: Naval Institute Press, 2000).
[49] Michael Mueller, *Canaris: The Life and Death of Hitler's Spymaster* (London: Chatham, 2007), pp. 10–33 and *passim*.

To supplement its cruisers, at the outbreak of war the German navy implemented long-standing plans to commission passenger liners and merchantmen to serve as commerce raiders. Of the sixteen vessels thus employed, seven eventually were sunk or scuttled, four ended up interned in neutral ports, and two were lost to shipwreck. The most successful was the 9,800-ton *Möwe*, which claimed forty-one enemy ships (186,100 tons) before being converted to a minelayer. The most famous of the German raiders – and the only sailing ship among them – was the three-masted windjammer *Seeadler*, commanded by Count Felix von Luckner. Commissioned later in the war, it sank sixteen vessels (30,100 tons) in an eight-month career before being wrecked on August 2, 1917 in the Society Islands. Among the larger converted cruisers, the 24,900-ton *Kronprinz Wilhelm* sank fifteen ships (60,500 tons) and the 16,000-ton *Prinz Eitel Friedrich* sank eleven ships (33,400 tons). Both were requisitioned from the North German Lloyd in August 1914, and both served until interned within days of each other at Newport News, Virginia, in April 1915.

Before the war, the British actively feared that German passenger liners, when armed, would be the scourge of the world's sea lanes, steaming too fast for any warship to track down. But prewar plans to arm large ocean liners as auxiliary cruisers failed to take into account the great cost and limited benefit of operating such vessels as warships. Their high rate of coal consumption was especially problematic for a German navy attempting to operate globally without a global network of secure bases.[50] Because the largest liners were the size of dreadnoughts or battle cruisers, like capital ships they required crews of several hundred men. And even those constructed most recently, with gun mountings and reinforced decks underneath, could not carry heavy guns. Thus, the largest converted German merchantmen had no more firepower than light cruisers, much smaller ships requiring far fewer men to operate on far less coal.

The voyage of the *Prinz Eitel Friedrich* illustrated the promise and problems of a large auxiliary cruiser. Equipped with four 4.1-inch (10.5-cm) and six 3.4-inch (8.8-cm) guns from two of the German gunboats abandoned at Tsingtao, it was very lightly armed for a vessel displacing 16,000 tons and could not afford to risk an encounter with

---

[50] Seligmann, *The Royal Navy and the German Threat*, p. 2. In prewar plans to convert their largest, fastest passenger liners into armed auxiliary cruisers the British, like the Germans, did not consider their high coal consumption. See *ibid.*, 2n.

an enemy warship. Thus, its cruise was in some ways more harrowing than that of Spee's squadron, in addition to being much longer. Initially ordered to operate in the East Indies, the ship left the islands at the end of September 1914, after the surrender of Kaiser-Wilhelmsland in New Guinea left it with no base in the area. Steaming across the Pacific to the coast of Chile, the *Prinz Eitel Friedrich* was reunited with Spee's cruisers but only for one day, on the eve of the Battle of Coronel, before operating separately again. After Spee's demise at the Falklands, the ship made it safely into the South Atlantic by skirting the coast of Antarctica, dodging ice floes between latitudes 60°S and 61°S, before breaking out to the north (thus showing a way that Spee could have done it). By the time the *Prinz Eitel Friedrich* gave itself up at Newport News, it had logged some 25,000 miles (40,000 km), but had little to show for it. Most of its eleven victims were relatively small, and if it had not captured cargoes of coal from some of them, it would have been dead in the water long before April 1915. The ship's first officer, Otto Brauer, called it a "useless coal-eater (*unnützige Kohlenfresser*)," and noted that its voracious appetite for fuel did not equate to impressive speed; indeed, by the end of its long cruise, with its machinery badly in need of cleaning and repair, it could manage just 13 knots.[51] Perhaps the lone advantage of using an armed ocean liner as a commerce raider was its capacity to take aboard and house, in relative comfort, the passengers and crews of the ships it captured and sank. It could thus afford to wage war entirely under the established standards of international law, destroying enemy ships and cargoes without taking civilian lives. Near the end of the *Prinz Eitel Friedrich*'s long voyage, Brauer quipped that it had become a "Noah's Ark" of nationalities, with separate communities of British, French, and other captives aboard, including so many babies and small children that the milk supply became a concern. By the time the ship reached Newport News, its population of prisoners had reached 350, outnumbering the crew.[52]

## Conclusion

By the time the *Prinz Eitel Friedrich* gave itself up for internment, Germany's initial campaign of unrestricted submarine warfare had

[51] Brauer, *Die Kreuzerfahrten*, pp. 49, 103.   [52] Ibid., pp. 99, 105 and *passim*.

already been underway for two months. Few of the navy's auxiliary surface raiders remained in service once the *Unterseeboote* (U-boats) were deployed against Allied commerce. In treating the subject of German attacks on Allied shipping during the First World War, scholars have traditionally focused on the British navy's lack of preparedness and slow response to the submarine threat. But the British were, indeed, prepared for an assault on their seagoing commerce, only from German cruisers, not from submarines. Their swift, decisive campaign against this threat exposed the hollow nature of German pretensions to world power. In the face of such unrelenting pressure, even a leader as heroic as Spee, extraordinarily courageous and resourceful though he was, could not overcome the reality that Germany had too few colonies and bases to sustain a global naval presence. Aside from the U-boat challenge in the North Atlantic, the Allies were free to use the rest of the world's oceans unmolested once the surface raiders were eliminated, and for all practical purposes, they were eliminated by the spring of 1915. Thus, the British dealt very effectively with the threat they had foreseen, only to falter later in the face of one neither they nor anyone else had envisaged.[53]

Indeed, judged within the broader context of a conflict of unprecedented cost that would drag on for nearly four and a half years, the British in particular (and the Allies in general) wasted little time in sweeping the world's oceans of German warships and armed auxiliary cruisers, effectively and expeditiously ending the naval war outside European waters and the North Atlantic. The consequences of this decisive early victory can hardly be overestimated. In addition to allowing the partition of Germany's Pacific colonies, it facilitated the free movement of troops from India to Africa and to the Middle East, where they shouldered much of the burden of the Allied war effort there, and additional millions of men from the British dominions, French colonies, and ultimately the United States to fight on the battlefields of Europe. In general terms, it allowed the Allies free movement of food, fuel, and other materials on a global basis. Finally, the overall failure of German surface raiders led directly to Germany's decision to use submarines against Allied shipping, arguably the most fateful decision taken by any of the belligerents during the war.

---

[53] See Seligmann, *The Royal Navy and the German Threat*, pp. 171–173 and *passim*.

Starting with the initial stalemate on the Western front in the fall of 1914, the war on land would unfold in trial-and-error fashion, as both sides introduced new technologies, which they then had to learn to use in the right measure and the right combination, in order for it to make a difference. The same would be true at sea. From the first shots in the summer of 1914 until it wound down the following spring, the global prelude of the Great War at sea was shaped by wireless telegraphy, the trial and error of its use figuring prominently in virtually every development. For Spee and his captains, for Cradock, Sturdee, and others who pursued him, and for individual raiders such as Müller, effective use of wireless made the difference between success or failure, even life or death. After making good use of the technology to coordinate his crossing of the Pacific, Spee manipulated his wireless traffic off Coronel to conceal the size of his squadron, leading Cradock to blunder into battle against a superior force. Then, at the Falklands, Sturdee used the same tactic against Spee, causing him to stumble into a fight he could not win.[54] When it came to targeting wireless stations and island stations on undersea cable lines, the Allies fared much better than the Germans. After cutting the German overseas cables in the North Sea, Allied warships succeeded in destroying important wireless stations on Yap, Samoa, and every German Pacific island colony in between, as well as at Swakopmund and Lüderitz Bay in Southwest Africa. In contrast, the Germans experienced their only success of the communication war at Fanning Island, cutting the Australia to Canada cable, while Müller's *Emden* was lost in a failed attempt to cut a cable and destroy a wireless station in the Cocos, and Spee's squadron likewise met its demise in an operation intended to destroy a wireless station at Port Stanley. The new technology gave the detached squadron or the individual raider an important new tool to make its way through hostile seas, especially to arrange for fuel and other supplies, but because it could not be used without transmitting clues as to the location of its user, the same technology made it more difficult for the hunted to hide.

Wireless would continue to evolve throughout the war. The range at which messages could be sent and received continued to improve, building upon the process begun by Marconi and Jackson in 1895–96, but other, equally important capabilities emerged, too. In the first months of the war, ships still had to guess the proximity of an

[54] Keegan, *Intelligence in War*, pp. 142–143.

enemy vessel by the strength of its wireless signal, and had no way of knowing from which direction it approached; by the end of 1914, as the war in European waters began to heat up, the British had developed direction-finding technology that enabled them to confirm when the Germans had sortied into the North Sea, and the Germans soon developed the same capability for use against the British.

# 4 EUROPEAN WATERS, 1914–15

While the search for Spee's squadron and individual commerce-raiding cruisers provided a focal point for the global prelude of the naval war, the battle cruiser *Goeben* and its escort *Breslau*, the only other German warships stationed beyond the Baltic and North Sea, became the dramatic centerpiece of the opening of the war in European waters. Following the lead of Winston Churchill, author of the first (and best-selling) history to address the flight of the *Goeben* from the central Mediterranean to the sanctuary of Constantinople, a century later historians continue to exaggerate its significance. Especially in the English-speaking world, it remains not uncommon to see this lone ship credited with bringing the Ottoman Empire into the war. The alliance of the Turks with the Germans certainly had far-reaching consequences. It blocked the Dardanelles and Bosporus to Allied shipping, cutting Russia's best supply route from the western Allies, thereby contributing to its collapse in 1917. Meanwhile, in the Middle East, it prompted Britain to seek friends among the Arabs while also promising Palestine to the Zionists, all in the quest to undermine Ottoman rule. But in attributing the German–Ottoman alliance to the *Goeben* alone, some writers go as far as to postulate a causal link between its opening maneuvers and the establishment of Soviet communism, as well as the modern-day Arab–Israeli conflict, as if these world-changing developments would not have occurred otherwise.[1] Yet Churchill himself

---

[1] See especially Dan van der Vat, *The Ship that Changed the World: The Escape of the* Goeben *to the Dardanelles, 1914* (Bethesda, MD: Adler & Adler, 1986).

foreshadowed such fanciful arguments by concluding that the *Goeben* steamed for Constantinople "carrying with her for the peoples of the East and Middle East more slaughter, more misery, and more ruin than has ever before been borne within the compass of a ship."[2]

Hyperbole aside, the escape of the *Goeben* to Constantinople in the early days of the fighting had at least an indirect connection to every other aspect of the European naval war of 1914–15. After its commander, Rear Admiral Souchon, became commanding admiral of the Ottoman navy, the *Goeben*, as Turkish flagship *Yavuz Sultan Selim*, fired the first shots of the war in the Black Sea. Meanwhile, by subtracting the *Goeben* from the German navy and bringing about the addition of two capital ships to the British navy – Ottoman dreadnoughts under construction in British shipyards, seized and incorporated into the Grand Fleet – the alignment of the Turks with the Germans further tipped the Anglo-German naval balance in the North Sea in Britain's favor, shaping the opening action there. And, finally, the German decision to send the *Goeben* to the Black Sea rather than to the Adriatic, where it would have strengthened the Austro-Hungarian fleet, left the Mediterranean more securely in Allied hands and made it easier for Italy to abandon its neutrality and join the Entente.

## Opening drama: the *Goeben* and *Breslau*

In November 1912, shortly after the start of the Balkan Wars, William II created a new naval command "to defend German interests in the Mediterranean."[3] The *Goeben* and *Breslau* were the only ships assigned to this "Mediterranean Division," and as new ships (completed in August 1912 and May 1912, respectively) neither would ever serve elsewhere. At 22,600 tons, the *Goeben* was significantly larger than any of the British battle cruisers at Malta, and it made a remarkable 28 knots in its sea trials. Thus, it was the fastest warship in the Mediterranean and, for the first eighteen months of its deployment, also the largest, a distinction it lost in May 1914 when Italy commissioned two slightly

---

[2] Winston S. Churchill, *The World Crisis*, 5 vols. (New York: Charles Scribner's, 1923), vol. I, p. 271.
[3] William II, Allerhöchste Kabinetts-Order (A.K.O.), November 5, 1912, text in Matti E. Mäkelä, *Souchon der Goebenadmiral greift in die Weltgeschichte ein* (Braunschweig: Friedrich Vieweg, 1936), p. 11.

larger dreadnoughts of the *Cavour* class. The *Breslau*, compared with other light cruisers, was also a formidable warship; at 4,570 tons it was significantly larger than the light cruisers serving with Spee's squadron or on other German overseas stations. The commander of the Mediterranean Division (Rear Admiral Konrad Trummler until October 1913, then Souchon) also had jurisdiction over other German warships temporarily assigned to the region; these included the *Hertha* and *Vineta*, old protected cruisers used as training ships for cadets, which cruised the Mediterranean in the winter months of 1912/13 and again in 1913/14, and the gunboat *Geier*, which left for the East African station in January 1914.[4] Thus, the division included just the *Goeben* and *Breslau* by the time William II arrived in the Mediterranean in March 1914 with the imperial yacht *Hohenzollern*, to be escorted by Souchon's ships on port calls to Trieste and Venice.

Owing to defective boiler tubes, the *Goeben* never came close to matching its top trial speed while in the Mediterranean. By the time Souchon took command, the ship was lucky to make 20 knots, causing the admiral to go to great lengths to hide his engine troubles from potential adversaries (apparently successfully, as the British and French never suspected the *Goeben*'s capabilities were in any way diminished). The *Goeben* was to be relieved by its sister *Moltke* later in 1914, but after the assassination at Sarajevo, Souchon feared the exchange might not take place as scheduled and arranged for the ship to be repaired in the Pola Arsenal. The boiler tubes were replaced, with representatives of the original German engine manufacturer on hand to supervise; work began on July 10, amid great secrecy, and was completed thirteen days later, just as Austria-Hungary submitted its ultimatum to Serbia. The *Goeben* lingered in the upper Adriatic for the following week, testing its machinery while also conducting gunnery practice and preparing for action. Austria-Hungary mobilized its fleet on July 26, two days before declaring war on Serbia; Souchon coaled the *Goeben* at Trieste on July 29, then put to sea on the evening of the 30th, headed south. Two days later, at Brindisi, he met the *Breslau*, which had been cruising in Greek waters. On August 2, the two ships proceeded to Messina, the assembly point for the Triple Alliance navies designated in the naval convention of 1913. There, Souchon learned that Germany was at war with Russia, hostilities with France were imminent, and that Italy had

---

[4] *Ibid.*, p. 11n.

declared neutrality. He took on coal and provisions, then put to sea again.[5]

Over the tense days that followed, several variables affected the decisions of Souchon and the other naval commanders in the region: Admiral Haus of Austria-Hungary, Vice Admiral Lapeyrère of France, Admiral Milne of Britain, and the commander of Milne's armored cruisers, Rear Admiral Ernest Troubridge. The sequence of who declared war on whom (and when) framed the action as it unfolded, but misinformation and confused orders affected everyone, especially when standing orders for the contingency of war were superseded by the course of events. Some orders were misunderstood, others disobeyed. Communication technology posed no problem, for all were within wireless reach of their admiralties.

Souchon's standing orders were straightforward enough. The Triple Alliance Naval Convention called for the joint Austro-German–Italian fleet to assemble at Messina, then steam into the western Mediterranean to engage the French fleet and block the French army's troop transports from Algeria. In the event that these plans were not implemented (and Italy's declaration of neutrality ensured they would not be), Souchon was to attempt to disrupt the transports with his own ships and, when no further good could be done in the Mediterranean, attempt to pass the Straits of Gibraltar and run for home.[6] After departing Messina, he steamed along the north coast of Sicily en route to the Algerian ports of Philippeville (Skikda) and Bône (Annaba), where he expected to find French transports awaiting their troops. Along the way, at 18:00 on August 3, Souchon received confirmation that Germany had declared war on France.

Lapeyrère's orders reflected the Mahanian ideal of securing command of the sea in the western Mediterranean by engaging, and defeating, the enemy fleet. The transports from Algeria were not to be escorted *per se* (thus freeing the navy from being tied to the army's mobilization timetable), but their route would be covered by a force of old battleships and cruisers deployed west of Sardinia. By the predawn hours of August 3, however, when the main body of Lapeyrère's fleet left Toulon, the admiral knew that Italy would be neutral and no Triple

---

[5] Ibid., pp. 53–64; Paul G. Halpern, *The Naval War in the Mediterranean* (Annapolis, MD: Naval Institute Press, 1987), pp. 12–13.
[6] Holger H. Herwig, "*Luxury*" *Fleet: The Imperial German Navy, 1888–1918* (London: Allen & Unwin, 1980; paperback edn. Prometheus Books, 1987), p. 153.

Alliance fleet would deploy to the western Mediterranean. Fearing the damage the *Goeben* could do to unescorted transports, he steamed for the Algerian ports intending to form convoys, despite receiving orders shortly after midnight on August 4 (confirming that Germany had declared war on France) which clearly forbade him to form convoys.[7]

On July 30, a full five days before Britain declared war on Germany, Churchill had ordered Milne to prepare to use the British Mediterranean Fleet to help to defend the French troop transports, against the *Goeben* in particular. Unless in combination with the French fleet, Milne was not to engage "superior forces," by which Churchill later contended he meant the Austro-Hungarian fleet with its three dreadnoughts, should it sortie from the Adriatic against Malta, but he did not state this explicitly in his orders.[8] On August 2, when Souchon left Messina, Milne received orders to track him with his battle cruisers, while Troubridge's armored cruisers were to watch the mouth of the Adriatic in case the Austro-Hungarian fleet came out.

On the night of August 3/4, while bearing down on the Algerian coast, Souchon received new orders via wireless from Berlin: "Alliance concluded with Turkey. *Goeben, Breslau* go immediately to Constantinople."[9] The admiral chose to interpret "immediately" rather loosely and proceeded to his intended targets. The *Breslau* opened fire on Bône at 05:30, the *Goeben* on Philippeville just after 06:00, but because the troop transports were assembling not at those ports, but at Algiers and Oran, the German shelling caused more alarm than damage. Souchon then headed back to Messina, to coal again before proceeding to Constantinople. Just before 11:00 on August 4, in the waters between Algeria and Sicily, Milne's battle cruisers *Indefatigable* and *Indomitable* intercepted the *Goeben*, then shadowed it for the next five hours, at one point pulling to within 9,000 m. Together, the two British ships mounted sixteen 12-inch (30.5-cm) guns to the *Goeben*'s ten 11-inch (28-cm) guns; fortunately for Souchon, Britain's ultimatum to Germany to evacuate Belgium or else face a declaration of war would not expire until midnight, leaving Milne powerless to act while

---

[7] Halpern, *The Naval War in the Mediterranean*, pp. 23–24.
[8] Churchill to Milne, July 30, 1914, text in Churchill, *The World Crisis*, vol. 1, pp. 237–238.
[9] Text in Mäkelä, *Souchon der Goebenadmiral*, p. 71. Mäkelä states that this message reached Souchon "the night before the attack" on the Algerian ports. Halpern, *The Naval War in the Mediterranean*, p. 13, places its receipt the following afternoon.

the German battle cruiser (whose engines were still not capable of top speed) gradually pulled away.[10] Reaching Messina on the morning of August 5, Souchon received a different reception now that a state of war existed in the Mediterranean, including Britain as well as France and Germany. Italian authorities informed him that, as belligerent warships calling at a neutral port, the *Goeben* and *Breslau* had to leave in twenty-four hours, too little time to load enough coal to make it all the way to Constantinople. Souchon negotiated a twelve-hour extension of the limit, but Milne soon added to his woes by posting cruisers at the northern and southern outlets of the Straits of Messina, to alert the rest of the British Mediterranean Fleet when the Germans put to sea again. Fearful of being blockaded, Souchon wired Haus at Pola, asking for Austro-Hungarian help. Within hours the request was repeated directly from Berlin to Vienna.[11]

The appeal placed Austria-Hungary in a dilemma, because it was not yet at war with either Britain or France; indeed, at that point it was only at war with Serbia, hostilities with Russia becoming official only on August 6. Diplomatic formalities aside, Haus also faced sobering realities of geography and relative naval strength. He had sufficient force to deal with the British Mediterranean Fleet, which in any event was under orders not to engage him, but the Anglo-French combination could easily overwhelm the combination of his own ships with the *Goeben* and *Breslau*. While Souchon's telegram assured Haus that "French forces are not here," on the previous day, August 4, the foreign ministry in Vienna had received a cipher telegram from the Austro-Hungarian consul in Naples confirming that the French fleet had left Toulon and at least some French units were already off Corsica "with orders to intercept Austro-Hungarian and German ships."[12] Thus, Haus knew the French were at sea in force, and that they, as well as the British, had much more firepower much closer to Messina than he did, putting him in no position to save the German ships. Souchon was on his own.

---

[10] Mäkelä, *Souchon der Goebenadmiral*, pp. 68–75.
[11] Halpern, *The Naval War in the Mediterranean*, pp. 13–14; Sondhaus, *The Naval Policy of Austria-Hungary*, p. 248.
[12] Souchon to Haus, August 5, 1914, text in Mäkelä, *Souchon der Goebenadmiral*, p. 89; Egon Pflügl (consul at Naples) to Ministerium des Äussern, August 4, 1914 (cipher telegram), Haus- Hof- und Staatsarchiv (HHStA), AR, F 44 – Marinewesen, Carton 13: Kriegsschiffe Frankreich, Kriegs-Operationen 2.

Figure 4.1 Admiral Anton Haus

To make matters worse for Souchon, he soon learned that his initial order to steam for the Dardanelles had been based on wishful thinking. Just before noon on August 6, he received a cable sent to Messina from Berlin the previous day, inexplicably not transmitted by wireless: "Entry into Constantinople at present not possible on political grounds."[13] The Ottoman Empire had agreed to the alliance with Germany on August 2, the day after Germany declared war on Turkey's historical archenemy, Russia, but the German ambassador in Constantinople, Baron Hans von Wangenheim, who signed the document on behalf of the Second Reich, had failed to convey to Berlin that the Turks had no intention of going to war until specific issues had been

[13] *Admiralstab* to Souchon, August 5, 1914, text in Mäkelä, *Souchon der Goebenadmiral*, p. 94.

resolved. At the insistence of the Turks the alliance remained secret, and for good reason. While their army had German advisors, their navy had British advisors, and the Ottoman fleet had three dreadnoughts under construction in British shipyards, two of which had been completed and were scheduled to be taken over within days by Turkish crews already standing by in Britain. Having just lost most of their remaining southeastern European lands in the Balkan Wars, the Turks were also not keen to commit themselves until the positions of their Balkan neighbors had been ascertained. There were misgivings in Berlin as well as in Constantinople. William II and the chief of the *Admiralstab*, Admiral Hugo von Pohl, did not want to send the *Goeben* and *Breslau* to the Dardanelles and had to be swayed by Tirpitz, who as state secretary of the Imperial Navy Office (the German equivalent of navy minister) had no authority over operational matters. The strongest pro-German voice in the Ottoman capital, war minister and chief of the general staff Enver Pasha, at this point lacked a similar influence. Thus, his party (the Committee of Union and Progress, or "Young Turks") remained divided on the wisdom of compromising Ottoman neutrality by giving sanctuary to the two German warships. The German–Ottoman alliance notwithstanding, the Turks were not yet ready to abandon their neutral status.[14]

Souchon resolved to proceed to the Dardanelles anyway, preferring to take his chances there over the alternatives of spending the war bottled up in the Adriatic with the Austro-Hungarian fleet, or likely destruction in a run for home. In the late afternoon of August 6, after a frantic day and a half spent taking on as much coal as possible from three German merchantmen anchored in Messina, the *Goeben* and *Breslau* left the port, steaming south. That evening, under a full moon, the *Breslau* exchanged fire with the British light cruiser *Gloucester*, posted by Milne to watch the southern outlet of the Straits of Messina, while the *Goeben* slipped by unchallenged. Both were soon in open waters, and after continuing southward for a short time they turned northeast, apparently headed for the Adriatic. To reinforce the ruse, a second German appeal for Austro-Hungarian help asked Haus to bring his fleet as far as Brindisi, at the mouth of the Adriatic, for a rendezvous

---

[14] Bernd Langensiepen, Dirk Nottelmann, and Jochen Krüsmann, *Halbmond und Kaiseradler: Goeben und Breslau am Bosporus, 1914–1918* (Hamburg: Verlag E. S. Mittler, 1999), p. 10.

with Souchon's ships. Haus responded early on August 7, putting to sea from Pola and Cattaro with a formidable force including his three dreadnoughts, three *Radetzky*-class pre-dreadnoughts, and an armored cruiser; he had steamed halfway down the Adriatic by the time Berlin informed Vienna that the *Goeben* and *Breslau* had changed course a second time shortly before midnight on August 6/7. Now steaming southeastward, they crossed the Ionian Sea and had reached Greek waters, having rounded Cape Matapan en route to the Dardanelles. The Germans urged Haus to follow Souchon's lead and take his fleet to the Black Sea, too, where it would better serve the common cause of the Central Powers against Russia. Ignoring the unsolicited advice, Haus had his ships back in port by August 8, but it took him another four days to quash the bizarre idea that he abandon the Adriatic for the Black Sea. Even if the Austro-Hungarian fleet could make it there, through an eastern Mediterranean soon to be guarded by a superior Allied fleet, he argued that Constantinople was too far from the Russian coast to be a suitable base of operations and, in any event, it lacked the facilities to repair capital ships. Worst of all, any Austro-Hungarian ships deployed to the Black Sea would be trapped there for the duration of the war (as the *Goeben* would be), leaving the Dual Monarchy's Adriatic coast undefended against the threat from Italy. Ironically, the Black Sea deployment scheme originated with one of Haus' own subordinates, Rear Admiral Erwin Raisp von Caliga, his liaison to the Austro-Hungarian army high command, who had suggested it to the German naval attaché in Vienna.[15]

The escape of the *Goeben* and *Breslau* infuriated Churchill, but the First Lord had only himself and his own Admiralty to blame. His orders to Milne had, indeed, emphasized the need to engage the *Goeben*, but within the context of assisting the French navy in preventing the German battle cruiser from attacking the Algerian troop transports. Thus, when Souchon put in a second time at Messina, Milne stationed his own battle cruisers off the northern and southern coasts of Sicily, to block the *Goeben* from returning to the western Mediterranean, leaving only the smaller *Gloucester* in a position to intercept it if it chose to head elsewhere. Worse yet, Churchill's admonition to avoid engaging "superior forces" ultimately was interpreted by Troubridge

---

[15] Mäkelä, *Souchon der Goebenadmiral*, pp. 93–109 *passim*; Sondhaus, *The Naval Policy of Austria-Hungary*, pp. 249–250.

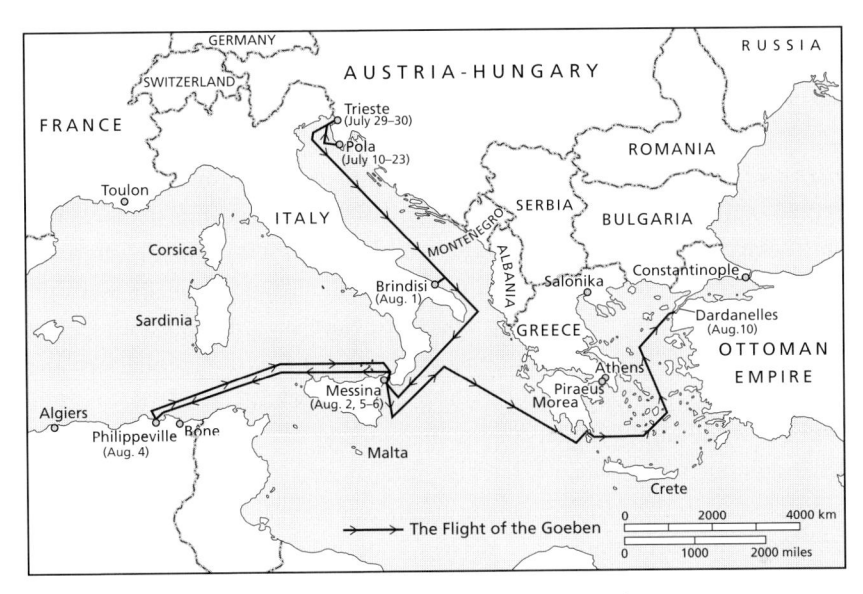

Map 4.1 Mediterranean Sea showing the flight of the *Goeben*

to mean avoiding the *Goeben* itself, at least for the armored cruisers under his command, whose 9.2-inch (23.4-cm) guns were outranged by the battle cruiser's 11-inch (28-cm) guns. Finally, after Souchon's ships passed Cape Matapan and were known to be heading for Constantinople, the British delayed pursuing them into the Aegean Sea for a full day because of a false report from the Admiralty, on August 8, that Austria-Hungary had declared war on Britain. This error prompted Milne, then belatedly steaming eastward with his battle cruisers, to break off the chase and order the concentration of the British Mediterranean Fleet for the defense of Malta, the deployment prescribed in his standing orders for the scenario of war with Austria-Hungary.[16] The failure to catch the *Goeben* ruined the careers of both Milne and Troubridge, whose connections and lineage (both were grandsons of admirals who had served in Nelson's navy) did not spare them from embarrassing inquiries. Milne lost his command later in August, and even though the Board of Admiralty ultimately upheld his conduct, he spent the rest of the war on half-pay. Troubridge lost command of his cruiser squadron the following month, was then exonerated by a court

---

[16] Halpern, *The Naval War in the Mediterranean*, p. 14; Mäkelä, *Souchon der Goebenadmiral*, p. 103. For Churchill's version of these events see Churchill, *The World Crisis*, vol. 1, pp. 270–275.

martial in November, but likewise never held another post at sea, serving from January 1915 as head of the British naval mission to landlocked Serbia.

Having given the Allies the slip, on August 9 Souchon refueled his ships from a collier in the Aegean Sea, then the following afternoon arrived off the Dardanelles. He was unsure of his reception there, but on the way from Messina he had wired Wangenheim that he intended to pass through the straits and enter the Black Sea with or without Turkish permission. He had no orders to take such a bold course, but his bravado only ensured that the ambassador and the officers of the German military mission would continue to work feverishly to arrange his reception. During his days en route, a series of events broke his way. On August 3, suspicious of Turkish intentions, Churchill had ordered the seizure of the Ottoman dreadnoughts *Reşadiye* (which became HMS *Erin*) and *Sultan Osman-i Evvel* (which became HMS *Agincourt*), and the destruction of the keel of the *Fatih Sultan Mehmed*, laid down just two months earlier. The realization that the ships, which the Turks had already paid for, were permanently lost naturally outraged Constantinople; at the same time, Turkish anxieties over the diplomatic situation in the Balkans diminished when Romania and Greece agreed to neutrality pacts with the Ottoman Empire, and Bulgaria showed signs of leaning toward an alliance with the Central Powers. On a more practical level, the Ottoman army put a pro-German officer in charge of the defense of the Dardanelles and Bosporus, who authorized the free passage of German and Austro-Hungarian warships but not the warships of other countries. Finally, Wangenheim's proposal that the *Goeben* and *Breslau* be sold to the Ottoman navy upon their arrival allayed Turkish fears about their status under international law. As German warships their presence would compromise Ottoman neutrality, but as Ottoman warships they would not, and the loss of the British-built dreadnoughts only made the prospect of acquiring a German battle cruiser that much more appealing to the Turks. Souchon did not yet know of these arrangements when he took aboard a Turkish pilot and entered the straits. At 19:35 on August 10, his ships dropped anchor at Çanakkale Roads. The following afternoon, the British light cruiser *Weymouth*, sent ahead by Milne to scout for the pursuing British forces, arrived at the mouth of the Dardanelles and was denied entry.[17]

[17] Langensiepen *et al.*, *Halbmond und Kaiseradler*, pp. 10–12.

Figure 4.2 Vice Admiral Augustin Boué de Lapeyrère

It remains unclear whether Haus' sortie down the Adriatic on August 7 inspired the premature Admiralty report that Anglo-Austrian hostilities had begun, but it soon became a moot point, as Britain and France both declared war on Austria-Hungary on August 12. Shortly thereafter, Lapeyrère brought the main body of the French fleet from the western Mediterranean to the mouth of the Adriatic to block Haus from coming out, while the British concentrated their Mediterranean forces at the Dardanelles to ensure that Souchon would not sortie into the Aegean Sea or threaten the Suez Canal. Standing watch off the Dardanelles proved to be tedious duty, even after August 15, when the sale of the two German ships (for 80 million marks) became official and they ran up the Turkish flag, the *Goeben* as *Yavuz Sultan Selim* and the *Breslau* as *Midilli*, with Souchon becoming an Ottoman vice admiral and fleet commander. Thereafter, the snail's pace of German–Turkish negotiations concerning the future role of Souchon, command and control over the *Yavuz Sultan Selim* and *Midilli*, and the German admiral's authority over the rest of the Ottoman navy ensured that the ships would not be used anytime soon. Technically Souchon became head of a new naval mission, including another 150 officers and technical specialists who arrived by rail from Germany on August 23, replacing the British mission, which finally left for home on September 16. Under the terms of a memorandum dated September 18, Germany remained in control of the *Yavuz Sultan Selim* and *Midilli*, making them Turkish in name only, and Souchon remained under German orders in the operation of the two ships. Their German crews, some 1,400 men, likewise remained personnel of the German navy. Souchon's authority over any other Ottoman navy ships would be determined on an *ad hoc* basis depending upon the situation. The German ambassador, who negotiated these terms, would have an ongoing role as liaison between Souchon and the Ottoman government.[18]

Even after these arrangements were formalized, the Ottoman Empire remained neutral and the *Yavuz Sultan Selim* and *Midilli* remained inactive, along with the rest of the Turkish fleet. On August 27, the same day that Milne was dismissed as commander of the British Mediterranean Fleet, the Admiralty ordered its forces off the Dardanelles to treat the two ships as German regardless of which flag they flew; the Asquith cabinet agreed, and a week later authorized the sinking of any Turkish warship that sortied from the straits. In mid-September, when Troubridge followed Milne home to face his court martial, Vice Admiral Sir Sackville Carden took command of the units keeping watch there, but Milne was not formally replaced, with the British Mediterranean command being held "in abeyance" until it was finally revived in August 1917. In the meantime, Carden and his successors in the eastern Mediterranean had the status of squadron commanders who, along with the local British commander at Malta, were subordinated to the French admiral (initially Lapeyrère) serving as Allied Mediterranean commander in chief. One of the three British battle cruisers assigned to the Mediterranean returned home with Milne, a second returned in December, leaving just the *Indefatigable* to serve as Carden's flagship, backed by armored cruisers. These reductions left the British amenable

---

[18] *Ibid.*, pp. 14–17.

to a French role in the eastern Mediterranean, filled later in 1914 by a squadron of old pre-dreadnoughts under Rear Admiral Emile-Paul Guépratte. Meanwhile, the Turks waited until September 26 to test the *de facto* Allied blockade, sending out a destroyer which Carden diplomatically opted to turn back rather than sink. Three days later the Turks responded by mining the open channel through their Dardanelles minefields, effectively closing the western approach to Constantinople.[19]

## The Black Sea, to the Allied attack on the Dardanelles

The closing of the Dardanelles and Bosporus to the Allies, on the heels of the formal acquisition of the German Mediterranean Division by the Ottoman navy, naturally raised expectations of an imminent Turkish decision to join the Central Powers. Yet the Turks continued to drive a hard bargain. The Ottoman government finally entered the war on the side of the Central Powers after Germany, on October 14, agreed to give the Turks a loan of 200 million francs (2 million Turkish pounds), payable in gold, to be shipped by rail from Berlin to Constantinople. Once the gold shipment arrived, Enver Pasha and the Ottoman navy minister, Cemal Pasha, agreed to allow Souchon to sortie, on a provocative raid against Russia's Black Sea ports, without a formal declaration of war.[20]

On the evening of October 27 the *Yavuz Sultan Selim* and *Midilli* left the Bosporus with four destroyers and two torpedo gunboats, ostensibly for maneuvers. They cruised eastward along the Anatolian coast before turning north to steam toward their targets. Souchon divided his forces and on the morning of October 29, between 03:00 and 07:00, they shelled and mined the ports of Odessa, Sevastopol, Novorossiysk, and Feodosia. His flagship did the honors at Sevastopol, where it dueled with the old pre-dreadnought *Georgi Pobiedonosets* and shore batteries. That afternoon, by prior arrangement with Enver Pasha and Cemal Pasha, Souchon wired Constantinople the lie that the Russian navy had "shadowed all movements of the Turkish fleet and systematically disrupted all exercises," and had thus "opened hostilities." The ships all reached home safely

---

[19] Halpern, *The Naval War in the Mediterranean*, pp. 50–51.
[20] Langensiepen *et al.*, *Halbmond und Kaiseradler*, p. 21.

by November 1. In addition to causing damage ashore, they sank a Russian gunboat, a minelayer, and a half-dozen merchantmen. After participating in the operation at Novorossiysk, the *Midilli* tried, and failed, to cut the undersea cable linking Sevastopol with Varna, Bulgaria, before returning to Constantinople.[21] Souchon's raid delivered the result the Ottoman war and navy ministers had wanted, allowing them to present a *fait accompli* to cabinet colleagues who had continued to drag their feet even after the Germans met all their conditions for activating the alliance. On November 2, Russia declared war on the Ottoman Empire, followed three days later by Britain and France. The Turks finally issued their reciprocal declarations of war on November 11, at which time Sultan Mehmed V, recognized as caliph by the world's Sunni Muslims, also proclaimed a jihad against the Triple Entente.

Thus, Souchon and his battle cruiser indeed served as the catalyst for bringing the Ottoman Empire into the war against Russia, but the admiral clearly acted as the agent of the leading pro-war, pro-German ministers in the Turkish government, and certainly not as a rogue agent of the Germans forcing the hand of the Turks with his actions. In any event, starting with their provocative opening raid on the Russian coast, the personnel and ships of the former German Mediterranean Division were the focal point of the conflict in the Black Sea. Without them, the Russian Black Sea Fleet enjoyed local superiority, its six pre-dreadnoughts easily outclassing the Ottoman pre-dreadnoughts *Barbaros Hayreddin* (ex-*Kurfürst Friedrich Wilhelm*) and *Torgud Reis* (ex-*Weißenburg*), purchased from Germany in 1910. The Turks had no armored cruisers, the Russians none in the Black Sea, and the Russians enjoyed a numerical or qualitative superiority in every other, smaller ship type. Thus, the *Yavuz Sultan Selim* alone changed the regional balance. At 22,600 tons, with ten 11-inch (28-cm) guns, it was much larger and had much more firepower than Russia's most formidable Black Sea pre-dreadnoughts, the 12,840-ton *Evstafi* and *Ioann Zlatoust*, which had a primary armament of four 12-inch (30.5-cm) guns. Even handicapped by its now chronic engine problems, the battle cruiser was still much faster than these or any other Russian Black Sea pre-dreadnoughts, none of which could make more than 16½ knots. Against such opponents, Souchon could risk the *Yavuz Sultan Selim* under almost any circumstances, confident that it could

---

[21] Ibid., pp. 21–26.

outrun any combination of ships that could outgun it. Meanwhile, his opposite number, Vice Admiral Ebergard, could not operate in open water except in force, because in a firefight the powerful battle cruiser alone could destroy one, two, or perhaps even three of his battleships. The Russians could take heart that the balance would soon swing back in their favor. The three dreadnoughts of the *Imperatritsa Maria* class, as large and fast as the *Yavuz Sultan Selim* but with twelve 12-inch (30.5-cm) guns – ships the Ottoman dreadnoughts seized by Churchill in August 1914 were supposed to counter – were nearing completion in the shipyards of Nikolaiev and were expected to join the Black Sea Fleet in 1915.

Ebergard had no intention of waiting until then to seek retribution for the surprise attacks of October 29. Two days after Russia declared war, he sortied with five of his pre-dreadnoughts (leaving behind only the old *Georgi Pobiedonosets*), two cruisers, a seaplane tender, and a flotilla of destroyers, crossing the Black Sea for a surprise coastal raid of his own. Ebergard's ships did their most important work at Zonguldak, a port on the "coal coast," 150 miles (240 km) east of Constantinople, where shelling led by the pre-dreadnought *Rostislav* caused damage to the local mines. They also intercepted and sank three unescorted Turkish steamers with supplies bound for the Ottoman Third Army on the Caucasus front via the port of Trebizond (Trabzon), 560 miles (900 km) east of the capital. Russian destroyers attempted to lay a minefield across the mouth of the Bosporus, but botched the operation with some mines detonating prematurely while others were sowed randomly enough to pose a future danger to both navies. Souchon responded to the attack by taking out the *Yavuz Sultan Selim* for a brief reconnaissance (November 6–7), but encountered none of Ebergard's ships, all of which made it safely back to Sevastopol. Afterward the loss of the three steamers enabled Souchon to persuade Enver Pasha of the need to convoy transport and supply ships even in coastal waters. It became the Ottoman navy's principal ongoing duty, because the shortcomings of the Anatolian road and rail infrastructure left Turkish forces on the Caucasus front heavily dependent on supply by sea.[22]

On November 17, Ebergard appeared off Trebizond with the same fleet that had shelled Zonguldak. After bombarding the port, he

---

[22] *Ibid.*, pp. 27–29.

ran for home, but the shelling prompted the Turks to dispatch Souchon in an attempt to intercept him. He took only his four fastest ships, the *Yavuz Sultan Selim* and *Midilli*, a second light cruiser, the *Hamidiye*, and the torpedo gunboat *Peyk*. Ebergard faced a voyage home to Sevastopol that was 65 miles (105 km) longer than Souchon's route from Constantinople to Sevastopol, and with ships that were much slower. The two forces drew closer by the hour, and at noon on November 19, just 20 miles (32 km) off Cape Sarych in the southern Crimea, Souchon intercepted the Russian column. Both sides opened fire at 12:18, in calm seas but with a thick fog limiting visibility. Souchon broke off the engagement after just 10 minutes, upon recognizing that he would not be able to block Ebergard's ships from reaching Sevastopol. In the brief artillery duel the *Evstafi* took four hits from the *Yavuz Sultan Selim*, scoring one in return, while all other ships emerged unscathed; casualties included thirty-three Russian dead against thirteen on Souchon's flagship. The limited damage on the Russian side vindicated Ebergard's strategy of only risking a sortie in force, but the episode also showed that Souchon could respond immediately to his moves. Ebergard, in turn, was powerless to intercept sorties by Souchon, for example, on December 10, when the *Yavuz Sultan Selim* steamed all the way to Batum, 100 miles (160 km) east of Trebizond, which it bombarded in support of an Ottoman army attack on the flank of the Caucasus front. But despite the weaknesses of the Russian Black Sea Fleet, Ebergard remained aggressive. He appeared again in force off the Bosporus on December 21 to cover minelayers, and off Zonguldak on December 23 to cover an attempt to sink four blockships. The latter operation caught the *Yavuz Sultan Selim* far to the east, escorting a convoy to Trebizond, but the *Midilli* appeared off Zonguldak in time to disrupt Russian plans there, sinking two of the blockships before they reached the harbor. The *Yavuz Sultan Selim* encountered no enemy warships on this occasion, but on December 26, when it returned from Trebizond and attempted to reenter the Bosporus, it struck two of the mines the Russians had sown five days earlier. The battle cruiser took on 600 tons of water before making it into port safely.[23]

The *Yavuz Sultan Selim* was never in danger of sinking, but the extent of the damage, and the lack of a dry-dock in Constantinople large enough to accommodate it, made repairs a challenge, and it

[23] *Ibid.*, pp. 29–34.

would not be ready to put to sea again until March 29, 1915. In its absence, Souchon never considered using the Ottoman navy's two old pre-dreadnoughts, instead leaving the *Midilli* and *Hamidiye* to shoulder the burden of escorting convoys to the Caucasus front and raiding the Russian coast. A third light cruiser, the refurbished *Mecidiye*, joined the fleet in January, only to be lost to a mine off Odessa on April 3. The Allies were never fully aware of the extent of the damage to the Ottoman flagship, but Ebergard took advantage of the respite to blockade Zonguldak and the "coal coast," thus disrupting the supply route from Constantinople to Trebizond as well as the shipment of fuel from the mines to the Ottoman capital.[24]

By the time the battle cruiser returned to service, the focus of the Turks shifted from the Russians to the western Allies, following their failed attempt, on March 18, to force the Dardanelles with a fleet consisting mostly of pre-dreadnoughts. The British had maintained a presence at the mouth of the Dardanelles since August 1914, reinforced by the French during the autumn, but made no attempt to attack with surface warships. Instead, from November 1914 into the new year, the Allies repeatedly attempted to infiltrate the Dardanelles with submarines. The British *B 11* (Lieutenant Norman Holbrook) scored an early success on December 13, sinking the 9,120-ton ironclad *Mesudiye* (built in Britain in the 1870s), which the Turks had anchored at Çanakkale as a guardship. Five French submarines deployed with Guépratte's battleships also probed the defenses, but none succeeded in transiting the Dardanelles into the Sea of Marmara, the enclosed waters between the Dardanelles and Bosporus.[25]

All things considered, in the opening phase of the war in European waters, the deployment of the German Mediterranean Division to the Black Sea and the incorporation of its ships into the Ottoman navy had not been decisive, even though they had, indeed, changed the regional naval balance. The *Yavuz Sultan Selim* and the *Midilli* enabled the Turks to operate anywhere in the Black Sea, but they could not prevent the Russians from doing likewise. The Germans increased the competence and capability of the Ottoman navy, but the transition was far from smooth. Few German officers, including Souchon himself, knew or cared about the culture of their hosts and took for granted

[24] *Ibid.*, pp. 39–47.
[25] *Ibid.*, p. 63; Halpern, *The Naval War in the Mediterranean*, p. 68.

that the relationship would function on their terms. Officers and sailors from the two German ships who were reassigned to other units of the navy were less than tactful in their criticism of everything from the competence of their Turkish counterparts to the quality of food and shipboard accommodations. The most serious incidents resulted from German sailors treating Turkish officers with disrespect, a problem so widespread that their numbers aboard ships other than the *Yavuz Sultan Selim* and *Midilli* had to be reduced. Because few Turkish naval officers (and none of the sailors) spoke German, even basic communication was problematic, ironically leaving French, which all educated Turks knew, as the default language of German–Turkish interaction.[26] In general terms, the operational challenges Souchon faced vindicated the decision of Admiral Haus not to send Austro-Hungarian warships to the Black Sea: at more than 300 miles (480 km) from the nearest point on the Russian coast, Constantinople left much to be desired as a base for offensive operations, and as Souchon learned once his flagship was mined, the lack of facilities made it difficult to repair a capital ship there. As the war dragged on and the material strength of the Russian Black Sea Fleet improved, Germany's warships at the straits – like the rest of its fleet in the North Sea – would become more significant as a deterrent fleet-in-being than as an actual offensive threat to Allied interests.

### The North Sea: First Helgoland Bight and Dogger Bank

The crisis that resulted in the First World War found the British navy in an enviable position: on July 15, 1914, the First, Second, and Third fleets of the Home Fleet began a "test mobilization" that had been scheduled months earlier, a massive undertaking that involved the activation of the entire Royal Fleet Reserve. While technically voluntary, as no state of war then existed, over 20,000 reservists heeded the call and reported for duty. King George V reviewed the mobilized fleet at Spithead on July 17 and 18, prior to a week of exercises at sea. The Third Fleet released its reservists the following weekend, just as Serbia gave its reply to the Austro-Hungarian ultimatum, but on Churchill's advice the First Sea Lord, Battenberg, ordered the First and Second fleets

---

[26] See examples in Langensiepen *et al.*, *Halbmond und Kaiseradler*, pp. 15–18.

to remain mobilized.[27] By July 28, the day Austria-Hungary declared war on Serbia, the decision had been made to relocate the First Fleet, concentrated at Portland on the Channel at the end of the test mobilization, to the Scottish bases of Rosyth, Cromarty, and Scapa Flow, from which it would be better placed to support the distant blockade of Germany on a line from the Orkneys eastward to the coast of Norway, under the strategy the British had adopted in the winter of 1912/13. Britain then moved to honor its naval commitments to France. On July 30, Churchill ordered Milne to prepare to contribute the British Mediterranean Fleet to the defense of the French troop transports, and on August 2 Britain informed Germany that it would not allow the German fleet to enter the Channel in order to attack the French coast. The following day, Jellicoe received a promotion to full admiral and command of the force now known as the Grand Fleet. Finally, on the morning of August 4, as Britain awaited Germany's response to its ultimatum concerning Belgium, Churchill ordered the Grand Fleet to sea, where it would be safest from a surprise torpedo attack or other preemptive strike, especially since the Scottish bases all lacked antisubmarine defenses and also did not have the extensive coastal artillery of the older installations farther south.

The British test mobilization of July 15–25 coincided almost exactly with the German High Sea Fleet maneuvers of July 14–25 conducted off the coast of Norway, observed at least part of the time by William II aboard the imperial yacht *Hohenzollern*. On the same weekend that Churchill and Battenberg decided to keep the British First and Second fleets mobilized, the emperor responded to the breach of diplomatic relations between Austria-Hungary and Serbia by cutting short his own summer cruise and ordering the fleet home. He was back in Berlin on July 27, and during the following week, as the best British warships were deployed to Scotland, the Germans used the Kiel Canal to send all dreadnoughts, battle cruisers, pre-dreadnoughts, and armored cruisers stationed in the Baltic to join their counterparts in the North Sea, where they had concentrated by the time the official mobilization order came on August 1.[28] In contrast to Britain's relatively undefended Scottish bases, the High Sea Fleet's primary anchorage at

---

[27] Churchill, *The World Crisis*, vol. 1, pp. 209–210.
[28] Reinhard Scheer, *Germany's High Sea Fleet in the World War* (London: Cassell, 1920), pp. 6–10.

Wilhelmshaven on the Jade was covered by the heavily fortified island of Helgoland, 70 miles (112 km) out to sea, and by a series of minefields laid to supplement the natural defenses provided by the shallow waters and sand bars common to the Elbe estuary. But these natural obstacles were a mixed blessing, as capital ships could only enter or leave Wilhelmshaven during high tide, and long before 1914 the fleet had grown too large for it to get into or out of the base on a single high tide.

In the first days of the war each navy expected, or feared, a bold strike from the other side that never came. Future High Sea Fleet commander Vice Admiral Reinhard Scheer, then a squadron commander under Ingenohl, later recalled the "universal . . . conviction that the English Navy would take the offensive,"[29] while on the British side Jellicoe counted himself among those who "found it difficult to imagine that the High Sea Fleet would adopt from the outset a purely passive role."[30] Yet the commanders of both navies felt they had legitimate reasons for caution. Jellicoe feared a surprise torpedo attack by German submarines or destroyer flotillas, and thus early in the war was "far more concerned for the safety of the Fleet when it was at anchor in Scapa Flow . . . than . . . when the Fleet was at sea."[31] Thus, he was comfortable with the distant blockade and, indeed, would not have favored a strategy requiring the fleet to be "moving continuously in the central and southern waters of the North Sea," where "the enemy could easily lay mines," a threat that ranked with torpedoes at the top of his list of concerns.[32] But Britain's distant blockade also invalidated the premises of the initial German strategy, which Scheer summarized as follows: "to damage the English Fleet by offensive raids against the forces engaged in watching and blockading the German Bight, as well as by mine-laying and submarine attack, whenever possible." The High Sea Fleet would "seek battle with the English Fleet only when a state of equality has been achieved by the methods of guerrilla warfare" thus described.[33] While the navy's strategists remained faithful to Tirpitz's conviction that the decisive battle for command of the North Sea could take place only after the British had been weakened, they departed from his vision of how that weakening would occur. Tirpitz had long assumed that

[29] *Ibid.*, p. 26.
[30] John Rushworth Jellicoe, *The Grand Fleet, 1914–1916: Its Creation, Development and Work* (New York: George H. Doran, 1919), pp. 38–39.
[31] *Ibid.*, p. 29.   [32] *Ibid.*, p. 19.   [33] Scheer, *Germany's High Sea Fleet*, p. 25.

Figure 4.3 Admiral Sir David Beatty

an aggressive regime of sorties by the High Sea Fleet would eventually enable it to catch and destroy part of the British fleet at sea, and through this means achieve what Scheer called "a state of equality." He rejected the notion that "guerrilla" methods could accomplish the same ends, because, as he later explained, "the prospects of such fighting depended on the enemy being kind enough to provide us with opportunities, which they were not likely to do. Guerrilla fighting would only have been feasible if the English had decided on a close blockade of our coasts," and the evidence from prewar British maneuvers had signaled it was "improbable that a close blockade of the German coasts would be undertaken."[34]

[34] Tirpitz, *My Memoirs*, vol. 2, p. 88.

Even though the two navies kept their largest warships hundreds of miles apart, each inflicted losses on its opponent within days of Britain's declaration of war. On August 5, the Germans sent their auxiliary minelayer *Königin Luise* to sow mines off Harwich, 55 miles (88 km) north of Dover, where half of Britain's destroyers were based as part of the light forces guarding the eastern approach to the Channel. One of the destroyers sank the *Königin Luise*, but on the morning of August 6 one of the mines it had laid sank the British light cruiser *Amphion*. The German navy opted not to challenge the Channel defenses for the sake of disrupting the transport to France of the British Expeditionary Force (BEF), which started on August 12 and continued unmolested thereafter. Scheer concluded that "we could only interfere with it at the price of a decisive battle with the English Fleet," a battle the Germans, because of their inferiority in capital ships, were not yet ready to fight.[35] Jellicoe, too, was in no rush to engage the enemy battle fleet, remaining obsessed with the danger from German torpedoes and mines. As soon as the main body of the BEF had crossed safely to France, removing the contingency that the Grand Fleet might have to sortie to the Channel to block the High Sea Fleet from attacking the transports, he moved his base temporarily from Scapa Flow to Loch Ewe, 120 miles (190 km) southwest of the Orkneys, on the northwest coast of Scotland. Over the weeks that followed the fleet returned only sporadically to Scapa Flow en route to and from patrols along the North Sea blockade line. Jellicoe did not feel reasonably secure at Scapa Flow until after February 1915, when work on the antisubmarine barriers there was finally completed.

In the absence of the dreadnoughts, lighter forces of the two navies finally met in combat on August 28, in the First Battle of Helgoland Bight. From the start of the war Commodore Reginald Tyrwhitt, commander of the light cruisers and destroyers based at Harwich, had conducted sweeps northeastward from the Straits of Dover across to the Dutch coast, then up toward Helgoland, roughly 350 miles (565 km) away. On August 28, his sweep was planned to coincide with a deployment of British submarines and have the support of Vice Admiral David Beatty's First Battle Cruiser Squadron, which Jellicoe had stationed farther south than his dreadnoughts (first at Cromarty, then Rosyth) to enable the battle cruisers to remain closer to potential action while the

[35] Scheer, *Germany's High Sea Fleet*, p. 19.

rest of the Grand Fleet withdrew temporarily to more secure waters. The battle lasted for eight hours after Tyrwhitt's first encounter with Rear Admiral Leberecht Maas' force of German light cruisers and destroyers just before 08:00 (German time), far to the west of Helgoland. Tyrwhitt pursued Maas and exchanged fire with him for 90 minutes, sinking one of his destroyers while sustaining extensive damage to his own flagship *Arethusa*. He broke off the action when they came within range of the fortress guns of Helgoland island, only to be pursued to the west by the light cruiser *Mainz*, which itself took several hits. Haze and intermittent fog plagued visibility for both sides all day. The opposing forces first sighted one another at a range of just 7,500 yards (6,860 m), and once the battle was underway few hits were registered at more than 5,000 yards (4,570 m). Poor visibility also effectively neutralized the guns of Helgoland, which played no role in the battle. Beatty's battle cruisers, led by his flagship *Lion* and accompanied by additional light cruisers, arrived shortly after 13:30 to take over from the beleaguered Tyrwhitt; meanwhile, Rear Admiral Franz Hipper's battle cruisers, summoned to reinforce Maas, remained trapped behind the bar at Wilhelmshaven by low tide and could not leave the Jade until after 13:00, delaying their arrival off Helgoland until after the battle had ended. Gunfire and torpedoes from Beatty's light cruisers sank the *Mainz* at 14:10. His battle cruisers then focused on Maas' flagship *Cöln*, which the *Lion* sank at 14:35, with casualties including the admiral and almost all hands (507 dead). The *Lion* subsequently mauled a third German light cruiser, the *Ariadne*, which was abandoned at 16:00. The British lost no ships, but afterward Tyrwhitt's *Arethusa* and two destroyers had to be towed back to Harwich.[36]

The First Battle of Helgoland Bight was important mostly for its effect on German morale; as Scheer later recalled, afterward "we were all burning to avenge the slap in the face we had received."[37] Yet the clear British victory also made William II less willing to allow his admirals to take risks, especially with the capital ships of the High Sea Fleet, leaving it less likely that the loss would be avenged anytime soon, at least by surface warships. While the submarines of both sides had been ineffective during the battle of August 28, the following

---

[36] Jellicoe, *The Grand Fleet*, pp. 110–112; Scheer, *Germany's High Sea Fleet*, pp. 43–46; Friedman, *Naval Firepower*, p. 106; Brooks, *Dreadnought Gunnery*, p. 217; Gröner, *Die deutschen Kriegsschiffe*, vol. 1, pp. 128, 135.

[37] Scheer, *Germany's High Sea Fleet*, p. 46.

month they showed their potential as individual hunters. On September 5, Germany's *U 21* (*Kapitänleutnant* Otto Hersing), operating off Beatty's battle cruiser base at Rosyth in the Firth of Forth, became the first U-boat to sink an enemy ship, torpedoing the British light cruiser *Pathfinder* (261 dead). Then, on the morning of September 22, 20 miles (32 km) off the Dutch coast, *U 9* (*Kapitänleutnant* Otto Weddigen) recorded the most spectacular and sobering success to date, sinking, in less than an hour, the 12,000-ton armored cruisers *Aboukir*, *Hogue*, and *Cressy* (1,459 dead). *U 9* went on to sink the 7,890-ton protected cruiser *Hawke* (524 dead) on October 15, securing the status of its commander, Weddigen, as the German navy's first hero of the Great War. These sinkings naturally reinforced Jellicoe's paranoia about submarine attacks on the capital ships of the Grand Fleet, especially with work on the antisubmarine defenses of Scapa Flow still far from complete. On October 22, he relocated his dreadnoughts from Loch Ewe all the way to Lough Swilly in Northern Ireland, another 155 miles (250 km) to the southwest, giving new meaning to the concept of "distant blockade." But even that remote location proved not to be safe. Just five days after the fleet arrived, the dreadnought *Audacious* struck a German mine off Lough Swilly and sank later that day, after efforts to tow it back to base failed; Jellicoe could take consolation only in that casualties were limited to one man killed. Meanwhile, the greatest success by a British submarine came on September 5, when *E 9* infiltrated the waters between Wilhelmshaven and Helgoland to torpedo the 2,050-ton German light cruiser *Hela*, which took so long to sink that all but three of her crew were saved. A month later *E 9* also sank the small destroyer *S 116*, the only other German vessel lost to a submarine attack during 1914.[38]

While the Germans registered almost all of the early successes in submarine and mine warfare, the surface victory they coveted remained elusive. The next Anglo-German encounter, the Battle of Texel Island (October 17, 1914), was no more significant than the First Battle of Helgoland but equally demoralizing for the German navy. A detachment from the British navy's Harwich force, consisting of the light cruiser *Undaunted* (Captain Cecil Fox) with four destroyers, was

---

[38] Jellicoe, *The Grand Fleet*, pp. 132, 145–149; Scheer, *Germany's High Sea Fleet*, p. 58; Otto Weddigen, "The First Submarine Blow is Struck," text available at: wwi.lib.byu.edu/index.php/U-9_Submarine_Attack.

conducting a sweep up the Dutch coast when it encountered Captain Georg Thiele's half-flotilla of four small destroyers, which had sortied from their base in the Ems River, on the German–Dutch border, on a mission to lay mines off the mouth of the Thames. The encounter took place on the morning of October 17, roughly 15 miles (24 km) west of the island of Texel, and did not last long. All four German vessels were sunk (218 dead, including Thiele) and thirty survivors taken prisoner, while the British force lost no ships and suffered no fatalities.[39]

Coinciding with these initial skirmishes in the North Sea, Germany's Schlieffen Plan failed to bring the desired victory on land. Following the French victory in the First Battle of the Marne (September 5–9) both sides dug in; trench lines quickly extended to the Flanders coast during the so-called "race to the sea," a series of failed attempts by each army to turn the northern flank of the other. Once the trenches reached the coast, a reallocation of forces left the BEF primarily responsible for the northern sector, including helping the remnant of the Belgian army defend western Flanders, the only part of Belgium not occupied by the Germans. The stalemate of trench warfare raised the value of artillery fire, opening a role for the British navy in providing fire support for the troops dug in within range of the coast. Fears of losing valuable warships to torpedoes or mines ultimately led the British to commission forty shallow-draft monitors for these coastal operations, ranging in size from the five units of the 355-ton *M-29* class, armed with two 6-inch (15.2-cm) guns, to the 6,700-ton *Marshal Ney* and *Marshal Soult*, each featuring two 15-inch (38-cm) guns. Most were commissioned during 1915, after which they saw action along the Belgian coast, at the Dardanelles, and, following Italy's entry into the war, in the upper Adriatic.[40] To bridge the gap while the monitors were still under construction, the British employed expendable pre-dreadnought battleships for inshore operations where the torpedo and mine dangers were the greatest. In October 1914, the *Revenge* (later renamed *Redoubtable*), built in 1891–93, became the forty-first and oldest British pre-dreadnought mobilized for the war. Along with other old battleships from the Channel Fleet, it participated in ineffective bombardments of the German-occupied Belgian coast on November 22

---

[39] Scheer, *Germany's High Sea Fleet*, p. 61. The German vessels lost in the battle, *S115*, *S117*, *S118*, and *S119*, at 400 tons were the size of the smallest destroyers of the First World War, but are called torpedo boats by some sources.

[40] *Conway, 1906–1921*, pp. 42–50.

and December 15–16. The following spring at the Dardanelles, the French navy joined the British in deploying pre-dreadnoughts in similar circumstances. Of course, expendable ships still had to be manned, and if the material loss of their sinking was not mourned, the human cost could be considerable. The old battleships tasked with bombarding the Belgian coast all returned unscathed, but two weeks after the second attack, on New Year's Day, the pre-dreadnought *Formidable* of the Channel Fleet had the distinction of being the first British ship of its type lost in the war, when it was torpedoed and sunk by *U 24* off Portland (547 dead).

While the British bombarded the Belgian coast, the Germans used Hipper's battle cruisers in two sorties against English coastal towns, hoping to draw British capital ships far enough to the south for the High Sea Fleet to engage them. The first raid, on November 3, led by three battle cruisers and Germany's largest armored cruiser, the 15,590-ton *Blücher*, targeted the town of Great Yarmouth on the coast of Norfolk. They caused no damage, the shells of Hipper's big ships landing harmlessly on the beach, but afterward mines sowed by one of the light cruisers accompanying his force sank the British submarine *D 5*, based in the port, when it attempted to pursue the Germans as they withdrew. The Germans suffered a far greater loss of their own the following day, when the 10,100-ton armored cruiser *Yorck*, which had sortied with Hipper's squadron, accidentally ran into a German minefield upon its return to Wilhelmshaven and sank (336 dead). In the second raid, on December 16, coinciding with the second British shelling of the Belgian coast, Hipper targeted the towns of Scarborough, Whitby, and Hartlepool, 165–185 miles (265–295 km) north of Great Yarmouth, with a force led by four battle cruisers and the *Blücher*. This time their shelling inflicted considerable damage, causing 137 deaths and nearly 600 injuries ashore, mostly civilian. Three of Hipper's ships took hits from shore batteries, while three British destroyers sustained damage.[41]

At least for the action of December 16, the greater story concerned the battle that did not happen. During the six weeks following

[41] Paul G. Halpern, *A Naval History of World War I* (Annapolis, MD: Naval Institute Press, 1994), pp. 39–40; Scheer, *Germany's High Sea Fleet*, pp. 64–73, Jellicoe, *The Grand Fleet*, pp. 174–179.

the first German raid, the Admiralty's Room 40 developed the ability to read most German naval wireless messages, an advantage that had already paid dividends in contributing to Spee's defeat at the Falklands on December 8. British naval intelligence based its work on three German code books that had fallen into Allied hands: one, from the wreckage of one of Thiele's destroyers sunk off Texel Island, in a chest netted by a British trawler; another, from a German merchant steamer seized in Australia at the beginning of the war; the third, via the Russian navy, from the German light cruiser *Magdeburg*, which ran aground off the Estonian coast in late August 1914.[42] By December 1914, the British had also established so-called "directional finding" or directional wireless stations on their North Sea coast, and had begun to analyze German wireless signals systematically in an effort to determine the composition and location of enemy forces that had put to sea. Such efforts, of course, represented a giant leap forward from the first weeks of the war, when an enemy ship's proximity could be ascertained from the strength of its wireless signal, but with the receiving ship having no way of knowing whether the threat was to the north, south, east, or west. On December 16, the combination of cracked German codes and directional wireless gave the British foreknowledge of Hipper's sortie and enabled Jellicoe to set an ambush at Dogger Bank, the rich fishing grounds in the central North Sea, with a force including four of Beatty's battle cruisers and six dreadnoughts, then based at Cromarty and Rosyth, which had not withdrawn to more distant waters with the rest of the Grand Fleet. The British also knew that Ingenohl (as it turned out, defying standing orders from the emperor) had sortied with most of the rest of the High Sea Fleet to a point east of Dogger Bank. The capital ships of the opposing fleets did not meet, as Hipper avoided the trap laid by the British, slipping away through a gap between their dreadnought squadron and battle cruiser squadron, and the British in turn avoided an encounter with Ingenohl's much larger force. By December 17 everyone had returned to their bases. Afterward Jellicoe remarked that "the escape of the enemy's force was most disappointing, seeing that our own squadrons were in a very favorable position for intercepting the raiders."[43]

[42] Halpern, *A Naval History of World War I*, pp. 36–37.
[43] *Ibid.*, p. 40; Jellicoe, *The Grand Fleet*, pp. 174–179; Scheer, *Germany's High Sea Fleet*, pp. 68–73.

But the battle that did not happen must be judged a greater missed opportunity for the Germans. As Jellicoe later noted, the British margin of superiority in capital ships available for action in the North Sea was narrower in December 1914 than at any other time in the war.[44] The British entered the war with twenty-nine capital ships and another thirteen building, the Germans with eighteen and another eight building. In the first four months of the war, the British completed another pair of dreadnoughts and a battle cruiser, and added the two battleships that British yards had built for the Turks, but lost the *Audacious* to a mine, leaving them with thirty-three; the Germans, meanwhile, had completed another three dreadnoughts and a battle cruiser but transferred the *Goeben* to the Turks, leaving them with twenty-one. While the German navy had all its capital ships in the North Sea, the British still had two battle cruisers in the Mediterranean and had detached three more to catch Spee's squadron, a quest that also occupied the battle cruiser *Australia*. Thus, the *de facto* British advantage as of December 16 was not 33:21, but just 27:21, at a time when mechanical problems plaguing Jellicoe's dreadnoughts left one or two of them refitting and unavailable on any given day. With good reason, Tirpitz concluded that "on December 16 Ingenohl had the fate of Germany in the palm of his hand."[45] The window of opportunity soon closed. Over the next two months, the return of another British battle cruiser from the Mediterranean (leaving just one there), plus the four involved in the hunt for Spee's squadron tipped the North Sea balance decisively toward Britain. Thereafter, new construction further widened the gap, reflecting the diverging numbers of capital ships the two countries had funded in their last prewar naval estimates (for 1912–13 and 1913–14), once Tirpitz had more or less conceded the naval race and the focus of German military spending shifted back in favor of the army. Thus, between the commissioning of the dreadnought *Kronprinz* (November 1914) and the Battle of Jutland, the German navy added just one capital ship, the battle cruiser *Lützow*, in the spring of 1916; during the same eighteen months, the British navy added another eight dreadnoughts: five of the 27,500-ton *Queen Elizabeth* class and the first two of the 28,000-ton *Royal Sovereign* class, plus the 28,600-ton *Canada* (ex-*Almirante Latorre*), which was under construction in Britain for Chile when the war began. All were not only larger, but also more

---

[44] Jellicoe, *The Grand Fleet*, pp. 48–49.   [45] Tirpitz, *My Memoirs*, vol. 2, p. 285.

heavily armed than any German dreadnought, *Canada* with ten 14-inch (35.6-cm) guns, the rest with eight 15-inch (38-cm) guns.

While the Germans, as of December 1914, had at least temporarily narrowed the gap in materiel in the North Sea, their disadvantage in the area of intelligence persisted. By the end of 1914, the Germans were aware that the British had directional wireless, but as Scheer's memoirs indicate, even after the war they still refused to believe that their codes had been broken. Thus, while they set to work developing their own directional wireless capability, they continued to use compromised codes well into the war. The SKM battle fleet code, in books captured from the *Magdeburg*, was not replaced with a new fleet code, FFB, until May 1917. After their capture in December 1914, survivors of Spee's defeat at the Falklands imprisoned in Britain managed to pass home their suspicion that the HVB code, used by German merchantmen to communicate with warships, had been broken (as, indeed, it was, after an HVB code book was taken from the steamer seized in Australia), yet it remained in use through much of 1915. Eventually, a German investigation of the compromised codes affirmed that they were unbreakable, and attributed their loss to "spies and traitors."[46]

While the German raid of November 3 fitted the "guerrilla" strategy Tirpitz detested, the raid of December 16, during which Ingenohl had sortied in an effort to trap part of the Grand Fleet with the main body of the High Sea Fleet, reflected his preference for using Germany's capital ships to even the odds in preparation for the eventual decisive encounter between the two battle fleets. The next sortie by Hipper's battle cruisers, once again followed by Ingenohl's dreadnoughts, resulted in the Battle of Dogger Bank (January 24, 1915), the war's first engagement between German and British capital ships. The British once again had advance warning thanks to an intercepted wireless message, this time from Ingenohl to Hipper, authorizing him to raid the fishing grounds in the central North Sea in order to disrupt the work of "intelligence trawlers" the Admiralty had deployed among the fishing boats.[47] Hipper left Wilhelmshaven shortly after midnight with a force including three battle cruisers and the armored cruiser *Blücher*, weaker than his December 16 squadron because the battle cruiser

---

[46] Scheer, *Germany's High Sea Fleet*, p. 73; Headrick, *The Invisible Weapon*, pp. 162–164.

[47] Tobias R. Philbin, III, *Admiral von Hipper, The Inconvenient Hero* (Amsterdam: John Benjamins, 1982), p. 109.

*Von der Tann* was undergoing a refit. He reached Dogger Bank by dawn and, at 08:15 (German time), before encountering any trawlers, his own light cruisers spotted British light cruisers steaming out of the northwest, one of which fired upon and struck the light cruiser *Kolberg*. It was the screening force for five battle cruisers under Beatty, approaching from Rosyth. At 08:30 Hipper turned away to the southeast, to run toward home while also luring Beatty into an engagement with Ingenohl's dreadnoughts. At 08:50 he radioed Wilhelmshaven to report his situation, and Ingenohl began to assemble the rest of the High Sea Fleet, a process that was completed by 10:30.[48]

It was a clear, crisp winter morning, with a light wind blowing from the northeast, making smoke no factor as the two squadrons steamed southeast on parallel courses, the British trailing leeward. These conditions enabled shots to be fired with reasonable accuracy at ranges even farther than the Battle of the Falklands, and much farther than prewar exercises had envisaged. Beatty's flagship *Lion*, leading the British column, at 09:52 opened fire on the *Blücher*, the last ship in Hipper's column, at a range of 20,000–21,000 yards (18,300–19,200 m), and scored the first hits at 19,000 yards (17,400 m), the greatest distance any naval gun had yet fired with accuracy. The battle raged for the next four hours, with Beatty's column, at one point steaming at 27 knots, gradually closing on Hipper's ships, which were forced to zigzag to avoid being struck. At 10:50 a salvo from the *Lion* bracketed the stern of Hipper's flagship *Seydlitz*, the lead ship in the German line, from a distance of at least 17,000 yards (15,500 m), igniting an ammunition fire that destroyed its two after turrets and killed 159 men. The ship was saved only by the timely flooding of its magazine. The *Lion* also struck the *Derfflinger* at a similar range but, after 11:00, took several hits as well, including salvoes from the *Derfflinger* between 11:35 and 11:50 that disabled its forward turret, reduced it to half-speed, and left it listing to port, without electricity, damage that was miraculously accompanied by just one death. The *Tiger*, next in the British line, then bore the brunt of German fire, losing the use of a turret. Beatty was not known for giving the most coherent flag signals, and once the *Lion* fell out of line the problem became worse. At noon Hipper contributed to their confusion by ordering his escorting torpedo flotilla into the fray. None of the British battle cruisers was hit, but afterward they failed to re-form a coherent line and, rather than continue to pursue the German

[48] Scheer, *Germany's High Sea Fleet*, pp. 77–80.

battle cruisers, focused on the *Blücher*, whose speed had been reduced around 11:30 by a hit from the *Princess Royal* that caused an ammunition fire and engine-room damage. The *Blücher* took a beating but continued to fire its guns, warding off the *Indomitable*, which at one point closed to within 6,000 yards (5,500 m), as well as light cruisers dispatched by Beatty for a torpedo attack. The armored cruiser finally capsized and sank at 13:13, with most of its crew (792 dead). Meanwhile, Beatty abandoned the crippled *Lion* at 12:20 and, after spending an hour aboard a destroyer, transferred his flag to the *Princess Royal* at 13:20, too late to resume the chase. The British lost sight of the fleeing Germans around 13:45, and by 15:30 Hipper had made contact with Ingenohl's ships, which had begun to steam northward only at 11:10 after a distress signal from Hipper following the near-sinking of the *Seydlitz*. By nightfall the German fleet was again safely behind the sandbars and minefields of the Elbe estuary. After losing contact with Hipper's ships, Beatty focused on shepherding the *Lion* home. Jellicoe and the dreadnoughts, belatedly steaming south from Scapa Flow, finally met the battle cruisers at 17:30 and escorted them the rest of the way.[49]

The outcome of the battle left both sides dissatisfied. The British had won, but Beatty felt he should have sunk Hipper's entire squadron, and believed he would have if his captains had not focused so much fire on the *Blücher* after it was already doomed, allowing the German battle cruisers to escape. British records indicate his flagship *Lion* fired 243 shells and scored just four hits, one each against the *Blücher* and *Derfflinger* and the two that almost sank the *Seydlitz*, but it took seventeen hits and had to be towed back to Rosyth by the *Indomitable*. The *Tiger* took seven hits, the *Indomitable* just one from the *Blücher*, the *Princess Royal* and *New Zealand* none at all. Aside from the lone death aboard the *Lion*, the crew of the *Tiger*, with ten dead, suffered the only fatalities on the British side. For his part, Jellicoe considered it a complete victory, remarking later that "the hit which disabled the *Lion* was a piece of luck for the enemy," and alleging in his own account of the battle that the German battle cruisers had suffered much more serious damage.[50]

---

[49] *Ibid.*, pp. 80–83; Jellicoe, *The Grand Fleet*, pp. 195–196, 490–493; Friedman, *Naval Firepower*, pp. 108–109; Brooks, *Dreadnought Gunnery*, pp. 219–221.
[50] Jellicoe, *The Grand Fleet*, p. 196.

Figure 4.4 Admiral Franz von Hipper

Meanwhile, on the German side, the three battle cruisers had fired nearly a thousand shells and scored twenty-two hits, all on the *Lion* and *Tiger*, while in turn the *Seydlitz* and *Derfflinger* each took three hits, the *Moltke* none. Despite the carnage aboard the *Seydlitz*, the damage to it did not affect its mobility and was quickly repaired afterward, leaving German recriminations to focus on the sinking of the *Blücher*, which Hipper's critics contended should not have been taken along on the sortie. Like the *Scharnhorst* and *Gneisenau* at the Falklands, its 8.2-inch (21-cm) guns and triple-expansion engines were no match for the heavier armament and turbine engines of British battle cruisers, which ultimately caught and destroyed it. But Hipper's defenders, then and among historians later, pointed out that the *Blücher* had accompanied the German battle cruisers on Hipper's raids of

November 3 and December 16, that its 8.2-inch guns had been modified to allow for a 30-degree elevation extending their range to 19,100 m, and that its engines were in very good shape, capable of 25 knots, the speed at which it was steaming when it took the debilitating engine-room hit from the *Princess Royal*. In his own assessment of the battle, Hipper claimed that poor quality coal had reduced the speed of his battle cruisers, which averaged 23 knots for the battle as a whole, insufficient speed to escape British battle cruisers unscathed.[51] It would not be the last time that German commanders lamented the poor quality of German coal stocks. Tirpitz, not surprisingly, considered the battle a missed opportunity for Germany. "The same mistake as usual was made in the preliminary thrust. The fleet was in port and not on the spot where the covering forces should have been."[52] Hipper, despite losing the *Blücher*, had drawn five British battle cruisers dangerously close to the High Sea Fleet, at a time when Jellicoe and the main body of the Grand Fleet were hundreds of miles away. Ingenohl had failed to come out in time to make Beatty pay for the risk he had taken, and thus squandered another chance to sink British capital ships and reduce the Grand Fleet's margin of superiority. More significant to the immediate future of the war in the North Sea, the loss of the *Blücher*, far more than the loss of the light cruisers at the First Battle of Helgoland Bight, made William II less willing to allow his admirals to take risks, especially with the capital ships of the High Sea Fleet. The defeat intensified the infighting endemic to the German naval hierarchy, as Pohl intrigued against Ingenohl, and Tirpitz against both of them. On February 2, the emperor intervened, sacking Ingenohl along with Vice Admiral Wilhelm von Lans, commander of a dreadnought squadron which, on Ingenohl's orders, had remained in the roadstead after clearing the bar rather than hasten to Hipper's aid. The dismissal of Lans, whom Tirpitz detested, suggests the state secretary was behind the changes, but the appointment of the chief of the *Admiralstab*, Pohl, to succeed Ingenohl satisfied no one. According to Tirpitz, the transfer of Pohl to the High Sea Fleet command "was received with the greatest astonishment."[53] Hipper, who remained commander of the German battle cruisers, corroborated the state secretary's assessment,

---

[51] Philbin, *Admiral von Hipper*, pp. 109–110.
[52] Tirpitz, *My Memoirs*, vol. 2, p. 295 (diary entry dated January 26, 1915).
[53] *Ibid.*, p. 126.

remarking of Pohl that "a more unlikely choice could not have been made."[54] Pohl could be counted upon to indulge William II's conviction that his capital ships should not be risked, and would accomplish nothing before giving way to Scheer in January 1916. Meanwhile, Tirpitz, who had hoped to succeed Pohl as chief of the *Admiralstab* (and thus gain a formal voice in operational matters), instead had to take consolation that Pohl's former post went to Vice Admiral Gustav Bachmann, one of his allies within the divided officer corps.

## The Adriatic, to the Italian declaration of war

Italy's declaration of neutrality made the Triple Alliance Naval Convention a dead letter and confined the Austro-Hungarian navy to the Adriatic, where it was blockaded by a vastly superior Allied force shortly after Britain and France declared war on the Dual Monarchy. Following his aborted sortie of August 7, coinciding with the *Goeben*'s feint toward the Adriatic, Admiral Haus concentrated his three dreadnoughts and nine newest pre-dreadnoughts at Pola, covering the main seaports of Trieste and Fiume (Rijeka), and sent his Cruiser Flotilla – three armored cruisers and three light cruisers – to Cattaro at the southern tip of Dalmatia. On August 13, the day after the declarations of war were delivered, the Allied Mediterranean commander, Lapeyrère, received orders to proceed to the Adriatic. At least initially, with Britain concentrating its Mediterranean forces at the Dardanelles and Italy not yet in the war, France assumed primary responsibility for the naval blockade of Austria-Hungary. On August 16, six days after the *Goeben* entered the Dardanelles, Lapeyrère passed through the Straits of Otranto and entered the Adriatic. His fleet included the dreadnoughts *Courbet* and *Jean Bart*, and the twelve newest French pre-dreadnoughts, accompanied by a token British force consisting of the armored cruiser *Defence* and one destroyer.

     Eventually the Allies would impose a "distant blockade" of Austria-Hungary, analogous to the British blockade of Germany in the North Sea, closing the Straits of Otranto between the southeastern tip of Italy and the coast of Albania. But on August 16, Lapeyrère steamed another 150 miles (240 km) northward into the southern

[54] Quoted in Philbin, *Admiral von Hipper*, p. 117.

Adriatic to the tiny coastal foothold of Montenegro, which had joined the war against Austria-Hungary on August 8. Because Montenegro practically surrounded the Austro-Hungarian base at Cattaro, commanding the heights all around the fjord-like anchorage, its entry into the war prompted Haus to reinforce the Cruiser Flotilla there with the three old *Monarch*-class coast defenders. Montenegro had just one small port, Antivari (Bar), 17 miles (27 km) south of Cattaro, which Austria-Hungary blockaded as soon as Cattaro was secured against attack from the land side. Because Montenegro owned no ships except the royal yacht *Rumija*, one light cruiser from the flotilla at Cattaro sufficed to stand watch there. On August 16, this duty fell to Captain Paul Pachner's *Zenta*, which the vanguard of Lapeyrère's fleet attacked and sank (179 dead). In perhaps the most extreme case of overkill in the entire war at sea, French battleships fired over 500 shells at the 2,300-ton cruiser, which went down with flags flying. Afterward, Lapeyrère's ships made no effort to pick up survivors, leaving Pachner and around 130 of his men to swim ashore, where they remained captives until 1916, when Austria-Hungary knocked Montenegro out of the war.

The action of August 16 opened Antivari to Allied ships, but the port had no facilities or defenses, and the French, soon in dire circumstances on the Western front, could not spare the manpower to secure it. A month later they landed 140 artillerymen and eight heavy guns, which the Montenegrins subsequently hauled to the heights above Cattaro. They shelled the harbor for several weeks until Haus added the pre-dreadnought *Radetzky*'s four 12-inch (30.5-cm) and eight 9.4-inch (24-cm) guns to the firepower already assembled in the waters below. The *Radetzky*'s salvoes knocked out two of the guns and forced the withdrawal of the rest, leading to the departure of the French mission in late November. Meanwhile, Lapeyrère faced the difficult task of sustaining operations with Malta, roughly 550 miles (890 km) to the southwest, as his nearest base, a distance as far from Cattaro as Scapa Flow was from Wilhelmshaven. By October, he had implemented a system for rotating warships back to Malta for resupply and refitting, increasingly using Corfu, 215 miles (345 km) south of Cattaro, just outside the Adriatic, as a forward anchorage, even though this violated the neutrality of Greece (and thus set the precedent for the Allies to use Lemnos, just west of the Dardanelles, as an advance base for operations there the following year). But the southern Adriatic remained the end of his tether. While Lapeyrère had more than enough strength to overwhelm Haus' fleet, the main Austro-Hungarian base at Pola, another 300 miles (480 km) up the coast from Cattaro, remained beyond the reach of a fleet operating out of Malta. Haus certainly had no intention of obliging the French by coming out to fight; indeed, as early as September 6 the admiral explained in a dispatch to Vienna that he had no intention of leaving Pola "so long as the possibility exists that Italy will declare war against us. I consider it my first duty to keep our fleet intact . . . for the decisive struggle against this, our most dangerous foe."[55]

Despite the extreme challenges he faced, Lapeyrère initially maintained an active regime of sorties into the southern Adriatic. After first appearing off Cattaro on September 1, when he bombarded the outer forts with his two dreadnoughts, ten of his pre-dreadnoughts, and four armored cruisers, he returned on a regular basis to threaten the Austro-Hungarian base there. On September 19 his armored cruisers ventured as far north as Cape Planka, 160 miles (260 km) up the Dalmatian coast from Cattaro. He could have taken and held a number of islands, but even after the Allied victory at the First Battle of the Marne saved Paris, the French army could spare no troops for amphibious operations in the Adriatic. Logistics alone kept Lapeyrère from dominating the Adriatic, at least until Haus bowed to pressure from his own submarine commander, Captain Franz von Thierry, and allowed Austro-Hungarian U-boats to be transferred from Pola to Cattaro. Like many flag officers of his age, Haus considered submarines to be defensive weapons, but the early successes of German U-boats, in particular *U 9*'s sinking of the three British armored cruisers off the Dutch coast in September, opened his eyes to their offensive potential. The first two Austro-Hungarian U-boats reached Cattaro later that month, and by the end of the year five of the seven boats then available were based there. They finally made their mark on December 21, when *U 12* torpedoed Lapeyrère's flagship, the 23,400-ton dreadnought *Jean Bart*, off Antivari.

The *Jean Bart* survived the attack, and despite taking on water made it safely back to Malta. Nevertheless, it remained out of action for several months, and Lapeyrère never recovered from the shock. Austro-Hungarian naval forces at Cattaro were strong enough that battleships

[55] Quoted in Halpern, *The Naval War in the Mediterranean*, p. 30.

had to be used to convoy supplies bound for the Montenegrin army via Antivari, and the new submarine threat made the use of battleships as convoy escorts too risky. The French navy went to the extreme of never again deploying a dreadnought or pre-dreadnought north of the Straits of Otranto, leaving Montenegro on its own until the Austro-Hungarian army finally overran the mountain kingdom in 1916. In the short term, the withdrawal of French battleships from the southern Adriatic enabled Austria-Hungary to be bolder in its use of the lighter forces stationed at Cattaro. They sowed mines off Antivari, which on February 24, 1915 sank a French destroyer. Then, on the night of March 1–2, an Austro-Hungarian destroyer infiltrated the harbor at Antivari, torpedoing the Montenegrin royal yacht. Finally, on the night of April 26–27, *U 5* (Lieutenant Georg von Trapp) torpedoed and sank the 12,500-ton French armored cruiser *Léon Gambetta* off Cape Santa Maria di Leuca, the southeastern tip of Italy (684 dead). This shocking loss prompted Lapeyrère to extend his caution to cruisers as well as battleships. For the next four weeks, until Italy's entry into the war gave the Allied fleet much more firepower and much better bases for the war in the Adriatic, he did not risk anything larger than a destroyer north of the parallel of the Ionian island of Cephalonia, 300 miles (480 km) south of Cattaro.

Italy entered the war under the terms of the Treaty of London, signed April 26, 1915, the day after the initial Allied landings at Gallipoli (see chapter six). An Anglo-French-Italian naval convention, concluded at Paris on May 10, created a new convoluted command structure taking into account Italy's insistence upon an Italian Allied commander for the Adriatic and direct control over its own five dreadnoughts. Admiral Luigi of Savoy, Duke of the Abruzzi, became commander of the First Allied Fleet, predominantly Italian and based at Brindisi, while Admiral Lapeyrère's existing force, now designated the Second Allied Fleet but still mostly French, received an advance base at Taranto. Lapeyrère remained the overall Allied Mediterranean commander with Abruzzi as his subordinate, but in the event that Lapeyrère took the Second Allied Fleet into the Adriatic, he would be under the command of Abruzzi. Austria-Hungary wasted no time responding to Italy's declaration of war, which followed on May 23. That evening, just hours after the onset of hostilities, Admiral Haus left Pola with most of his fleet, including all three dreadnoughts and nine pre-dreadnoughts, to conduct a punitive bombardment along 300 miles

(480 km) of central Italy's Adriatic coastline. The raid disrupted the subsequent mobilization of the Italian army inasmuch as it damaged stations of the coastal railway at Ancona, Rimini, and Senigallia, and bridges at Senigallia and at the mouth of the Potenza River. Seaplanes based at Pola supplemented the shelling with bombing raids on Ancona and Venice. The Italian navy offered little opposition to the sortie. A small force at Venice, led by three old pre-dreadnoughts, remained in port. The night's only naval action involved light cruisers and destroyers of the two navies, in the Italian case sent northward from Brindisi, and resulted in the sinking of one of the Italian destroyers off the island of Pelagosa.[56]

The sortie marked the first time that Haus had risked a dreadnought, pre-dreadnought, or even an armored cruiser to the possibility of battle with the overwhelmingly superior Allied fleet. Yet Austria-Hungary thus far had managed to secure the Adriatic Sea, making it the most frustrating theater of the war for the Allies. Nowhere else did they have such a preponderance of power that they were unable to bring to bear for any constructive purpose. These frustrations had provided the context for the Anglo-French negotiations with the Italians over the winter of 1914/15, and contributed to the overestimation of the value of Italy as an ally, at sea as well as on land. Haus' opening sortie of the campaign, though not repeated, set the tone for what was to come, as from the start the Italians, even more so than the French, seemed willing to concede the Adriatic to the enemy. Abruzzi soon kept only pre-dreadnought battleships at Brindisi, moving his dreadnoughts farther from harm's way to Taranto, his caution reinforced by the Austro-Hungarian navy's uncanny knack of anticipating Allied actions. Though the Dual Monarchy generally viewed its own Italian minority with suspicion, it had better luck in recruiting agents to infiltrate into Italy than Italy had in developing its own network of spies among the Italians living in Austria-Hungary. A special office of the naval intelligence service, operating out of the Austro-Hungarian consulate in Zurich from May 1915 onward, provided a constant stream of valuable information from within Italy and also orchestrated periodic acts of sabotage in Italian ports. The first, most spectacular example of the latter came four months into the campaign, when Austrian agents infiltrated Brindisi and blew up the pre-dreadnought *Benedetto Brin*

[56] Sondhaus, *The Naval Policy of Austria-Hungary*, pp. 272–276.

(456 dead).[57] Meanwhile, at sea further Italian losses by the end of 1915 included two auxiliary cruisers, one destroyer, four submarines, and three torpedo boats, while Austria-Hungary lost just two destroyers and two submarines. Italian timidity and successful further appeals for reinforcements from the French and British enabled the Austro-Hungarian "fleet in being" to tie down an ever-greater number of Allied warships that could have been put to better use elsewhere. Fatefully, Italy's disappointing performance in the war would leave the British and French with fewer scruples about breaking the territorial promises included in the Treaty of London to bring the Italians into the war in the first place, and thus laid the foundation for postwar developments that would have profound consequences not just for Italy, but for Europe as a whole.

## Conclusion

For a German navy that, by December 1914, had achieved near-parity with the British in the North Sea, the loss of the *Goeben* to the Ottoman navy was no different from having it sunk. From Churchill onward, authors writing about the flight of the German battle cruiser to Constantinople have focused on its significance to the Ottoman decision to enter the war, extrapolating from there its broader impact on the war ranging from Russia to the Middle East. But before it took on an operational significance as a one-ship "fleet-in-being" at Constantinople, the *Goeben*'s greatest significance was as a ship missing from the High Sea Fleet – which it could have joined had it steamed for home as soon as its repairs at Pola were finished on July 23, 1914 – that also did not join the Austro-Hungarian fleet. We may only speculate about how much difference another battle cruiser would have made for Hipper at Dogger Bank, or if the outcome of that battle would have been different had it been there instead of the ill-fated *Blücher*, whose sinking had an out-of-proportion impact on William II, dooming the High Sea Fleet to a year of inactivity after January 1915. The absence of the *Goeben* was also felt in the Adriatic, where it would have added another weapon to

---

[57] Hans Hugo Sokol, *Österreich-Ungarns Seekrieg 1914–1918*, 2 vols. (Graz: Akademische Druck- und Verlagsanstalt, [1933] 1967), vol. 1, pp. 465–467; Sondhaus, *The Naval Policy of Austria-Hungary*, p. 304.

the arsenal available to Admiral Haus. Though the Germans typically were insufferable as allies, the German navy held the Austro-Hungarian navy in higher regard than the German army did the Austro-Hungarian army, and the two would cooperate closely from 1915 onward in using the Adriatic to stage a formidable submarine threat to the Allies in the Mediterranean; had the *Goeben* fled to the Adriatic, its presence might have further energized the relationship. At least in some small measure, the battle cruiser would have enabled either the High Sea Fleet or the Austro-Hungarian fleet to assume a more aggressive posture, and thus its absence contributed to the inactivity of the surface fleets of the Central Powers, an inactivity that would be corrosive to the morale of the men aboard the idle big ships, who accounted for the majority of the manpower in both navies.

From the perspective of the late winter or early spring of 1915, the war at sea (like the war on land) looked very different from the conflict that had been anticipated the previous summer. The British and German navies entered the war assuming the effective range for their heaviest guns would be somewhat less than 9,000 yards (roughly 8,000 m), the maximum range at which Russian and Japanese guns had scored hits in the war of 1904–5. But Spee's armored cruisers registered hits at 13,000 yards (11,900 m) at Coronel, and had straddled their pursuers at 15,000 yards (13,700 m) at the Falklands; then, at Dogger Bank, British guns scored their first hits at 19,000 yards (17,400 m). After Dogger Bank, Beatty recommended that Dreyer Tables and other range-finding instruments be modified to accommodate ranges up to 25,000 yards (22,900 m), and guidelines regarding when to commence firing were revised upward for both the British and German navies.[58] After emphasizing intensity of fire in their own exercises in the immediate prewar years, the British were nevertheless surprised by the rate of fire they encountered from German ships in the battles of 1914–15. At Dogger Bank, the German battle cruisers each fired an average of nearly 100 shells more than their British counterparts during the same number of hours; at the unanticipated longer ranges, with hit rates in the area of 2–3 percent, more rapid fire logically became the key to scoring more hits and damaging or sinking enemy ships.

Aside from the range and rate of gunfire, the complete ineffectiveness of torpedoes fired by larger warships ranked as the war's

[58] Friedman, *Naval Firepower*, p. 108.

greatest early surprise. As a legacy of the torpedo scare of the first years of the century (1900–5), when it was feared that the effective range of torpedoes would outstrip the effective range of guns, capital ships were given torpedo tubes as a secondary armament; HMS *Dreadnought* had five, the first two classes of German dreadnoughts had six, later dreadnoughts and battle cruisers fewer. The late-model torpedoes of 1914 had a theoretical range of 10,000–11,000 yards (9,100–10,000 m), leading the British and German navies to assume their capital ships would make effective use of their torpedoes in battle. Yet it became clear early on that no battleship or cruiser would ever get close enough to another battleship or cruiser to actually use its torpedoes, while the guns carried by these larger types more than sufficed to keep destroyers and smaller surface ships at a distance. Torpedoes fired by submarines posed the greatest – indeed, the only – torpedo threat to larger warships, and other than submarine-fired torpedoes, mines had proven to be the only real danger to battleships and cruisers, aside from the gunfire of other battleships and cruisers. By the first months of 1915, submarines had been decisive in the Adriatic, mines in the Black Sea, and both submarines and mines in the North Sea. In their days of disappointment after Dogger Bank, the Germans made the fateful decision to use submarine warfare systematically not just against Allied warships, but against Allied shipping, declaring their own undersea "blockade" of the British Isles to counter the British blockade of Germany.

# 5 SUBMARINE WARFARE: THE GREAT EXPERIMENT, 1915

"Firing from a submarine is extraordinarily difficult," Tirpitz reminded Admiral Pohl, chief of the *Admiralstab*, adding that this was especially so if the target of the torpedo "maintains a higher speed and changes course frequently."[1] The admonition came in a letter dated October 1, 1914, nine days after *U 9*'s spectacular sinking of the British armored cruisers *Aboukir*, *Hogue*, and *Cressy* off the Dutch coast made the submarine's commander, *Kapitänleutnant* Otto Weddigen, the German navy's first war hero. Tirpitz downplayed the success by pointing out to Pohl that the *Aboukir* was steaming "at ten knots," and furthermore, "the *Hogue* and *Cressy* were stationary when attacked," making them very easy to sink. He conceded that, going into the war, the offensive potential of the submarine had been "underestimated, but... it is now exaggerated as a result of the success of *U 9*."[2] These remarks came in a preamble to a lengthy defense of the battle fleet Tirpitz had worked so hard to build, a legacy that now seemed threatened by the unexpected effectiveness of the navy's smallest vessels, which the Germans (like everyone else) had developed before the war for short-range defensive purposes. But when the focus shifted to attacking merchant vessels, Tirpitz's position on U-boats began to change. After

---

[1] Tirpitz to Pohl, October 1, 1914, text in Alfred von Tirpitz, *Erinnerungen* (Leipzig: Verlag von K. F. Koehler, 1920), p. 313. Note: the English translation of this key sentence, in Tirpitz, *My Memoirs*, vol. 2, p. 97, reads "Shooting from a submarine is extraordinarily difficult if the vessel attacked maintains a good speed and changes direction frequently when near submarines."

[2] Tirpitz to Pohl, October 1, 1914, text in Tirpitz, *My Memoirs*, vol. 2, p. 97.

*U 17* torpedoed and sank the British merchantman *Glitra* off the Norwegian coast on October 20, German submarine commanders gradually became more aggressive in their targeting of unarmed ships. Having initially respected norms devised for commerce raiders – which called for crews to be allowed to abandon ship, and obligated the attacker to provide for their safety – U-boats on occasion began to sink their targets without warning, or leave survivors to fend for themselves.

Once it became clear that Britain, in its quest to close Germany's ports, had no intention of honoring the provisions of the prewar Declaration of London that allowed food and other non-military cargoes to pass through a blockade, the Germans began to consider ways to use the U-boat threat to inflict a similar hardship on the British. Tirpitz later recalled that, as early as November 7, Pohl circulated "a draft of a declaration for a submarine blockade of the whole coast of Great Britain and Ireland."[3] But a policy of retribution came with risks. It could be emotionally satisfying to the Germans while doing little real damage to the Allies, with the collateral effect of offending neutral powers, especially the United States. With the permission of the German Foreign Office, Tirpitz sought to test American public opinion on the matter by granting an interview to Karl von Wiegand, a German-American war correspondent working for the Hearst newspaper chain, in which he openly contemplated unrestricted submarine warfare, asking the rhetorical question, "If pressed to the limit, why not?"[4] The interview, conducted on November 21, appeared in several leading US newspapers just before Christmas, but it failed to elicit much sympathy; indeed, the American public, like the US government, would never accept the German argument that unrestricted submarine warfare against Britain was no less moral or legal than the British blockade of Germany. Meanwhile, Pohl considered the interview an ill-conceived leak of secret discussions then underway among German naval and political leaders, an error compounded when the interview was published in Germany, where it stirred public support for a U-boat campaign against Allied commerce. During January 1915, as the German government implemented bread rationing, such sentiments naturally grew stronger, and the public's expectation that unrestricted submarine warfare would happen became a factor in swaying the chancellor, Bethmann Hollweg, to support it.[5]

[3] Tirpitz, *My Memoirs*, vol. 2, p. 139.   [4] Quoted in Kelly, *Tirpitz*, p. 395.   [5] *Ibid.*

## The first round of unrestricted submarine warfare

A combination of factors caused the food shortage that Germany began to feel in the winter of 1914/15. As the only continental European power that was a net importer of food, Germany was vulnerable not just to blockade by sea, but to the general disruption of trade caused by the war on land. Russia had become its main supplier of grain, and hostilities with Russia naturally ended that trade. Austria-Hungary ranked as Germany's next most important source of food, in particular Hungary, which also served as a net supplier for Austria, but for the predominantly agrarian Dual Monarchy, as for Russia, the general mobilization of August 1914 compromised that fall's harvest and resulted in less land being cultivated thereafter. As early as 1915, Hungary was barely keeping Austria supplied and sending very little on to Germany. The Germans had done very little before the war to prepare for this scenario, and at least some of the blame rested at the doorstep of Tirpitz, who had long warned of the prospect of a British blockade but only to justify a larger battle fleet. At his direction, the Imperial Navy Office had even "discouraged economic preparations" on the home front because such measures would appear easier, and certainly less expensive, than building more battleships.[6]

Unable to depend upon their own agricultural base or their leading prewar sources of food, the Germans quickly became dependent on their neutral neighbors – the Scandinavian countries, the Netherlands, and Switzerland – for whatever they could either provide themselves or transship from sources abroad. From the start, Berlin's policies to address the food question often made matters worse; as a British government report noted later in the war, "the German genius for organization appears to have had a disastrous effect upon agriculture."[7] Avner Offer, author of the landmark study on agrarian policy and the Great War, concludes that "rationing in Germany was mechanical," failing to account for such basic factors as age, gender, and economic inequality.[8] Thus, among all the belligerents eventually adopting some form of rationing, Germany's policies spread the burden least equitably

---

[6] Offer, *The First World War: An Agrarian Interpretation*, p. 336.
[7] "Appreciation of the Attached Western and General Report, No. 30," August 1917, UK National Archives (TNA): Public Record Office (PRO) CAB 24/147/5, p. 10.
[8] Offer, *The First World War: An Agrarian Interpretation*, p. 54.

across society. But despite the complex nature of the food problem, from the start the German public, regardless of social class, focused on the British as the primary cause of the shortages, and because the blockade effectively prevented Germany from seeking relief from new sources of food overseas, throughout the war the blockade would remain the most tangible symbol of privation on the home front.

While public opinion figured most prominently in Bethmann Hollweg's decision to support a more aggressive submarine campaign, for William II it was the navy's defeat at Dogger Bank. Under the circumstances, the emperor considered the possibility of inflicting serious harm to the Allied war effort without exposing the dreadnoughts and battle cruisers of the High Sea Fleet to be particularly appealing. Tirpitz, too, came all the way round, recovering fully from his initial view that submarine warfare threatened the strategic primacy of the battle fleet. In any event, by January he considered the High Sea Fleet's window of opportunity for victory to have closed. Britain's newly launched dreadnoughts would soon reinforce Jellicoe's Grand Fleet, and the battle cruisers returning from the Mediterranean and from the pursuit of Spee further strengthened Beatty's squadron, redesignated the Battle Cruiser Fleet in February 1915. Together, these British North Sea forces had far better than a 3:2 ratio of capital ship superiority over the Germans. The German navy did not yet have enough U-boats to be deployed systematically for any purpose, but their effect against undefended merchantmen was likely to be far greater than against enemy warships, which now operated much more carefully (in the North Sea as well as the Adriatic) whenever submarines were in the vicinity, after so many were torpedoed in the first months of the war. Skeptics within the German navy conceded that, if nothing else, a U-boat campaign would keep the sea lanes in play for Germany at a time when the last of its surface raiders was being hunted down.

Because the decision to undertake the campaign came during the days of infighting and intrigue between Dogger Bank and the resulting changes in the German naval leadership, the rollout left much to be desired. As late as January 27, Bethmann Hollweg led Tirpitz to believe that he would not approve the onset of unrestricted submarine warfare "before the spring or summer of 1915,"[9] leaving the admiral shocked when it was announced just one week later, after Pohl secured the

[9] Tirpitz, *My Memoirs*, vol. 2, p. 143.

consent of the emperor and chancellor. On February 4, two days after he succeeded Ingenohl as commander of the High Sea Fleet, Pohl issued the official declaration of Germany's undersea blockade of the British Isles, to take effect in two weeks: "The waters around Great Britain and Ireland, including the English Channel, are hereby proclaimed a war region. On and after February 18th every enemy merchant vessel found in this region will be destroyed, without it always being possible to warn the crews or passengers of the dangers threatening." The declaration further warned that "attacks intended for hostile ships may affect neutral ships also," but as a concession to neutral Norway and the Netherlands, exempted from the threat "the sea passage to the north of the Shetland Islands" as well as a strip of the North Sea along the Dutch coast.[10]

Among the German admirals, Bachmann joined Tirpitz in opposing the decision to undertake such an ambitious campaign with so little advance preparation. Bachmann learned of the declaration on February 2, the day of his appointment to succeed Pohl as chief of the *Admiralstab*, and on that occasion had "expressed unreservedly to Admiral von Pohl" his "objections to so early an introduction of submarine warfare," owing to "the small number of our submarines, the lack of bases in Flanders or elsewhere, inexperience of submarine warfare against merchant ships, etc." Not only did Germany have too few U-boats to make a difference at this stage, their use in a role not envisaged prior to the war meant that strategy and tactics would have to be developed on the fly. But Bachmann's concerns "all were rejected by the admiral, who stated that the matter was already decided."[11] Tirpitz worried that the declaration "had the appearance of bluff," and found troubling "the ambiguity arising from our obvious efforts to spare neutrals, coupled with our threats not to spare them."[12] The United States responded within a week of the declaration, not waiting for the campaign to actually begin. President Woodrow Wilson's note, dated February 10, asked the German government "to consider, before action is taken, the critical situation ... which might arise were the German naval force[s] ... to destroy any merchant vessel of the United States or cause the death of American citizens." Wilson then cut to the heart of

---

[10] "German Declaration of Naval Blockade Against Shipping to Britain," Berlin, February 4, 1915: www.firstworldwar.com/source/pohl_uboatwar1915.htm.
[11] Tirpitz, *My Memoirs*, vol. 2, p. 145.   [12] *Ibid.*, p. 144.

the revolutionary nature of the German declaration, observing that "to declare or exercise a right to attack and destroy any vessel entering a prescribed area of the high seas without first certainly determining its belligerent nationality and the contraband character of its cargo would be an act... unprecedented in naval warfare."[13] The American reaction did not surprise Tirpitz, but shook both William II and Bethmann Hollweg. On February 15, the emperor ordered U-boat commanders not to sink neutral ships in the war zone, and two days later the chancellor sent a conciliatory response to Wilson, implying that the submarine campaign would end if the United States could prevail upon Britain to observe the Declaration of London in its blockade of Germany. These actions had the effect of uniting the naval leadership. Tirpitz criticized "the vacillating nature of our policy" and "our all too humble answer to America," and joined Bachmann in supporting Pohl's position that unrestricted submarine warfare, "once it had been announced to the world... must be stood by at all costs."[14]

In its quest to stay the course, the German navy had to overcome the limitations Bachmann and Tirpitz cited in their initial criticism of the declaration. Germany entered the war with thirty-six submarines, and by February 1915 had added nine more, but during the same six months seven were lost to accidents or to enemy action, and the oldest four (*U 1–U 4*) were removed from active service. This left thirty-four on hand when the campaign began, some of which were too small for the cruises required to enforce the undersea blockade. The navy's *UB* boats, designed for coastal use, had a surfaced displacement of just 130 tons and measured 92 feet long by 10 feet deep, with a beam of barely 10 feet (28 m × 3 m × 3.2 m). Manned by two officers and a crew of twelve, they had a surface speed of only 6–7 knots. The smallest submarines Germany considered ocean-going – the seven boats remaining from among the dozen numbered *U 5–U 16* – were giants by comparison, though very small by later standards. Each displaced approximately 500 tons, measuring just under 190 feet long by 12 feet deep, with a beam of 20 feet (58 m × 3.5 m × 6.0 m). They were manned by two officers and a crew of twenty-seven. With a top speed of 13–15 knots surfaced, they were still several knots slower than high-profile targets

---

[13] "Text of U.S. 'Strict Accountability' Warning to Germany," February 10, 1915: www.firstworldwar.com/source/wilsonwarningfeb1915.htm.

[14] Tirpitz, *My Memoirs*, vol. 2, pp. 149, 152.

such as battleships and ocean liners, which could simply outrun the threat when they were aware of its presence. Lighter warships, such as destroyers and torpedo boats, moved at twice the speed of the fastest submarines and thus posed a danger to any they were deployed to hunt. All of these U-boats moved significantly slower when submerged, using power from batteries that recharged when the submarine's engines operated on the surface. The smallest of the ocean-going submarines carried enough fuel for a surfaced range of 1,800–2,100 nautical miles (3,330–3,890 km), but their batteries allowed them just 80–90 nautical miles (148–167 km) submerged. The first *UB* boats operated on an even shorter leash, with a range of just 1,500 nautical miles (2,780 km) surfaced and 45 nautical miles (83 km) submerged. Both types were so small that the crew had to sleep on hammocks hung throughout the interior of the boat, which they shared because crews worked and slept in shifts. By one estimate only fifteen of the German submarines on hand in the spring of 1915 (those which burned diesel fuel rather than gasoline or kerosene) were capable of operating away from their bases for up to three weeks at a time. They carried few torpedoes (two for the *UB* boats, six for the others) and had to save them for encounters with warships or attacks against merchantmen in dangerous circumstances, for example, when enemy warships or aircraft were in the vicinity. This made a submarine's deck gun the weapon of choice whenever its commander felt confident enough to attack while surfaced, but none of the smallest dozen U-boats had one until retrofitted with a 2-inch (5-cm) gun on the foredeck, a process not completed until May 1915.[15]

Further compromising the effectiveness of a campaign waged with relatively small numbers of small submarines, the German navy after February 1915 did not use all serviceable U-boats for commerce raiding but still deployed some off British naval bases, hoping to ambush and sink enemy warships. The cruise of the new *U 29* serves as an example of this divided focus. Commanded by *Kapitänleutnant* Weddigen, whose *U 9* had sunk the British armored cruisers the previous autumn, *U 29* sortied from Ostend in occupied Belgium on March 10, and two days later sank three merchantmen totaling 10,000 tons while cruising off the coast of Cornwall. After Weddigen took great pains to rescue the survivors of these ships (at one point towing their

[15] Kelly, *Tirpitz*, p. 393; see also *Conway, 1906–1921*, pp. 175, 180. See also: www.uboat.net.

lifeboats, before leaving them safely aboard a French barque he had stopped), he broke off commerce raiding and made for Scapa Flow to stalk the capital ships of the Grand Fleet. On March 18, in the nearby Pentland Firth, *U 29* was rammed and sunk by HMS *Dreadnought* (ironically in the great ship's only encounter with a German naval vessel of any kind) shortly after Weddigen launched an unsuccessful torpedo attack on the dreadnought *Neptune*. Like most lost submarines, *U 29* went down with all hands, thus taking the life of the navy's first U-boat hero before he could play much of a role in the unrestricted campaign.[16]

During the first round of unrestricted submarine warfare, the Germans rarely were able to maintain more than six U-boats on patrol around the British Isles at any given time. Over the seven months of the campaign, they sank 787,120 tons of merchant shipping (89,500 in March 1915, 38,600 in April, 126,900 in May, 115,290 in June, 98,005 in July, 182,770 in August, and 136,050 in September), against a total loss of fifteen submarines. Because Britain had entered the war with over 21 million tons of merchant shipping capacity, the loss to U-boats of 787,120 tons (not all of it British-flagged) had little practical effect on the war effort. While the campaign demonstrated the potential of the submarine as a commerce raider, the material damages were far less significant than the diplomatic consequences, in particular, the irreparable harm done to Germany's relationship with the United States.

Shortly after its introduction, unrestricted submarine warfare expanded to include Austria-Hungary as well as Germany, but at the start of the campaign the Austro-Hungarian navy had just five U-boats capable of offensive action, and additional U-boats under construction for the Dual Monarchy at Kiel had been expropriated for use by the German navy. By the end of 1914, these five submarines had been forward-deployed from Pola down the Adriatic to Cattaro, but clearly Austria-Hungary could not threaten Allied commerce in the Mediterranean without help from their allies. During March the German navy sent the partially completed submarines *UB 7* and *UB 8* by rail from Kiel to Pola, where they were assembled and placed in commission the following month, manned by German crews likewise sent overland.

[16] Otto Eduard Weddigen, *Otto Weddigen und seine Waffe: aus seinen Tagebüchern und nachgelassenen Papieren* (Berlin: Marinedank-verlag, 1915), pp. 44–47; Paul Kemp, *U-boats Destroyed: German Submarine Losses in the Two World Wars* (Annapolis, MD: Naval Institute Press, 1997), p. 12.

Figure 5.1  *U 53* surfaced with crew

The German navy also tested the feasibility of sending a submarine directly from home waters to the Adriatic. On April 25, *Kapitänleutnant* Hersing's *U 21* left Wilhelmshaven for Cattaro, reaching its destination eighteen days later after refueling in neutral Spanish waters. Shortly after Hersing's boat left Germany, Lieutenant Trapp's Austro-Hungarian *U 5* had sunk the French armored cruiser *Léon Gambetta* off the Italian boot heel, prompting Admiral Lapeyrère to pull the Allied blockade line southward to the parallel of Cephalonia; thus, when *U 21* arrived it had no trouble passing the Straits of Otranto and entering the Adriatic. In May, with the action heating up at Gallipoli and the Dardanelles (see Chapter 6), *U 21* moved into Greek waters. During the same month, Austro-Hungarian warships towed the smaller *UB 7*, *UB 8*, and *UB 3* (the latter sent overland from Germany in mid-April) from Pola down the Adriatic before releasing them to make their way to Greek waters as well; the light cruiser *Novara* (Captain Miklós Horthy) did the honors for *UB 8*, on May 2 towing the submarine all the way to Cephalonia, 300 miles (480 km) south of Cattaro, on what would be the war's longest sortie outside the Adriatic by any Austro-Hungarian surface vessel. Three of these submarines (*U 21*, *UB 7*, and

*UB 8*) soon turned up off the coast of Asia Minor, but *UB 3* never reached its destination and its fate remains a mystery.[17]

In contrast to the wartime interaction between the German and Austro-Hungarian armies, in which the former typically held the latter in contempt, the naval cooperation featured a far greater degree of mutual respect from the start. Indeed, the Germans admired the professionalism of their allies and, at least to a degree, envied their traditions. *Kapitänleutnant* Max Valentiner, who spent much of the war operating in partnership with Austro-Hungarian forces, later recalled that "the naval officer corps impressed me a great deal. I would describe it as exemplary. The officers were all well-mannered" and "the old naval tradition was important to them. There were many officers whose father or grandfather had fought in 1866 under Admiral Tegetthoff at the Battle of Lissa and helped him to defeat the Italians." He considered "the training of the Austrian naval officers" to have been "outstanding." They also spared little expense as hosts, at least as long as wartime food supplies held up. Upon his arrival in Cattaro late in 1915, Valentiner was surprised and impressed by the sumptuous fare in the officers' mess of the depot ship *Gäa*. The hospitality and "friendly warmth of all Austrian comrades" made a lasting impression on him.[18] Along with the bonds they forged with their allies, German submariners based in the Adriatic also developed their own quirky camaraderie. *Oberleutnant* Martin Niemöller credited Hersing and his subordinates in *U 21* with starting the custom that all German submarine officers ashore in Pola "irrespective of rank and real name" addressed each other as "Heinrich."[19]

In addition to sending their own submarines to the Adriatic, in May 1915 the Germans strengthened their ally's small undersea force by shipping the submarines *UB 1* and *UB 15* by rail to Pola, where they soon became *U 10* and *U 11* in the Austro-Hungarian navy. The Dual Monarchy added another U-boat when the French submarine *Curie*, sunk on a daring raid of Pola harbor in December 1914, was raised, repaired, and commissioned as *U 14*. Italy's entry into the war (May 23,

---

[17] Sondhaus, *The Naval Policy of Austria-Hungary*, p. 268; Halpern, *The Naval War in the Mediterranean*, pp. 110–111, 116.

[18] Max Valentiner, *Der Schrecken der Meere: Meine U-Boot-Abenteuer* (Leipzig: Amalthea-Verlag, 1931), pp. 118–119.

[19] Martin Niemöller, *From U-Boat to Pulpit*, trans. D. Hastie Smith (Chicago, IL: Willett, Clark, 1937), p. 84.

1915) made unrestricted submarine warfare in the Mediterranean a great deal more complicated, as the Italians did not declare war on Germany until August 1916, and the Germans decided not to force the issue by declaring war on Italy. To ensure the greatest possible freedom of action, during the intervening fifteen months German U-boats operating in southern European waters were double-numbered as Austro-Hungarian U-boats. Each had a German commander and crew, but carried a second false set of papers and, when possible, an Austro-Hungarian junior officer aboard to give the ruse a fig-leaf of international legality. The submarines shipped overland from Germany but commissioned by Austria-Hungary likewise included a mixture of personnel, at least for their initial Adriatic training cruise, often a German officer as commander and a German machinist or two with an Austro-Hungarian crew. The ensuing confusion left the true identity of some attacking submarines a mystery to the Allies until after the war, or to researchers until decades later, especially for studies attempting to credit individual U-boat commanders for tonnage sunk. For example, Lieutenant Heino von Heimberg, destined to finish his career as a vice admiral in the Third Reich, was in command of the training cruise of German *UB 15* (actually Austro-Hungarian *U 11*) on June 10, 1915, when it sank the Italian submarine *Medusa*, but had returned to his position as commander of Austro-Hungarian *U 26* (actually German *UB 14*) by July 7, when that submarine sank the 9,800-ton armored cruiser *Amalfi* off Venice. Leaving the Adriatic (and his boat's false identity) behind, Heimberg next took *UB 14* to the Greek islands, where on August 13 it sank the 11,100-ton British troopship *Royal Edward* (866 dead) before moving on through the Dardanelles and Bosporus to a successful run against Russian targets in the Black Sea (see Chapter 6). Later in the year France also lost a troopship to a U-boat attack in the Mediterranean, as *Kapitänleutnant* Valentiner's *U 38*, which at times masqueraded as an Austro-Hungarian submarine of the same number, torpedoed the *Calvados* (740 dead) off Oran on November 4, shortly after arriving from northern waters. Even after both the Central Powers were at war with Italy, the inconsistency of declarations of war by other countries (for example, the United States against Germany in April 1917, but not against Austria-Hungary until December 1917) kept alive the justification for double-numbering all German submarines operating in the Mediterranean. By the time the war ended, fifty-six of them had been given Austro-Hungarian numbers, but aside from *U 10* (ex-*UB 1*) and *U 11* (ex-*UB 15*) none actually served in the Austro-Hungarian navy.[20]

The Allies may have been confused about whether these submarines were German or Austro-Hungarian, but, in any event, they usually knew where they were thanks to the volume of wireless traffic that U-boats generated. Compared with surface warships, submarines faced greater challenges finding targets and avoiding life-threatening dangers, the latter including not just enemy warships and mines, but also their own navy's warships and mines when returning to port. In the German navy, standing orders required U-boats to check in via wireless whenever they sank an enemy merchantman, encountered an enemy warship, or were approaching home and needed to pass through a German minefield. In northern waters all these signals gave away U-boat positions to British directional wireless – accurate to within 50 miles (80 km) in the Atlantic and 20 miles (32 km) in the North Sea – but the Germans considered the transmissions worth the risk. The German navy eventually built its own directional wireless stations on the Helgoland Bight at Sylt and Borkum in the Frisian Islands, near Cuxhaven at Nordholz, and on the island of Helgoland itself, as well as at Bruges in occupied Belgium, joined later by additional stations at Tondern in Schleswig and at Cleves in Westphalia, but these were used less to detect the enemy than to help U-boats and surface warships to navigate their way home through the German minefields, or to bring home zeppelins lost in bad weather. In the directional wireless race, the British enjoyed the advantage not just of having it first, but also had a geographical advantage: from the British Isles, they could scan the seas for enemy ship signals in every direction, whereas for the Germans, the British Isles blocked any signals emitted by ships farther west, limiting the usefulness of their directional wireless to the North Sea. When it came to deciphering (rather than simply tracking) enemy wireless activity, the German navy started the war well behind the army in its capabilities and did not open its own cryptographic center (at Bruges) until July 1915. After a central headquarters for code deciphering was established in Holstein, at Neumünster, in February 1916, the Bruges installation, covering the Channel, became part of a second tier of regional cryptographic stations, the others being located at Tondern (for the North Sea), Libau,

---

[20] Sondhaus, *The Naval Policy of Austria-Hungary*, pp. 268, 279–280; Halpern, *The Naval War in the Mediterranea*n, p. 154. See also www.uboat.net.

in occupied Latvia (for the Baltic), Skopje, in occupied Macedonia (for the Mediterranean), and the main Austro-Hungarian base at Pola (for the Adriatic). After the war the Germans claimed Neumünster could decrypt two-thirds of intercepted British messages at least partially, but they never succeeded in breaking the Grand Fleet's code. Confident as ever that their own codes were unbreakable, the Germans continued to be slow to introduce new codes even when faced with evidence that old codes had been compromised. Thus, the unrestricted campaign opened with U-boats still communicating in HVB code (the same one used by German overseas cruisers and merchantmen, and suspect after November 1914), a security breach not corrected until the summer of 1915, when the new FVB code replaced it.[21]

The first phase of unrestricted submarine warfare climaxed on May 7 when *U 20* (*Kapitänleutnant* Walther Schwieger) torpedoed and sank the British passenger liner *Lusitania* off the south coast of Ireland. The 30,400-ton vessel, owned by the Cunard Line, had been in service since 1907 on the Liverpool–New York route; at the time of its demise, it was homeward bound on its 202nd crossing overall, and third crossing since the German declaration of the submarine blockade of the British Isles. Built to naval specifications, with gun mountings on a reinforced deck and turbine engines capable of 25 knots, the *Lusitania* was requisitioned as an armed merchant cruiser at the outbreak of war, painted grey, then promptly returned to the Cunard Line after the Admiralty realized that the ship, at or near top speed, consumed nearly 1,000 tons of coal per day. The high cost of fuel and of the crew of 800 required to man her could be taken in its stride by a private firm charging top-of-the-market prices in peacetime for the ship's 2,100 berths, but was prohibitive for a navy in wartime. Returned to civilian duty and a civilian paint scheme, the *Lusitania* remained profitable amid declining wartime passenger traffic only because so many other liners were requisitioned for use as troopships or hospital ships, or voluntarily laid up by their owners. The onset of unrestricted submarine warfare found the *Lusitania* in New York; it made its way back to Liverpool unscathed, its captain shunning Admiralty overtures for a destroyer escort through the danger zone, then left British waters unescorted for another voyage to New York in early April. Nine days prior to its scheduled return departure of May 1, the German embassy posted

---

[21] Headrick, *The Invisible Weapon*, pp. 164–166.

warnings in fifty US newspapers reminding prospective transatlantic passengers that "vessels flying the flag of Great Britain, or any of her allies, are liable to destruction in those waters and that travelers sailing in the war zone on the ships of Great Britain or her allies do so at their own risk."[22] The ship sailed for Liverpool significantly under-booked, but the general wartime decline in transatlantic passenger traffic makes it impossible to ascertain the impact of the German warnings, some of which (at least in the New York press) were printed adjacent to Cunard advertisements for the *Lusitania*. The sinking occurred 11 miles (18 km) off the Irish coast on the afternoon of May 7, two hours after the *Lusitania*'s captain acknowledged a warning from the Admiralty of U-boat activity in the area. The ship sank in just 18 minutes after *U 20*'s torpedoes found their mark, taking with it nearly two-thirds of those aboard. For its final voyage the ship had embarked nearly a thousand fewer people than its full capacity of passengers and crew, yet the dead still numbered a staggering 1,198 (among them 128 American citizens), with 764 survivors. Never before had a single act of war caused so many noncombatant deaths.[23]

Though the *Lusitania* was not an American ship and American citizens accounted for barely 10 percent of the dead, its sinking proved to be a key event in turning American public and political opinion against Germany. Three weeks after the sinking, responding to a formal protest from President Wilson, Foreign Secretary Gottlieb von Jagow justified *U 20*'s actions on the grounds that the *Lusitania* had "Canadian troops and munitions on board."[24] While Jagow's allegation regarding the Canadians proved to be false, the ship's own manifest revealed that it had left New York with 5,671 cases of cartridges and ammunition in its cargo hold, along with 189 containers of unspecified "military goods." Nevertheless, most Americans rejected the German position that the *Lusitania* was a legitimate target of war, as did

---

[22] Text in Diana Preston, *Lusitania: An Epic Tragedy* (New York: Walker Publishing, 2002), p. 91.

[23] While all sources agree on the number of dead, the number of Americans lost ranges from 123 to 128, depending upon whom one counts as "American." Figures for the number of survivors vary more widely, owing to discrepancies between the passenger list and persons actually aboard. As many as 188 passengers had some claim to American citizenship.

[24] "The Sinking of the *Lusitania*: Official German Response by Foreign Minister Gottlieb von Jagow," Berlin, May 28, 1915, available at: www.firstworldwar.com/source/lusitania_germanresponse.htm.

virtually everyone in Britain. Indeed, one recent analysis confirms that the issue of whether the ship "was carrying munitions...was absolutely beside the point" to the British public, which considered the sinking "the greatest single atrocity of the war."[25] The suggestion that Churchill, in his role as First Lord, had orchestrated the disaster to incite the United States into declaring war on Germany aroused the passions of conspiracy theorists at the time and has continued to do so ever since. Churchill himself stoked these fires by writing, twenty-two years after the fact, that "in spite of all its horror, we must regard the sinking of the *Lusitania* as an event most important and favourable to the Allies."[26] While the record does not support allegations of the First Lord's direct complicity in the disaster, the Admiralty must bear responsibility for the cynical calculation that Britain had nothing to lose by shipping war materiel aboard the *Lusitania* and other civilian liners. Most of these shipments would make it through, and every passenger vessel sunk by a U-boat hastened the day that the United States would enter the war on the side of the Allies.

## American neutrality and German U-boats

Wilson's initial protest to the German government following the *Lusitania* sinking, dated May 13, also included condemnation of three earlier German attacks involving American shipping or American loss of life: the sinking of the British steamer *Falaba* by *U 28* off the coast of Wales (March 28) with one American casualty; the bombing of the American tanker *Cushing* by a German airplane off the Dutch coast (April 28); and the torpedoing of the American tanker *Gulflight* by *U 30* off the coast of Cornwall (May 1), with the loss of three lives. As it turned out, the three casualties aboard the *Gulflight* would be the only American deaths caused by a U-boat in an attack against an American ship prior to the start of the more robust second round of unrestricted submarine warfare in February 1917; nevertheless, Wilson's protest emphasized the broader principles at stake rather than what he considered the finer point of which flag had been flying aboard the vessel in which

---

[25] Adrian Gregory, *The Last Great War: British Society and the First World War* (Cambridge University Press, 2008), p. 61.
[26] Quoted in Preston, *Lusitania*, p. 5.

American citizens had been attacked or killed. Citing "the sacred freedom of the seas," he asserted that "American citizens act within their indisputable rights... in traveling wherever their legitimate business calls them upon the high seas, and exercise those rights in what should be the well-justified confidence that their lives will not be endangered by acts done in clear violation of universally acknowledged international obligations." Wilson also condemned the German embassy's warnings, posted in the American press prior to the sinking of the *Lusitania*, on the grounds that "no warning that an unlawful and inhumane act will be committed can possibly be accepted as an excuse or palliation for that act or as an abatement of the responsibility for its commission." He ended with an absolute rejection of the use of the submarine as a commerce raider: "Manifestly, submarines cannot be used against merchantmen, as the last few weeks have shown, without an inevitable violation of many sacred principles of justice and humanity."[27]

Wilson's message elicited widespread approval in the United States, but failed to satisfy his chief political opponent, former president Theodore Roosevelt, who considered anything short of a declaration of war cowardly, or his own secretary of state, pacifist William Jennings Bryan, who wanted a more even-handed response also criticizing the morality of Britain's blockade of Germany. The British ambassador in Washington, Sir Cecil Spring-Rice, confirmed that Wilson's middle course – condemning German behavior, but not threatening war – reflected the sensibilities of most Americans, inasmuch as these were reflected in the embassy's compilation of nearly a thousand newspaper editorials from across the country published in the first three days after the sinking of the *Lusitania*, only six of which advocated war.[28] As had been the case with Wilson's response to the initial declaration of unrestricted submarine warfare in February, the president's remarks following the sinking of the *Lusitania* had a profound effect on William II and Bethmann Hollweg. The chancellor went as far as to inform the admirals that he "refused to be responsible for the campaign in its

---

[27] "U.S. Protest Over the Sinking of the *Lusitania*," Washington, May 13, 1915, available at: www.firstworldwar.com/source/bryanlusitaniaprotest.htm. This source attributes the protest note to Secretary of State William Jennings Bryan, but Justus D. Doenecke, *Nothing Less Than War: A New History of America's Entry into World War I* (Lexington, KY: University Press of Kentucky, 2011), p. 77, is the most recent of many historians to identify Wilson as the author.

[28] Doenecke, *Nothing Less Than War*, pp. 73, 78–79.

existing form."[29] While Jagow's reply, dated May 28, defended not just the sinking of the *Lusitania* but also the less sensational demise of the *Falaba*, at Bethmann Hollweg's direction the foreign secretary promised further investigation of the cases involving the two American tankers. He followed up three days later with an apology for the attacks on the tankers, citing mistaken identity in both cases, and promised to pay for damages incurred by the *Gulflight*, which had limped into British waters without sinking. Restitution was not needed in the case of the *Cushing*, which sustained no damages after the bombs intended for it missed their mark.[30]

Bethmann Hollweg had supported unrestricted submarine warfare in the first place largely because of its popularity with the German public, and Tirpitz concluded that, at this stage, public opinion alone was keeping the chancellor from abandoning the policy. "He wanted to keep up the appearance of maintaining it," while at the same time making it toothless enough to cause no offense to the Americans. Toward this end, Bethmann Hollweg persuaded William II to follow Jagow's apology for the attacks on the American tankers with a directive that U-boat commanders henceforth should target no vessel without first ascertaining whose flag it flew. The emperor complied, then, on June 6, forbade the sinking of large passenger liners regardless of their flag. These orders prompted both Tirpitz and Bachmann to submit their resignations, which the emperor refused to accept.[31] Forced to acquiesce in a campaign that was far from "unrestricted," they remained of one mind with the chancellor only in urging William II to keep the new orders secret, Bethmann Hollweg for domestic reasons, and the admirals for the sake of the campaign's credibility on the high seas. To the further detriment of German–American relations, the emperor agreed, and in the end even the German embassy in Washington was not informed of the change of policy. This secrecy had profound consequences in the United States, where Bryan, on June 8, resigned his cabinet post rather than support the position Wilson had taken, which he considered to be both ineffective and overly belligerent. Bryan enjoyed considerable popularity, having been the Democratic Party's nominee for president in three of the four elections preceding Wilson's 1912 victory, and at

[29] Tirpitz, *My Memoirs*, vol. 2, p. 156.
[30] Doenecke, *Nothing Less Than War*, pp. 69–70.
[31] Tirpitz, *My Memoirs*, vol. 2, pp. 157–158.

least for the next twenty-two months he attempted to mobilize his followers behind the cause of peace. Meanwhile, his successor as secretary of state, Robert Lansing, emerged as the cabinet's leading voice for intervention on the side of the Allies.[32]

The day after Bryan's resignation, Wilson, not knowing the impact of his first *Lusitania* note, sent a second communication to Berlin, a lengthy response to Jagow's notes of May 28 and June 1, in which he expressed "gratification" at Germany's acknowledgment of wrongdoing in the attacks on the American *Gulflight* and *Cushing*, but rejected the justification of the sinking of the British *Falaba* and *Lusitania*. As for Jagow's contention that munitions had been aboard the latter, Wilson confirmed that, as far as the United States was concerned, "these contentions are irrelevant to the question of the legality of the methods used by the German naval authorities in sinking the vessel."[33] Jagow waited until July 8 to respond, then issued little more than a recapitulation of his previous note of May 28.[34] Wilson's next rebuttal, dated July 21, acknowledged the apparent (though officially still secret) modifications of German unrestricted submarine warfare, which had resulted in fewer incidents involving neutrals and, of course, no repeat of the *Lusitania* disaster with a ship of comparable size: "the events of the past two months have clearly indicated that it is possible and practicable to conduct [German] submarine operations…in substantial accord with the accepted practices of regulated warfare." Yet Wilson's closing remarks made this third *Lusitania* note the harshest of all, warning that the United States would uphold the maritime rights of neutrals "at any cost" and view "as deliberately unfriendly…repetition by the commanders of German naval vessels of acts in contravention of those rights."[35]

Thereafter tensions subsided for nearly a month, until August 19, when *U 24* torpedoed and sank the 15,800-ton British passenger liner *Arabic*, of the White Star Line. The attack came off the southern coast of Ireland, very near the place where the *Lusitania* had been sunk, but because the *Arabic* was outbound from Liverpool to New York at

[32] Doenecke, *Nothing Less Than War*, pp. 79–84.
[33] "Second U.S. Protest Over the Sinking of the *Lusitania*," Washington, May [sic. June 9], 1915, at www.firstworldwar.com/source/lusitania_2ndusprotest.htm.
[34] Doenecke, *Nothing Less Than War*, pp. 85–86.
[35] "Third U.S. Protest Over the Sinking of the *Lusitania*," Washington, July 21, 1915, at: www.firstworldwar.com/source/lusitania_3rdusprotest.htm.

the time, the Germans could not argue that it had contraband aboard. Even though it was half the size of the *Lusitania* and carried far fewer passengers, most of whom were saved, the forty-four dead included two American citizens. Those closest to Wilson counseled a response in keeping with his note of July 21: Secretary of State Lansing and Colonel Edward House, the president's personal advisor, both urged breaking diplomatic relations with Germany and preparations for war. At this point Wilson was prepared to break relations only after giving Germany a chance to disavow the sinking of the *Arabic*. But in conveying this message to the German ambassador, Count Johann von Bernstorff, Lansing strengthened the threat to a declaration of war that could be avoided only if Germany stopped unrestricted submarine warfare altogether.[36]

On August 26–27, in meetings held at Pless in Silesia, the German army's Eastern front headquarters, Bethmann Hollweg informed the admirals of his intention to assure Washington that henceforth "submarine commanders had definite orders not to torpedo passenger steamers without warning, and without opportunity being given for the rescue of passengers and crews." Tirpitz and Bachmann argued that such a declaration would concede "the correctness of the enemy contention that the submarine campaign was unlawful," but the chancellor secured William II's approval to proceed despite their objections, and managed to minimize the negative domestic reaction by timing his retreat to coincide with the end of the Reichstag's summer session on August 27.[37] This time there would be no papering over the breach between the political and naval leadership. The so-called "*Arabic* pledge" prompted Tirpitz and Bachmann once again to submit their resignations. This time the emperor accepted the resignation of Bachmann, but insisted that Tirpitz stay on, though the state secretary's run of nearly two decades as the leading voice within the German navy had clearly reached its end. Further evidence that Tirpitz's sun had set came on September 5, when his old rival Admiral Henning von Holtzendorff, who had retired in 1913 after spending the previous four years as commander of the High Sea Fleet, was called back to active duty to fill Bachmann's role as chief of the *Admiralstab*. William II granted Tirpitz a personal audience and assured him that he would

[36] Doenecke, *Nothing Less Than War*, pp. 116–118.
[37] Tirpitz, *My Memoirs*, vol. 2, pp. 162–165.

continue to seek his advice "on all important questions of naval policy," but henceforth, the architect of Germany's naval expansion would reside in Berlin rather than at headquarters, and thus would not be in a position to function in his customary advisory role.[38]

Holtzendorff soon formed a common front with the chief of the army High Command, General Erich von Falkenhayn, and Bethmann Hollweg opposing a continuation of unrestricted submarine warfare. After they persuaded William II that the level of antagonism generated in the United States and other neutral countries far outweighed the material losses that Germany's small undersea force could cause, new orders issued on September 18 subjected further German U-boat activity against unarmed ships to traditional prize rules.[39] Germany thus abandoned its great experiment with unrestricted submarine warfare after just seven months, even though the most recent two (August, with 182,770 tons sunk, and September, with 136,050 tons sunk) had been the most successful months of the campaign. In the end, Bachmann proved to be correct in his prediction that the first round of unrestricted submarine warfare, pursued with inadequate resources and a lack of resolve by German civilian authorities, would have "no effect in securing the ultimate victory of the German people," but was "enough to create incidents and quarrels with the Americans."[40]

With the new restrictions in place, during the autumn months the only diplomatic incident involving submarine warfare followed the torpedoing, on November 6, of the 8,200-ton Italian passenger liner *Ancona*, homeward bound from New York, off the coast of Sicily, with the loss of twenty-seven lives, including nine Americans. Because the attacking boat, *U 38* (*Kapitänleutnant* Valentiner), was flying the Austro-Hungarian flag at the time, the incident nearly led to a diplomatic breach between Washington and Vienna. Valentiner had stopped the *Ancona* while surfaced, as required under the new restrictions, but its crew alone took to the lifeboats, leaving the passengers to their fate; after waiting 45 minutes, and with other ships approaching the site, he torpedoed the liner in its bow rather than amidships, inflicting fatal damage but in a manner that allowed those aboard another 45 minutes to abandon ship. Though Valentiner's actions ultimately allowed for the survival of 545 of the 572 persons aboard, both Italy and the

[38] *Ibid.*, pp. 165–167; Kelly, *Tirpitz*, pp. 400, 403–404.
[39] Tirpitz, *My Memoirs*, vol. 2, pp. 169–170. [40] *Ibid.*, p. 151.

United States equated the sinking of the *Ancona* with the *Lusitania*; ultimately, in order to placate the Americans, the Austro-Hungarian foreign minister, Count István Burián, promised Lansing that his government would pay an indemnity and punish the commander of the U-boat.[41] Valentiner, of course, was not punished, and by war's end submarines under his command had sunk nearly 300,000 tons of Allied shipping, enough to rank him as Germany's third most successful U-boat commander of the Great War. His next controversial sinking came on December 30, just one day after Burián's correspondence appeasing the Americans, when *U 38*, cruising off Crete, torpedoed the 7,950-ton British liner *Persia* without warning. The 334 dead included two Americans, but the US consulate in Egypt soon confirmed that the *Persia* had mounted a 4.7-inch (12-cm) gun, thus justifying Valentiner's decision to treat it as an auxiliary cruiser rather than as a passenger ship.[42]

During these months, from his quasi-exile in Berlin, Tirpitz remained the leading proponent of unrestricted submarine warfare, advocating the construction of an undersea force sufficient to do real damage to Britain. Germany would require hundreds of U-boats, not dozens, built in sufficient numbers to account for their very short service lives. Manpower likewise would have to be considered expendable, and trained in sufficient numbers to make good the high losses at sea. Thus, a truly decisive submarine campaign would require not just a considerable redirection of the navy's human resources, but a lot more money; indeed, the largest U-boats constructed in 1917, after the resumption of unrestricted submarine warfare, would have a per ton cost 40 percent greater than the German capital ships commissioned that year, and in order to afford the requisite number of U-boats the navy would have to cease work on all dreadnoughts and battle cruisers not close to completion. After Tirpitz presented this calculus to the leading generals in a series of meetings held at the Prussian war ministry (December 30–January 5), Falkenhayn recognized that it followed the same grim logic of the campaign of attrition he planned to unleash in 1916 on the Western front, focusing on Verdun. Holtzendorff, also in Berlin for these meetings, likewise reconsidered his position of the previous autumn. Even though the number of U-boats on

---

[41] Doenecke, *Nothing Less Than War*, pp. 127–128; Valentiner, *Der Schrecken der Meere*, pp. 109–113.
[42] Doenecke, *Nothing Less Than War*, p. 128.

hand at the start of the new year (fifty-four, including fourteen *UB* boats and eleven minelaying *UC* boats) remained far short of Tirpitz's ideal, on January 7 the *Admiralstab* issued the first of a series of memoranda justifying a more aggressive course, culminating on February 29 in orders for an "intensified" submarine campaign. But the best efforts of Falkenhayn and Holtzendorff could not persuade Bethmann Hollweg. When the three met with William II on March 4, the chancellor carried the day, the emperor agreeing with him that unrestricted submarine warfare should be "postponed indefinitely." Tirpitz, doubly wounded by being excluded from the meeting and by its outcome, resigned eight days later, finally ending his nineteen-year reign as state secretary.[43]

Meanwhile, under Holtzendorff's order of February 29, individual U-boat commanders grew increasingly aggressive, some attacking Allied merchantmen without warning. The matter came to a head after *UB* 29 torpedoed the French passenger ferry *Sussex* in the Channel on March 24. Two dozen Americans were aboard and, though none was killed, on April 18 Wilson issued an ultimatum demanding that Germany "abandon its present methods of submarine warfare against passenger and freight-carrying vessels" or else suffer a breach of diplomatic relations with the United States. At this point Bethmann Hollweg's reasoning prevailed, and a week later Admiral Scheer, Pohl's successor as commander of the High Sea Fleet (see Chapter 7), recalled all U-boats for service in fleet operations, on the grounds that the reimposition of traditional prize rules made commerce raiding too risky for the submarines. On May 4, the German Foreign Office informed the American government of the change in policy, its so-called "*Sussex* pledge" reiterating the "*Arabic* pledge" of the previous September, laying the issue to rest until February 1917.[44]

## American neutrality and the British blockade

Because the United States did enter the war against Germany eventually, the tense Anglo-American wartime exchanges over the issue of the

---

[43] Tirpitz, *My Memoirs*, vol. 2, pp. 171–176; Robert M. Grant, *U-boats Destroyed: The Effect of Anti-Submarine Warfare, 1914–1918* (London: Putnam, 1964), p. 29.

[44] Doenecke, *Nothing Less Than War*, pp. 167–172, Wilson quoted at p. 169; Scheer, *Germany's High Sea Fleet*, pp. 129–130.

blockade and freedom of the seas have been largely forgotten. Until the onset of unrestricted submarine warfare in February 1915, Wilson was far more critical of the British than of the Germans, at least when it came to their policies on the high seas, and though the sinking of the *Lusitania* did turn American public opinion in favor of the Allies, it was not the absolutely decisive determining event that countless general histories of the First World War have held it to be. The aftermath of the sinking did find the United States drawing closer to the Allies in general and the British in particular, in part because Wilson (in contrast to Bryan) refused to keep the British on a par with the Germans once the Germans started the unrestricted U-boat campaign, and in part because the Allies, over the summer of 1915, grew to appreciate their own growing dependence on American resources. Ultimately, even when the United States protested what it considered to be British violations of international law at sea, the obvious difference was that these protests concerned damage to American economic interests rather than the death of American citizens, and thus generated fewer newspaper headlines with far less impact on US public opinion.

As early as August 17, 1914, Admiralty instructions regarding the implementation of the blockade of Germany emphasized that "it is of prime importance to keep the United States of America as a friendly neutral."[45] Later that month the foreign secretary, Sir Edward Grey, allayed fears about British warships seizing American cargoes deemed contraband by promising that in such cases, Britain would purchase the cargoes, thereby *de facto* insuring American exporters against any loss. He felt he could afford to be magnanimous because, compared with Britain, the United States had a very small merchant marine, lacked the capacity to expand it, and thus traded at Britain's mercy. The massive British merchant fleet carried six times as many US cargoes to overseas destinations as the American merchant marine, and in the last prewar year British shipbuilders had launched nine times as much new mercantile tonnage as American shipbuilders.[46] But the British underestimated both American sensitivity on the shipping question and American resolve to change the status quo, especially when the outbreak of war led to an immediate decline in the share of British tonnage available to carry US exports, thus causing goods to pile up at the docks in American ports.

[45] Quoted in Lambert, *Planning Armageddon*, p. 237.    [46] *Ibid.*, pp. 239–240.

This shipping emergency caused the first great Anglo-American confrontation of the war, after Wilson proposed to purchase the 1.3 million tons of German shipping that had sought refuge in US ports. Germany was keen to sell the ships because, under international law, neutral countries billed the shipowners for the cost of berthing and maintaining ships under internment, raising the specter of bankruptcy for the leading German shipping companies unless the war were to end very quickly. The transaction appealed to the United States because it would gain, at one stroke, as much mercantile tonnage as its own shipyards could build in seven years (at current rates of production), and make it far less dependent on British shipping to carry its exports. Wilson urged Congress to authorize the purchase of the interned vessels to serve as the fleet of a new government-owned shipping line, naively believing Britain would not object. Churchill, as First Lord of the Admiralty, counseled a hard line, advising Grey that "very great pressure should be exerted" on the United States to block the sale of the ships, but because Grey had not objected to the sale of smaller numbers of interned German merchantmen in Spain, Sweden, and Chile – which, in the latter case, enabled the use of some of them to supply Spee's squadron at Easter Island in October 1914 – he felt he could not protest their sale in the United States. It did not help matters that the Board of Trade had already approved dozens of requests from various companies to transfer British merchantmen to American registry, thus making Britain appear hypocritical in protesting the transfer of German merchantmen to American registry. Similarly, British arguments citing the illegality of the proposed sale of the interned ships under the Declaration of London rang hollow at a time when Britain was disregarding provisions of the same document in its own blockade of Germany. In the end Grey issued only a weak admonition that the United States should not use former German merchantmen in trade with European ports. Ultimately, Britain's ambassador in Washington, Spring-Rice, exploited his close friendships with powerful Republican opponents of Wilson, including former president Theodore Roosevelt and Senator Henry Cabot Lodge of Massachusetts, to lobby against the shipping bill, which soon ran into trouble in Congress. It still had not passed as of February 1915, when Wilson let the matter drop amid the furor over the introduction of unrestricted submarine warfare.[47]

[47] *Ibid.*, pp. 240–248, Churchill quoted at p. 244.

In response to the delay (and ultimate failure) of Wilson's proposal to form a US government shipping line from interned German merchantmen, private American firms addressed the shipping shortage by purchasing aging British steamers and transferring them to US registry. Thus, over 200 ships had left British registry by the end of 1914 alone, and despite repeated attempts by the British government to prevent the transfer of these merchantmen to foreign flags, the practice continued at least until 1916. By October 1914, the British concluded that it would be easier (and likely more effective) to pressure neutral countries in Europe to restrict the re-export of items to the Germans than to challenge the United States over cargoes bound for those countries, especially the Netherlands, where Rotterdam had become the leading port for wartime Germany's overseas trade. Later that month, Britain further appeased the United States by allowing its most important export, cotton, through the blockade. Meanwhile, a remarkable amount of trade continued to flow from Germany to the United States. After a serious disruption in the first two months of the war, by March 1915 German exports to the United States had rebounded to 60 percent of their prewar level.[48]

Throughout the winter of 1914/15, Churchill and Grey remained the principal antagonists in the infighting over Britain's blockade policy. Even though the blockade, as early as January 1915, had become effective enough to force Germany to start rationing, the German food shortage could be attributed to other factors as well, in particular the loss of agricultural imports from Russia, Germany's leading prewar source of grain, and Austria-Hungary, which faced a blockade of its own. The Admiralty believed that the enemy's food situation would have been much worse if the Foreign Office had not routinely ordered the release of most of the ships detained by the British navy on suspicion of carrying food cargoes intended for Germany. Indeed, most were released without even being inspected, infuriating Jellicoe, who under the circumstances, justifiably, questioned the cost and benefit of the navy's blockade effort. It took the introduction of unrestricted submarine warfare – ostensibly Germany's response to the British blockade – to inspire Britain to enforce its own policies more vigorously. On March 12, the Asquith government announced the "retaliation blockade," a "complete interdiction" of German seagoing commerce. Grey

[48] *Ibid.*, pp. 251, 263, 267, 436.

and the Foreign Office, out of concern not to offend the United States, continued to restrain the Admiralty when it came to the interdiction of American goods suspected of having Germany as their ultimate destination, but gave free rein to the navy to choke off German exports to the United States. Because the "retaliation blockade" considered all exports of German origin to be contraband and subject to seizure, it thus had an immediate impact on German exports to the United States, which by the end of June 1915 had collapsed to just 13 percent of pre-war levels. Though the "retaliation blockade" would have been more strongly enforced if not for the ongoing row between the Admiralty and the Foreign Office, Wilson still considered it objectionable enough to warrant a protest, at least until the sinking of the *Lusitania* changed his thinking on the matter. By then Churchill's departure from the cabinet in the wake of the debacle at the Dardanelles (see Chapter 6) had eased tensions between the Admiralty and Foreign Office, but the infighting over the inefficiency of the blockade continued until Asquith, in February 1916, gave responsibility for it to a new Ministry of Blockade headed by Lord Robert Cecil.[49]

The growing importance of the United States as a source of supplies for the Allies further softened the earlier acrimony in Anglo-American relations. As late as July 1915 most of Asquith's ministers dismissed as ridiculous the notion that "the Allies were dependent upon the United States," but shortly thereafter, during August, Britain negotiated its first loan from New York banks.[50] France borrowed in New York as early as November 1914, and from August 1915 both countries benefited from Wilson's decision to allow their war bonds to be sold on the American financial market. Over the next twenty months, until the United States entered the war, the Allies managed to raise $4.6 billion there, over half through the sale of their bonds, the remainder through the liquidation of some of their existing American investments. The increasing volume of Allied purchases in the United States pumped most of this money back into the US economy. The total value of American munitions exports, which stood at just $40 million in 1914, boomed to nearly $1.3 billion in 1916, while the total value for exported manufactured goods rose from $2.4 billion (or 6 percent of the gross national product) in 1914 to $5.5 billion (or 12 percent of GNP) in 1916, almost exclusively because of increased trade with the

[49] *Ibid.*, pp. 366, 369, 374, 424, 436, 443, 477, 496.   [50] *Ibid.*, pp. 374, 460.

Allies. While J. P. Morgan, which brokered most of the transactions, led a long list of American firms that reaped enormous profits from this trade, millions of ordinary Americans, from workers to farmers, benefited as well. Long before it entered the war in April 1917, the United States had become neutral in name only.[51]

## Antisubmarine warfare in its infancy: Q-ships and barrages

The British navy's initial response to the submarine threat centered around merchant cruisers with concealed deck guns, sent into the sea lanes to attract enemy submarines by pretending to be helpless freighters. Eventually called "Q-ships" after a numbering system introduced by the Admiralty late in 1916, they were the most lethal of a host of former civilian craft forming the Auxiliary Patrol of Britain's wartime navy, a motley fleet that included trawlers and drifters from the fishing fleet as well as yachts and motorboats from the well-to-do.[52] The British navy deployed its first Q-ship, the former freighter *Vittoria*, in late November 1914, just six weeks after the first sinking of a merchantman by a U-boat, only to decommission it after two months of futile cruising. The Admiralty chose a former submariner, Lieutenant Commander Godfrey Herbert, to captain its second Q-ship, the *Antwerp*, commissioned in January 1915, reasoning that "a submarine officer would naturally in his stalking be able to realize at once the limitations and possibilities of his opponent."[53] Like the *Vittoria*, the *Antwerp* was paid off without ever sinking a German submarine, but the Admiralty remained intrigued by the prospects of "mystery" or "decoy" ships in antisubmarine warfare and redoubled their efforts after the loss of the *Lusitania*.

On July 24, a newly commissioned Q-ship registered the first success. The former collier *Prince Charles* (Lieutenant Mark Wardlaw) encountered *U 36* off remote North Rona Island, about 55 miles (90 km) north of the Scottish mainland, enticed it to surface, then opened fire and sank it before its crew could man its deck gun to launch

---

[51] Sondhaus, *World War I*, p. 310.
[52] E. Keble Chatterton, *Q-Ships and their Story* (London: Sidgwick & Jackson, 1922), p. 7; Gordon Campbell, *My Mystery Ships* (Garden City, NY: Doubleday, Doran, 1929), p. 7.
[53] Chatterton, *Q-Ships and their Story*, p. 8.

an attack. On August 15, the converted fishing smack *Inverlyon* used similar tactics to sink *UB 4* off Yarmouth.[54] The former submariner Herbert, commanding the new Q-ship *Baralong*, soon launched a more audacious (and controversial) attack, ironically on August 19, the same day that *U 24*'s sinking of the *Arabic* marked the beginning of the end of the first round of unrestricted submarine warfare. The *Baralong* was on patrol roughly 70 miles (115 km) off the south coast of Ireland when it encountered *U 27* (*Kapitänleutnant* Bernard Wegener), which had surfaced to stop the British freighter *Nicosian*. Though not required to do so under orders then in force, Wegener allowed the crew to abandon ship, a process still underway when the *Baralong*, flying the American flag, closed to within point-blank range of the two vessels, ostensibly to rescue the *Nicosian*'s survivors. The *Baralong* then ran up the British flag, revealed its previously hidden guns, and opened fire. After *U 27* was sunk, at least twelve of its survivors were shot and killed rather than taken prisoner, including the boat's commander, Wegener, actions that stood in sharp contrast to Wardlaw's conduct after the sinking of *U 36*, from which fifteen men were rescued. Several Americans among the *Nicosian*'s crew eventually reported the incident, which Wilson called "horrible" and Lansing "shocking," yet neither lodged a protest with the British government even though the *Baralong* had approached *U 27* under cover of the American flag.[55] The *Baralong* was also responsible for that summer's fourth sinking of a U-boat, on September 24, roughly 145 miles (235 km) west of Land's End, Cornwall. By then operating as *Wyandra*, under Lieutenant Commander A. Wilmot-Smith, the ship approached *U 41* shortly after it had torpedoed the British merchantman *Urbino*, again using the American flag and with the apparent mission of rescuing survivors as cover for its attack. Two of the thirty-seven men aboard *U 41* survived to be taken prisoner, including an officer who eventually made it home to Germany via a prisoner exchange, to tell his story.[56]

The war's most successful Q-ship captain, Lieutenant Commander Gordon Campbell, took command of the *Farnborough* (ex-*Loderer*)

[54] *Ibid.*, pp. 14–16; Grant, *U-boats Destroyed*, p. 27.
[55] Chatterton, *Q-Ships and their Story*, pp. 20–23; Doenecke, *Nothing Less Than War*, p. 122.
[56] Iwan Crompton, *Englands Verbrechen an U 41: Der zweite "Baralong"-Fall im Weltkrieg*, ed. Werner von Langsdorff (Gütersloh: C. Bertelsmann, 1941), pp. 105–123; Chatterton, *Q-Ships and their Story*, pp. 26–30.

in October 1915, shortly after the initial suspension of unrestricted submarine warfare, and had to wait until March 22 to claim his first victim, *U 68*, sunk off the west coast of Ireland during the German navy's brief "intensified" campaign during the spring of 1916. The *Farnborough* was the first Q-ship to use depth charges in action, supplementing Campbell's ingenious tactics, including dispatching a "panic party" in a lifeboat after sighting a U-boat, to more accurately simulate a freighter's reaction to an approaching submarine, while remaining aboard ship with the rest of his crew, manning their hidden guns.[57] Q-ships under Campbell's command would sink two more U-boats after the resumption of unrestricted submarine warfare. By war's end the British navy would employ more than 180 "mystery ships of all sorts,"[58] raising the question of whether their eleven confirmed U-boat victims (far less than one-tenth of the total submarines Germany lost) justified their cost. It would not be unreasonable to argue that their deployment was a mixed blessing at best for the Allied merchant fleet, because the presence of such ships in the sea lanes made U-boat commanders adopt an even more aggressive attitude of "shoot first, ask questions later" when approaching any potential target.

The question of cost versus benefit also applied to the use of trawlers and drifters for antisubmarine warfare, initially on barrages across the straits of Dover and Otranto, and by war's end along the North Sea blockade line between Scotland and Norway. From the start of the war the British navy's Auxiliary Patrol included hundreds of fishing vessels, mostly manned by their civilian crews, the trawlers adapted primarily for minesweeping, and the drifters, designed to drag deep-sea nets, instead dragging underwater barriers for enemy submarines. The first drifters assembled at Dover in January 1915, and by June over 130 were in service there. They patrolled the straits dragging steel nets constructed in mesh patterns of 10-foot (3-m) squares, with the typical drifter trailing 1,000 yards (900 m) of nets extending to a depth of as much as 120 feet (36 m).[59] Because the strait was just 21 miles (34 km) wide at its narrowest point and 180 feet (55 m) deep at its deepest, but with a mean depth of 108 feet (33 m), theoretically a line of three dozen drifters could cover the entire passage. Nature made

[57] Chatterton, *Q-Ships and their Story*, pp. 40–42.
[58] Campbell, *My Mystery Ships*, p. 302.
[59] Reginald Bacon, *The Dover Patrol, 1915–1917*, 2 vols. (New York: George H. Doran, 1919), vol. 2, pp. 105–108.

this practically impossible, as even in calm weather the tides and current posed almost insurmountable difficulties. The drifters, armed with nothing heavier than a 6-pounder apiece, and sometimes only heavy machine guns, also could not defend themselves against even the smallest enemy warships and had to be protected by destroyers (always in short supply) or armed auxiliary steamers. During the first phase of unrestricted submarine warfare the Dover drifters registered just one confirmed success, on March 4, 1915, forcing *U 8* to surface and surrender after it became entangled in the nets.[60] Nevertheless, enough U-boats appeared to be avoiding the Channel for the longer passage around the north of Scotland to persuade the Admiralty that a barrage of drifters across the Straits of Dover, though porous, was still very useful. In addition to their stationary duties, drifters accompanied the British navy's pre-dreadnoughts and monitors on bombardments of the Belgian coast; in one case, in August 1915, eighty of them dragged 16 miles (26 km) of antisubmarine nets on three sides of a force dispatched to shell Zeebrugge.[61] The French navy's modest Channel forces also used dragged torpedo nets but for local harbor defense, for example, at Le Havre, where *UB 26* was caught on April 5, 1916 and scuttled by its crew, all of whom survived. The French later raised and repaired *UB 26*, recommissioning it under the name *Roland Morillot*.[62]

    The British proposed the creation of a drifter barrage across the Adriatic Sea at the Straits of Otranto in May 1915, as soon as Italy entered the war, but the Italian commander, the Duke of the Abruzzi, refused the offer. Italian attitudes toward the submarine threat changed after the sinking of the armored cruiser *Amalfi* off Venice on July 7 by the German submarine *UB 14* (masquerading as Austro-Hungarian *U 26*), followed eleven days later by the sinking of the armored cruiser *Garibaldi* off the lower Dalmatian coast by Austro-Hungarian *U 4*, by which time the suspicion that German U-boats were using Pola and Cattaro as bases mustered further support for the project at the Admiralty. During the last week of September, sixty British drifters reached Taranto. They soon moved to Brindisi, where they became the responsibility of Rear Admiral Cecil Thursby, commander of the British Adriatic Squadron under Abruzzi's First Allied Fleet. Thursby

---

[60] Grant, *U-boats Destroyed*, p. 22.
[61] Bacon, *The Dover Patrol*, vol. 1, p. 118, vol. 2, p. 112.
[62] Grant, *U-boats Destroyed*, p. 32.

Figure 5.2 Admiral Duke of the Abruzzi

separated the drifters into three divisions, hoping to rotate two to sea and one in port, thus keeping as many as forty on station at any given time. He rarely had that many drifters at his disposal, however, especially after the intervention of Bulgaria on the side of Germany and Austria-Hungary resulted in the Central Powers crushing Serbia in the autumn of 1915, leaving Allied naval forces scrambling to evacuate 133,000 Serbian troops who had sought refuge in neutral Albania. In the winter of 1915/16 they were transported from the Italian-occupied ports of Durazzo (Durrës) and Valona (Vlorë) to Corfu, before moving on to Salonika (Thessaloniki) the following spring, where they joined British and French contingents in opening up a new Macedonian front. Lapeyrère's successor as French (and overall Allied) commander, Vice Admiral Louis Dartige du Fournet, commandeered every available transport and escort vessel for these operations, including several of Thursby's drifters, making it impossible for him to cover the designated patrol area. But the investment proved to be worth the price. The evacuation to Corfu took two months and involved nearly 250 individual steamer passages, well within range of hostile surface forces and U-boats based at nearby Cattaro, yet just four of the transports were sunk, all by mines. During December Austro-Hungarian destroyers sank two French submarines, the only Allied warships lost escorting the operation. The Central Powers also failed to sink a single transport during the subsequent redeployment of the Serbian army to Salonika, to which Thursby contributed two dozen drifters as escorts.[63] On May 13, 1916, before those boats were finally returned, the Otranto drifters registered their only confirmed catch of the war, when Austro-Hungarian *U 6* blundered into their nets and was abandoned by its crew, all of whom survived to be taken prisoner. Other submarines continued to evade the barrage, among them Austro-Hungarian *U 5* (Lieutenant Friedrich Schlosser), which on June 8 torpedoed and sank the 7,930-ton troopship *Principe Umberto* off the coast of Albania. The 1,750 dead, almost all Italian soldiers, were the most to lose their lives in a single U-boat action in the entire war.[64]

Physical realities made the goal of covering the Straits of Otranto with a drifter barrage far more ambitious (and far less realistic) than the plans for Dover. The passage at the mouth of the Adriatic was 45 miles (72 km) wide at its narrowest point and 2,600 feet (800 m) deep at its deepest; by comparison, the Straits of Dover were less than half as wide and dramatically shallower. The currents were also much stronger, making it not uncommon for gaps of as much as 10 miles (16 km) to open up in the drifter line during the course of a single night. To make matters worse for the Allies, after the loss of *U 6*, Austro-Hungarian light cruisers, destroyers, and torpedo boats based at Cattaro increased the frequency of raids against the Otranto barrage, sinking one drifter on the night of May 31/June 1 and two more on July 8–9. Because the drifters were British and the warships that protected them (light cruisers, auxiliary cruisers, and destroyers) were mostly French and Italian, the issue of protecting the barrage strained inter-Allied relations. Rear Admiral Mark Kerr, who succeeded Thursby in May 1916, increased

[63] Halpern, *The Naval War in the Mediterranean*, pp. 163–164, 215–219, 278.
[64] See www.uboat.net.

the number and the security of the drifters under his command. By that September the contingent had grown to include ninety-six boats, based at Taranto rather than at Brindisi, regularly deployed on a line running eastward from Cape Santa Maria di Leuca, the southeastern tip of Italy, to Corfu, farther south than the original Otranto barrage line and thus more secure from the Austro-Hungarian warships based at Cattaro, but also a much greater distance to cover, measuring roughly 80 miles (130 km) across. Activity in the Mediterranean by U-boats obviously based in the Adriatic hardly abated, leaving Kerr to conclude that 300 drifters were needed for a serious effort to block the passage.[65]

After seeing how effective minefields could be in blocking the passage of surface ships, the Allies came round to the view that the barrages should have not just nets to catch submarines, but underwater mines to blow them up. Rear Admiral Reginald Bacon, commander of the Dover Patrol from 1915 to 1917, emerged during 1916 as the leading advocate of a multilayered mine barrage across the Straits of Dover, an underwater "vertical wall of mines," as he called it, but serious planning for its assembly did not begin until after Germany resumed unrestricted submarine warfare, and owing to the number of mines required it was not completed until the end of 1917.[66] By then, the Allies had also supplemented the Otranto barrage with mines, and in the war's last year would undertake another brainchild of Bacon's, the ambitious project of constructing a chain of underwater mines on the North Sea blockade line from Scotland to Norway.

## Conclusion

The sinking of the *Lusitania*, for Britain "the greatest single atrocity of the war,"[67] and, for the United States, a key event in turning public and political opinion against Germany, without question ranks as the most important development in the initial great experiment with unrestricted submarine warfare. Because of the proximity of the sinking to the Irish coast, in the days after May 7, 1915, hundreds of the dead washed ashore, a disproportionate number of them women and children, whose survival rate in such a disaster was naturally significantly

---

[65] *Ibid.*, pp. 279–285.   [66] Bacon, *The Dover Patrol*, vol. 1, p. 106.
[67] Gregory, *The Last Great War*, p. 61.

Figure 5.3 Admiral Sir Reginald Bacon

lower than that of adult males. Photographs of the dead published in British newspapers only reinforced the shock and horror, and helped to steel the resolve of the home front to persevere in history's costliest war to date. In the spring of 1915, unrestricted submarine warfare overshadowed the concurrent horror of Germany's introduction of poison gas to the trench warfare of the Western front, indeed, joining it to deepen the British (and overall Allied) conviction that victory was the only acceptable outcome against a foe capable of such crimes.

The deliberate employment of submarines as high seas raiders brought a sudden and dramatic change in the nature of the war not just for the victims of German commerce raiding, but for the perpetrators as well. Just two months before the sinking of the *Lusitania*, when the German auxiliary cruiser *Prinz Eitel Friedrich* docked at Newport

News, Virginia, having operated for seven months under the standards that traditionally governed raiders at sea, the Americans interning the ship noted that the prisoners aboard outnumbered the crew, and that its captain had seen fit to assign a reserve lieutenant to care for the large number of children among them. One of the female captives affirmed that the personnel aboard "consisted of gentlemen, from the captain down to the last stoker and sailor."[68] German officers and seamen, like their counterparts in other navies, as early as 1914 had engaged in actions that could be labeled inhuman, and as late as 1918 demonstrated an ability to show compassion toward their foes; nevertheless, the spring of 1915 ranks as a watershed in their adoption of the requisite mentality for what a later generation would call "total war."

The German navy learned valuable lessons during the first round of unrestricted submarine warfare. U-boat officers who survived those seven months would put their tactical expertise to good use later in the war, while those in charge of submarine design recognized that larger, more heavily-armed U-boats with a greater range would not only be more lethal weapons, but could also be more livable for the men aboard, thus increasing the amount of time that a boat could be kept at sea. In the months to come, German naval leaders had to balance the quest to build larger submarines with the need to build more of them, as Tirpitz, in retirement, had the satisfaction of seeing the triumph of his view that Germany could do serious harm to Britain only by deploying a far greater number of U-boats.

[68] Brauer, *Die Kreuzerfahrten*, pp. 99, 109.

# 6 COMBINED OPERATIONS, 1915

"We are going to get through," confided Commodore Sir Roger Keyes to his diary, ten days before the Allied fleet he helped direct made its ill-fated attempt to force the Dardanelles, "but it is a much bigger thing than the Admiralty or anyone out here realized."[1] Keyes served as chief of staff to Vice Admiral Carden, commander of the reinforced British Eastern Mediterranean Squadron, tasked with opening the Turkish straits to the Allies, in the hope that by threatening Constantinople the Ottoman Empire could be forced out of the war. The following evening Carden sent the Admiralty a clear assessment of the "much bigger thing" and the challenges he faced: "The methodical reduction of the forts is not feasible, without expenditure of ammunition out of all proportion to that available... We are for the present checked by absence of efficient air reconnaissance, the necessity of clearing the minefield, and the presence of a large number of movable howitzers on both sides of the straits, whose positions up to the present we have not been able to locate."[2]

On March 18, 1915, the combination of formidable forts, minefields, and mobile batteries foiled the Allied attempt to force the Dardanelles using naval power alone, much to the dismay of the First Lord of the Admiralty, Winston Churchill, who had been promoting the attack for several months, all the while insisting that no troops

---

[1] Roger Keyes, *The Fight for Gallipoli: From the Naval Memoirs of Admiral of the Fleet Sir Roger Keyes* (London: Eyre & Spottiswoode, 1941), pp. 31–32.

[2] Carden to the Admiralty, March 9, 1915, text in Keyes, *The Fight for Gallipoli*, p. 33.

would be needed in the assault and relatively few would be needed to secure the Gallipoli Peninsula once the fleet had taken the straits. But troops would be needed, and a great many of them, to take the Turkish forts on the peninsula that commanded the Dardanelles. Five months later, as the first great Eastern front offensive of the Central Powers was winding down, the Germans faced a similar challenge in their quest to take Riga, the largest port in Russia's Baltic provinces. In contrast to the Dardanelles, at Riga it was the army that had assumed that it could achieve the objective with little help from the navy, only to realize that ships would be needed, and a great many of them, to secure the Gulf of Riga and force the Russians out of the city. In those circumstances Admiral Prince Henry of Prussia, younger brother of the emperor and overall commander of German Baltic forces, filled the role of willing partner for the generals, arguing that capital ships idled by the prevailing caution vis-à-vis the British fleet in the North Sea should be put to use against the Russians. Thus, aside from the first round of unrestricted submarine warfare and the measures undertaken against it, the most extensive endeavors of the naval war in 1915 involved combined operations to secure objectives on land, for the Allies at the Dardanelles and Gallipoli, and for the Germans at Riga.

## The Allies and the Dardanelles campaign

In the autumn of 1914, after the onset of trench warfare on the Western front, Churchill began to advocate the decisive use of British power around the periphery of Europe as an alternative to pouring more resources into the stalemate in northeastern France. In the first months of the war the Germans had demonstrated that a relatively modest investment in the Ottoman Empire – the battle cruiser *Goeben*, now *Yavuz Sultan Selim*, its light cruiser escort, a naval mission sent overland, and a cash subsidy to seal the deal – could alter the strategic situation in the Black Sea, allowing the Turks, under German command, to seize the initiative in a region that the Russians would otherwise have dominated. Churchill believed the Allies, without compromising their interests elsewhere, could gain a decisive advantage in the region. Over the winter of 1914/15 he promoted the idea that a squadron of Allied warships, most of them pre-dreadnoughts, could force its way past the forts and through the minefields of the Dardanelles, then transit the Sea of Marmara to deploy off Constantinople, the metropolis straddling the Bosporus. The bold stroke might compel the Ottoman Empire to sue for peace, opening up the Turkish straits as a supply route from the western Allies to Russia. At the least, Churchill calculated, it would force the Turks to concentrate their power on the defense of their capital, relieving pressure not only on the Russians in the Caucasus, but also on the British in Egypt. Best of all, he insisted, the operation could be accomplished with naval power alone.

As the plan incubated, Churchill did not let sobering geographic realities get in his way. The first step of the operation, transiting the Dardanelles, required navigating against the current up a waterway flowing 38 miles (61 km) northeast-to-southwest from the Sea of Marmara to its mouth at the Aegean Sea, measuring 3.7 miles (6 km) across at its greatest width, but just 1,300 yards (1,200 m) wide at the Narrows, a heavily fortified bend in the channel. The shoreline, hilly in most places and wooded in some, was dotted with villages; in addition to the Narrows, the most formidable forts were at the Aegean mouth of the strait and on the higher ground of the northern shore, on the Gallipoli Peninsula. Its average midstream depth of 180 feet (55 m) was more than sufficient for battleship operations, making the Narrows, the coastal forts, and mines sown in the channel the greatest obstacles. After successfully transiting the Dardanelles, the Allied fleet would make its way across the Sea of Marmara, a substantial body of water measuring nearly 110 miles (175 km) from east to west and 45 miles (70 km) from north to south, to attack Constantinople, located at the sea's northeastern corner, astride the Bosporus. A much shorter and narrower, but somewhat deeper, waterway than the Dardanelles, the Bosporus flows almost due south across the 19 miles (31 km) separating the Black Sea from the Sea of Marmara, through an area heavily populated since antiquity. Its average midstream depth of 213 feet (65 m) made the Bosporus easily passable by the largest ships, including Souchon's *Yavuz Sultan Selim*, based in the strait, but it was not wide enough – just 765 yards (700 m) across at its narrowest, 2 miles (3.3 km) at its widest – to be forced by an enemy fleet, and thus Churchill never contemplated asking the Russians to do so. Instead, as the plan evolved, it included a demonstration by the Black Sea Fleet off the Bosporus to coincide with the Anglo-French attempt to force the Dardanelles.

Churchill's idea gained support when the stalemate on the Western front continued into 1915. Admiral Fisher, called out of retirement after the war began to resume the duties of First Sea Lord, remained skeptical of the prospects, but Vice Admiral Carden, despite eventually acknowledging the problems posed by the forts, minefields, and mobile batteries ashore, always believed that a strengthened British Eastern Mediterranean Squadron, with the support of French forces already on hand, could force the straits, and prepared the plans Churchill used to persuade Prime Minister Asquith and other key cabinet figures of the scheme's feasibility. Upon returning from the Falklands in January 1915, the battle cruiser *Inflexible* relieved the *Indefatigable* off the Dardanelles, becoming Carden's flagship, but soon relinquished this honor to the newly commissioned *Queen Elizabeth*, the navy's first dreadnought with 15-inch (38-cm) guns, which arrived in early February at Churchill's insistence, but over the objections of most of the sea lords. Carden also received the remaining two pre-dreadnoughts of the China and East Indies stations as well as most of the pre-dreadnoughts of the Channel Fleet. British marines occupied the Greek island of Lemnos, 30 miles (50 km) west of the mouth of the Dardanelles, where the bay at Mudros was large enough to provide a forward base for the reinforced squadron. On February 3, British Imperial forces (mostly Australians and New Zealanders) satisfied another prerequisite for the operation by routing an Ottoman army sent to attack the Suez Canal, thus securing Egypt and creating an opening for the British to redeploy most of the manpower they had assembled there. Even if Churchill were correct and Carden's ships forced the straits, troops would have to be landed to take and hold the forts they had bypassed, and those troops were now available. More formidable naval reinforcements were not forthcoming, as the British navy's best capital ships could not be spared from the North Sea, and the French navy's dreadnoughts had to stay in the central Mediterranean to counter the presence of Austro-Hungarian dreadnoughts in the Adriatic. When the Allied bombardment of the outer forts of the Dardanelles began on February 19, Carden's force included just two modern capital ships – the *Queen Elizabeth* and the *Inflexible* – backed by twelve British pre-dreadnoughts and the four French pre-dreadnoughts commanded by Rear Admiral Guépratte, on station since late in 1914. Carden also received the seaplane carrier *Ark Royal*, whose six aircraft served as spotters for the battleship guns. On March 11, after three weeks of preparatory shelling, Churchill ordered Carden to proceed with the operation on March 18. During the intervening week, however, Carden fell ill, succumbing to an ulcer that kept him from ever holding another command at sea. His second-in-command, Rear Admiral John de Robeck, thus assumed responsibility for the attack just two days before it was launched.[3]

De Robeck sent his battleships into the Dardanelles on the morning of March 18, after being assured that the night before minesweepers had cleared all mines to within 8,000 yards (7,300 m) of the Narrows, the main obstacle to the operation's success, some 12 miles (20 km) inside the straits.[4] The lead ships entered the straits at 10:30, accompanied by a flotilla of minesweepers which were to continue their work while the battleships silenced the guns ashore. By 11:30 they were 6 miles (10 km) inside the straits, close enough to shell the Narrows forts. The plan called for divisions of ships to bombard the forts in turn, while those awaiting rotation to the front continued to engage other Turkish installations. From the start the operation suffered from the persistent and effective fire of mobile howitzers. Because these horse-drawn batteries could be moved as soon as the Allied guns found their mark, little could be done to counter their efforts; they targeted the larger ships as well as the minesweepers, but their fire proved to be most effective in disrupting the minesweeping effort. Nevertheless, the operation proceeded more or less as planned through the second rotation of the bombardment, undertaken by Guépratte's division, which took a pounding from the Narrows forts in the hour following 12:30. By the time they were relieved by a British division, the pre-dreadnought *Gaulois* had been holed at the waterline by a Turkish shell and had taken on so much water that it barely made it out of the straits, unfit

---

[3] Keyes, as chief of staff, provides a first-hand account of the change of command in *The Fight for Gallipoli*, pp. 43–45.

[4] Julian Corbett, *History of the Great War: Naval Operations*, 5 vols. (London: Longmans, Green, 1920–31), vol. 2, pp. 213–230, remains the most detailed account of the Allied side of the engagement of March 18, and has largely survived the scrutiny of time. See also Keyes, *The Fight for Gallipoli*, pp. 56–72. Recent accounts include Victor Rudenno, *Gallipoli: Attack from the Sea* (New Haven, CT: Yale University Press, 2008); Robin Prior, *Gallipoli: The End of the Myth* (New Haven, CT: Yale University Press, 2009); Peter Hart, *Gallipoli* (Oxford University Press, 2011), each of which follows what has become the standard approach of giving relatively little coverage to the naval campaign and much greater attention to the action on the Gallipoli Peninsula after the landings.

for further action. Guépratte's flagship *Suffren*, likewise badly damaged by shellfire, had to be towed back to Mudros. But the greatest loss came shortly before 14:00, when the *Bouvet*, while rotating to the rear, struck a mine in waters the Allies had considered cleared; it sank in less than 2 minutes, with almost all hands still aboard (639 dead). Even though the Allied shelling failed to destroy any of the forts and none of his ships succeeded in approaching the Narrows, de Robeck persisted in the attack until 16:05, when the battle cruiser *Inflexible* struck a mine and had to be towed to safety. Some 10 minutes later, the British pre-dreadnought *Irresistible* also struck a mine and had to be abandoned. At 16:50, once de Robeck had ascertained that these losses had come from mines rather than from torpedoes fired from the shore, he ordered the forward division to break off its shelling of the Narrows forts and fall back; an hour later, he ordered a general withdrawal from the straits. A second British pre-dreadnought, the *Ocean*, struck a mine at 18:05, during the retreat, and had to be abandoned, while another four sustained damages but were able to withdraw under their own power. Of the eighteen Allied warships deployed in the Dardanelles, only the *Queen Elizabeth* and seven pre-dreadnoughts (six British and one French) emerged unscathed.

De Robeck initially planned to repeat the attack, and Keyes, his chief of staff, remained enthusiastic despite the clear failure of March 18, recalling later his feeling that "in spite of the misfortunes of that day, success was now within our reach."[5] But General Sir Ian Hamilton, commander of the Mediterranean Expeditionary Force (MEF) then being assembled on Lemnos, had been on hand to witness what Keyes called "the spectacle of the *Inflexible* and *Gaulois* limping out of the straits, apparently in a sinking condition," and it affected him profoundly. On March 19, Hamilton telegraphed the Secretary of State for War, Lord Kitchener, stating that in his opinion "the straits are not likely to be forced by battleships," and indeed, "the army's part will be more than mere landing parties to destroy the forts; it must be a deliberate and prepared military operation, carried out at full strength, so as to open a passage for the navy."[6] By March 22, de Robeck concurred that "it will be necessary to take and occupy the Gallipoli Peninsula

---

[5] Keyes, *The Fight for Gallipoli*, p. 72.
[6] Hamilton to Kitchener, March 19, 1915, text in Keyes, *The Fight for Gallipoli*, p. 84.

**Figure 6.1** French battleship *Bouvet*

by land forces before it will be possible for first-rate ships, capable of dealing with the *Goeben* [sic], to get through..."[7] The Allied navies then shifted their focus to transporting troops to Lemnos and then on to Gallipoli, where they would facilitate the opening of the straits by storming the Turkish forts.

Thus, amid the disappointment, the need for naval forces capable of taking on the former German battle cruiser remained high on the list of British considerations. For his part, Vice Admiral Souchon considered the Allied debacle of March 18 as confirmation that the Dardanelles had been made impassable to enemy surface vessels, and hoped to renew his focus on the Black Sea and the defense of the Bosporus and Constantinople from Russian attack. With the *Yavuz Sultan Selim* temporarily out of action after being mined late in 1914, Souchon had not been able to stop Vice Admiral Ebergard and the Russian Black Sea Fleet from blockading Zonguldak and the "coal coast" for the winter months, during which time the Russian presence off the north coast of Anatolia had disrupted the supply route from Constantinople to Trebizond and the Caucasus front, as well as the shipment of fuel from

---

[7] De Robeck to the Admiralty, March 22, 1915, text in *ibid.*, p. 83.

the mines to the Ottoman capital. Souchon intended to resume a more robust posture after March 29, when his battle cruiser finally returned to service, only to have his plans compromised by the Allied landings on the Gallipoli Peninsula and, on the same day, April 25, confirmation that the first Allied submarine, the Australian *AE 2*, had breached the Dardanelles barrage and entered the Sea of Marmara.[8] The Turks had been aware of Allied attempts to send submarines through the straits ever since the previous November, with two running aground in the Dardanelles: the French *Saphir* on January 15 and the British *E 15* on April 17, the latter giving up codebooks and maps of British minefields in the North Sea and Channel which the Germans subsequently found very useful.[9]

A Turkish torpedo boat sank *AE 2* just five days after it entered the Sea of Marmara, but British submarines based at Mudros soon followed its course. Operating, in effect, at the rear of the Ottoman army deployed along the heights of the Gallipoli Peninsula, their activity disrupted the flow of supplies and reinforcements across the enclosed sea between the two straits and also hampered the evacuation of the sick and wounded. The threat from Allied submarines also made Souchon anxious about the security of the Bosporus anchorage used by his best warships, the *Yavuz Sultan Selim* and the light cruisers *Midilli and Hamidiye*.

During the Gallipoli landings of April 25, British and French warships provided fire support for one French, two British, and two Australia–New Zealand Army Corps (ANZAC) divisions, carried to their beachheads not in purpose-built landing craft, like their counterparts in the Second World War, but in columns of longboats towed by steam launches. A British infantry division landed at Cape Hellas, the tip of the Gallipoli Peninsula, and the ANZAC divisions landed on the peninsula's Aegean coast. As diversions, the French division landed south of the mouth of the Dardanelles at Kum Kale prior to moving on to Cape Hellas, and the second British formation, the marines of the Royal Naval Division, put ashore much farther up the peninsula at Bulair. The defending forces, organized by General Otto Liman von Sanders, head of the German military mission in Constantinople,

---

[8] Langensiepen *et al.*, *Halbmond und Kaiseradler*, pp. 39–47.
[9] *Ibid.*, p. 64; Headrick, *The Invisible Weapon*, p. 166. Headrick erroneously places the stranding of *E 15* in May 1915.

initially consisted of six divisions of the Turkish Fifth Army, 84,000 men in all, of which the division commanded by General Mustafa Kemal (later known as Atatürk) held the key high ground south of Suvla Bay, just across the peninsula from the Narrows forts, above what would soon be called Anzac Cove. By the end of the day on March 25, 20,000 ANZACs had secured a beachhead of 0.75 mile² (2 km²), where they were contained by Kemal, who recognized that their landing was not a feint. Once the initial landings were completed, the Allies had put 70,000 men ashore, too few to break out of their coastal enclaves. The bloodiest fighting occurred between the initial landings and May 3, during which time the ANZAC divisions, reinforced by four battalions of British marines from the Bulair beachhead, suffered heavy casualties, including 8,700 killed. The Turks lost twice as many men, nearly 20,000, by reinforcing Kemal and allowing him to counterattack repeatedly in an effort to push the ANZACs into the sea. Afterward both armies dug trench lines, the Allies on the slope just above the beaches and the Turks on the higher ground beyond. Meanwhile, the British 29th Division lost 6,500 men in securing its beachhead at Cape Hellas and establishing trench lines 3.5 miles (5.5 km) inland from the tip of the cape; the front remained there even after the French division arrived to provide additional support. Thus, Churchill's antidote for the stalemate on the Western front had only resulted in another stalemate at Gallipoli.

    Accounts of the endless recriminations that plagued the amphibious phase of the Dardanelles campaign have traditionally focused on mutual British–ANZAC criticism, but this paled in significance against the inter-service acrimony between the army and navy. Indeed, the overall campaign's main significance to history came in the negative examples it set for how not to conduct combined operations. While the war minister, Lord Kitchener, had held a number of meetings with the Admiralty in London throughout the winter months, Hamilton met his naval counterparts at the Dardanelles for the first time on March 16, just two days before Allied warships attempted to force the straits.[10] On the day of the Gallipoli landings one Australian colonel at Anzac Cove complained that "amateur yachtsmen could handle boat traffic better" than the British navy. British army officers likewise were scathing in their criticism of the navy, and army–navy exchanges, even

---

[10] Keyes, *The Fight for Gallipoli*, pp. 47–50.

Figure 6.2 Gallipoli landing, 1915

on the record, were often terse and sarcastic, especially over the issue of fire support. Even when officers of the two services met face to face to discuss operations, their exchanges suffered from what one historian has called "the curious gap between the mental worlds of the navy and army," which extended to misunderstandings over the definitions of terminology as basic as the time of day. For example, the army considered "morning" everything up to noon, whereas to the navy "morning" meant 04:00 to 08:00, with 08:00 to noon being "forenoon." Such a simple semantic difference could cause considerable confusion in the timing of a bombardment. It also did not help matters that the British army had moved slower than the navy in embracing the latest communication technology, leaving much of the shore-to-ship signaling (especially early on) to flags rather than to wireless, increasing the likelihood of fatal shelling errors. Naval gunners, like the troops ashore, had poor maps, and the opposing trench lines were so close that it was difficult to shell the enemy without the occasional friendly-fire hit. This factor, plus the crowded conditions on the beaches, meant that any "shorts" were liable to cause considerable death and destruction, leading cautious gunners, more often than not, to overshoot the mark, blanketing the heights with shells that fell harmlessly to the rear of the Turkish trenches. The lack of adequate aerial spotting worsened after the arrival offshore of German submarines during May, prompting the navy to withdraw the *Ark Royal* and its seaplanes. Sightings of U-boats (here, as elsewhere, often false sightings) caused de Robeck to disperse his ships frequently, thus removing the army's fire support without warning. This quite naturally added to the inter-service tensions, especially when the fleet suddenly disappeared while operations were underway on land.[11]

The failure of the Allied troops to move beyond their initial beachheads put Churchill at the center of a political firestorm. The First Lord's position at the Admiralty became untenable after May 15, when Fisher unleashed a salvo of criticism against him upon resigning as First Sea Lord. The bad news from Gallipoli, combined with a crisis over war production, shook Asquith enough to prompt the prime minister to form a coalition government. In exchange for cooperation with the Liberals, the Conservatives demanded Churchill's resignation from the cabinet, which followed on May 25. The sea lords at the Admiralty, who had never wanted to risk new capital ships at the Dardanelles, wasted no time in recalling the *Queen Elizabeth* and *Inflexible* to the North Sea. To make good the lost firepower, de Robeck received the eight remaining pre-dreadnoughts of the Channel Fleet, which were joined in July and August by newly commissioned monitors of various sizes. Not surprisingly, old battleships considered expendable accounted for most of the navy's losses after March 18. On the night of May 12–13, a Turkish torpedo boat sank the pre-dreadnought *Goliath* (570 dead). Then, the first German submarine to appear off Gallipoli, Hersing's *U 21*, sank two pre-dreadnoughts shortly after its arrival, the *Triumph* on May 25 and the *Majestic* two days later. These attacks came in broad daylight while both ships were anchored off Gaba Tepe providing fire support for troops ashore, circumstances that allowed most of each crew to be saved. *U 21* went on to a successful career in the Mediterranean, operating for the most part out of Cattaro, at times as Austro-Hungarian *U 36*. Hersing eventually sank a third Allied warship, the French armored cruiser *Amiral Charner* (427 dead) on February 8, 1916, off the coast of Syria.[12]

[11] Timothy H. E. Travers, "When Technology and Tactics Fail: Gallipoli 1915," in Stephen D. Chiabotti (ed.), *Tooling for War: Military Transformation in the Industrial Age* (Chicago, IL: Imprint Publications, 1996), pp. 106–109.

[12] Otto Hersing, *U 21 rettet die Dardanellen* (Leipzig: Amalthea-Verlag, 1932), pp. 51–60, 81–84.

Of the Allied submarines active during the Gallipoli campaign, the most successful was *E 11* (Lieutenant Commander Martin Nasmith), which infiltrated the Sea of Marmara to sink a dozen Turkish vessels of various sizes between May 20 and June 8, a feat that earned Nasmith a Victoria Cross. On a subsequent sortie on August 8, Nasmith's *E 11* torpedoed and sank the pre-dreadnought *Barbaros Hayreddin* (253 dead). By the autumn months the underwater incursions through the Dardanelles minefields were almost exclusively British; the last French submarine to make the attempt, the *Turquoise*, ran aground in the straits on October 30. By the end of the Gallipoli campaign, Allied submarines operating in the Sea of Marmara had sunk 29,000 tons of Turkish shipping, including twenty-five steamers that accounted for most of the figure. British submarines were responsible for all the Ottoman warships sunk; in addition to the *Barbaros Hayreddin*, these included a destroyer and five gunboats.[13]

Meanwhile, both sides poured troops into the Gallipoli Peninsula, almost tripling their numbers. At the peak of the summer action the Allies had fourteen divisions deployed against sixteen for the Turks, in trench lines as close as 5–6 miles (8–10 km) across the peninsula from the forts they were supposed to attack. The Battle of Sari Bair (August 6–21), named after a ridge dominating both Anzac Cove and Suvla Bay, followed an attempt by Hamilton to surprise the Turks by opening a third beachhead with eight of his divisions. In support of the campaign's most intense fighting since early May, the ships offshore fired 6,000 shells during the first three days of the battle, by comparison, one-third of the daily total fired by the US Navy at the height of the battle for Iwo Jima in July 1945, but still very impressive for the time. The battle also included the war's greatest documented range of effective naval fire support for inland forces, when the 9.2-inch (23.4-cm) guns of a British monitor destroyed a Turkish battery from a distance of 21,000 yards (19,200 m).[14] The engagement proved to be indecisive, however, as the Allies sustained another 20,000 casualties in return for very minor gains. Hamilton did not attempt another offensive before General Sir Charles Monro succeeded him as MEF commander on October 15.

---

[13] Langensiepen *et al.*, *Halbmond und Kaiseradler*, pp. 64–94 *passim*; Halpern, *The Naval War in the Mediterranean*, pp. 161, 189.

[14] Travers, "When Technology and Tactics Fail," pp. 107–110.

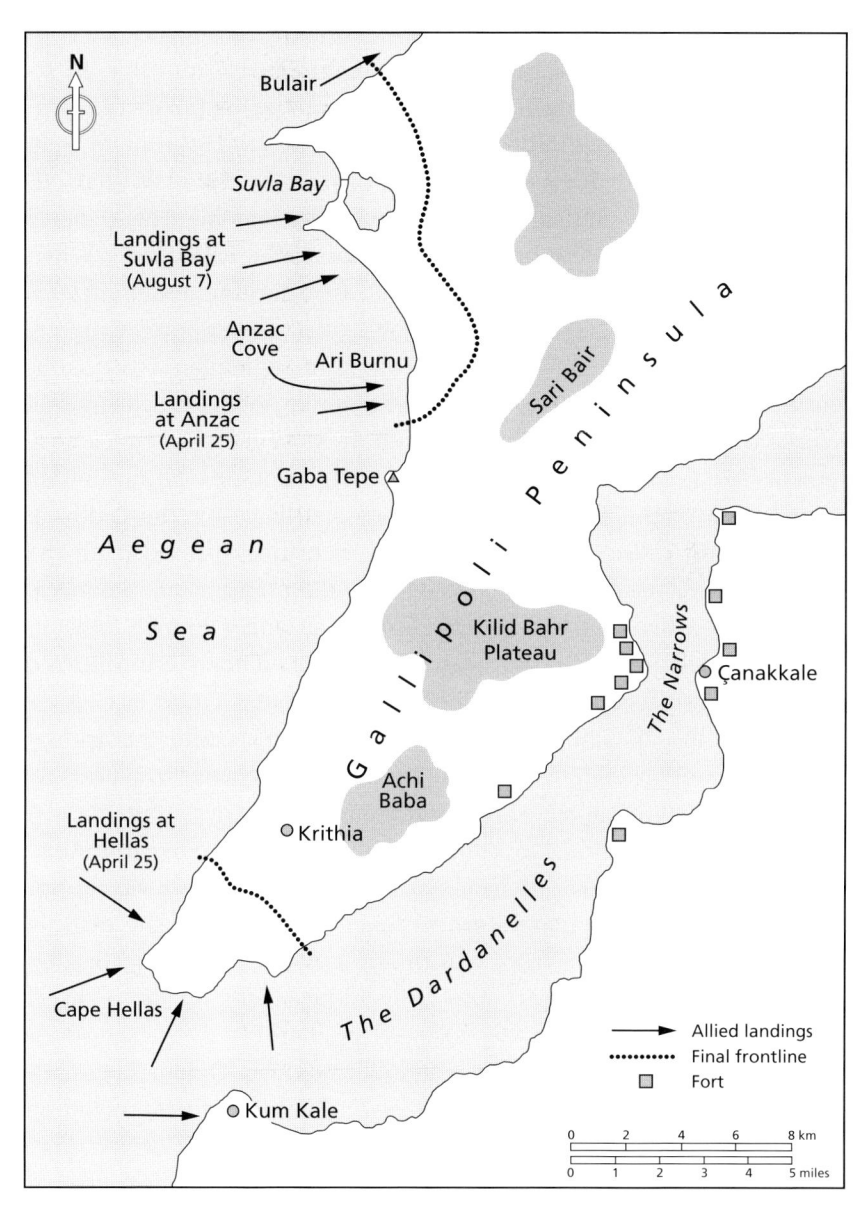

Map 6.1 Gallipoli and the Dardanelles

By then, Bulgaria's entry into the war on the side of the Central Powers had prompted the Allies to decide to abandon the Dardanelles campaign, in order to free up manpower to support Serbia. Assuming that a Bulgarian invasion of Serbia would activate a Greco-Serbian defensive alliance that dated from the Balkan Wars, thus bringing

Greece into the war on the side of the Allies, Britain and France concluded an agreement with the pro-Allied Greek prime minister, Eleftherios Venizelos, to allow them to land troops at Salonika (Thessaloniki). But from the beginning of the war Greek sympathies had been sharply divided, with King Constantine, brother-in-law of William II, seeking to preserve neutrality, while Venizelos and his liberal party attempted to bring the country into the war on the Allied side. When Austria-Hungary declared war on Serbia, Constantine and Venizelos had agreed that Greece was under no obligation to support the Serbs, but after Bulgaria joined the Central Powers in September 1915, Constantine remained committed to neutrality while Venizelos considered Greece bound by treaty to support Serbia. In any event, the Greek government had already accepted the Allied occupation of Corfu as a base at the mouth of the Adriatic and Lemnos as a base for the Gallipoli campaign, and those violations of Greek neutrality provided all the precedent the Allies needed to proceed with their landings at Salonika, starting with a British division from Suvla Bay and a French division from Cape Hellas, which arrived on October 5. They were followed by troops sent directly from Britain and France that could have reinforced the army at Gallipoli. Sizing up the situation after he arrived to replace Hamilton, Monro soon advised Lord Kitchener to withdraw the remaining troops. The war minister confirmed the decision after visiting the peninsula in mid-November. Many of those leaving continued to land at Salonika, even after it became clear that Greece would not enter the war and Serbia could not be saved. Naval forces successfully evacuated the last of the troops from Anzac Cove and Suvla Bay on the night of December 19/20, and from Cape Hellas on the night of January 8/9, 1916.

The Battle of Gallipoli generated 251,000 Ottoman casualties, including 87,000 dead, and 141,000 Allied casualties, including 44,000 dead (among them 21,000 British, 10,000 French, 8,700 Australians, and 2,700 New Zealanders). The British navy lost five of the twenty pre-dreadnoughts it deployed in the Dardanelles campaign, the French navy, one of five, and the Ottoman navy, two of three. The Allied navies also torpedoed over 56,000 tons of Turkish shipping in and around the straits, just over half of it in the Sea of Marmara, at a cost of eight submarines (four British and four French), most of which were lost to mines. While they had inflicted far more human and material damage than they absorbed, the Allies afterward faced the reality that their effort at the Dardanelles had done nothing to change the course of the war. Decades later, even after his role as Britain's prime minister in the Second World War came to define his place in history, the futile campaign remained a stain on Winston Churchill's legacy. His supporters blamed everyone but him for the debacle; Keyes, for example, still insisted a quarter of a century later that a second attempt to force the straits, after March 18, would have succeeded in breaking through with the loss of "two or three [battleships]... possibly none if we were lucky," and "would have shortened the war by two years, and spared literally millions of lives."[15]

Given the results of March 18 and the formidable nature of the obstacles, Churchill's scheme for the Dardanelles must be considered naively overambitious at best, and certainly doomed to fail. The landing of significant forces on the Gallipoli Peninsula on April 25, and their dramatic reinforcement in the months that followed, shifted the focus from the sea to the land; as a result, most accounts of the campaign say little about the naval dimension after the failure of the initial plan to force the straits. Criticism of the conduct of the landing itself and of the reliability or consistency of battleship fire support thereafter, while certainly legitimate, has overshadowed the navy's remarkable feat of putting five divisions of troops ashore on a defended coast with barely a month to prepare, then keeping that force supplied as it tripled in size. And by focusing overwhelmingly on what the Allies did wrong, the English-language literature on the campaign typically ignores what the enemy did right, missing the central point that at Gallipoli, no less than in the initial attempt to force the Dardanelles, the Allies failed because they underestimated the Turks. For the Turkish nation, Mustafa Kemal, as Atatürk, remains the iconic figure of the victory, but the emphasis on the great leader should not obscure his broader significance as a symbol of the defenders of the Dardanelles and Gallipoli, whose tenacity, resilience, and ingenuity took the Allies by surprise.

## The war in the Black Sea, 1915

While it could not be a priority for the Turks as long as Allied troops remained ashore at Gallipoli and Allied submarines remained active

---

[15] Keyes, *The Fight for Gallipoli*, p. 547.

in the Sea of Marmara, the war in the Black Sea continued throughout 1915. By prior arrangement with the western Allies, on the day of the initial landings at Gallipoli a Russian squadron appeared off the Bosporus, and Vice Admiral Ebergard's battleships closed to shell the Bosporus forts for about an hour. On May 2–4, Ebergard returned with a force including the pre-dreadnoughts *Panteleimon* (ex-*Potemkin*), *Rostislav*, and *Tri Sviatitelia* for a second bombardment of the Bosporus forts, after which he shelled other targets along the Black Sea coast of European Turkey up to the Bulgarian border. A third Russian sortie to the mouth of the Bosporus, on May 10, included all five of Ebergard's operational pre-dreadnoughts plus the cruisers *Kagul* and *Pamiat Merkuria*. On that occasion, the *Yavuz Sultan Selim* raised steam to challenge the attackers, and in a 20-minute duel sustained two hits while scoring just one of its own, out of 126 shells fired. In each of the three Russian operations, seaplanes launched from two tenders accompanying Ebergard's squadron dropped bombs to supplement the shelling delivered by the battleships.[16]

Because the Bosporus forts were stripped of troops to reinforce the defenses at Gallipoli, the Turks suffered few casualties in these attacks. Some 80,000 troops were thus redeployed from the forts and other works defending Constantinople against attack from the Black Sea side, leaving Souchon and the navy more completely responsible for the security of that flank of the Ottoman capital. At the same time, the desperate need for manpower prompted the Turks to draft men from the mines of the "coal coast" for service in the army, causing coal production to fall precipitously. While this left Souchon with less traffic to convoy from Zonguldak to Constantinople, it also left the capital (and the navy) increasingly short of fuel. Indeed, during 1915 the Turks had to start importing coal from Germany, which ultimately supplied over one-third of their monthly needs.[17]

During the summer of 1915, submarines changed the way both Souchon and Ebergard approached operations in the Black Sea. After Russian submarines were deployed to supplement surface vessels preying upon the coastal trade off northern Anatolia, fears of losing the *Yavuz Sultan Selim* or *Midilli* to torpedo attacks led Souchon to end the earlier practice of having them escort coastal convoys, except under rare

---

[16] Langensiepen *et al.*, *Halbmond und Kaiseradler*, pp. 47–49.
[17] *Ibid.*, pp. 48, 58; Halpern, *A Naval History of World War I*, p. 238.

circumstances. During one such occasion, on July 19, the *Midilli* struck a Russian mine, sustaining damage that put it out of action until February 1916. The light cruiser's months of inactivity had a fateful impact on at least one of its junior officers, Lieutenant Karl Doenitz, who transferred home for U-boat training, thus embarking on a new career path that eventually made him the Third Reich's leading submariner. With Souchon continuing to hold back the *Yavuz Sultan Selim* out of fear of the submarine threat (and as the last line of defense for Constantinople against another Allied attempt to force the Dardanelles), the temporary loss of the *Midilli* left the light cruiser *Hamidiye* as the largest serviceable Ottoman warship. Meanwhile, Russian intelligence had learned of the arrival of the first German submarines at Constantinople, prompting Ebergard to show more caution in the deployment of his larger warships, including the dreadnought *Imperatritsa Maria*, commissioned in early July. During the summer of 1915, he kept his battleships at Sevastopol, using only destroyers to supplement his submarines in the campaign against enemy shipping between the "coal coast" and the Ottoman capital. In September, Souchon retaliated by deploying *UB 7* and *UB 8* against Russian coastal trade around the Crimea. Later that month, after converting the *Hamidiye* to a training ship for Turkish recruits, Souchon resumed use of the *Yavuz Sultan Selim* to escort transports and supply ships between Constantinople and Zonguldak. Ebergard likewise gradually grew less cautious with his larger warships, and on October 1 dispatched the *Imperatritsa Maria* on its first mission, a raid on Zonguldak with the pre-dreadnoughts *Evstafi, Ioann Zlatoust*, and *Panteleimon*. Ebergard's lone dreadnought returned to the "coal coast" for another raid on November 24, escorted only by the cruiser *Pamiat Merkuria*. His boldness came despite evidence of increasing German submarine activity in Russian waters; on October 7, Lieutenant Heimberg's *UB 14* sank a Russian steamer and tanker off the Crimea, the first significant victims of German U-boats in the Black Sea. The U-boats soon extended their range into the eastern Black Sea. In a bold raid on November 23, *UC 13* shot up the harbor at Sochi, only to fall victim to a storm on the Anatolian coast just five days later. It was the first submarine lost by either side in the war in the Black Sea.[18]

    Bulgaria's entry into the war on the side of the Central Powers extended Souchon's responsibilities, since the Bulgarians had a very

---

[18] Langensiepen *et al.*, *Halbmond und Kaiseradler*, 50–57.

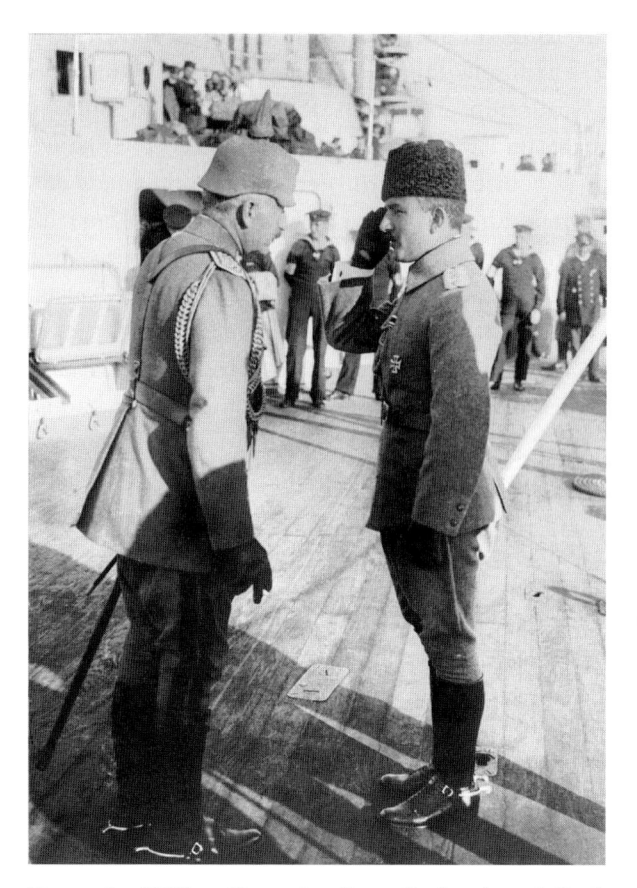

Figure 6.3 William II meeting Enver Pasha aboard *Goeben*

small navy – six torpedo boats supplemented by armed yachts, patrol boats, and minesweepers – and subsequently depended on their allies to defend their principal port, Varna, and the rest of their coastline against enemy attack.[19] On October 15, nine days after hostilities between Russia and Bulgaria began, Souchon took the *Yavuz Sultan Selim* on a one-day visit to Varna, where the Bulgarians welcomed him with great fanfare. By late October, he had U-boats operating out of Euxinograd, 5 miles (8 km) north of Varna. The new base had the advantage, compared with Constantinople, of being 105 miles (170 km) closer to Odessa, Russia's busiest Black Sea port. Ebergard did not wait long to attack Bulgaria, appearing in force off Varna and Euxinograd on October 27. In the Russian Black Sea Fleet's largest operation of the war,

[19] *Conway, 1906–1921*, pp. 411–412.

the *Imperatritsa Maria*, pre-dreadnoughts *Evstafi*, *Ioann Zlatoust*, and *Panteleimon*, cruisers *Kagul* and *Pamiat Merkuria*, fifteen destroyers, three minelayers, and the seaplane tenders *Nikolai I* and *Almaz* participated in the day-long shelling, bombing, and mining of the Bulgarian coast.[20]

Long before Russia had a dreadnought in the Black Sea, Ebergard had not hesitated to challenge Souchon and the Ottoman navy. After the *Imperatritsa Maria* joined the fleet, the Russians seized the initiative in the Black Sea, and would hold it for the next two years until revolution caused the collapse of their fleet. Indeed, in the wake of the army's crushing defeat in the spring and summer of 1915, and the ensuing loss of Poland and Lithuania, the navy's performance in the Black Sea became Russia's only bright spot.

## Germany, Russia, and Riga

The strategic imperative of defending Petrograd (the new, less "German" name given to St. Petersburg shortly after the war began) kept the Russian navy from ever taking the initiative in the Baltic as it had in the Black Sea. The timid posture continued even after the four pre-dreadnoughts and six armored cruisers of their Baltic Fleet were joined, in December 1914, by the four dreadnoughts of the 23,360-ton *Gangut* class, formidable ships which, like the *Imperatritsa Maria* class being built for the Black Sea, featured twelve 12-inch (30.5-cm) guns. Tsar Nicholas II underscored the caution by admonishing his Baltic Fleet commander, Admiral Essen, to avoid "a second Tsushima."[21] Theoretically four *Gangut*-class dreadnoughts gave Russia the strength to act as master of the Baltic, just as Austria-Hungary's dreadnoughts enabled it to dominate the enclosed waters of the Adriatic, yet Essen and his colleagues faced the sobering reality that the High Sea Fleet could at any time send enough units from Wilhelmshaven via the Kiel Canal to overwhelm whatever forces Russia deployed in the Baltic. Scheer did not hesitate to attribute Russian behavior to psychological factors, speculating that "their lack of confidence in their own efficiency may

---

[20] Langensiepen *et al.*, *Halbmond und Kaiseradler*, pp. 55–56.
[21] Quoted in Halpern, *A Naval History of World War I*, p. 184.

be responsible for the fact that the Russians refrained from taking the offensive."[22]

At the start of the war the Russians concentrated the Baltic Fleet at its main base, Kronstadt in the Gulf of Finland, to ensure the defense of the capital. On August 2, one day after the onset of hostilities, German light cruisers arrived off Libau, the fleet's forward base on the Latvian coast, but found no Russian warships there. Both navies laid extensive minefields, in their own waters for defensive purposes, and also off the ports of the enemy, and both used vessels as large as cruisers to escort minelaying operations or for general reconnaissance, but for the next nine months, until the Central Powers launched their spring offensive of 1915 on the Eastern front, Russian and German surface vessels never encountered one another at sea. Nevertheless, as in other theaters, ships were damaged or lost because of mines and torpedoes, along with accidents such as the fateful grounding of the light cruiser *Magdeburg* on August 28, in a fog off the Estonian island of Odenholm, which yielded to the Russians the first German naval code books that eventually found their way to the British Admiralty. The Russians lost their first warship on October 11, the armored cruiser *Pallada*, which sank with all hands (597 dead) after being torpedoed by *U 26* (*Kapitänleutnant* Baron Egewolf von Berckheim) at the mouth of the Gulf of Riga. The following month, on November 17, the Germans likewise lost an armored cruiser when the *Friedrich Carl*, flagship of Rear Admiral Ehler Behring's cruiser squadron, based at Danzig, sank after striking a Russian mine in the coastal waters of East Prussia, but with almost everyone aboard surviving.[23]

Unable to spare any of their capital ships for service in the Baltic, the Germans used old battleships mobilized from the reserve for their first attempt to lure Essen's fleet out of Kronstadt. On September 3–9, Prince Henry sent Vice Admiral Erhard Schmidt with seven units of the *Wittelsbach* and *Braunschweig* classes (commissioned between 1902 and 1904) and the armored cruiser *Blücher*, escorted by five light cruisers and two dozen destroyers, all the way to the mouth of the Gulf of Finland; Essen came out with the Baltic Fleet's four pre-dreadnoughts (the *Gangut*s not yet being in commission) but not until

---

[22] Scheer, *Germany's High Sea Fleet*, p. 58.
[23] Lutz Bengelsdorf, *Der Seekrieg in der Ostsee 1914–1918* (Bremen: Hauschild, 2008), pp. 16–21, 28–29, 35–36.

September 8, by which time Schmidt's squadron was already on its way home.[24] The following month Prince Henry received temporary use of Scheer's squadron of the High Sea Fleet, consisting of the eight newest pre-dreadnoughts of the *Braunschweig* and *Deutschland* classes (commissioned 1905–8), for a raid on Libau, but the operation was canceled after the Germans received intelligence that British submarines had deployed to the Baltic.[25]

Even though the Russians had entered the war with more submarines than the Germans, they were slow to break with the prewar notion that their purpose was defensive; thus, the British navy's *E 1* and *E 9* were the first Allied submarines to hunt for German targets in the Baltic. During October 1914 the two boats made their way from Britain to Russian waters, where they operated out of a base at Lapvik on the Gulf of Finland. Essen soon had them on patrol as far west as Danzig, but without effect.[26] Aside from the special challenges of Baltic submarine operations during the icy months, the British quickly learned, as had the Germans in the war's first weeks, that the lower level of salinity especially in the eastern Baltic could have dramatic effects on the handling of a submarine regardless of the time of the year, for example, making diving much faster and surfacing much slower.[27] While Russian bases would continue to host British submarines for as long as Russia remained in the war, the British never sent surface vessels into the Baltic. It is likely they would have, had Fisher remained as First Sea Lord deeper into the war. During his return to office in 1914–15, Britain resumed construction of his favorite capital ship type, the battle cruiser, laying down another five, of which three (the future *Courageous*, *Glorious*, and *Furious*) were designed with a shallower draught and intended by Fisher for Baltic operations.[28]

Aside from a handful of British submarines, the Russians had no help on the maritime flank of the Eastern front when the Central Powers launched their spring offensive. With no prospect for success on the Western front in 1915, Falkenhayn reinforced the German and Austro-Hungarian armies in the east for a decisive push that he hoped would knock Russia out of the war, freeing the German army to focus on France. Their breakthrough followed the Battle of Tarnów-Gorlice

[24] *Ibid.*, pp. 21–23.    [25] Scheer, *Germany's High Sea Fleet*, pp. 64, 66.
[26] Halpern, *A Naval History of World War I*, pp. 188–190.
[27] Valentiner, *Der Schrecken der Meere*, pp. 45–46.
[28] *Conway, 1906–1921*, pp. 39–40.

(May 2–10), fought east of Cracow, Austria-Hungary's largest Polish city, which Russian troops had threatened in their autumn 1914 offensive. After Austro-Hungarian troops retook Lemberg (L'viv) on June 22, the entire Eastern front stood on Russia's prewar soil, prompting Falkenhayn to pause the advance while Bethmann Hollweg, through a Danish intermediary, made a peace overture to the tsar based on the *status quo ante*. Nicholas II rejected the proposal, citing the pledge the Triple Entente powers had made (on September 5, 1914) not to conclude a separate peace. Falkenhayn then faced the dilemma of how to define victory in the current campaign. In July the offensive resumed, with the new goal of conquering (or liberating) Russian Poland; even if the Poles could not be turned against the Russians, the elimination of the Polish salient would dramatically shorten the Eastern front and enable the Central Powers to hold it with fewer troops, facilitating operations on other fronts. The Latvian port of Riga was now seen as the natural anchor for the Baltic flank of the new front. While Falkenhayn had no intention of sending German troops any farther east in 1915, as Scheer noted, possession of this key port would open up for the Germans "the use of the more suitable sea route for the transport of troops and war materiel to the Gulf of Riga." Given the problems of moving overland in a country with too few roads and railways, Riga was essential to any future strike in the direction of Petrograd, another 300 miles (480 km) to the northeast.[29]

At the outbreak of war Riga ranked as the Russian Empire's busiest seaport, its third largest industrial center after Petrograd and Moscow, and trailed only those cities and Odessa in population. Unlike Petrograd, its harbor remained ice-free in winter. The city and its suburbs straddled the mouth of the River Dvina (German: Düna; Latvian: Daugava) on the south shore of the Gulf of Riga, a large enclosed bay measuring, at its largest, 90 miles (145 km) from north to south and 80 miles (130 km) from west to east. A large island, Ösel (Saaremaa), on the northwest side of the gulf, separates it from the Baltic Sea. The broad Irben (Irbe) Straits, south of Ösel, 40 miles (65 km) long and 20 miles (32 km) wide at their narrowest, are the main channel providing access to Riga from the west. East of Ösel, between the island and the west coast of Estonia, a narrower channel consisting of

---

[29] Quoted in Scheer, *Germany's High Sea Fleet*, p. 58; see also Sondhaus, *World War I*, pp. 143–146.

Kuiwast Roads and, to the north, Moon Sound provides access to Riga from the north, through waters dotted by smaller islands, principally Moon (Muhu) and Dagö (Hiiumaa). Coinciding with the onset of the spring offensive of the Central Powers, the Russians mined the Irben Straits, where the depth, 35–65 feet (10–20 m), allowed passage to the largest warships, and also began to dredge a deeper channel to enable their own battleships to transit the much shallower Moon Sound and Kuiwast Roads. These projects reflected their strategic priorities of foiling a German attack on the gulf from the west while ensuring the access of any large warships they would send from the north to defend it.

In contrast to the Allied effort at the Dardanelles, which started as a naval operation that would not require troops and ended as a military operation with the navies playing a peripheral role, the German drive for Riga started as an army offensive with the naval role limited to coastal fire support and ended as a naval operation intended to force the evacuation of the city. While Falkenhayn and the High Command directed the Tarnów-Gorlice offensive and the subsequent conquest of Poland, responsibility for the German drive from East Prussia into Russia's Baltic provinces was delegated to the eastern command (*OberOst*) of Field Marshal Paul von Hindenburg and his chief of staff, General Erich Ludendorff. Their troops included the Eighth Army (General Otto von Below), the Tenth Army (General Hermann von Eichhorn), and the Niemen Army (General Otto von Lauenstein), of which the latter, named for the river that formed the border between East Prussia and Russian Lithuania, was soon amalgamated with the Eighth Army and subordinated to Below. Hindenburg and Ludendorff launched the Baltic offensive on April 26, a week before the start of Tarnów-Gorlice, in order for it to have some value as a diversion. Jumping off from a frontline just over the Russian border, some 90 miles (145 km) southwest of Riga at its nearest point, the Niemen Army operated closest to the coast, while the Tenth Army, to its south, advanced toward Kovno (Kaunas), and the Eighth Army, farther south, pushed for Grodno. The Niemen Army, tailored for action in the relatively flat coastal plain, included seven cavalry and five infantry divisions, against which the Russian Fifth Army was eventually reinforced to nine infantry and nine cavalry divisions. Libau, just 70 miles (110 km) up the coast from the easternmost Prussian port, Memel, was the first city in the path of the advancing German front. After enduring a shelling from two German light cruisers on April 27, Libau was subjected to a heavier bombardment on May 7. As German troops approached from the land side, Rear Admiral Albert Hopman arrived with a squadron led by the old *Siegfried*-class coastal battleship *Beowulf* and the armored cruisers *Prinz Adalbert*, *Prinz Heinrich*, and *Roon* to shell the city and its defenses. Hopman's attack was covered by a screen of light cruisers deployed north of Libau; in the first surface engagement of the war between the German and Russian navies, one of these cruisers, the *München*, exchanged shots with a force under Rear Admiral Mikhail Bakhirev led by the armored cruisers *Admiral Makarov* and *Bayan*. Rather than fight to hold Libau, the Russians withdrew, and German forces occupied the city and port on May 8, at no cost except the loss of a destroyer that struck a mine in the harbor.[30]

At this crucial moment the Russian Baltic Fleet experienced an unexpected change in command when Admiral Essen, aged fifty-four, succumbed to a respiratory infection on May 20 after a brief illness. Vice Admiral Viktor Kanin, previously in charge of mining operations, succeeded him, a fitting choice since mine warfare remained Russia's strong suit. Indeed, as the German army inched closer to Riga, both navies remained aggressive in their use of mines, and both lost minelayers. On June 4, during a failed German attempt to mine the northern passage into the Gulf of Riga, Berckheim's *U 26* torpedoed and sank the Russian minelayer *Yenisei* (297 dead) as it headed to the same waters from the Gulf of Finland. Then, on July 1–2, Bakhirev's squadron, including the *Admiral Makarov*, *Bayan*, and a third armored cruiser, the 15,190-ton *Rurik*, broke up a German attempt to sow mines in the Aaland Islands, pursuing the minelayer *Albatross* and the squadron escorting it, led by the *Roon*, southward to the waters between the west coast of Latvia and the Swedish island of Gotland. The *Albatross*, badly damaged, saved itself only by steaming into neutral Swedish waters for internment. The Russian pursuit, which the Germans called the "Gotland Raid," continued as far south as 56°N, and included a firefight and exchange of hits between the armored cruisers *Roon* and *Bayan*, as well as an attack by the British submarine *E 9* (Lieutenant Commander Max Horton) on the *Prinz Adalbert*, which was torpedoed but not sunk when it sortied from Danzig to support the outnumbered Germans.[31]

---

[30] Bengelsdorf, *Der Seekrieg in der Ostsee*, pp. 50–54; Sondhaus, *World War I*, p. 146; Halpern, *A Naval History of World War I*, pp. 191–192.
[31] Bengelsdorf, *Der Seekrieg in der Ostsee*, pp. 56–65.

Meanwhile, in the action on land, the Russian army did not attempt a counterattack against the advancing Germans until June 9, when they reached Schaulen (Šiauliai), 75 miles (120 km) south of Riga on the railway linking the city to Vilna (Vilnius). The offensive advanced no further before Falkenhayn called a halt to it, to facilitate the peace overture to the tsar.[32] After the German advance resumed, on July 13, *OberOst*'s armies faced an enemy gradually strengthened by troops withdrawn from Poland. On July 18, elements of the Niemen Army took Windau (Ventspils) near the western approach to the Irben Straits, 70 miles (110 km) up the coast from Libau, after it had been shelled by cruisers. German troops then occupied the south shore of the straits and began to make their way eastward along the gulf coast toward Riga; meanwhile, Germans advancing up the railway from the south soon threatened Mitau (Jelgava), just 15 miles (24 km) southwest of Riga, which fell on August 1. As the Russian army began to dig in west and south of the city, the navy sent the pre-dreadnought *Slava* (Captain Sergei Viazemsky) to reinforce the smaller ships and submarines already deployed in the gulf. Because the dredging of Moon Sound had not yet been completed, the *Slava* had to round Ösel Island to enter the gulf from the west, through the Irben Straits, and did so on July 31 escorted (at least to the mouth of the straits) by the dreadnoughts *Gangut* and *Petropavlovsk*, which for the first time sortied beyond Helsinki, the base to which the Russian Baltic dreadnoughts had been forward deployed.[33]

The *Slava* became key to the defense of Riga against the German naval assault launched eight days later. For the main strike force the Germans used Vice Admiral Schmidt and the same seven pre-dreadnoughts of the *Wittelsbach* and *Braunschweig* classes involved in his bold sortie to the mouth of the Gulf of Finland in September 1914. To support them in case the *Gangut*s came out of Helsinki, the High Sea Fleet loaned Prince Henry's Baltic command a squadron of eight dreadnoughts plus the battle cruisers *Seydlitz*, *Moltke*, and *Von der Tann*, commanded by Hipper (recently promoted to vice admiral). As a further precaution, Pohl's flagship and another squadron of dreadnoughts moved from Wilhelmshaven to the Elbe River, leaving them

---

[32] Norman Stone, *The Eastern Front, 1914–1917* (New York: Charles Scribner's, 1975), p. 172.
[33] George M. Nekrasov, *Expendable Glory: A Russian Battleship in the Baltic, 1915–1917* (Boulder, CO: East European Monographs, 2004), pp. 41, 43.

closer to the Baltic via the Kiel Canal in case of emergency.[34] Like de Robeck's planned thrust through the Dardanelles to appear off Constantinople, Schmidt's incursion into the Gulf of Riga was based on the premise that the mere appearance of a powerful fleet off the targeted city would suffice to produce the desired result, in this case, a Russian evacuation of Riga, rendering unnecessary an assault from the land side by the army, which in any event did not have a sufficient number of troops on hand to accomplish the task. Schmidt's attack on Riga, like de Robeck's attempt to force the Dardanelles, hinged on minesweepers clearing the way for the battleships, in this case through the heavily mined Irben Straits. The German plan also included the mining, from the south or gulf side, of the northern (Moon Sound) passage into the gulf; unaware that the Russians had not yet completed the dredging of Moon Sound to allow the passage of battleships, the Germans considered this step crucial to the success of the overall operation against the threat of significant Russian reinforcements entering the gulf from the north. The plan also called for blockships to be sunk in the harbor of Pernau (Pärnu), the gulf's second largest port.[35]

Schmidt's minesweepers began their work in the Irben Straits at 03:50 on the morning of August 8, with the plan calling for them to complete their task in three hours, enabling the minelayer *Deutschland* to enter the Gulf of Riga, cross it to the mouth of the northern passage, and sow mines there shortly after noon. But the sweeping was still underway at 10:30, when Viazemsky brought the *Slava* out into the Irben Straits, where it exchanged shots with Schmidt's pre-dreadnoughts *Elsass* and *Braunschweig* at a range of 17,500 yards (16,000 m) before retiring. The minesweepers took six hours to clear a channel 550 yards (500 m) wide through the westernmost band of mines, only to encounter another minefield 2 miles (3.2 km) into the straits. Mines had claimed two of the minesweepers by 13:45, when Schmidt called off the operation for that day. Schmidt sent his ships to Windau and Libau to coal, and by the time they reappeared at the mouth of the Irben Straits on August 10, the Russians had re-laid the minefields. German activity on that day was limited to the armored cruisers *Roon* and *Prinz Heinrich* shelling a Russian airfield and wireless station on Ösel Island, while Hipper sent the *Von der Tann* and a

---

[34] Scheer, *Germany's High Sea Fleet*, p. 91.
[35] Bengelsdorf, *Der Seekrieg in der Ostsee*, p. 69.

light cruiser all the way to the coast of Finland, where they shelled a battery at Utö.[36]

Schmidt tried to run the Irben Straits a second time on August 16, starting at 04:00, this time with a force led by the dreadnoughts *Nassau* and *Posen*. Hipper remained outside in the Baltic with his three battle cruisers, the other six dreadnoughts, and the two newest pre-dreadnoughts, while the remaining five older battleships stood by at Libau. The minesweeping again took longer than expected, especially since the Russians had laid fresh mines to replace those swept on August 8, and was again disrupted by the *Slava*, which Viazemsky brought out shortly after noon. Schmidt broke off the minesweeping operation at 17:00 and that evening sent two destroyers into the gulf to torpedo the *Slava*, but they lost their way in the dark and failed to find their target. Around 07:40 on the morning of August 17, the *Nassau* and *Posen* dueled with the *Slava* in the Irben Straits, this time scoring three hits at a range of 17,800 yards (16,300 m), forcing Viazemsky to withdraw. This exchange sufficed to cow the Russians, who did nothing to disturb German minesweeping operations over the next two days. By August 19 a path had been cleared and the dreadnoughts entered the Gulf of Riga; that evening at 17:30 the *Deutschland*, escorted by a light cruiser, finally reached the mouth of the northern passage and began to sow its mines, only to be driven off within 30 minutes by a vigorous attack by Russian destroyers. That evening and into the night, the *Nassau*, *Posen*, and lighter warships Schmidt had sent into the Gulf of Riga skirmished with Russian units. The following day, the Germans carried out their plan to sink blockships at Pernau, but fresh minefields laid off the mouth of the River Dvina deterred them from closing to shell Riga. Ultimately an incident outside the gulf prompted Schmidt to end the operation and order a general withdrawal: on the morning of August 19, west of Dagö Island, the British submarine *E 1* (Lieutenant Commander Noel Laurence) torpedoed the *Moltke*. The battle cruiser took on only 450 tons of water and withdrew under its own power, ultimately transiting the Kiel Canal to go into dry-dock in Hamburg; nevertheless, the attack called into question the German decision to expose so many capital ships to the risks posed by mines and submarines, in an operation that appeared increasingly unlikely to succeed. The *Nassau*, *Posen*, and the rest of the German ships left

---

[36] *Ibid.*, pp. 70–73.

the gulf on the afternoon of August 20, without engaging the Russians further. Overall, the action in and around the Gulf of Riga between August 8 and August 19 cost the Germans two destroyers and three minesweepers, while the Russians lost two gunboats.[37]

The naval operation against the Gulf of Riga failed because it had not been sufficiently coordinated with the army's advance on the city of Riga. Indeed, throughout the German offensive of the spring and summer of 1915, genuine cooperation between the navy and the army had been limited to the shelling by warships that helped prepare the way for troops to take Libau and Windau, both of which were peripheral to the army's main objective. The elimination of the Polish salient, which enabled the Central Powers to cover the Eastern front with far fewer troops, likewise enabled the Russians to bolster the defenses on their side of the newly shortened lines. While Prince Henry refused to call the operation a failure, seeing a moral or psychological victory in Schmidt's ultimate success in clearing the Irben Straits and deploying dreadnoughts into the gulf, Hipper and the rest of the admirals thought nothing had been gained.[38] They were not keen to try again, either, at least not until the army was willing to make Riga a priority and allocate the manpower necessary to take it, including troops for the navy to land on Ösel and Dagö islands, which had to be occupied in order for the gulf to be secured.[39] The Baltic phase of the 1915 offensive of the Central Powers ended with the Germans in possession of the western half of Latvia, with the coastal terminus of the front fluctuating between the towns of Kemeri (Kemmern) and Tukums, 27–37 miles (44–59 km) west of Riga; to the south of the city, on the left (south) bank of the Dvina, the front stood within 10 miles (16 km) of Riga at one point. During the operation in the Gulf of Riga, the Tenth Army took Kovno on August 18 before pushing on to take Vilna on September 19, leaving all of Lithuania in German hands. Meanwhile, farther south, the Eighth Army took Grodno on September 3. The offensive left the Central Powers in possession of all of Poland as well, and contracted the Eastern front to around 800 miles (1,280 km) in length, along a line extending from the coast just west of Riga, along the Dvina into

---

[37] Nekrasov, *Expendable Glory*, pp. 49–54; Bengelsdorf, *Der Seekrieg in der Ostsee*, pp. 73–79; Scheer, *Germany's High Sea Fleet*, p. 92.
[38] Halpern, *A Naval History of World War I*, p. 198.
[39] Bengelsdorf, *Der Seekrieg in der Ostsee*, p. 85.

eastern Latvia, then south to Czernowitz (Chernovtsy), the capital of the Austrian province of Bukovina, bordering neutral Romania.[40]

Following the German failure at Riga, the dreadnoughts and battle cruisers deployed to the Baltic all returned to the North Sea, not to return for two years, when the High Command, by then under Hindenburg and Ludendorff, finally put sufficient resources behind taking the city and securing the gulf. After the German capital ships withdrew, the Russians became less cautious with their own dreadnoughts, repeatedly sending them in pairs as far south as the waters off Gotland to cover minelaying. Additional layers of minefields soon stretched from the southwestern tip of Finland due south to Dagö Island, across the narrow passage separating it from Ösel Island, and across the Irben Straits separating Ösel from the Latvian mainland, formidable defenses that gave the Russians a secure coastal route to resupply and reinforce the front at Riga directly from Petrograd. At the same time, the British strengthened the Allied hand in the open Baltic by sending more submarines.

These formidable mine and torpedo threats claimed the two largest German warships lost in the theater during the rest of 1915: the armored cruiser *Prinz Adalbert*, torpedoed by *E 8* (Lieutenant Commander F. H. J. Goodhart) off Libau on October 23 (672 dead), and the light cruiser *Bremen*, mined off Windau on December 16 (250 dead).[41] With no German capital ships or pre-dreadnoughts to challenge it, during the autumn months the *Slava* became the source of the most robust fire support provided by any warship in the Riga campaign, repeatedly shelling German positions west of Riga, though it was not entirely unmolested as it did so, as a bomb dropped by a German airplane hit the ship's bridge during a bombardment on September 25, killing Viazemsky and most of his staff.[42] Captain Aleksandr Kolchak, temporarily in charge of the naval forces in the gulf during the autumn, subsequently orchestrated the landing of 536 troops on October 22 at the village of Petragge, near Cape Domesnes at the eastern end of the Irben Straits, over 70 miles (110 km) behind the German lines. Kolchak later said of the landing party that "we were compelled to withdraw it quickly, as it was too negligible; but in any case, it produced a panic

---

[40] Sondhaus, *World War I*, pp. 146, 148.
[41] Gröner, *Die deutschen Kriegsschiffe*, vol. 1, pp. 78, 131.
[42] Nekrasov, *Expendable Glory*, pp. 59–61.

Figure 6.4 Captain (later Admiral) Aleksandr Kolchak

among the Germans."[43] Ironically, Russia's "Petragge Raid" was the only amphibious landing carried out in the Gulf of Riga during 1915.

## Conclusion

The battles of 1915 at the Dardanelles and Gallipoli and at Riga are difficult to analyze as early attempts at combined operations because, like so many actions in the Great War, they evolved while underway, with the decision-makers on each side reacting to circumstances in an era of new and rapidly changing technologies and tactics. Indeed, as

---

[43] Ibid., p. 61; Aleksandr Vasiliyevich Kolchak *et al.*, *The Testimony of Kolchak and Other Siberian Materials* (Palo Alto, CA: Stanford University Press, 1935), p. 32.

early as the Second World War large-scale engagements rarely had the ad hoc character typical of the campaigns of 1914–18. Thus, especially for combined operations, the importance of inter-service planning (along with inter-allied planning, where applicable) ranks first among the lessons learned from these experiences. Particularly in the case of Gallipoli, the impulse to place blame failed to take into account that the operation featured countless examples of the trial-and-error warfare typical of the war as a whole. No one had ever attempted to land so many troops on the beaches of an actively defended shoreline, at least not since industrialization had revolutionized weaponry. Minus the steamers towing the longboats, the landings more resembled British amphibious operations in the Napoleonic Wars than the various Allied landings conducted just a generation later, during the Second World War. When it came to tactics, commanders at sea as well as on land often were making it up as they went along.

In both cases, meaningful inter-service planning well in advance of operations simply did not take place. Churchill conceived of the Dardanelles as a naval operation and Carden designed it as such, with a plan involving a significant degree of inter-allied same-service cooperation between the British and French navies; only after the failure of the initial naval operations were all parties involved persuaded of the need to land troops. The quest to take Riga, in contrast, was viewed by the German High Command and by Hindenburg's and Ludendorff's *OberOst* as a land campaign like any other, with the naval role limited to fire support (by cruisers rather than battleships) when the beach flank of the advancing front reached a port city or town. Such reasoning worked well enough at Libau and Windau, but did not hold when the front approached Riga, a much larger port city that the Russians were determined not to lose. Only after the army's advance stalled did German leaders acknowledge that naval power was indispensable to achieving the objective.

As an obstacle to be transited, the Irben Straits were roughly the same length as the Dardanelles, but much wider and with no traditional fortifications along the shores. Because German troops had already taken the south shore of the straits by the time the navy arrived, the attacking ships faced hostile fire only from Ösel Island, where the Russian batteries were far weaker than the artillery mounted in the Turkish forts along the Dardanelles. Coincidentally, in each case the naval forces deployed by the attackers included eighteen capital ships or battleships.

At the Dardanelles, the core of the Allied force consisted of one dreadnought, one battle cruiser, and sixteen pre-dreadnoughts, all of which went into the straits. For the Riga operation, the Germans deployed eight dreadnoughts, three battle cruisers, and seven pre-dreadnoughts, of which just two dreadnoughts and two pre-dreadnoughts went into the straits, not on the same day; in the case of Riga, however, the bulk of the naval force was sent in the first place to deter the dreadnoughts of the Russian Baltic Fleet from compromising the operation from outside the straits, a factor that did not exist at the Dardanelles, where the Aegean and eastern Mediterranean were secure for the Allies, except for the U-boat threat. The Germans, of course, succeeded where the Allies had failed at the Dardanelles in actually sweeping the minefields of the Irben Straits and entering the Gulf of Riga, only to find that additional minefields laid off the port and elsewhere in the gulf, combined with tenacious and determined resistance from the hodgepodge flotilla they faced, prevented their big ships from playing their intended role in achieving the objective. Ultimately, in both cases, damage to a battle cruiser (the mining of the *Inflexible* in the Dardanelles, and the torpedoing of the *Moltke* outside the Irben Straits) triggered the decision to call off the attack, at least to the extent that the potential loss of a modern capital ship caused a reappraisal of the cost and benefit of continuing the operation.

The Great War afforded just one further opportunity for the combined operations lessons of 1915 to be applied on a large scale, when the Germans took Riga in 1917 (see Chapter 9), but the premium subsequently placed on meticulous planning for operations against coastal targets was also reflected in the British navy's unsuccessful raids on Ostend and Zeebrugge in 1918 (see Chapter 10). Amphibious warfare innovations, such as purpose-built landing craft, would have to wait until the Second World War, by which time minesweeping operations as a prerequisite for combined operations were taken for granted because they had become so professionalized, extensive, and commonplace; for example, the work of a host of British and Canadian boats in sweeping the Channel of mines before the Normandy landings of June 1944, which usually goes unacknowledged in D-Day histories. In wars to come, more sophisticated mines required more sophisticated tactics for neutralizing them, but from a tactical perspective they would remain the weaker party's best bet for coastal defense against a stronger naval power attempting amphibious operations, as witnessed in their use in the Persian Gulf by Saddam Hussein's Iraq against the United States in 1991 and again in 2003. Just as future practitioners of combined operations could learn much from studying the Allied and German failures of 1915, those seeking to foil such attacks could profit by emulating the mine-based defensive operations of the Turks in the Dardanelles and the Russians in the Gulf of Riga.

# 7  THE YEAR OF JUTLAND: GERMANY'S FLEET SORTIES, 1916

"There seems to be something wrong with our bloody ships today," Vice Admiral David Beatty remarked to Captain Ernle Chatfield, as they stood on the bridge of HMS *Lion*, flagship of the Battle Cruiser Fleet.[1] It was 16:26 on the afternoon of May 31, 1916, and the British and German navies had finally met, roughly 100 miles (160 km) west of Denmark's Jutland peninsula, in the fleet-scale battle both had anticipated for nearly two years. The sortie by the German High Sea Fleet, now under the command of Vice Admiral Reinhard Scheer, had begun in the predawn hours of that morning, marking the third of six times between March and November 1916 that it would attempt to challenge the British Grand Fleet. Jutland was the biggest battle any German fleet would ever fight, and for the British, the biggest and most important since Trafalgar in 1805. From the Grand Fleet commander, Admiral Jellicoe, to Beatty, the squadron and ship commanders, and down to the lowliest ensign, the British naval officer corps entered the battle fully expecting a triumph as decisive as Lord Nelson's victory over the Franco-Spanish fleet 111 years earlier. But two hours into the engagement things were not going well. Indeed, Beatty's incredulous remark to Chatfield came in reaction to seeing the battle cruiser *Queen Mary* explode after being struck by a German salvo, 24 minutes after the battle cruiser *Indefatigable* had met the same fate. The Germans sank a third British battle cruiser, the *Invincible*, later in the afternoon,

---

[1] Ernle Chatfield, *The Navy and Defence: The Autobiography of Admiral of the Fleet Lord Chatfield*, 2 vols. (London: Heinemann, 1942–47), vol. 1, p. 143.

and would not lose a capital ship of their own until the predawn hours of the following day, during Scheer's withdrawal to Wilhelmshaven.

The chain of events that led to the greatest battle of the Great War at sea began nearly five months earlier, with an unanticipated change of leadership in the High Sea Fleet. On January 8, 1916, Admiral Hugo von Pohl, appointed commander just eleven months earlier, following the German defeat at Dogger Bank, fell seriously ill and had to be taken from his flagship to hospital. Specialists in Berlin soon confirmed that the 60-year-old admiral had cancer of the liver, and in late February he died. As soon as he fell ill, Pohl's command passed to Vice Admiral Scheer on an interim basis; on January 18, after it became clear that Pohl's illness was terminal, William II removed the interim designation and made the appointment permanent.[2] This fateful turn of events had profound consequences. Scheer, just eight years younger than Pohl but far more energetic, assumed his new duties determined to end the High Sea Fleet's general inactivity of the past year. He had spent the entire war with the fleet and knew it well, having served as commander of a pre-dreadnought squadron under Ingenohl before being upgraded to a dreadnought squadron under Pohl. He soon persuaded William II to allow a return to the strategy pursued before the defeat at Dogger Bank, in which Hipper's battle cruisers would be used to bait a portion of the British Grand Fleet into battle with the main body of the High Sea Fleet. Unlike Ingenohl during the Dogger Bank action, Scheer intended to place the German dreadnoughts in a position to intervene quickly once a battle developed.

## Scheer and the spring sorties

Scheer's appointment came a full year after Tirpitz concluded that the High Sea Fleet's window of opportunity for victory had closed once the concentration of British capital ships in home waters, plus a greater number of new units commissioned early in the war, had left Britain with far better than a 3:2 ratio of superiority over Germany in dreadnoughts and battle cruisers. The calculus had not improved between January 1915 and January 1916; indeed, Britain now had thirty-seven capital ships (twenty-seven dreadnoughts and ten battle cruisers), all

[2] Scheer, *Germany's High Sea Fleet*, pp. 94–95.

Figure 7.1 Vice Admiral Reinhard Scheer

with the Grand Fleet at its North Sea bases, against which Germany could muster just twenty-one (seventeen dreadnoughts and four battle cruisers). Yet Scheer's fundamental motivation for steering a more active course was no different from that which Tirpitz had articulated earlier: a need to demonstrate "the utility of our High Sea Fleet" in order "to justify its existence and the vast sums exacted... for its maintenance."[3]

The program devised by Scheer and his staff called for the island of Helgoland, 70 miles (112 km) north of Wilhelmshaven, to be a defensive hub rather than an outpost, at the center of a great arc stretching from the Dutch barrier island of Terschelling to the Danish coast of Jutland at Horns Reef. The new perimeter at long

[3] *Ibid.*, p. 97.

last addressed the perennial (though far-fetched) German fear, dating from the early years the prewar naval buildup, of a surprise attack by the British fleet destroying the German fleet at anchor. On a more practical level, it created a secure area behind which the squadrons of the High Sea Fleet could be organized for sorties in relative security from British submarines. Fresh minefields were laid and aggressive torpedo flotilla patrols instituted to secure this perimeter, while more formidable minesweeping forces were deployed to clear British mines sown in the North Sea beyond it. Meanwhile, to provoke the Grand Fleet (or at least part of it) into venturing southward from the safety of its bases at Scapa Flow, Cromarty, and Rosyth, the coastal bombardments of southeastern England would resume. The Naval Airship Division (*Marine-Luftschiff-Abteilung*), which had entered the war with just one zeppelin, had operated a total of nineteen since then, twelve of which remained available for raids against inland as well as coastal targets. Scheer also planned to use submarines in conjunction with fleet operations, especially a new U-boat flotilla based in occupied Flanders. Thanks to a new general code (AFB) introduced early in 1916, German naval communications promised to be more secure than they had been since the first months of the war. And at least the newest (*Kaiser*- and *König*-class) dreadnoughts, late in 1915, had been fitted with new range-finders, further enhancing their firepower.[4]

The opening blow of the new German offensive against Britain came in the air rather than at sea, in a raid by nine zeppelins conducted on the night of January 31/February 1. Eight of the airships returned home safely, their captains reporting that they had bombed Liverpool and the industrial centers of the Midlands, though the evidence on the ground (61 civilians killed and 101 injured, roughly half of them in Tipton and Wednesbury) indicated that the Germans had mistaken smaller towns for large cities.[5] Like previous airship actions the raid caused more alarm than damage, but afterward German reconnaissance noticed the British deploying more small vessels to Dogger Bank, which Scheer suspected were to serve as a distant early warning cordon against further zeppelin raids. Most turned out to be minesweepers sent to counter the more aggressive minelaying operations on the

---

[4] *Ibid.*, pp. 94, 98–103; Headrick, *The Invisible Weapon*, p. 163.

[5] Scheer, *Germany's High Sea Fleet*, p. 105; Tom Morgan, "The Great Zeppelin Raid, 31 January 1916," available at: http://net.lib.byu.edu/estu/wwi/memoir/zeppelin.html; "Damage in the Raid," *The Times*, February 5, 1916.

new German defensive perimeter that, at the northwestern edge of its arc, extended into the central North Sea. In any event, on the night of February 10/11 Scheer targeted these vessels in a sweep conducted by Captain Johannes Hartog with three torpedo flotillas (twenty-five small destroyers) from the High Sea Fleet. They made contact with four British warships initially mistaken for light cruisers, which turned out to be much smaller (1,270-ton) minesweeping sloops. Hartog's vessels sank one of the sloops, the *Arabis* (fifty-six dead), and dispersed the rest before returning to Wilhelmshaven. This skirmish, called the Second Battle of Dogger Bank in some histories, hardly warranted the title; indeed, it was most significant because the British navy misread the German destroyer sweep as the prelude to a sortie by the High Sea Fleet and responded in force. Jellicoe's dreadnoughts and Beatty's battle cruisers raised steam at Scapa Flow and Rosyth, and by the evening of February 11 had effected a rendezvous halfway between the Firth of Forth and Dogger Bank, about 100 miles (160 km) from where the German flotillas had been reported. Tyrwhitt's light cruisers and destroyers also came up from Harwich. Once it became clear that Scheer's capital ships were not coming out, they all returned to their respective ports, but not before the British lost a second ship. On February 12, on the return voyage to Harwich, Tyrwhitt's flagship *Arethusa* sank after striking a mine sown by one of the U-boats based in Flanders; all but a dozen of its crew were saved.[6]

For the first sortie by the High Sea Fleet, on March 5–6, Scheer's plan called for Hipper's battle cruisers to steam westward from Wilhelmshaven, near the coast as far as Terschelling, then southwestward to attack patrolling units of the Harwich force in the eastern approach to the Channel. To further provoke the Grand Fleet into coming out, the sortie was coordinated with a raid on Hull by two zeppelins conducted the night before (March 4/5). The four German battle cruisers were accompanied by the destroyers of two torpedo flotillas, with additional support from a dozen U-boats deployed from Flanders. Scheer followed Hipper at a distance of 30 miles (48 km) with the flagship *Friedrich der Grosse* and the navy's remaining sixteen dreadnoughts, escorted by additional destroyer flotillas; on this occasion he left behind the II Squadron, Germany's six newest pre-dreadnoughts, which remained at

---

[6] Scheer, *Germany's High Sea Fleet*, p. 107; Jellicoe, *The Grand Fleet*, pp. 269–270; Halpern, *A Naval History of World War I*, p. 311.

Figure 7.2 German dreadnought *Friedrich der Grosse*

the ready in Helgoland Bight. The entire fleet cleared the bar well before dawn, and Hipper reached Terschelling at 07:00 on March 5 just as the airships passed overhead on their flight home, but to Scheer's surprise, and "in spite of good visibility," the sortie brought "no encounter with the enemy." The commander treated the operation as "an occasion for different exercises in maneuvering the fleet in fighting formation," before the appearance of British submarines prompted a return to Wilhelmshaven on March 6. During these same days the Grand Fleet also sortied, but north of Dogger Bank. On March 5, Jellicoe sent out the seven pre-dreadnoughts of the III Battle Squadron (the *King Edward VII* class, minus the lead ship, which had been lost to a mine in January), then followed with the rest of the fleet on March 6, before all returned to their bases on March 7.[7]

Scheer's second fleet sortie, on April 24–25, retraced the route of the first, but with Hipper's battle cruisers steaming all the way to the southeastern coast of England to bombard the towns of Great Yarmouth and Lowestoft, in the hope of provoking a response by the

---

[7] Scheer, *Germany's High Sea Fleet*, pp. 113–117, quoted at p. 117; Jellicoe, *The Grand Fleet*, pp. 275–276.

Grand Fleet. Great Yarmouth, undamaged in the German navy's first attempt at coastal bombardment (November 3, 1914), was home to a British submarine base, while Lowestoft, on the Suffolk coast, 9 miles (14 km) to the south, hosted a detachment of minesweepers. Once again, Scheer coordinated his sortie with an air attack, this time by eight zeppelins departing with (rather than ahead of) the fleet. The German battle cruisers – now five in number, with the addition of the newly commissioned *Lützow* – were accompanied by six light cruisers and two flotillas of destroyers, as before with additional support from the U-boats stationed in Flanders. Scheer followed this more robust striking force with the rest of the High Sea Fleet, including the six pre-dreadnoughts of the II Squadron. The operation began at 12:00 on April 24, with the goal of having the battle cruisers off Great Yarmouth and Lowestoft at dawn on the 25th. Just four hours out of Wilhelmshaven, the battle cruiser force was reduced to four when the lead ship in the German column, Hipper's flagship *Seydlitz*, struck a mine off the Dutch coast, took on water at the bow, and had to return home, escorted by a zeppelin and two destroyers. Hipper transferred his flag to the *Lützow*, and the sortie proceeded as planned. In the immediate predawn hours of April 25, six of the zeppelins bombed Harwich, Norwich, Lincoln, and Ipswich; Hipper's battle cruisers followed with their bombardments, starting at Lowestoft at 05:00 (04:00 GMT) and finishing at Great Yarmouth at 06:00. The raiders were challenged off Lowestoft by Tyrwhitt with a detachment of four light cruisers and a dozen destroyers from the Harwich force, which fled back to the south as soon as they recognized that the attacking force included battle cruisers. One of the cruisers, HMS *Conquest*, survived a direct hit from one of Hipper's ships. After shelling the two ports, Hipper's squadron rejoined the main body of the High Sea Fleet nearer the Dutch coast, west of Terschelling, but when no British surface forces challenged them, and submarines appeared to shadow his movements, Scheer took his ships home.[8]

The attack, indeed, provoked a British response, but too late to bring about a battle. Jellicoe had just taken the Grand Fleet out on a sortie of his own from April 21 to April 24, steaming across the North Sea all the way to Horns Reef on the Jutland coast before heavy fog (in which the battle cruisers *New Zealand* and *Australia* collided, badly

---

[8] Scheer, *Germany's High Sea Fleet*, pp. 123–129.

damaging the latter) forced him back to his bases. As soon as he had returned home, intelligence that Scheer had left Wilhelmshaven in force at midday on April 24 prompted Jellicoe to put to sea again later that afternoon, as soon as his ships had refueled. Tyrwhitt's report of contact with German battle cruisers off Lowestoft, received before dawn on April 25, prompted Jellicoe to order full speed in an attempt to intercept the attackers on their homeward run. By 12:00 (11:00 GMT) on April 25 the main body of the Grand Fleet was 225 miles (360 km) south of Scapa Flow and 100 miles (160 km) due east of the Firth of Forth, with the III Battle Squadron (the *King Edward*s) 35 miles (56 km) farther to the south, the V Battle Squadron (the *Queen Elizabeth*s) 35 miles beyond them, and Beatty's Battle Cruiser Fleet even farther to the southeast, all steaming toward Terschelling. This dispersal of the British fleet, of course, would have worked to Scheer's advantage had the two forces met in battle, with Jellicoe's squadrons arriving piecemeal against a concentrated enemy, but the chase ended that afternoon, when British submarines reported the High Sea Fleet heading for Wilhelmshaven, and on April 26 the ships of the Grand Fleet returned to their bases. Jellicoe's postwar account credited Beatty with "having evidently only just barely missed cutting off the enemy from his base," but the British battle cruisers likely never drew closer than 200 miles (320 km) from the Germans at any time on April 25.[9]

Compared with the navy's December 1914 shelling of Scarborough, Hartlepool, and Whitby, and a number of zeppelin raids against major British cities since January 1915, the toll taken by the bombing and shelling of April 25, 1916, was light indeed: four civilians killed, nineteen injured. The zeppelins did little damage to the four coastal towns they attacked and on this occasion their bombs took none of the lives. Nevertheless, "owing to the alarm of the inhabitants," as Jellicoe later noted, the attack brought immediate political pressure on the Admiralty, to which the admiral responded by transferring the III Battle Squadron, the last pre-dreadnoughts serving with the Grand Fleet, to Sheerness in Kent, at the mouth of the Thames, to support the Harwich force in the event of a future attack by German capital ships.[10] The ships were expendable in part because five newly commissioned dreadnoughts of the *Queen Elizabeth* and *Royal Sovereign* classes joined the

---

[9] Jellicoe, *The Grand Fleet*, pp. 284–287, quoted at p. 287.   [10] Ibid., p. 287.

fleet between February and May 1916. Of the squadron's seven *King Edward VII*-class battleships, two were sent on to the Mediterranean, but the remaining five were joined at Sheerness by HMS *Dreadnought*, which became the squadron flagship. Thus, the ship whose construction had started the prewar international naval race was no longer with the Grand Fleet in late May, when it steamed out to meet the High Sea Fleet in the Battle of Jutland.

Four weeks before his great encounter with Scheer's fleet, Jellicoe conducted another sortie to the Jutland coast of Denmark, once again to the vicinity of Horns Reef. His ships began the operation on the afternoon of May 2, and all were at sea by daybreak on the 3rd. The force included twenty-eight dreadnoughts and seven battle cruisers, backed by armored cruisers, light cruisers, destroyer flotillas, and submarines, along with the seaplane carriers *Vindex* and *Engadine*, whose aircraft were to bomb the zeppelin base at Tondern in Schleswig, in retaliation for the recent zeppelin raids against Britain. On the morning of May 4, when the time came to launch the seaplanes, the seas were heavy enough to prevent all but one from becoming airborne, and it dropped just one bomb on Tondern, which did no damage. One airborne zeppelin, forced down by gunfire from two light cruisers, was destroyed just off the Danish coast by the deck gun of the submarine *E 31*. Overall the operation accomplished little and failed to draw out the High Sea Fleet; on the afternoon of May 4, Jellicoe ordered his ships back to their bases.[11]

Scheer's first two fleet-scale sorties of 1916 certainly showed a willingness, if not an eagerness, to fight, but the second in particular showed how unlikely it would be for all or part of the two fleets to meet somewhere off the Dutch coast as a result of a German provocation against the coast of Britain. Even if the British took the bait, the realities of fuel consumption and the submarine torpedo threat meant that Scheer could not stay out long enough for Jellicoe to steam so far south from his bases. Meanwhile, Jellicoe's own spring sorties across the North Sea to Horns Reef demonstrated that he was more comfortable seeking battle north of Dogger Bank, somewhere between his own bases and the Jutland coast of Denmark. If Scheer sortied that way, in the direction of the Skagerrak rather than the Channel, the likelihood of a battle would be much greater. On May 31, he did.

[11] *Ibid.*, pp. 288–290.

## The Battle of Jutland

After the High Sea Fleet's sortie of April 24–25, the timetable for Scheer's next operation hinged on the return to service of the *Seydlitz*, which had taken on 1,400 tons of water while limping home from being mined off the Dutch coast. The hole in the battle cruiser's hull measured almost 1,000 ft² (90 m²) and took over a month to repair. Scheer had no intention of going out again without the *Seydlitz*; during the wait, he laid plans for another operation, repeating his general strategy of March and April, to bring about a battle through a provocative attack by zeppelins and battle cruisers. This time, however, he targeted the northeastern coast of England, focusing on Sunderland, much closer to the bases of the Grand Fleet. But by May 28, when the *Seydlitz* finally rejoined the fleet, the weather had intervened to change Scheer's plans. Captain Peter Strasser, head of the Naval Airship Division, advised the admiral that prevailing wind patterns would make it impossible to send any zeppelins aloft in the direction of Britain for the next several days. Rather than wait for the weather to change, Scheer opted to send the fleet north instead of west, up the Jutland coast toward the Skagerrak.[12] His decision resulted in the only fleet-scale engagement of the war, the battle that the British called "Jutland," the Germans "Skagerrak."

The operation began at 01:00 GMT on May 31, when Hipper's battle cruisers left the Wilhelmshaven roadstead escorted by six light cruisers. In the hours that followed, Scheer's dreadnoughts crossed the bar from the harbor to the roadstead, and by dawn had joined up with the pre-dreadnoughts of the II Squadron, steaming out from their anchorage in the nearby Elbe estuary. By morning Hipper was underway some 50 miles (80 km) ahead of Scheer and the main body of the fleet. The return of the *Seydlitz* meant that the High Sea Fleet was at full strength except for the dreadnought *König Albert*, left behind because of a condenser problem. Thus, the Germans sortied with a total of sixteen dreadnoughts and five battle cruisers, supplemented by six pre-dreadnought battleships, eleven light cruisers, and sixty-one destroyers. Scheer's orders called for Hipper "to show himself off the Norwegian coast before dark [on May 31], to cruise in the Skagerrak during the night, and at noon the next day [June 1] to join up with the Main Fleet." To conceal their movements from detection for as long as

[12] Scheer, *Germany's High Sea Fleet*, pp. 129, 135.

possible, Hipper's ships, and the rest of the fleet behind them, were to steam northward parallel to, but well out of sight of, the Jutland coast. The Naval Airship Division had ten zeppelins available to support the sortie, five of which went up on the afternoon of May 31, but mist and haze rendered them useless for reconnaissance. As Scheer later noted, "neither did they see anything of their own Main Fleet, nor of the enemy, nor hear anything of the battle."[13]

The Germans, still confident in the security of their own codes, deluded themselves into believing that they could keep the British ignorant of their movements. Indeed, in his retrospective of the sorties of the spring of 1916, Scheer credited German intelligence with intercepting and deciphering British wireless messages while at the same time assuming any British intelligence of German ship movements was coming from "agents or from submarines in the North Sea."[14] But on May 29, the Admiralty's Room 40 achieved its first breakthrough in decrypting messages in the new German AFB code. Even though the British did not completely master the new code until September 1916, after an AFB codebook was recovered from the wreckage of a downed zeppelin, this capability plus decryptions of the older SKM and VB codes gave the British precise knowledge of German movements throughout the ensuing battle. On May 30, when Scheer issued the orders to the fleet to sortie, Room 40 read his signals, and British directional wireless stations subsequently confirmed that the ships of the High Sea Fleet were putting to sea. The British intelligence advantage was compromised only by a fundamental disconnect between the Admiralty's code-breakers and the commanders of the fleet; the naval staff did not always forward all Room 40's discoveries to Jellicoe and Beatty in a timely fashion, and the admirals did not always believe the intelligence they were sent. Ironically, this intra-mural British distrust mitigated the potentially devastating effects of the unfounded confidence of the Germans in the security of their own codes. As Daniel Headrick has observed, just as "the German admirals could not get themselves to believe that enemy code breakers consistently decrypted their messages," on the British side "neither Jellicoe nor Beatty... were prepared to let the results of a great battle hinge on decrypts produced by lowly civilians" in the Admiralty's Room 40.[15]

---

[13] *Ibid.*, pp. 140–141.   [14] *Ibid.*, p. 123.
[15] Headrick, *The Invisible Weapon*, p. 163.

Figure 7.3 Admiral Sir John Jellicoe

Their general skepticism of Admiralty intelligence services notwithstanding, on the evening of May 30 the British commanders acted on the evidence that Scheer was preparing a major fleet sortie and put to sea before him. At 22:30 Jellicoe left Scapa Flow with the main body of the Grand Fleet, and 30 minutes later Beatty departed Rosyth with the Battle Cruiser Fleet. Their ships included twenty-eight dreadnoughts and nine battle cruisers, every British capital ship except the recently reassigned HMS *Dreadnought*, three other dreadnoughts then fitting out or being refitted, and the battle cruiser *Australia*, still not repaired from its collision with *New Zealand* five weeks earlier. The British fleet also included eight armored cruisers, twenty-six light cruisers or flotilla leaders, seventy-eight destroyers, and one minelayer. The ships under Jellicoe's direct command included twenty-four dreadnoughts and three battle cruisers, the latter, under Rear Admiral Horace Hood, recently sent to Scapa Flow from Rosyth for gunnery practice. Before the battle Beatty's six battle cruisers were supplemented by the navy's most formidable dreadnoughts, the five *Queen Elizabeth*s, under Rear Admiral Hugh Evan-Thomas, sent to Rosyth to replace Hood's ships. The exchange, which Beatty had been lobbying for since February, had finally occurred on May 22, at which time the *Queen Elizabeth* itself went into the dock at Rosyth for maintenance, thus numbering among the dreadnoughts that would miss Jutland. Far more significant than the absence of this one powerful ship, in the days between the arrival of Evan-Thomas at Rosyth and the sortie eight days later, Beatty inexplicably never met with him or shared with him the Battle Cruiser Fleet Orders, which were much more flexible than the Grand Fleet Orders prescribed by Jellicoe.[16] The disconnect between Beatty and Evan-Thomas became evident as soon as the battle began.

As in his most recent sorties of April 21–24 and May 2–4, Jellicoe struck out across the North Sea, on a line stretching southeastward from Scapa Flow that would have brought the Grand Fleet to the Jutland coast of Denmark just north of Horns Reef had it not encountered the High Sea Fleet first.[17] Light vessels screening for Beatty and Hipper first sighted one another at 14:20 GMT on

---

[16] Brooks, *Dreadnought Gunnery*, p. 231.
[17] The accounts of the commanding admirals are available in Jellicoe, *The Grand Fleet*, pp. 304–387, and Scheer, *Germany's High Sea Fleet*, pp. 136–168. The most recent of a host of English-language accounts of the battle include: N. J. M. Campbell, *Jutland: An Analysis of the Fighting* (Annapolis, MD: Naval Institute Press, 1986); V. E. Tarrant, *Jutland: The German Perspective* (Annapolis, MD: Naval Institute Press, 1995); Keith Yates, *Flawed Victory: Jutland 1916* (Annapolis, MD: Naval Institute Press, 2000); H. W. Fawcett and G. W. W. Hooper (eds.), *The Fighting at Jutland: The Personal Experiences of Sixty Officers and Men of the British Fleet* (Annapolis, MD: Naval Institute Press, [1921] 2001); and Daniel Allen Butler, *Distant Victory: The Battle of Jutland and the Allied Triumph in the First World War* (Westport, CT: Praeger Security International, 2006). The most recent German account is Michael Epkenhans, Jörg Hillmann, and Frank Nägler, *Skagerrakschlacht: Vorgeschichte, Ereignis, Verarbeitung* (Munich: Oldenbourg, 2009). On gunnery ranges at Jutland see Sumida, "The Quest for Reach," p. 77 and *passim*. Other sources for the following paragraphs include: Andrew Gordon, *The Rules of the Game: Jutland and British Naval Command* (Annapolis, MD: Naval Institute Press, 1996), pp. 76–151, 433–499; Gröner, *Die deutschen Kriegsschiffe*, vol. 1, pp. 46, 85, 129, 137, 139–140; *Conway, 1906–1921*, pp. 13, 22, 25, 27–36, 140, 146, 148, 152, 154.

the afternoon of May 31, at 56°48′N, 5°21′E, a location just over 100 miles (160 km) west of Jutland and 110 miles south-southeast of the southern tip of Norway. Owing to their earlier start, by the time of first contact the British were farther from their bases – 350 miles (560 km) from Scapa Flow and 310 miles (500 km) from Rosyth – than the Germans, who were 210 miles (340 km) north-northwest of Wilhelmshaven. The first exchange of fire came at 14:28, between the light cruisers. At the time the two battle cruiser forces were still almost 50 miles (80 km) apart, delaying their first exchange until 15:48. After sighting the British battle cruisers, Hipper turned away to the south-southeast, running back toward Scheer in an effort to draw Beatty into a battle with the entire High Sea Fleet. At that point, Scheer was 46 miles (74 km) south of Hipper, while Jellicoe was 53 miles (85 km) northwest of Beatty. More significant was the gap that had opened up within Beatty's force as he raced to the point of contact, then began his pursuit of Hipper. Owing to a series of questionable turning maneuvers by Evan-Thomas, which recent scholarship blames on poor signals from Beatty,[18] the four *Queen Elizabeth*s, which had been steaming just 5 miles from the British battle cruisers, fell roughly 10 miles behind them. The superior speed of the battle cruisers caused the gap to widen after Beatty began to chase Hipper into the German trap.

The first phase of the battle, known to history as the "run to the south," lasted roughly 50 minutes. An officer aboard the *New Zealand*, the fifth ship in Beatty's column, remarked that the opening was "so like Battle Exercise, the way in which we and the Germans turned up on to more or less parallel courses and waited for the range to close." With a patience that "seemed very cold-blooded and mechanical," the ship's personnel "in the control position, all [were] sitting quietly at their instruments waiting for the fight to commence."[19] Steaming on parallel courses to the south-southeast, the battle cruisers in the opposing columns opened fire at distances of up to 18,500 yards (16,900 m) before settling into a duel at a range of 12,000–16,000 yards (11,000–14,600 m). In the first 12 minutes of the exchange, the Germans registered fifteen hits, the British just four. At 16:00 a shell from Hipper's flagship *Lützow* destroyed a turret on Beatty's flagship *Lion*, which

---

[18] See Gordon, *Rules of the Game*, p. 101; Brooks, *Dreadnought Gunnery*, p. 234.
[19] Fawcett and Hooper (eds.), *The Fighting at Jutland*, p. 34.

was saved from a likely explosion only because the order was given to flood the magazine underneath. The *Lützow* went on to score thirteen hits on the *Lion*; meanwhile, the *Moltke* scored nine hits on the *Tiger* within a span of just 12 minutes, taking four hits in return. The first casualty of the battle, the *Indefatigable*, sank at 16:02 (1,017 dead) after a horrific magazine explosion ignited by four shells from the *Von der Tann*, fired from a range of just under 13,500 yards (12,300 m). Evan-Thomas' *Queen Elizabeth*s, heretofore too far to Beatty's rear to score hits, at 16:08 began to fire at distances of 19,000–23,000 yards (17,400–21,000 m) from the rear of Hipper's column. Within minutes, their 15-inch (38-cm) shells had struck the *Von Der Tann* and *Moltke*, forcing both to start zigzagging to disrupt enemy targeting. At 16:26, two or three shells from the *Derfflinger* struck the battle cruiser *Queen Mary*, which exploded and sank (1,266 dead), prompting Beatty's famous remark. While just two men survived on the *Indefatigable*, which blew up immediately upon being hit, twenty survived the *Queen Mary*, which was fatally crippled by an initial explosion before being destroyed by a second one minutes later. Ernest Francis, a gunner's mate in the *Queen Mary*'s X-turret, remembered an eerie calm after the initial "big smash," during which "everything in the ship went quiet as a church." But from what he could see around him, it seemed clear that the battle cruiser could not fight on: "the floor of the turret was bulged up, and the guns were absolutely useless." Orders went out to abandon ship, and by the time the survivors reached the deck, the *Queen Mary* already "had an awful list to port." Francis recalled that even after the ship began to capsize, "there seemed to be quite a fair crowd" clinging to the hull, one of whom shouted confidently that "she will float for a long time yet." He had just managed to swim clear "when there was a big smash," another great explosion, which destroyed the sinking wreck.[20] No doubt more would have survived if they, too, had not lingered on the hull.

    Those aboard the *New Zealand* were close witnesses to the demise of both the *Indefatigable*, which was next in line astern, and the *Queen Mary*, two ships ahead. About 10 minutes after the *Queen Mary* was hit, the *New Zealand* passed within 100 yards (91.5 m) of the wreck, just before the second explosion. An officer aboard noted that "there was a blinding flash, a dull heavy roar ... followed by a few

---

[20] *Ibid.*, pp. 46–47.

seconds' silence, and then the patter of falling debris. All that was left of the *Queen Mary* was a great mushroom-shaped cloud of smoke about 600 to 800 feet high."[21] But according to the ship's navigation officer, the sobering sight did not discourage the men aboard the *New Zealand*. "In spite of the fact that they had all plainly seen the *Queen Mary* blow up, the idea of defeat did not seem to enter their heads."[22] Around 16:30, the destroyer escorts of Beatty and Hipper engaged, with each side sinking two destroyers. At this time the *Seydlitz* was hit by a British torpedo, but was not seriously damaged. At 16:38, the first of Beatty's ships sighted the main body of the High Sea Fleet steaming up from the south. Beatty promptly reversed course to the north, hoping to draw the entire German fleet onto Jellicoe's advancing force. Evan-Thomas' dreadnoughts completed the turn at 16:54, ending the opening phase of the action.

The second phase of the battle, the "run to the north," featured exchanges at a range of 17,000–21,000 yards (15,500–19,200 m). After Beatty's flagship *Lion* fired the first shots at 16:48, the 15-inch (38-cm) guns of the *Queen Elizabeth*s, now at the rear of his column, closest to the enemy, did the bulk of the damage for the British, overmatching the 11- and 12-inch (28- and 30.5 cm) guns of Hipper's battle cruisers, which now formed the vanguard of Scheer's fleet. The *Lützow*, *Derfflinger*, *Seydlitz*, and *Von der Tann* all suffered damage, the latter so severe that all its heavy gun turrets were temporarily inoperable, but they returned the favor to the two dreadnoughts bringing up the British rear, the *Warspite* and *Malaya*, the latter taking at least five hits between 17:27 and 17:35 alone. The first contact between Jellicoe's force and the Germans came at 17:36, when a light cruiser attached to Hood's Battle Cruiser Squadron (which Jellicoe had sent on ahead of the rest of his fleet) met light cruisers of Hipper's group. Just before 18:00, the German light cruisers came within range of Hood's battle cruisers; two were hit and the *Wiesbaden* completely disabled (589 dead). No capital ships were sunk during the "run to the north," but a steering problem aboard the *Warspite* forced it to withdraw from the action just as the two main fleets met. The only other British casualty was the destroyer *Nomad*, whose survivors, picked up by the Germans, provided them with confirmation that they were now in battle with the entire Grand Fleet.

[21] *Ibid.*, p. 35.   [22] *Ibid.*, p. 40.

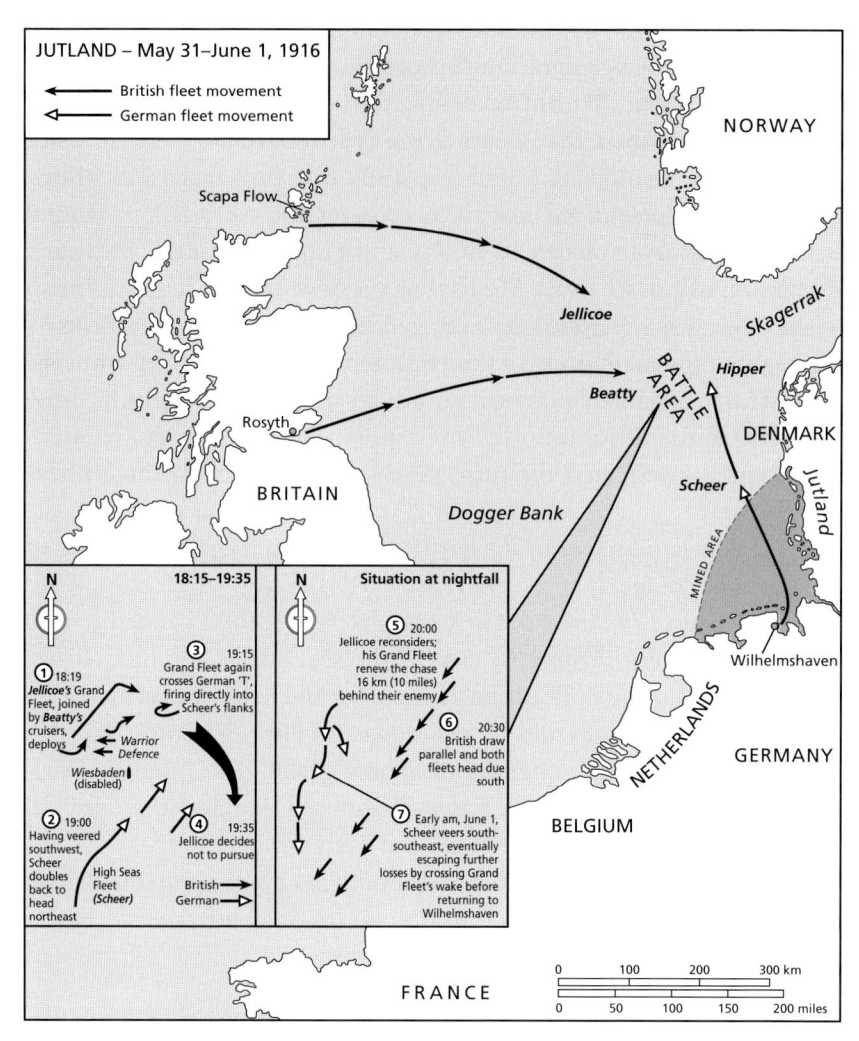

Map 7.1 Battle of Jutland

By 18:15, Evan-Thomas' remaining three *Queen Elizabeth*s had fallen into line at the rear of Jellicoe's twenty-four dreadnoughts, while Beatty's four surviving battle cruisers raced to the front of the line, where they joined Hood's three battle cruisers as the entire British force executed a crossing of the German "T," steaming eastward in an east–west line. At the onset of this phase of the battle the old armored cruisers *Defence* and *Warrior*, deployed with Beatty at the head of the column, came under heavy fire from the German capital ships while trying to finish off the stricken *Wiesbaden*. At 18:20, at a range of barely 8,000 yards (7,300 m), a shell from the *Friedrich der Grosse* ignited the magazine of the *Defence*, which exploded and sank with all hands (903 dead). The *Warrior* survived fifteen hits to be towed from the scene, only to founder and sink the next morning. Meanwhile, Hipper's battle cruisers, still heading the German column, came within 9,000 yards (8,200 m) of Hood's battle cruisers before turning away. The *Lützow* took eight hits in 8 minutes but remained in the fight, and moments later fired a salvo that landed squarely on the deck of Hood's flagship *Invincible*, blowing off one of its turrets amidships and igniting the magazine below. At 18:32, a thunderous explosion tore the ship in two, killing Hood and most of his crew (1,026 dead).[23] Because the Germans were getting the worst of it at the time, the spectacular blast drew cheers aboard many British ships on the assumption that one of Hipper's battle cruisers had been sunk. On the bridge of Beatty's *Lion*, close enough to see what had really happened, anticipation that the battle had finally turned in Britain's favor gave way to gloom.

> Just when the defeat of the enemy appeared certain, the *Invincible* was hit by a salvo ... and split in two. It happened, literally speaking, in a flash: one moment she was the flagship leading her squadron ... [which] seemed likely to annihilate the enemy battle cruisers; the next moment she was merely two sections of twisted metal, the fore end and the after end floating apart on the water.[24]

There were just six survivors.

Between 18:33 and 18:45, Scheer's entire column executed a turn-away to the southwest, covered by a smoke screen from his destroyers. At 18:57, the dreadnought *Marlborough* was hit by a torpedo, most likely fired by the disabled light cruiser *Wiesbaden*, but continued to move under its own power. The British assumed Scheer was running for Wilhelmshaven, but just before 19:00 he ordered his column to double back to the northeast. Only the badly damaged *Lützow*, abandoned by Hipper and his staff, fell out of line to continue its homeward course. Scheer subsequently gave a variety of explanations for his decision to turn back toward the enemy, none of which seem very

---

[23] An officer aboard the *Derfflinger* later claimed that his ship, next in the German line, was responsible for the sinking of the *Invincible*, which some sources place 2 minutes later, at 16:34. See Brooks, *Dreadnought Gunnery*, p. 261.

[24] Fawcett and Hooper, *The Fighting at Jutland*, pp. 385–386.

convincing to historians. Some have noted that Scheer's new course, if maintained, would have led him into the Baltic via the Skagerrak, but not before his line crossed the wake of Jellicoe's column (by this time steaming southeastward), enabling him to inflict more damage on the British.

The battle resumed around 19:05, and the ensuing fourth phase lasted some 40 minutes. By slowing his column to 15 knots, Jellicoe, not Scheer, achieved the desired crossing of the "T," as the lead ships of Scheer's column headed directly into Jellicoe's starboard flank. Within minutes the entire British line was concentrating fire on the approaching Germans. Their vanguard, once again Hipper's battle cruisers, again closed to within 9,000 yards (8,200 m) of the British line, only this time with dreadnoughts passing before them. Shells rained down on the entire front half of Scheer's column, with hits being registered as far back as the eleventh ship, the dreadnought *Helgoland*. The *Derfflinger*, heading the column, was struck by fourteen shells; among the other battle cruisers, the *Seydlitz* took five hits, the *Lützow* (not yet safely away) five, and the *Von der Tann* one. The dreadnought *Grosser Kurfürst* sustained between five and seven hits, the *Kaiser* two, the *König* and *Markgraf* one apiece. Returning fire, the Germans managed just two hits against the British line, both on the dreadnought *Colossus*. At 19:13, in the thick of the fight, Scheer ordered the German battle cruisers to sacrifice themselves against Jellicoe's line, but 5 minutes later he rescinded the order and his entire force again turned away, this time to the west, in considerable disarray. A destroyer flotilla covered the maneuver by launching torpedoes at the British line; none of them found their mark, but the threat forced Jellicoe to turn away to port at 19:20, leaving his ships farther to the east, opening up some distance between his fleet and the Germans, with whom he temporarily lost contact. By 19:35 all British ships had ceased firing. Scheer soon altered his course from west to southwest, then by 20:10, due south, running for home. Beatty, whose surviving battle cruisers (at the head of the British line) had steamed too far southeastward to be fully engaged in the most recent collision with the enemy, meanwhile turned southwestward, then due west, toward the Germans, imploring Jellicoe to follow with the rest of the fleet. For reasons that remain open to debate, he waited until 20:00 to do so.

The fifth and final phase of the battle began with the High Sea Fleet already enjoying a lead of 10 miles (16 km) over its pursuer, but once the Germans committed to their southward course the British closed fast. Their light cruisers sighted the German column just minutes before the sun set at 20:19, by which time Beatty was leading the British line steaming westward, into the port flank of the Germans. Between 20:18 and 20:36, in the battle's last exchange between capital ships, the battle cruisers *Princess Royal*, *Tiger*, and *New Zealand* scored as many as seven hits, their victims including the already-battered *Derfflinger* and *Seydlitz*, along with the pre-dreadnoughts *Schleswig-Holstein* and *Pommern*. Up to that point Scheer had kept the II Squadron, consisting of five pre-dreadnoughts of the *Deutschland* class and the older pre-dreadnought *Braunschweig*, out of danger at the rear of his column; now, he committed them, along with his light cruisers and destroyers, to cover the retreat of the rest of his ships. In the misty twilight, return fire from the *Schleswig-Holstein* and *Pommern* included one shell that struck the *Princess Royal*, but the Germans refused to be lured back into battle, breaking off to the southwest. As early as 20:42 Hipper's battle cruisers were once again leading Scheer's line due south. Now in full darkness, the British continued to steam southwestward until after 21:00, and were not all headed south again until 21:30. They assumed the Germans were still somewhere to their west, but starting at 21:10, Scheer had altered the course of his column to the east-southeast, back toward the Jutland coast, and did not turn south again until later in the evening. In the course of these maneuvers, most of the British fleet, for perhaps an hour, was between the Germans and Wilhelmshaven, without ever realizing it; Scheer's turn to the east-southeast took him across Jellicoe's wake as the main body of the Grand Fleet passed to the southwest.

  In the confusion that set in after dark, the cruisers and destroyers inflicted and suffered most of the damage. At 23:35, the cruiser *Southampton* torpedoed and sank the light cruiser *Frauenlob* (324 dead). Around midnight, the Germans sank two more British warships, the armored cruiser *Black Prince* (857 dead) and the flotilla leader *Tipperary* (185 dead), after they blundered into Scheer's dreadnoughts. The losses of June 1 were all German. At 00:30 the dreadnought *Posen* accidentally rammed and severely damaged the light cruiser *Elbing*. Between 02:45 and 03:00, the light cruiser *Wiesbaden* finally sank after 8 hours dead in the water, the *Elbing* was scuttled, and the Germans gave up on the *Lützow*. The crippled battle cruiser, which had been struck by at least two dozen heavy shells during the battle, remained

**Figure 7.4** The badly damaged *Seydlitz* after Jutland

underway until the burden of more than 8,300 tons of water left it riding so low at the bow that its stern and propellers were almost exposed. After its crew abandoned ship, leaving behind 115 dead, it was sent to the bottom by a torpedo from a German destroyer. Minutes later, at 03:13, a British destroyer torpedoed and sank the pre-dreadnought *Pommern* (839 dead). Before dawn another British destroyer torpedoed and disabled the light cruiser *Rostock*, which German destroyers sank after it was abandoned. Finally, the dreadnought *Ostfriesland* struck a mine at 05:20 on the final approach to Wilhelmshaven, but took on just 400 tons of water and was able to make it into port under its own power. During the long final phase of the battle, the British lost four destroyers, the Germans one. After giving up on the *Lützow*, the Germans successfully shepherded home two other battle cruisers damaged almost as badly. The *Derfflinger*, struck by twenty-one heavy shells, took on over 3,300 tons of water and slowed to a crawl, while the *Seydlitz*, recipient of twenty-two hits, took on over 5,300 tons of water, ran aground twice, and finally made Wilhelmshaven a day late, listing so heavily to port that she almost capsized before being taken in hand by salvage vessels. Early on June 1, the German navy sent aloft its remaining five available zeppelins in the hope that their reconnaissance might help the fleet make its way safely home, but a low cloud ceiling limited their usefulness; finally, by mid-morning, they were able to report that the British had headed back to their bases. Jellicoe's account confirms that after British directional wireless had indicated that the High Sea Fleet had passed the minefields and was securely behind its defense perimeter, he ordered the Grand Fleet home.

The postwar memoirs of Jellicoe and Scheer contain detailed accounts of the battle, in each case riddled with inaccuracies and omissions, but giving some indication of how history's largest and most complex naval battle to date was perceived from the bridge of the flagships *Iron Duke* and *Friedrich der Grosse*. Scheer, for example, witnessed the "powerful explosion" that destroyed the *Queen Mary*, but did not learn of the sinking of the *Invincible* and *Indefatigable* until later that evening.[25] Jellicoe, for his part, reported the "certain" sinking of two German dreadnoughts, when none had been sunk, and also believed that U-boats were actively engaged in the battle, claiming the "certain" sinking of one submarine and "probable" sinking of three others.[26] Scheer, who read Jellicoe's memoir before writing his own, confirmed that "with regard to the submarines he was totally mistaken, as none took part in the battle."[27] Indeed, the failure of the U-boats to affect the course of the action frustrated Scheer as much as the negligible role of his zeppelins, but in at least one case a German submarine's efforts paid dividends shortly after the battle. *U 75* (*Kapitänleutnant* Curt Beitzen) laid over three dozen mines off Scapa Flow just before the Grand Fleet came out, none of which did any harm to Jellicoe's ships leaving the base or returning to it after the battle, but on June 5 one of his mines claimed the 10,850-ton armored cruiser *Hampshire*, bound for Archangel, carrying Secretary of State for War Lord Kitchener on a mission to Russia. All but twelve of the 655 men aboard drowned, including Kitchener and his staff.[28]

In the Battle of Jutland, the Germans clearly inflicted more damage than they suffered, sinking the battle cruisers *Invincible*, *Indefatigable*, and *Queen Mary*, the armored cruisers *Defence*, *Warrior*, and *Black Prince*, one flotilla leader and seven destroyers, while losing the battle cruiser *Lützow*, the pre-dreadnought battleship *Pommern*, four light cruisers and five destroyers of their own. Of the warships

---

[25] Scheer, *Germany's High Sea Fleet*, p. 145.    [26] Jellicoe, *The Grand Fleet*, p. 489.
[27] Scheer, *Germany's High Sea Fleet*, p. 168.
[28] *Ibid.*, p. 200; Halpern, *A Naval History of World War I*, p. 329; *Conway, 1906–1921*, p. 12.

engaged at Jutland that sustained damage but survived the battle, seven British and nine German capital ships needed repairs extensive enough to require dry-docking; of these, all but one British and two German vessels were back in service within two months. Having lost so many more of their larger warships, the British suffered far higher casualties, including 6,097 dead compared with 2,551 for the Germans. Hood was the only flag officer killed in the battle. On the German side, Rear Admiral Paul Behncke, commander of the III Squadron, sustained a severe wound from a fragment of one of the shells that hit his flagship *König* and remained hospitalized for weeks afterward.

Putting aside Jellicoe's caution and Scheer's luck, explanations of the outcome of Jutland typically focus on the superior construction of the larger German warships, the unsafe handling of unstable propellants aboard the larger British warships, and inferior fire control especially on the British side. Four of the five German battle cruisers sustained heavy damage, but only the *Lützow* sank, while among the German dreadnoughts the newest units of the *König* class absorbed the most punishment (the *König* ten hits, the *Grosser Kurfürst* eight, and the *Markgraf* five), but none was seriously compromised. As for the shipboard management of propellants, the poor quality of British cordite and the lack of flash-tight doors below heavy gun turrets on the British battle cruisers are frequently cited, along with the insufficiently strict protocols for the transfer of propellants between magazines and turrets. The battle cruisers *Invincible*, *Indefatigable*, and *Queen Mary*, and the armored cruiser *Defence* all succumbed to catastrophic magazine explosions that brought instant death to most of their crews; just twenty-eight of the 3,367 men aboard the three battle cruisers survived the ships' destruction. Unfortunately for Britain, the loss of these ships did nothing to change what became, by war's end, the worst record for any navy with such explosions, even for ships at anchor. Thus, the earlier losses of the pre-dreadnought *Bulwark* at Sheerness in November 1914 (738 dead) and the cruiser *Natal* at Cromarty in December 1915 (421 dead) were followed by the explosion and sinking of the dreadnought *Vanguard* at Scapa Flow in July 1917 (804 dead) and the monitor *Glatton* at Dover in September 1918 (79 dead).

In the area of fire control, the battle touched off the debate, still ongoing today, over the prewar selection of British range-finding devices, and also raised questions over the adequacy of British gunnery training, especially for the battle cruisers; indeed, performances such as the *New Zealand*'s four hits out of 420 rounds fired defied explanation. At the same time, Jutland appeared to prove the superiority of German range-finding and vindicate German gunnery training methods. Nevertheless, among recent analyses British gunnery has its defenders.[29] At least one account finds "not much difference in gunnery performance between the fleets," and attributes the relative German success to good luck amid rapidly changing visibility. While weather conditions remained generally good throughout the battle, at times mist and haze complicated visual spotting and compromised the data being entered manually into range-finding devices. Indeed, aside from the four vessels sunk by magazine explosions, the ships of the Grand Fleet held up well enough, though in the immediate aftermath of the battle the British assumption that the Germans had better heavy-caliber shells prompted the development, by 1918, of improved shells at least for their newest capital ships, shells that remained standard through the Second World War.[30]

## The summer and autumn sorties; restricted submarine warfare

Four days after the Battle of Jutland, William II visited Wilhelmshaven to inspect the High Sea Fleet. Aboard Scheer's flagship *Friedrich der Grosse*, the emperor gave "a hearty speech of welcome to divisions drawn from the crews of all the ships, thanking them in the name of the Fatherland for their gallant deeds." The kings of Bavaria and Saxony led the list of subsequent visitors from among the crowned heads of the smaller German states, while Scheer reported that "congratulations on the success of the fleet poured in from all divisions of the army in the field, from every part of the country and from all classes of the people."[31] The German celebration of what was, at most, a tactical victory contrasted sharply with the disappointment on the other side of the North Sea. Ever since the prewar arms race the British navy, from the admirals down to the sailors and stokers, had fully expected that a fleet-scale encounter with the Germans would end in a glorious victory, a modern-day Trafalgar. While no one considered Jutland a defeat, it

---

[29] For a spirited defense of British fire control at Jutland, see Brooks, *Dreadnought Gunnery*, pp. 284–288 and *passim*.
[30] Friedman, *Naval Firepower*, pp. 110–111.
[31] Scheer, *Germany's High Sea Fleet*, pp. 175–176.

also did not feel like a victory, even though the outcome, in practical terms, was just as decisive: as one journalist put it, the prisoner may have succeeded in assaulting its jailer, but was now safely back in its cell.[32] King George V expressed his continued confidence in Jellicoe, but would not go so far as to congratulate him, instead sending the admiral a telegram blaming the weather for the missed opportunity to crush the German fleet: "I regret that the German High Sea Fleet in spite of its heavy losses was enabled by the misty weather to evade the full consequences of the encounter they have always professed to desire, but for which when the opportunity arrived they showed no inclination."[33] Jellicoe echoed the same theme in his own post-battle message to the fleet: "Weather conditions of a highly unfavourable nature robbed the fleet of that complete victory which I know was expected by all ranks."[34]

Scheer did not send his full, formal account of the battle to William II until July 4, by which time the reality of how little had been accomplished had set in. In the preamble to his concluding remarks, he argued that "the far-reaching heavy artillery of the great battleships was the deciding factor, and caused the greater part of the enemy's losses... The big ship – battleship and battle cruiser – is therefore, and will be, the main strength of naval power. It must be further developed by increasing the gun calibre, by raising the speed, and by perfecting the armor." But Scheer followed this vigorous defense of the battle fleet built under the Tirpitz plan with a telling rejection of the strategic premise for building it, admitting that "even the most successful result from a high sea battle will not compel England to make peace." Like Tirpitz a year and a half earlier, Scheer had come round to the view that the only hope for victory at sea lay in a U-boat war against British commerce. Thus, he advocated a resumption of unrestricted submarine warfare, pursued this time "with the greatest severity." But until the navy had the means and the mandate to wage such a campaign, Scheer planned to continue regular sorties with the surface fleet. For lack of a better strategy, he persisted with the concept of leading with his battle cruisers, followed by the rest of the fleet, hoping

[32] Roger Chickering, *Imperial Germany and the Great War, 1914–1918* (Cambridge University Press, 1998), pp. 91–92.
[33] George V to Jellicoe, June 3, 1916, text in Jellicoe, *The Grand Fleet*, p. 388.
[34] Jellicoe, Memorandum to the Grand Fleet, June 4, 1916, text in Jellicoe, *The Grand Fleet*, p. 412.

to provoke a British response that would enable him to engage part of Jellicoe's fleet with all of his own. The only difference was that he hoped to make better use of submarines in conjunction with these future sorties.[35]

Scheer made good on his promise to the emperor, included in the same report, that "by the middle of August the High Sea Fleet ... will be ready for fresh action."[36] By then, the refitting of the *König Albert* and the commissioning of the new *Bayern* left him with eighteen dreadnoughts, supplemented by the *Moltke* and *Von der Tann*, the only German battle cruisers not still in dry-dock. Rather than devise something new, Scheer revised his plan for the raid on Sunderland intended for late May. On August 18, at 22:00 (German Summer Time, 20:00 GMT), the fleet left the Wilhelmshaven roadstead and struck out on a westnorthwest course leading some 400 miles (640 km) across Dogger Bank to the northeastern coast of England, on a timetable for Hipper's lead ships to shell Sunderland at dusk on August 19. As substitutes for the absent battle cruisers, Scheer gave Hipper the *Bayern* and the *König*-class dreadnoughts *Grosser Kurfürst* and *Markgraf*, and followed behind with the remaining fifteen dreadnoughts. This time he kept the main body of the fleet just 20 miles (32 km) behind Hipper's advance group "to ensure immediate tactical co-operation in the event of our meeting the enemy," which he considered more likely this time because Sunderland was so much closer to Rosyth and Scapa Flow than the targets of the previous raids. As in the March sortie, Scheer left behind the pre-dreadnoughts of the II Squadron and, as in April, the zeppelins (eight, this time) went aloft to accompany the fleet rather than bomb British coastal towns ahead of it. The main difference came in Scheer's inclusion of two lines of U-boats directed by a submarine officer aboard one of his battleships, which were to protect the port and starboard flanks of the German column on the outbound voyage, then deploy to ambush pursuing British capital ships when the High Sea Fleet made for home under cover of darkness following the shelling of Sunderland.[37]

At least initially the plan appeared to be working to perfection. Scheer felt more comfortable being just 20 miles behind Hipper, indeed, so close that "the smoke of the cruisers was visible all the time." The

---

[35] Scheer, *Germany's High Sea Fleet*, pp. 167–169.
[36] Ibid., p. 169.   [37] Ibid., pp. 180–181.

submarine pickets provided him with intelligence and also claimed two of the British light cruisers sent out to monitor his advance: the *Nottingham*, torpedoed and sunk by *U 52* at 09:10 (07:10 GMT) on the morning of August 19, and the *Falmouth*, torpedoed by *U 66* that afternoon (and finished off the following day by *U 63*, while being towed back to port). Just after 07:00 (05:00 GMT) on August 19, the British submarine *E 23* torpedoed the last dreadnought in the German line, the *Westfalen*, causing damage significant enough to force its return to Wilhelmshaven, but Scheer pressed on with the rest of his ships. The navy's cryptography center at Neumünster provided evidence that the sortie had provoked a considerable response, and by the early afternoon of the 19th Scheer's U-boats and zeppelins had also reported British forces of various sizes approaching from the south as well as the north. Jellicoe, acting on intelligence that the High Sea Fleet was coming out, had brought the Grand Fleet out for a southward sweep of the North Sea the previous day, and Tyrwhitt's Harwich force had also put to sea. Unfortunately for the Germans, summer thunderstorms intervened to punctuate an otherwise clear day, disrupting the intelligence flow from the airships, while reports from the U-boats grew too inconsistent to be considered reliable. Scheer later recalled his frustration that "from all the information received, no coherent idea of the countermeasures of the enemy could be formed." Finally, just after 14:20, he ordered Hipper to fall back on the main body of the fleet so that all of them could alter course to the southeast, to meet what seemed to be a significant British force coming up from the south, from the direction of Harwich and Sheerness. Ironically, had Scheer continued on his intended course toward Sunderland, he would have run right into Jellicoe, who calculated that at one point the two fleets were just 42 miles (68 km) apart. But two hours on his new course brought no contact with British warships, and at the same time left the High Sea Fleet too far from Sunderland to make landfall there at sunset, as planned. At 16:35, Scheer again altered course, this time to the east-southeast, to return to Wilhelmshaven. By 18:00 (16:00 GMT) Jellicoe had Beatty break off his pursuit, and the British forces, too, returned to their bases.[38]

---

[38] Jellicoe, *The Grand Fleet*, pp. 434–440; Scheer, *Germany's High Sea Fleet*, pp. 181–184, quoted at pp. 181 and 182.

In a strategic sense the battle that did not happen on August 19 was more significant than Jutland, in that it marked the last time the Grand Fleet would be so aggressive in sweeping the North Sea in search of the High Sea Fleet. "The ease with which the enemy could lay a submarine trap for the fleet had been demonstrated on the 19th of August," Jellicoe later noted, "and risks which we could afford to run earlier in the war were now unjustifiable." The loss of the *Nottingham* and *Falmouth* prompted him to argue that, in the future, light cruisers should not be used as a screen for capital ships without, in turn, being screened by destroyers. He cited the "general agreement ... between the flag officers of the fleet and the Admiralty" that "it was unwise to take the fleet far into southern waters" unless accompanied by a far larger destroyer force than Britain then had.[39] Beatty concurred, and in a letter to Jellicoe on September 6, quoted the adage "when you are winning, risk nothing." By mid-September the two admirals had agreed not to send British dreadnoughts and battle cruisers south of 55°30′N, a line stretching across the North Sea from Newcastle to the German–Danish border.[40]

A stormy September forced the postponement of Scheer's fifth fleet sortie of 1916 until October, by which time the new chief of the army High Command, Hindenburg, and his chief of staff, Ludendorff, had been invested with sweeping powers not just over the German war effort, but over that of the other Central Powers as well, exercised in the name of William II, whom Germany's allies had agreed to accept as titular supreme allied commander. Recognizing the economic dimension of the struggle, the new leadership militarized German war industries under the "Hindenburg Program," and also authorized the resumption of restricted submarine warfare against Allied commerce, preliminary to another unrestricted campaign to be launched early in 1917. Scheer could not complain, having advocated unrestricted submarine warfare in his July memorandum to the emperor, but the change in strategy meant that U-boats would no longer be available for operations with the High Sea Fleet. His improvised strategy called for destroyers to scout the Dogger Bank area and "capture prizes," while the capital ships acted "as a support to the light craft that were sent out." As in

---

[39] Jellicoe, *The Grand Fleet*, p. 443.
[40] Beatty to Jellicoe, September 6, 1916, quoted in Halpern, *A Naval History of World War I*, p. 331.

August, Scheer had eighteen dreadnoughts and two battle cruisers at his disposal, and once again left behind the pre-dreadnoughts of the II Squadron. When the sortie finally came, on October 18–19, rough seas forced the destroyer operation to be scaled back, and it failed to provoke a response from the Grand Fleet (which, under the "risk nothing" line Jellicoe and Beatty had adopted a month earlier, would not have steamed that far south in any event). Afterward, Scheer concluded that his destroyers would be of more use against British antisubmarine defenses at the eastern approach to the Channel, and sent two of the High Sea Fleet's torpedo flotillas to Zeebrugge on the coast of Flanders, where a half-flotilla was already based. On the night of October 26/27, this combined force attacked the Dover Barrage, sinking ten drifters, two destroyers, and one transport steamer without losing any of its own ships.[41]

Scheer's sixth and final sortie of the year involved just half of his capital ships, and had the limited purpose of covering a half-flotilla of destroyers sent to rescue two U-boats stranded on the coast of Jutland, north of Horns Reef. The drama unfolded after *U 30*, on the morning of November 3, reported engine trouble while off the coast of Norway, near Bergen. The crippled boat was soon met and escorted by *U 20*, homeward bound around the northern tip of Scotland from a cruise in the Irish Sea. British naval intelligence, reading German wireless traffic, became aware of their situation during the day on November 3 and alerted Jellicoe, who dispatched light cruisers and destroyers on sweeps of the Norwegian and Danish coasts to intercept them. *U 20* accompanied *U 30* across the Skagerrak to the Danish coast, where both boats ran aground in a fog after nightfall on November 4. If the stranded U-boats were found first by the British navy, they were likely to be shelled until destroyed; if they survived intact until the following morning, to be found by Danish authorities, they would be interned with their crews for the duration of the war. *U 30* soon managed to work itself free of the sand, but was too damaged to submerge, and in any event its commander refused to leave while *U 20* remained aground. Shortly after 22:00, news of their predicament reached Wilhelmshaven, prompting Scheer to dispatch the destroyers on their rescue

---

[41] Scheer, *Germany's High Sea Fleet*, pp. 186–189, quoted at p. 187. The account of the raid of October 26–27 in Bacon, *The Dover Patrol*, vol. 2, pp. 25–30, claims six drifters were sunk, with three drifters and a trawler damaged.

mission, with a robust escort consisting of the battle cruiser *Moltke* and eight dreadnoughts.[42]

Scheer was especially concerned for *U 20*, which had torpedoed the *Lusitania* eighteen months earlier and was still commanded by the same officer, *Kapitänleutnant* Schwieger, whom the Allies considered a war criminal. The German destroyers reached the scene shortly after 07:00 on November 5, and for four hours tried to pull *U 20* free, but gave up after high tide passed with the boat still stranded. *Moltke* and the dreadnoughts continued to stand guard while Schwieger and the crew of *U 20* were rescued, *U 30* taken under tow, and *U 20* blown up by a demolition team. The operation proceeded without interruption until 13:00, just after the ships put to sea for the return voyage to Wilhelmshaven, when the British submarine *J 1* (Lieutenant Commander Noel Laurence) arrived on the scene to torpedo the dreadnoughts *Grosser Kurfürst* and *Kronprinz*. Laurence's *E 1* had torpedoed the *Moltke* in August 1915, without sinking it, but in the process had prompted the decision to end the German navy's Riga operation; on this occasion, too, neither German capital ship was badly damaged and each made it safely home under its own power, but the realization that they might have been lost for the sake of saving two submarines prompted William II to forbid Scheer to take such a risk in the future. On November 22, the admiral defended the sortie in person at an audience with the emperor, at Pless in Silesia, the German army's Eastern front headquarters, warning him that, once unrestricted submarine warfare resumed, "the fleet will have to devote itself to one task, to get the U-boats safely out to sea and bring them safely home again," thus likely necessitating similar operations in the future. Scheer concluded "every U-boat is of such importance that it is worth risking the whole available fleet to afford it assistance and support." While at Pless, Scheer had his first meetings with Hindenburg and Ludendorff at which "it was agreed that, if the war should drag on for so long, February 1, 1917, was the latest date at which to start the unrestricted U-boat campaign." The generals wanted to postpone the campaign for the moment because the Central Powers were on the verge of crushing Romania, which had just joined the Allies in August, and there was at least some hope that this turn of events might lead to peace talks. They also shared with Scheer the fears (ultimately unfounded) of Germany's

---

[42] Scheer, *Germany's High Sea Fleet*, pp. 191–192.

ambassador to The Hague that a resumption of unrestricted submarine warfare would prompt the Netherlands to join the Allies.[43]

By the time Scheer went to Pless to meet with the emperor and the generals, the resumption of restricted submarine warfare already had taken a heavy toll on Allied shipping, claiming 231,573 tons in September, 341,363 tons in October, and 326,689 tons in November. The latter figure included the largest Allied ship sunk in the war, when, on November 21, the 48,160-ton *Britannic*, sister of the *Titanic*, serving as a hospital ship, struck a mine laid by *U 73* in the Aegean Sea; because it was running empty at the time, just thirty lives were lost. German submarines went on to claim another 307,847 tons in December, then 328,391 tons in January 1917. Even though the U-boats were adhering (albeit at times only loosely) to internationally accepted prize rules, the damage inflicted was much greater than during the first round of unrestricted submarine warfare because Germany now had many more submarines in service. The total deployed German undersea force topped 100 boats early in the new year, and in the five months to the end of January they had sunk roughly twice the tonnage that had been taken in the seven months of unrestricted submarine warfare in 1915. Almost all of the damage was done by surfaced U-boats, with 80 percent of the victims warned before being sunk, and 75 percent sunk by the deck gun rather than by torpedoes. Remarkably, during these five months Germany lost just ten submarines, three of which were sunk by the Russians in the Black Sea. After Jellicoe turned over command of the Grand Fleet to Beatty on November 28, 1916, to take office as First Sea Lord, addressing Britain's dismal record in antisubmarine warfare became his top priority, entrusted to a new Anti-Submarine Division in the Admiralty. Germany's resumption of unrestricted submarine warfare soon added a greater sense of urgency to such efforts.[44]

## The war in southern European waters, 1916

The months between Jutland and the resumption of unrestricted submarine warfare were an eventful time elsewhere in the naval war,

---

[43] *Ibid.*, pp. 192–194, quoted at pp. 193 and 194; Jellicoe, *The Grand Fleet*, pp. 456–457.

[44] Halpern, *A Naval History of World War I*, pp. 335–336, 343; see also data at: www.uboat.net.

with things generally going the way of the Central Powers. The failure of Austria-Hungary's spring offensive in the Alps left the Italian front stalemated, and the rival fleets did not attempt to engage one another in the Adriatic, yet the Austrians managed to keep the Italians on their heels. On August 2, the Italian navy lost a second battleship to Austrian sabotage, the dreadnought *Leonardo da Vinci*, sunk at anchor in Taranto harbor, then on December 11 suffered the loss of the pre-dreadnought *Regina Margherita*, which fell victim to a minefield off Valona, Albania. The French navy likewise lost two battleships: the pre-dreadnought *Suffren*, torpedoed by German *U 52* off Lisbon on November 26, and the pre-dreadnought *Gaulois*, torpedoed by German *UB 47* in the Aegean on December 27. Austro-Hungarian espionage in Italy remained a valuable asset to the Central Powers in the Adriatic and beyond, but the advantage did not last long into the new year. The Italians finally traced the enemy's covert operations to the Dual Monarchy's consulate in Zurich, which their own agents raided in February 1917, securing evidence that led to the arrest of scores of Austrian agents, effectively breaking the spy network.[45]

In the Black Sea, the Russian navy spent the first half of 1916 supporting a Russian army offensive in the Caucasus. Russia's second Black Sea dreadnought, the *Imperatritsa Ekaterina Velikaya*, saw its first action in this role in February 1916, leading a group including many of the pre-dreadnoughts that had been so active in 1914 and 1915. The same month, to support the Ottoman army retreating in the face of the Russian offensive, Vice Admiral Souchon took the *Yavuz Sultan Selim* as far east as Trebizond for the first time since December 1914, joined by the *Midilli*, finally back in action after being mined in July 1915. On April 4, off Suermene Bay on the coastal flank of the Caucasus front, the *Midilli* encountered the *Imperatritsa Ekaterina Velikaya*, whose 12-inch (30.5-cm) guns far out-ranged its own 5.9-inch (15-cm) guns, and miraculously emerged unscathed after being bracketed by a salvo. Russian naval support played a role in the fall of Trebizond, which the Turks abandoned on April 18. Afterward, the Black Sea Fleet convoyed 35,000 troops to Trebizond to secure the gains, in the process losing just one small transport, the 760-ton *Merkury*, which sank on June 20 off Odessa after striking a mine laid by *UC 15*

---

[45] Sokol, *Österreich-Ungarns Seekrieg*, vol. 1, p. 467.

Zu der ruhmvollen Tätigkeit der türkischen Flotte im Schwarzen Meere:
Konteradmiral Souchon mit seinem Stabe.
(Phot. Sébah & Joaillier, Konstantinopel.)
Von links nach rechts: Türkischer Chef des Admiralstabes Fregattenkapitän
Enver-Bei (nicht zu verwechseln mit dem gleichnamigen türkischen Kriegsminister),
I. Admiralstabsoffizier Korvettenkapitän Busse, Konteradmiral Souchon, II. Admiralstabsoffizier Korvettenkapitän Büchsel, Flaggleutnant Oberleutnant z. S.
Wichelhausen, türkischer Flaggleutnant Oberleutnant z. S. Hakki.

Figure 7.5 Vice Admiral Souchon with staff

(272 dead). Despite facing an opponent that now included two dreadnoughts, Souchon remained responsive to Turkish appeals to use the *Yavuz Sultan Selim* and *Midilli* not just to convoy, but to carry troops and supplies to the front. These were risky operations, taking them farther from Constantinople than Sevastopol was from Constantinople,

and thus leaving them vulnerable to being cut off on their way home. On a homeward voyage in early July, the two warships were nearly intercepted by Vice Admiral Ebergard's superior force, including the *Imperatritsa Maria* and *Imperatritsa Ekaterina Velikaya*, waiting for them off the coast between Zonguldak and Constantinople, but Souchon managed to avoid the trap and reach base safely. Russian naval authorities used the episode as a pretext to sack Ebergard in favor of Aleksandr Kolchak. The forty-one-year-old Kolchak, a rising star within the officer corps, was already well known for his prewar exploits as an Arctic explorer and, more recently, his service in the Gulf of Riga in 1915. Promoted to rear admiral early in 1916, he received a second, extraordinary promotion to vice admiral when given command of the Black Sea Fleet.[46]

The initial success of Russia's summer offensive against Austria-Hungary, led by General Aleksei Brusilov, prompted Romania's entry into the war on the Allied side (August 27, 1916). While its army invaded Transylvania, its negligible navy was no match for the forces Souchon had based on the Bulgarian coast, at Varna and Euxinograd. Kolchak thus had to focus on the western Black Sea, and after the armies of the Central Powers counterattacked and quickly occupied most of Romania, the pre-dreadnought *Rostislav* on October 22 covered the evacuation of the main port, Constanza. Coinciding with the disappointment over Romania's poor performance in the brief campaign, on October 20 the Russian navy suffered its greatest material loss of the war when a magazine explosion sank the dreadnought *Imperatritsa Maria* at anchor in Sevastopol, killing 200 and injuring 700.[47] The demoralizing disaster came just as the Russians had begun to enjoy the benefits of their capital ship superiority in the Black Sea; afterward, they focused on replacing the lost dreadnought by accelerating work on its sister-ship, *Imperator Aleksandr III*, then still under construction at Nikolaiev.

Meanwhile, during 1916, Allied naval power played a central role in the increasingly heavy-handed attempts to coerce Greece to declare war on the Central Powers. By the end of 1915, the Allied

---

[46] Langensiepen *et al.*, *Halbmond und Kaiseradler*, pp. 135–141; Halpern, *A Naval History of World War I*, pp. 243–246.

[47] Langensiepen *et al.*, *Halbmond und Kaiseradler*, pp. 148–152; Halpern, *A Naval History of World War I*, pp. 248–249.

bases on the islands of Corfu (for Adriatic operations) and Lemnos (for the Dardanelles) had been joined by an ever-growing army in the mainland enclave at Salonika, established for the belated attempt to save Serbia from being overrun by the Central Powers after Bulgaria entered the war. In December 1915, as Corfu became home to Serbia's government-in-exile and the evacuated remnants of the Serbian army, King Constantine finally sacked the prime minister, Venizelos, and suspended the liberal Greek parliament. Lacking a pro-Allied advocate in any official capacity in Athens, the Allies nevertheless shipped the Serbian army to Salonika in the spring of 1916 and reinforced their own troops there, with an eye toward the eventual creation of a Macedonian front. After failing to disrupt the transport of the Serbs, the Germans had better luck against French troopships bound for Salonika, which ran unescorted, armed as auxiliary cruisers. *U 35* alone sank the 13,750-ton *Provence* (990 dead) in February and the 14,970-ton *Gallia* (1,338 dead) in October, elevating its commander, *Kapitänleutnant* Lothar von Arnauld de la Perière, to the status of most successful U-boat captain.[48]

During 1916 the British actively recruited Greek irregulars for use in raids along the Turkish coast, and while the Allies did not recognize a rival government established by Venizelos at Salonika in August, they used the threat of recognizing it as leverage to demand that the Greek army provide their Salonika force with batteries of mountain artillery for use against the Bulgarians. When Constantine refused, the Allied Mediterranean commander, Dartige du Fournet, appeared off Piraeus on December 1 with a force including the dreadnought *Provence* and four *Danton*-class pre-dreadnoughts. He shelled Athens (with at least one round falling close to the Greek royal palace), then landed troops. Loyal Greek forces drove the Allied landing parties back to their ships, inflicting over 200 casualties, but the king finally conceded the mountain artillery and, the following month, agreed to withdraw the Greek army to the Morea, allowing the Allies to operate freely in the northern part of the country. Dartige du Fournet became the scapegoat for the bungled operation and at the end of 1916 gave way to Vice Admiral Dominique-Marie Gauchet. Greece finally entered the war on the Allied side in July 1917, after a French squadron landed

---

[48] See data at: www.uboat.net.

9,500 troops at Piraeus, this time unopposed, to force Constantine to abdicate.[49]

## Conclusion

With some justification, the Germans could point to the Allied violation of Greek neutrality as being no different from their own earlier violation of Belgian neutrality, but the analogy could not be carried too far, of course, because there was no Belgian Venizelos and no pro-German faction within Belgium clamoring for an alliance with the Central Powers. Indeed, while both sides in the First World War bullied weak neutral countries, just as both used poison gas on battlefields, used submarines to attack unarmed enemy ships, and used airplanes or airships to drop bombs on cities, the Germans bore the onus of having done all of these things first, of having, in each case, raised the stakes or escalated the conflict. As 1916 gave way to 1917, they prepared to do so yet again.

Under Scheer's leadership, the Germans had maintained the initiative in the North Sea throughout the year of Jutland, but his six sorties had resulted in just one battle, a tactical victory that had not altered the strategic situation. Scheer's defense of his decisions on November 4–5, coming after his admission four months earlier that U-boats, rather than the battle fleet, represented Germany's best hope in the war at sea, signaled the direction the German navy would take during the conflict's last two years. Given the increasing disparity in strength between the British and German surface fleets, Scheer had no alternative. During 1916, the addition of eight new capital ships (six dreadnoughts and two battle cruisers) on the British side more than compensated for the three battle cruisers lost at Jutland; meanwhile, during 1916 the German navy added just the battle cruiser *Lützow* and dreadnought *Bayern*, only to lose the *Lützow* at Jutland less than three months after it was commissioned. At the end of the year Britain enjoyed a 2:1 ratio of superiority over Germany in capital ships, with forty-four in commission (thirty-three dreadnoughts and eleven battle cruisers),

---

[49] Halpern, *The Naval War in the Mediterranean*, pp. 289–300, 367; Sondhaus, *The Naval Policy of Austria-Hungary*, p. 289; *Conway, 1906–1921*, pp. 192, 196, 256, 259.

of which all but HMS *Dreadnought* were with the Grand Fleet at its North Sea bases, against which Germany could muster just twenty-two (eighteen dreadnoughts and four battle cruisers). The British battle fleet also enjoyed a growing qualitative advantage, including eleven capital ships armed with 15-inch (38-cm) guns against just one (the *Bayern*) on the German side. A reorganization of the High Sea Fleet late in the year eliminated the last squadron of pre-dreadnoughts, ships Scheer had left behind on four of his six sorties during 1916. Their manpower would be needed for the growing armada of submarines to be deployed when unrestricted submarine warfare resumed.

# 8 SUBMARINE WARFARE: THE GREAT GAMBLE, 1917–18

On July 29 of the war's last year, at the railway station in Elberfeld, near Wuppertal on the fringe of the Ruhr, two German submarine officers exchanged farewells after spending two days with friends on leave. They had entered the navy in 1910 and had been Naval School classmates; now, aged twenty-six, both were veterans of four years of war and held the rank of *Oberleutnant*. As they parted ways, Hans Jochen Emsmann boarded a train for occupied Flanders and a U-boat command at Zeebrugge, while his friend on the platform, Martin Niemöller, would soon return to the Adriatic and his own U-boat command at Pola. The disastrous, irreversible breakdown of Germany's Western front at Amiens – on what Ludendorff called "the black day of the German army" – was still a week and a half away, but both Emsmann and Niemöller had experienced enough to know that the prospects for victory were no longer very good, even though U-boats had sunk nearly 8 million tons of Allied shipping in the eighteen months since the resumption of unrestricted submarine warfare. At the close of what Niemöller remembered as "a serious talk about the general situation," Emsmann's mood suddenly shifted to an exculpatory light-heartedness: "If the war is lost, it will certainly not be due to anything you and I have done!" he assured his friend.[1]

Emsmann died three months later, when his *U 116* sank with all hands on a suicidal attempt to infiltrate the harbor at Scapa Flow in the war's last days. Niemöller died in 1984 at the age of ninety-two, after

---

[1] Niemöller, *From U-Boat to Pulpit*, p. 98.

becoming more famous for his second career as a Protestant pastor and survivor of eight years' imprisonment in concentration camps for his principled condemnation of Nazi Aryan racism. Through all that came afterward, Emsmann's words remained with him, and for Niemöller, ever the patriotic German, they rang true. But the irony, for Germany, was that they and other U-boat commanders did their duty all too well. The war, indeed, would be lost, with the intervention of the United States and its massive reservoir of fresh manpower the key to the Allied victory. At the Armistice, 1.4 million American troops stood on the Western front, where their numbers had long since exceeded the French and, in the war's last days, grew to surpass the total number of British and Imperial troops. Behind them, another 700,000 Americans had landed in France but were not yet deployed to the front, and 2 million more had been mobilized at various camps in the United States. In the bloody war of attrition, American intervention ranked first among the factors causing the defeat of the Central Powers, and the resumption of the campaign of unrestricted submarine warfare was the issue that caused the United States to declare war on Germany.

## Unrestricted submarine warfare and the US declaration of war

On January 9, 1917, at Pless in Silesia, William II met with Hindenburg, Ludendorff, Bethmann Hollweg, and the chief of the *Admiralstab*, Holtzendorff, to discuss the renewal of the unrestricted campaign. The German navy had been moving toward consensus on resuming the campaign ever since Scheer, a month after Jutland, had urged the emperor to allow submarine warfare to be pursued "with the greatest severity."[2] Holtzendorff, whose opposition to the first round of unrestricted submarine warfare had been crucial to ending it in September 1915, at this stage took the lead in persuading German leaders to reintroduce it, arguing that the great gamble would be worth the risk of the United States entering the war. In dismissing the danger of American intervention, the army High Command took note of the time it would take for the United States to mobilize and ship an army to the Western front. Ludendorff later recalled that the calculation was "to reduce enemy tonnage [so] that the quick transport of the new American armies was

---

[2] Scheer, *Germany's High Sea Fleet*, p. 167.

out of the question." In any case, it would be difficult for the United States to stay the course after "a certain proportion of the transports had been sunk. The navy counted upon being able to do this."[3] In this regard, Holtzendorff reflected the views not only of Scheer but also of Hipper and other leading admirals. The emperor, chancellor, and High Command agreed with them, and chose the date of February 1, first proposed the previous November by Scheer and the generals, for the change in policy. Holtzendorff had also lobbied for that date in a detailed memorandum sent to Hindenburg on December 22, 1916, in which he calculated that if U-boats averaged sinking 600,000 tons of Allied shipping for five months, Britain would have to sue for peace. He justified "the risk of war with America, so long as the U-boat campaign is begun early enough to ensure peace before the next harvest, that is, before August 1." He concluded that "an unrestricted U-boat campaign, begun soon, is the right means to bring the war to a victorious end for us. Moreover, it is the only means to that end."[4]

To facilitate the construction of the additional submarines needed to pursue the campaign to a successful conclusion, the admirals agreed to abandon two dreadnoughts and five battle cruisers then at various stages of completion, freeing up shipyard personnel and resources to build U-boats. Their decision to give up on the capital ship program marked the definitive end of the Tirpitz plan, twenty years after its birth. While the outcome of the conference at Pless was never in doubt, the decision also could not have been made much sooner. Given the massive sums Germany had invested in its battle fleet since the 1890s, it had to remain the central focus of the country's effort at sea until after Jutland demonstrated, to the fleet's own commander, that even in a big battle in which it inflicted more damage than it absorbed, it could not change the overall strategic situation.

At the conclusion of the conference, Holtzendorff accompanied the foreign secretary, Arthur Zimmermann, to Vienna to secure the participation of Germany's ally. At a meeting on January 20 with Austro-Hungarian leaders, they benefited from the enthusiastic endorsement of Admiral Haus, up from Pola for the session. Emperor Charles, who had succeeded Francis Joseph the previous November, and Count Ottokar

---

[3] Erich Ludendorff, *Ludendorff's Own Story*, 2 vols. (New York: Harper, 1919), vol. 2, p. 20.
[4] Holtzendorff to Hindenburg, December 22, 1916, text in Scheer, *Germany's High Sea Fleet*, pp. 248–252.

Czernin, whom he had appointed to succeed Burián as Habsburg foreign minister, were both skeptical but accepted the *fait accompli* after Holtzendorff admitted that German U-boat commanders had already received their orders. Six days later, Charles accompanied Haus to Pless for more detailed discussions, during which they pledged to disarm aging cruisers at Cattaro to free up the manpower needed to service the anticipated increase in German submarine traffic. They also promised to deploy their own submarines in the central Mediterranean, to operate against Allied shipping between Malta and Salonika. But the campaign soon lost its most ardent Austrian supporter when Admiral Haus, then sixty-five, succumbed to pneumonia on the trip home from Germany. He died on February 8, shortly after returning to his flagship in Pola. Charles remained convinced, at heart, that the decision to resume unrestricted submarine warfare was a mistake, and soon came round to the view that his empire could be saved only via a separate peace with the Allies, which he began to pursue weeks later using his brother-in-law, Prince Sixtus of Bourbon-Parma, to open a secret channel to France. Meanwhile, Austria-Hungary remained outwardly committed to its alliance with Germany and to the unrestricted campaign, pursued under the direction of Haus' successor, Admiral Maximilian Njegovan. Even Czernin remained unaware of the "Sixtus Affair" until the French government made it public the following spring.[5]

The Central Powers were much better prepared for unrestricted submarine warfare in February 1917 than they had been in February 1915. Counting U-boats commissioned in January, Germany had 136 (including twenty-seven *UB* boats and fifty-nine *UC* minelayers), of which 105 were ready to sortie, to which Austria-Hungary added twenty more. The quality of the submarines at their disposal also differed dramatically from those deployed two years earlier. They included the first of a class of "submarine cruisers" numbered *U 151* through *U 157*, which had a surfaced displacement of just over 1,500 tons and dimensions of 213 feet long by 17 feet deep, with a beam of 29 feet (65 m × 5.3 m × 8.9 m). Each carried a complement of eight officers, including a surgeon, and a crew of around seventy, enough to take prizes deemed too valuable to sink. Owing to their size, their speed (12 knots surfaced, 5 knots submerged) was similar to that of their smaller predecessors, but their diesel engines and large fuel tanks gave

---

[5] Sondhaus, *The Naval Policy of Austria-Hungary*, pp. 293–294, 302, 332–333.

them a surfaced range of 25,000 nautical miles (46,300 km), more than enough to reach American or Equatorial waters and return home to Germany without refueling; indeed, the class featured two boats that had crossed the Atlantic in the summer of 1916 as merchantmen, in a propaganda exercise demonstrating a blockaded Germany's ability to trade with the United States. Their armament included eighteen torpedoes along with two 5.9-inch (15-cm) and two 3.45-inch (8.8-cm) deck guns, and they could also lay mines. The "submarine cruisers" reflected the culmination of the quest for a more lethal U-boat with a greater range that could remain at sea longer because conditions aboard were more livable for the crew. Ultimately, however, the navy accepted Tirpitz's notion that in a truly ruthless commerce war submarines and submariners had to be considered expendable, and thus replicated a larger number of smaller boats that were more formidably armed than the war's early submarines but did not require such large crews. Of the designs introduced in 1917, the most popular boats were the twenty-two of Type *U 93*, each of which displaced approximately 840 tons. They measured 235 feet long by 13 feet deep, with a beam of 21 feet (71.6 m × 3.9 m × 6.3 m), and were manned by three officers and a crew of thirty-six. They were faster surfaced (with a top speed of nearly 17 knots) and submerged (8–9 knots) than earlier submarines, and their sixteen torpedoes plus 140 rounds for a 4.1-inch (10.5-cm) deck gun gave them much more firepower. They carried enough fuel for a surfaced range of 8,300 nautical miles (15,370 km), but their batteries allowed them just over 50 nautical miles (93 km) submerged. Along with these larger U-boats the navy still built *UB* coastal submarines and *UC* minelayers, but by 1917 the newest of these types displaced over 500 tons, and thus exceeded the displacement of the ocean-going U-boats of 1914–15.[6]

The Type *U 93* boats and the "submarine cruisers" had the fuel capacity to extend the U-boat war far into the Atlantic, but this theoretical threat took on a practical significance only because wartime advances in German long-wave wireless telegraphy enabled them to receive orders from home at unprecedented distances. The German navy directed its submarines in northern and Atlantic waters using transmitters at Nauen near Berlin, at Eilvese in Hanover, and at Bruges, while those in the Mediterranean, Adriatic, and Black Sea used smaller

---

[6] *Conway, 1906–1921*, pp. 180–182; see also at: www.uboat.net.

transmitters at Pola and Damascus (which were also used to direct Austro-Hungarian U-boats). By 1917, an increase in Nauen's power to 400,000 watts enabled U-boats to pick up its signal as far away as the Cape Verde Islands, a distance of roughly 3,200 miles (5,200 km). The stronger signal also enabled U-boats to receive it underwater at depths nearing 100 feet (30 m). More powerful wireless sets installed aboard German submarines likewise enabled them to send messages home from farther away. During the first half of the war a typical 500-watt unit allowed U-boats to send signals up to 300 miles (500 km), but the 1-kilowatt unit standard in 1917–18 allowed transmissions home from as far away as the Canary Islands (2,100 miles, or 3,400 km). Without these breakthroughs, the geographic scope of the second round of unrestricted submarine warfare would have been as limited as the first, notwithstanding the other qualities of the newer, larger U-boats.[7]

German leaders could count on the public to welcome the renewal of the unrestricted campaign, all the more so because in recent months the British blockade had been felt as never before. After his appointment as head of the new Ministry of Blockade early in 1916, Lord Robert Cecil broke the deadlock between the Admiralty and the Foreign Office over blockade policy. At his insistence, Britain formally abrogated the Declaration of London (July 7, 1916) and thereafter asserted the international legality of the blockade. Compared with Grey, Cecil was far less circumspect about the rights of the smaller neutral states and, thanks to his carrot-and-stick diplomacy, by the end of the year Germany could no longer depend as much on its neutral neighbors to supplement its own agricultural output. While the results remained mixed in the Scandinavian countries, Cecil achieved a major victory when the Netherlands bowed to British pressure and curtailed food exports to Germany. Grey remained unreconciled to the new course, but continued to weaken vis-à-vis Cecil until he resigned in December 1916, shortly after Asquith gave way to David Lloyd George. The new prime minister moved Balfour to the Foreign Office to replace Grey, then appointed another prominent Conservative, Sir Edward Carson, to replace Balfour at the Admiralty, changes which had the effect of unifying the key cabinet ministries behind a more vigorous blockade policy.[8]

---

[7] Headrick, *The Invisible Weapon*, p. 164.
[8] Eric W. Osborne, *Britain's Economic Blockade of Germany, 1914–1919* (London: Frank Cass, 2004), pp. 127–145, 153, 159–160.

During the winter of 1916/17 – the "turnip winter" of the Central Powers, named for the readily available vegetable that figured ever more prominently in the average diet – reduced rations provided the average German civilian with just over 1,300 calories per day, significantly less than the prewar peacetime average of nearly 2,300. Government-run soup kitchens fed the masses in Berlin and other major cities. Inflation also became a serious problem, with the increase in wages trailing far behind the increase in the prices of food and other essentials.[9] In announcing the renewal of the campaign to the Reichstag on January 31, Bethmann Hollweg assured the representatives that "the number of our submarines has very considerably increased... and thereby a firm basis has been created for success." The chancellor emphasized that the decision to resume unrestricted submarine warfare had not been taken lightly, but that the time had come "to employ the best and sharpest weapon."[10]

In an effort to elicit sympathy in the United States, the Germans had made no secret of the deterioration in conditions on their home front. Consequently, by the time of Bethmann Hollweg's speech, US leaders expected Germany to retaliate against the Allied blockade by resuming unrestricted submarine warfare, unless the war ended soon in a negotiated peace. Woodrow Wilson, narrowly elected to a second term as president in November 1916, thereafter redoubled his efforts to mediate the conflict, appealing, in a speech before the US Senate on January 22, for the warring powers to accept a "peace without victory."[11] The president was thus outraged when, nine days later, within hours of Bethmann Hollweg's Reichstag speech announcing the renewal of the campaign, the German ambassador in Washington, Count Bernstorff, delivered a note to Secretary of State Lansing formally conveying the same message, only couched as a response to Wilson's speech of the 22nd. After a preamble that condemned Britain for "using her naval power for a criminal attempt to force Germany into submission by starvation," Bernstorff informed the United States that "from

---

[9] *Ibid.*, p. 161; see also Keith Allen, "Food and the German Home Front: Evidence from Berlin," in Gail Braybon (ed.), *Evidence, History and the Great War: Historians and the Impact of 1914–18* (New York: Berghahn, 2003), pp. 172–197.
[10] "Theobald von Bethmann-Hollweg's Speech to the Reichstag Regarding Unrestricted Submarine Warfare," Berlin, January 31, 1917, available at: www.firstworldwar.com/source/uboat_bethmann.htm.
[11] Doenecke, *Nothing Less Than War*, pp. 242–243.

February 1, 1917, sea traffic will be stopped with every available weapon and without further notice in the... blockade zones around Great Britain, France, Italy and in the Eastern Mediterranean," the boundaries of which were outlined specifically in the remainder of the document. Germany would allow the continuation of unmolested passenger travel between the United States and Britain, but under conditions so restrictive (one American-flagged liner each way per week, following a specific route, bearing markings prescribed by the Germans) that they were certain to be rejected.[12] Wilson, indeed, rejected the change in policy, and wasted no time in doing so. Before a joint session of Congress on February 3, the president quoted at length from the text of Germany's "*Sussex* pledge" of May 4, 1916, issued in response to his own ultimatum of April 18, 1916, that Germany "abandon its present methods of submarine warfare" or else suffer a breach of diplomatic relations. Because those methods had now resumed, Wilson announced the recall of his ambassador from Berlin and the expulsion of Bernstorff from the United States. He also threatened the Germans with war "if American ships and American lives should in fact be sacrificed by their naval commanders in heedless contravention of... international law and the obvious dictates of humanity."[13]

The high expectations attached to the new campaign left Germany's submariners under considerable pressure to produce dramatic results quickly, and the leading crews and commanders did not disappoint their superiors. In February alone, *U 35* (*Kapitänleutnant* Lothar von Arnauld de la Perière) sank sixteen ships (36,800 tons) and *U 39* (*Kapitänleutnant* Walter Forstmann) sank eight (21,990 tons), both while operating in the Mediterranean. *U 21* (*Kapitänleutnant* Otto Hersing), recalled to northern waters after nearly two years in the Mediterranean, sank thirteen ships (36,510 tons). New boats with novice commanders also made their mark, most notably the Flanders flotilla's *UC 65* (Lieutenant Otto Steinbrinck), which claimed thirty-two victims (27,070 tons) in February, then another fifteen (19,320 tons) on March 1 alone. The vessels sunk by these four boats included Dutch, Norwegian, Swedish, and American ships, reflecting the German

---

[12] "Germany's Policy of Unrestricted Submarine Warfare," Washington, January 31, 1917, at: www.firstworldwar.com/source/uboat_bernstorff.htm.

[13] "President Wilson's Speech to Congress Regarding Unrestricted U-Boat Warfare," Washington, February 3, 1917, at: www.firstworldwar.com/source/uboat_wilson.htm.

intention this time around to give no quarter to neutrals caught trading in the forbidden zones.[14] At the same time, U-boats continued to attack armed as well as unarmed targets. These included the largest Allied warship sunk by a submarine torpedo in the Great War, the 18,320-ton *Danton*, namesake of the last, largest class of French pre-dreadnoughts, which fell victim to *U 64* (*Kapitänleutnant* Robert Moraht) on March 19 off Sardinia, while en route from a refit at Toulon to blockade duty at the mouth of the Adriatic (296 dead). Overall, the campaign destroyed 520,410 tons of Allied shipping in February, 564,500 tons in March, and 860,330 tons in April, in the latter case, a monthly total not topped even by Nazi Germany's much larger submarine force during the Second World War. The sinking of over 1.9 million tons of shipping in three months put the U-boats on pace to claim better than the 600,000 tons per month that Holtzendorff had calculated would bring peace before the next harvest.

German submariners had just begun racking up their record figure for the campaign's third month when Wilson, on April 2, asked Congress for a declaration of war. Over the eight weeks since the severance of diplomatic relations every American ship sunk by a U-boat had brought the two countries closer to hostilities, but there had been no equivalent to the dramatic attacks of 1915–16 on the *Lusitania*, *Arabic*, and *Sussex*. Instead, a German diplomatic gaffe of the highest order escalated tensions to breaking point. On February 19, the British shared with the Americans a telegram from the German foreign secretary, Zimmermann, to the German embassy in Mexico City, which the Admiralty's Room 40 had intercepted and decoded.[15] This "Zimmermann telegram," drafted in anticipation of an American declaration of war against Germany, promised Mexico the return of three southwestern US states in exchange for its entry into the war, and sought Mexican help in getting Japan to quit the Allies and join the Central Powers. On March 1, as soon as he was satisfied that the telegram was not a British forgery, Wilson released the text to the American press. While the telegram has traditionally been interpreted as having turned public opinion decisively in favor of US intervention on the side of the Allies, recent scholarship supports the conclusion that it affected Wilson more than

[14] See lists of ships sunk by individual commanders and submarines at: www.uboat.net.
[15] Nicholas Black, *The British Naval Staff in the First World War* (Woodbridge: Boydell Press, 2009), p. 2.

anyone else. While the president continued to hope that war could be avoided, most of his cabinet, Congress, and the public had made up their minds, with majorities already favoring war; at the same time, the telegram made little difference to the non-interventionist minority, whose skepticism was fueled by Britain's role in the affair.[16] Zimmermann himself removed any remaining doubts about the authenticity of the telegram in a Reichstag speech later in March, when he admitted writing it. By then, the initial revolution in Russia and the abdication of Nicholas II removed the embarrassment Wilson would have felt in bringing the United States into a war against autocracy as an ally of the leading autocratic state. On March 20, Wilson's cabinet gave its unanimous endorsement for war with Germany, only to see the president waver for two weeks before submitting his request to Congress. In contrast to the American entry into the Second World War, when Congress gave Franklin Roosevelt a quick declaration of war with only one dissenting vote the day after Japan bombed Pearl Harbor, entry into the First World War came after days of debate. The final votes for war, by the Senate on April 4 (82:6) and the House of Representatives on April 6 (373:50), were decisive but far from unanimous.[17]

The United States joined the Allies as an "associated power" rather than by concluding a treaty linking itself to the Triple Entente, a decision reflecting Wilson's desire to go to an eventual postwar peace conference not bound by the territorial promises the Allies had made to each other since 1914. At this point Wilson also wanted war with Germany alone, not the rest of the Central Powers. The United States eventually declared war on Austria-Hungary (December 7, 1917), but went no further than breaking diplomatic relations with Germany's remaining allies, Bulgaria and the Ottoman Empire. Starting with Cuba, one day after the United States, eight Latin American countries also entered the war on the Allied side as "associated powers," while another four broke diplomatic relations with Germany, but did not declare war. Of those joining the Allies only Brazil sent armed forces, deploying a naval division for Atlantic convoy duty. The rest contributed by following the lead of the United States in seizing German merchant ships that had been granted internment in their neutral ports, thus adding

---

[16] See Thomas Boghardt, *The Zimmermann Telegram: Intelligence, Diplomacy, and America's Entry into World War I* (Annapolis, MD: Naval Institute Press, 2012).

[17] Doenecke, *Nothing Less Than War*, pp. 289–296.

precious tonnage to the Allied shipping total once these vessels (rusting at anchor since 1914) were refitted for further service.

The American entry into the war also deprived the remaining neutrals of the most powerful champion of their international rights at sea. The Netherlands suffered the most, as the United States eventually joined Britain in requisitioning Dutch merchant ships for its own wartime use. Wilson likewise followed the British lead in closing loopholes that allowed transshipments to the enemy by imposing an embargo on American exports to Germany's neutral neighbors in October 1917. Such measures further worsened the food crisis on the German home front, where as early as the summer months another reduction in rations left the average civilian with 1,100 calories per day, less than half the prewar norm.[18]

## The US Navy and the convoy system

Wilson had made naval expansion the cornerstone of his peacetime "preparedness" program after developments in 1914–15 – international norms defied by Germany's use of submarines and Britain's blockade of Germany, plus Japan's occupation of so many formerly German Pacific islands – persuaded him that the United States would need a much stronger fleet regardless of the outcome of the war. Though the final version of the bill introduced in Congress in the spring of 1916 included ten light cruisers, fifty destroyers, and sixty-seven submarines among a total of 157 vessels of all sizes to be laid down no later than 1919, capital ships – ten dreadnoughts and six battle cruisers – were the centerpiece of the program and accounted for most of its $315 million cost. The bill was in trouble, ironically, until the Battle of Jutland. The great North Sea clash that persuaded the Germans, despite their tactical victory, to give up further battle fleet expansion in favor of submarine warfare had the opposite effect for the cause of capital ship construction in the United States. Supporters of an American battle fleet "second to none" had difficulty in making their case until after the only two larger battle fleets finally met at sea, thus appearing to prove that battle fleets still mattered. Congress passed the Naval Act in August 1916, and subsequent legislation funded it by increasing federal income tax (introduced

[18] Osborne, *Britain's Economic Blockade*, pp. 161, 163.

three years earlier) for wealthier Americans. By war's end, the last six of the dreadnoughts were designated as the 43,200-ton *South Dakota* class, and the six battle cruisers as the 43,500-ton *Lexington* class. By adding another sixteen capital ships, including these dozen giants, to the nineteen that had already been built, laid down, or authorized, the Naval Act of 1916 put the United States on course to become the world's leading naval power, surpassing Britain by 1922 or 1923.[19]

After the declaration of war, Wilson delegated responsibility for its conduct to his generals and admirals, and, more so than any other wartime US president, allowed them to set strategies and policies, with the caveat that the United States must have a clear role in determining the outcome in order to ensure his own leading role in making the peace. This general directive left American military and naval leaders at odds with their British and French counterparts, who wanted American manpower and naval assets committed piecemeal as soon as possible, to meet immediate needs, serving under their command. In keeping with Wilson's overall goals, the head of the American Expeditionary Force (AEF), General John J. Pershing, resisted the proposed "amalgamation" of American troops, insisting instead on deploying an American army on an American sector of the Western front, even though such an army could not possibly be ready until the summer of 1918 at the earliest. Likewise, the commander of the US Atlantic Fleet, Admiral Henry T. Mayo, initially took an all-or-nothing approach to the deployment of his forces. He could cite Mahan to defend the position that a battle fleet had to stay together, and point to the British and German North Sea examples of fidelity to that principle. He therefore resisted British appeals for a division of American dreadnoughts to join the Grand Fleet, even though it would facilitate a series of battleship redeployments which, when the last dominoes fell, would allow for the paying off of the oldest active pre-dreadnoughts, freeing British manpower to serve on antisubmarine patrols in 119 new destroyers then nearing completion. Mayo also rejected a British request for direct American participation in the antisubmarine effort through the deployment to European waters of as many US Navy destroyers as possible, instead promising to send just six.[20]

[19] Doenecke, *Nothing Less Than War*, pp. 198–200; *Conway, 1906–1921*, pp. 118–119.
[20] Jerry W. Jones, *U.S. Battleship Operations in World War I* (Annapolis, MD: Naval Institute Press, 1998), pp. 3, 9–12.

Figure 8.1 Admiral William S. Sims

Rear Admiral William S. Sims, well-respected head of the Naval War College in Newport, Rhode Island, soon became the central figure in overcoming Anglo-American naval differences. The Canadian-born Sims, the navy's leading anglophile, had distinguished himself at sea most recently as a destroyer flotilla commander (1913–15), but had served earlier as naval attaché in Paris and St. Petersburg, and thus was well suited to play an inter-Allied diplomatic role. He was already on his way to Britain when the United States entered the conflict, having been ordered there by Wilson in late March on a secret mission to establish contact with British naval leaders. After the US declaration of war, Wilson made Sims commander of American naval forces in European waters; in that capacity he worked well with the new First Sea Lord, Jellicoe, and with Admiral Sir Lewis Bayly, serving since

1915 as "Commander-in-Chief, Coast of Ireland," headquartered at Queenstown on Cork Harbor. Sims had met Jellicoe in China during the Boxer Rebellion, and later renewed the acquaintance on annual prewar visits to Britain when both were working on problems related to gunnery ranges and range-finding. Bayly did not know Sims before the war, but had a similar career path, having served as British naval attaché in Washington and, more recently, head of the Royal Naval College, Greenwich, as well as in a destroyer flotilla command among his posts in the fleet. In addition to securing an American naval deployment that fitted British (and broader Allied) needs, Sims also helped the common cause by becoming a mediator between Jellicoe and Bayly, who did not get along well.[21] Bayly's contempt for Jellicoe dated from their service together as lieutenants, when, according to Bayly, Jellicoe had difficulty staying awake on night duty.[22]

In his first meeting with Jellicoe, on April 10, Sims received the sobering details of just how much shipping tonnage the Allies had lost since the renewal of unrestricted submarine warfare, with projections of how much more they were likely to lose that spring. The British government had kept the magnitude of the losses secret in order not to alarm the public. The situation was certainly far grimmer than anyone in the United States had realized, but also not yet as bad as the Germans assumed it was, because they had been overly optimistic in their projections of January 1917, underestimating how much tonnage the Allies had available to them and overestimating how much they required to continue their war effort at present levels. Thus, at the start of the year the Allies had a surplus of 6 million tons of shipping (21.5 million, against the 15.5 million then needed to sustain their efforts), or double the 3 million tons (600,000 times five) that Holtzendorff had assumed was their margin of security. Nevertheless, in the first three months of the campaign U-boats had destroyed nearly 2 million tons, and were sinking Allied shipping at a rate that would eliminate even the larger margin before the end of 1917. A solution had to be found to reverse their record of success, and Jellicoe conceded to Sims that there was "absolutely none that we can see now." Indeed, Sims found "a general

[21] Elting E. Morison, *Admiral Sims and the Modern American Navy* (Boston, MA: Houghton Mifflin, 1942), pp. 280, 341–342, 377–381 and *passim*.
[22] Lewis Bayly, *Pull Together! The Memoirs of Admiral Sir Lewis Bayly* (London: George G. Harrap, 1939), p. 62. In his *Memoirs* Bayly refers to Jellicoe as his "friend," but misses few opportunities to criticize him.

belief in British naval circles that [Germany's] plan would succeed," because "it was a matter of very simple arithmetic to determine the length of time the Allies could stand such a strain." If the U-boats came close to averaging the 860,000 tons sunk in April 1917 for another six months, "the limit of endurance would be reached around November 1, 1917," just three months beyond Holtzendorff's target date of August 1.[23]

The systematic adoption of convoys as a solution to the submarine menace coincided with the US entry into the war and, specifically, the presence of Sims in London. The Allied navies had escorted convoys of troopships since 1914, but for a variety of reasons key voices had always resisted the extension of the practice to include cargo ships. Prewar opponents of convoys as an antidote to commerce-raiding cruisers included the influential strategist Corbett, who believed they only offered tempting, vulnerable targets for the enemy.[24] Such sentiments grew even stronger when the submarine superseded the cruiser threat. Because submarines were much slower than cruisers, most merchant captains preferred to take their chances at outrunning any they encountered rather than tie their fate to a convoy, which had to move at the speed of its slowest ship. For their part, authorities in charge of managing ports cited logistical problems dockside that convoys could pose if too many merchantmen entered the same harbor at the same time. Senior British naval authorities doubted merchantmen were capable of steaming in close formation, as required in a convoy. The same skeptics at the Admiralty cited the inability of the navy to protect convoys against submarines with the forces available at that time. While a cruiser or two sufficed to defend a convoy of a dozen or more ships against surface raiders (a threat dramatically diminished after the spring of 1915), a much larger number of destroyers and other smaller warships would be needed to escort convoys against U-boats.

Sizing up the status of the debate during his first two weeks in Britain, Sims found Jellicoe siding with the skeptics, while the current Grand Fleet commander, Beatty, was among the few senior officers who supported convoys. Lloyd George favored convoys, but had gotten nowhere with the Admiralty. A number of junior officers at the

---

[23] William Snowden Sims, *The Victory at Sea*, with Burton J. Hendrick (Garden City, NY: Doubleday, Page, 1920), pp. 9–11.

[24] Julian Stafford Corbett, *Some Principles of Naval Strategy* (London: Longmans, Green, 1911), pp. 261–279.

Admiralty, led by Commander Reginald Henderson, likewise favored convoys and mustered evidence to support their case. On April 29, Sims visited the Admiralty to review a report ordered by Jellicoe and presumably compiled by Henderson, demonstrating the feasibility of a convoy system. The following day, Lloyd George went to the Admiralty and secured from Jellicoe and the sea lords a commitment to initiate convoys at least on a trial basis. At a dinner with Sims on the evening of April 30, the prime minister credited the American admiral with the breakthrough, and an aide of Sims later claimed that British junior officers considered him their champion. Afterward Sims went no farther than to take credit for persuading Jellicoe to order the report on the feasibility of convoys. When pressed on the matter, he concluded, diplomatically, that "in the absence of an authorized statement from the Admiralty" or a very high-ranking officer serving within it, which he doubted would be forthcoming, "it would be a mistake [to] claim that the influence of our officers was the determining factor in the adoption of the convoy."[25]

A recent, exhaustive account of British naval staff work during the First World War rejects the notion that convoy policy changed decisively with Lloyd George's visit to the Admiralty on April 30, and makes the case instead for a gradual transformation from December 1916 onward, after the changes that brought the new prime minister to Downing Street and Jellicoe to the post of First Sea Lord. Nicholas Black points out that Jellicoe approved the convoying of coal supplies to France on January 16, long before the Americans were a factor, and the convoying of Britain's Scandinavian trade on April 21, before the supposedly decisive meeting with Lloyd George. Finally, on April 27, again before the prime minister's visit to the Admiralty, Jellicoe approved a memorandum written the previous day by the head of the Anti-Submarine Division, Rear Admiral Alexander Duff, which cited the success of the French coal convoys, along with the entry into the war of the United States, as reasons to adopt a convoy system. Black's account cites further evidence of Admiralty planning for "trial

---

[25] Morison, *Admiral Sims*, pp. 348–353, Sims quoted at p. 352. Corbett, *History of the Great War: Naval Operations*, vol. 4, p. 324, credits Henderson as the leader of the officers at the Admiralty who favored convoys. Lloyd George, *War Memoirs*, 6 vols. (Boston, MA: Little, Brown, 1933–37), vol. 3, pp. 105–107, acknowledges Sims but takes much of the credit for establishing the convoy system.

convoys" long before April 30. He acknowledges, but also minimizes, the role of Henderson, and does not mention Sims at all.[26]

The first convoy from the United States reached Britain on June 10, and others soon made the crossing from American ports directly to France, one of which carried Pershing and his staff, along with 14,000 troops of the US 1st Division. Irrespective of his role in the British decision to implement transatlantic convoys, Sims played an unmistakable part in facilitating operations once they began. Thanks largely to his efforts, by the end of June the US Navy had sent twenty-eight of its fifty-two available destroyers to join the antisubmarine patrols operating under Bayly's command. By the end of the year a division of four American dreadnoughts had joined the Grand Fleet at Scapa Flow; two more eventually served there, and another three were deployed to Berehaven, Ireland, to stand guard against the unlikely event of a sortie by German battle cruisers into the Atlantic sea lanes.[27] The arrival of these battleships, in turn, enabled the British to decommission older pre-dreadnoughts and to reassign manpower to their own expanding destroyer force, the deployment of which was crucial to the Allied antisubmarine effort for the remainder of the war. Most of the American contribution did not fall into place until later in 1917, but, thanks to Sims, the British navy eventually received precisely the sort of help it had requested in the first place. Bayly considered the assistance indispensable and, alone among British admirals, never hesitated to praise the work of Sims, with whom he developed a lifelong friendship. The only problem not remedied by the arrival of the Americans concerned what Bayly called the "leakage of important information from Queenstown," which he attributed to the anti-English sentiments of the local Irish population who were "practically all Roman Catholics... including the dockyard workers." This "leakage" actually worsened once Sims secured the deployment of additional American destroyers to the base at Queenstown, as evidenced by the uncanny ability of the Germans to make sure that the entrance to Cork Harbor "was mined the night before they arrived." This led Bayly to conclude that the "leakage" came from pro-German or anti-British sources in the United States as well as locally in Queenstown.[28]

[26] Black, *The British Naval Staff*, pp. 173–183.
[27] Jones, *U.S. Battleship Operations*, pp. 6, 16–18.
[28] Bayly, *Pull Together!*, pp. 182–185.

In the Second World War, the transatlantic range of most German submarines required the Allies to provide escort for their convoys all the way across the North Atlantic, usually in tag-team or relay fashion by separate forces operating out of Newfoundland, Iceland, and the British Isles. But in the First World War the seven "submarine cruisers" were the only U-boats capable of reaching American waters, making the escorting of convoys in the western Atlantic less crucial. Convoys thus usually left New York or other North American ports in the company of an American, British, or French cruiser, to guard against the remote possibility of attack by a German surface raider. They were picked up in mid-ocean by a group of destroyers (typically eight or ten) operating out of Queenstown, escorting an outbound group of empty troopships and merchantmen; the latter ships then would continue westward with the cruiser escort, while the destroyers turned to accompany the fully loaded, eastbound convoy to some British or French port. The scheme left convoys most vulnerable to attack or accident during the mid-ocean rendezvous, especially in bad weather or if destroyers had to leave an empty westbound convoy with no cruiser escort in sight in order to pick up an eastbound convoy. One such case, on May 10, 1918, resulted in *U 90* (*Kapitänleutnant* Walter Remy) sinking the 18,170-ton *President Lincoln*, en route home to New York after unloading troops at Brest, just after its escorting destroyers had turned to protect an eastbound convoy. It was the largest American troopship sunk in the war, but, being empty at the time, just twenty-six lives were lost. Because destroyer commanders on North Atlantic convoy duty were under orders to give priority to protecting fully loaded convoys, just three eastbound troopships were sunk. Their ships soon ranked as the war's busiest naval vessels. Each destroyer spent five days at sea for every two or three in port, and on average cruised 6,000 miles (10,000 km) per month.[29]

To serve the needs of convoy escort and antisubmarine warfare, the United States suspended work on the dreadnoughts and battle cruisers of its 1916 program in order to increase and accelerate the number of destroyers under construction. Six *Caldwell*-class destroyers, already under construction, entered service in 1917 and provided the

---

[29] Thomas Hughes, "Learning to Fight: Bill Halsey and the Early American Destroyer Force," *Journal of Military History*, 77(1) (January 2013): 83–84; Walter S. Delany, *Bayly's Navy* (Washington, DC: Naval Historical Foundation, 1980), p. 12. See also data at: www.uboat.net.

prototype for the "flush-deck" design of the fifty *Wilkes*-class destroyers authorized in the 1916 program. An amendment to the Naval Act added another sixty-one vessels to the *Wilkes* class and also authorized 162 *Clemson*-class destroyers, bringing the total of the two new classes to 273, of which ninety-eight were launched before the Armistice, nearly tripling the number of US Navy destroyers in service. Less publicized, but equally impressive, the United States doubled the size of its submarine force in 1917–18, adding forty-nine boats to the fifty already in commission at the end of 1916.[30] By the Armistice over one-third of the dramatically expanded American destroyer force had been sent to the war zone, along with a token number of submarines. Some of the destroyers operated out of Brest and some were sent to Gibraltar and the Mediterranean, but most were based at Queenstown. In all, the US Navy contribution to Bayly's command alone included forty-seven destroyers and seven submarines, served by two destroyer tenders and one submarine tender. Three tugs, one minelayer, the lone American Q-ship *Santee*, and thirty small patrol-torpedo boats dubbed "submarine chasers" rounded out the contingent.

With Sims typically in London, the American ships at Queenstown were under the direct command of Captain Joel R. P. Pringle, whom Bayly made his chief of staff, for the First World War an unusual inter-Allied arrangement, but one that would become common in the Second World War.[31] Even at a distance, however, Sims brought to bear the experience of his prior assignment as a destroyer flotilla commander, a key similarity between his own résumé and that of Bayly. He knew the best American destroyer captains and pressed for their transfer to Bayly's force. These included William "Bull" Halsey and Frank Fletcher, prominent admirals in the Second World War who saw their first action at sea on North Atlantic convoy duty in 1917–18.[32] The destroyer *Fanning* was the first American ship to sink a U-boat, using depth charges to destroy *U 58* off Milford Haven on November 17, 1917. The destroyer *Jacob Jones* was the first American warship sunk by a U-boat, falling victim to *U 53* off the Scilly Isles on December 6, 1917.[33]

---

[30] *Conway, 1906–1921*, pp. 123–131.   [31] Delany, *Bayly's Navy*, p. 8.
[32] Hughes, "Learning to Fight," pp. 73–76, 81–86.
[33] Grant, *U-Boats Destroyed*, p. 153; *Conway, 1906–1921*, p. 123; see also at: www.uboat.net.

Long before these actions, the effectiveness of the convoy system had been demonstrated in the declining totals of Allied tonnage lost to U-boat attacks. After reaching 616,320 tons in May and 696,725 tons in June, the toll taken by unrestricted submarine warfare fell to 555,510 tons in July, 472,370 tons in August, and 353,600 tons in September, before rebounding to 466,540 tons in October. Thus, the U-boat force had surpassed Holtzendorff's goal of destroying 600,000 tons per month for the first five months of the campaign, February through June, but because the chief of the *Admiralstab* had underestimated by half the surplus of enemy tonnage over absolute need, Germany did not force Britain to breaking point by his target date of August 1, before another harvest could be brought to bear. And thanks to the effectiveness of the convoy system, by the time of the breaking point initially projected by Jellicoe to Sims, November 1, the U-boats had fallen short of claiming the 6 million tons of shipping necessary to force a reduction in the Allied war effort, instead destroying just over 5 million tons. In November 1917, the toll taken by German submarines fell to 302,600 tons, the lowest monthly total since September 1916, and it became clear that the campaign would not force an end to the war on Germany's terms. Nevertheless, the tonnage lost in December (411,770 tons) underscored the continued seriousness of the U-boat threat. German submarines never caused Britain to experience anything like the sort of hunger that the British blockade inflicted upon Germany, but in January 1918 Lloyd George finally introduced food rationing as a precaution. On the first anniversary of the resumption of unrestricted submarine warfare, the overall shipping tonnage at the disposal of the Allies was still decreasing, despite the commissioning in the US merchant marine of dozens of interned German ships and the best efforts of American shipyards to build new vessels. The Emergency Fleet Corporation, established by Congress in April 1917, ultimately claimed credit for the construction of 507 ships totaling 2.8 million tons, but of these, just 151 were built from scratch specifically for the war effort, the rest being requisitioned from among vessels already under construction when the United States entered the conflict.[34]

[34] United States Congress, Senate, Committee on Commerce, *United States Shipping Board Emergency Fleet Corporation: Hearings Before the Committee on Commerce, United States Senate, Sixty-fifth Congress, Second [and Third] Session, on S.Res. 170* (Washington, DC: US Government Printing Office, 1918), Pt 3, pp. 56–57.

In addition to food for the British Isles and supplies for the war effort in general, by the end of 1917 the transatlantic convoys included ever-greater numbers of troopships. In this capacity converted German ocean liners idled in American ports since 1914 were among the most useful. The largest of these, the 54,280-ton *Leviathan* (ex-*Vaterland*), formerly of the Hamburg-Amerika Line, made its first crossing in December 1917. Originally designed for 1,165 passengers, it was reconfigured to carry a maximum of 14,000 troops and transported a total of 119,000 Americans to Europe by the end of the war, far more than any other single ship. British-flagged ships carried 49 percent of all AEF troops, American-flagged ships 45 percent, with Italian, French, and Russian ships (the latter under British control after the Russian Revolution) accounting for the remainder. The overwhelming majority of the AEF (79 percent) left via New York, with Newport News (14 percent) a distant second. After crossing the Atlantic, roughly half of all American troops disembarked in French ports, the other half in British ports, from where they were shipped on to France. Liverpool received just over 40 percent of the arriving Americans, more than any other port, followed closely by Brest (38 percent), with St. Nazaire (just under 10 percent) ranking third. From the sailing of the first convoy until the Armistice, the AEF sealift transported 2,079,880 men.[35]

The Americans, of course, were not the first troops shipped to the war's various fronts by sea, but, unless one counts the BEF crossing the Channel as going "overseas," the sheer size of the force transported was unprecedented in both raw numbers and in the number of men shipped per month. In comparison, over the course of the entire war less than 1.5 million troops from Britain's dominions and colonies were transported on the high seas to a war zone; these included 580,000 Indians, 424,600 Canadians, 331,800 Australians, 100,400 New Zealanders, and 30,000 South Africans. Beyond the United States and the British Empire, France's sub-Saharan African colonies sent the most troops to Europe, some 135,000 men. Non-combatants shipped to the various war zones by sea included nearly a million Asian and African workers and laborers, among them 400,000 Indians, 150,000 Chinese, and 100,000 Egyptians. Unless their numbers are included, too, the

---

[35] Walter Kudlick, "Sealift for the AEF," at: www.worldwar1.com/dbc/sealift.htm#a; see also data in Leonard P. Ayres, *War with Germany: A Statistical Summary* (Washington, DC: US Government Printing Office, 1919).

total figure of men shipped overseas for the Allied war effort retains its American majority.

Between June 1917 and November 1918, the transatlantic convoys also transported 7,453,000 tons of supplies for the AEF, a figure that would have been much higher if not for a strategic decision to use the available shipping tonnage to carry as many men as possible. Most American units arrived in France with no arms other than their rifles, and used French machine guns and artillery, British and French tanks, and were supported by American pilots flying British and French planes. Thus, further training at camps in France was needed to ensure a basic competence and familiarity with the weaponry. The 1st Division finally deployed to a quiet sector of the Western front in October 1917, four months after its arrival; owing to similar delays in the preparation of the ever-growing numbers that followed them, the impact of the AEF at the front would be negligible until May 1918. Germany, which by November 1917 had lost the great gamble at sea, thus had its window of opportunity to win the war on land extended in the additional months that would pass before sufficient numbers of American troops were deployed to turn the tide on the Western front.

## U-boats and antisubmarine warfare

Germany commissioned another eighty-seven U-boats during 1917, as many as any one country had built in all the years before 1914 combined, but this barely sufficed to maintain the force at the size at which it had begun the campaign. Sixty-three U-boats were lost in action during the year, almost three times as many as in 1916, all but two of them after the renewal of unrestricted submarine warfare. The navy also lost the services of another fifteen for a variety of reasons: two transferred to Austria-Hungary (to replace two U-boats it lost during 1917); eight converted to training purposes; two given up for internment in neutral countries; and three lost in accidents. The net result was that Germany entered the last year of the war with 142 U-boats, including forty-nine coastal *UB* boats and thirty-two *UC* minelayers, just six boats more than it had eleven months earlier when the campaign resumed.[36]

[36] Grant, *U-Boats Destroyed*, p. 72.

Of the sixty-three U-boats lost as a result of Allied action during 1917, forty-three were sunk in the last five months of the year, evidence of the success of the more robust antisubmarine warfare methods whose development coincided with the introduction of convoys. The Admiralty dedicated its new Intelligence Division 25 (ID 25) to the tracking of submarines, using the information fed from the directional wireless stations built earlier in the war plus new ones constructed in Ireland, in Bayly's command jurisdiction. An amalgamation of Room 40 and the Enemy Submarine Section, ID 25 issued warning messages of U-boat activity to Allied ships at sea in ever-increasing numbers, from thirty-nine per month when unrestricted submarine warfare resumed to 172 per month during the last year of the war. Even though directional wireless intelligence helped convoys to avoid U-boats and enabled destroyers to hunt them down, U-boats continued to maintain a greater presence on the airwaves than surface vessels, following standing orders that required them to check in via wireless whenever they sank an enemy merchantman or encountered an enemy warship. In a forerunner of the "wolf pack" tactics of the Second World War, the Germans eventually tried to counter the convoys by coordinating the operations of U-boats at sea, but these efforts only added to their wireless traffic and made them that much easier to avoid, or to attack. Meanwhile, convoys were able to conceal their location, at least to more distant U-boats, by having their ships communicate with each other using low-power radios.[37]

Once the Allies knew where submarines were, they were able to take advantage of new or improved ways to destroy them. During the first round of unrestricted submarine warfare, the British had accelerated prewar experiments with depth charges, cans of explosives detonated by the water pressure at a pre-selected depth. The most common depth charge of the war, known as Type D, carried 300 lb (140 kg) of TNT. Introduced in January 1916, these depth charges were in such short supply that vessels on antisubmarine patrol – destroyers, sloops, and Q-ships – initially carried just two, and as late as June 1917 were only issued four. Thanks to the priority placed on increased production, a year later it was not unusual for warships on convoy duty to

---

[37] Headrick, *The Invisible Weapon*, pp. 164–165, 167; Black, *The British Naval Staff*, p. 187.

carry thirty to fifty depth charges apiece, and the British navy alone had dropped a total of 16,451 by the end of the war. The underwater shock waves from a depth charge sufficed to pop rivets and induce leaks, making it an effective weapon even when it did not detonate in the immediate vicinity of a submarine. Figures for confirmed kills of U-boats resulting from depth charges range from thirty to thirty-eight, with the first undisputed success coming on December 13, 1916, when the British destroyer *Landrail* sank *UB 29* off the south coast of Ireland. Depth charges likely played some role in many more sinkings, especially those in which a U-boat responded to leaks and other structural damage by surfacing, after which gunfire finished it off. Because most were dropped during the war's last year, not surprisingly the vast majority of the U-boats definitely sunk by them, at least twenty-two, were lost in 1918.[38]

Not until the Second World War did aircraft surpass destroyers and other small surface warships to become the submarine's worst enemy. Nevertheless, it was during the First World War that low-flying planes were first used in antisubmarine warfare, once it became clear that, because a submerged submarine typically ran just below the surface, its silhouette could be easily visible from the air even while it remained unseen by nearby ships. On September 15, 1916, the Austro-Hungarian navy became the first to destroy a submarine in an air attack, when one of its seaplanes bombed and sank the French submarine *Foucault* off Cattaro. Just over a year later, on September 22, 1917, the British sank their first German U-boat from the air, when a Curtis H-12 flying boat operating from the Royal Naval Air Service's base at Dunkirk bombed and sank *U 32* off the Dutch coast. While Britain ultimately deployed more aircraft in antisubmarine warfare than any of the other belligerents of the Great War, *U 32* was the only submarine sunk by a British plane unassisted by warships. Yet long before the end of the war, fear of attack by aircraft served as a deterrent to U-boat operations whenever they were known to be in the area.[39] Aircraft also affected the submarine campaign by damaging an undetermined number of boats

---

[38] Fraser M. McKee, "An Explosive Story: The Rise and Fall of the Depth Charge," *Northern Mariner*, 3 (1993): 49–50; Grant, *U-Boats Destroyed*, pp. 39, 152, 159, 164.

[39] John J. Abbatiello, *Anti-Submarine Warfare in World War I: British Naval Aviation and the Defeat of the U-Boats* (London: Routledge, 2006), pp. 1–3.

they did not sink. For example, Martin Niemöller's first mission as commanding officer of a U-boat, in *UC 67* out of Pola during the early summer of 1918, called for him to lay mines and hunt for targets off Marseilles, but he had to turn back just west of Malta after his submarine was damaged in an attack by a British plane operating out of the base there.[40]

When compared with aircraft, Q-ships sank more U-boats but did nothing to deter them from operating against merchantmen, indeed, it was more likely that they encouraged German submariners to be more ruthless when approaching any ship that appeared suspicious. Over half of the confirmed losses of U-boats to Q-ships (six of eleven) came in the ten months between November 1916 and September 1917, starting with the successes of the *Penshurst* (Commander F. H. Grenfell) which sank *UB 19* on November 19, 1916, and *UB 37* on January 14, 1917, both in the Channel, during the "restricted" prelude to the resumption of unrestricted submarine warfare. Britain's most successful Q-ship commander, Gordon Campbell, still commanding the *Farnborough*, sank *U 83* on February 17, 1917, but in that engagement it suffered damage that forced its withdrawal from service. Campbell and his crew subsequently manned the Q-ship *Pargust*, which sank *UC 29* on June 7, 1917. The *Stonecrop* (Commander M. B. R. Blackwood) managed just one sinking, on September 5, 1917, but it was *U 88* (*Kapitänleutnant* Walther Schwieger), thus avenging the *Lusitania* at least inasmuch as it took the life of the officer who, as commander of *U 20*, had been responsible for torpedoing the Cunard liner. Finally, on March 17, 1917, the *Privet* (Lieutenant Commander C. G. Matheson) sank *U 85* in the Channel, then remained in service long enough to claim *U 34* in the Mediterranean on November 9, 1918, just two days before the Armistice. That sinking was also the only one after Schwieger's *U 88* in September 1917, reflecting the new reality that the widespread Allied use of convoys left the lone "mystery" ship looking too suspicious for most U-boat commanders to risk approaching.[41]

---

[40] Niemöller, *From U-Boat to Pulpit*, pp. 87–97.
[41] Chatterton, *Q-Ships and Their Story*, passim; Campbell, *My Mystery Ships*, passim. Grant, *U-Boats Destroyed*, pp. 153–154, lists *U 88* as victim of a mine rather than a Q-ship, and instead has *UC 18*, sunk on February 19, 1917 by "gunfire of decoy," as the eleventh victim of a Q-ship. Data in www.uboat.net identifies this Q-ship as the *Lady Olive*, a vessel not mentioned by Chatterton, Campbell, or Grant.

Throughout the second round of unrestricted submarine warfare, the Allies continued to pour considerable resources into antisubmarine barrages despite slight evidence of a return on the investment; at the same time, the existing barrages remained vulnerable targets to the enemy's surface warships. In the year after the Otranto barrage claimed its only confirmed victim, *U 6* in May 1916, the Austro-Hungarian navy periodically raided the drifter line at the mouth of the Adriatic, but Rear Admiral Kerr's decision to move it farther south, to the parallel of Santa Maria di Leuca, the southeastern tip of Italy, 200 miles (320 km) south of Cattaro, improved its security somewhat, though not its effectiveness. Despite the deployment of additional drifters, the line claimed no more victims, although Austria-Hungary's *U 30* went missing in the area on March 31, 1917, en route to its first Mediterranean cruise, and may have been sunk by the barrage. Thereafter the cruiser command at Cattaro began to plan a raid against the drifters which grew to include three light cruisers, led by Captain Miklós Horthy in the *Novara*, supplemented by a diversion on the coast of Albania by two destroyers, commanded by Captain Prince Johannes von und zu Liechtenstein, with one German and two Austro-Hungarian U-boats staking out the Allied bases at Brindisi and Valona to torpedo warships attempting to respond to the raid.

This plan resulted in the Battle of the Otranto Straits (May 15, 1917), the war's most extensive high-sea action in the Adriatic. The battle opened with a predawn attack by Horthy against the drifter line, sinking fourteen of the forty-seven boats deployed that night, and damaging four others; meanwhile, Liechtenstein's destroyers sank three ships in an Italian convoy off the Albanian coast, along with a destroyer escorting them. The U-boats failed to target a single Allied ship coming out to pursue the raiders, and by daylight the Allies had deployed three cruisers and thirteen destroyers to search for Horthy's cruisers, while two cruisers and five destroyers hunted Liechtenstein's destroyers. For much of the morning, most of these Allied ships were between the Austro-Hungarian ships and the safety of Cattaro. A running battle lasting from 09:00 until 12:00 left the *Novara* battered and Horthy badly wounded after he ordered his 3,500-ton ship, armed with 3.9-inch (10-cm) guns, to close with the 5,300-ton British cruiser *Dartmouth*, which featured 6-inch (15.2-cm) guns. The German *UC 25* (*Kapitänleutnant* Johannes Feldkirchner) intervened to torpedo the *Dartmouth*, which had to be towed back to Brindisi; Horthy's *Novara* likewise had to be

Figure 8.2 Captain (later Rear Admiral) Miklós Horthy

towed back to Cattaro after the battle. Liechtenstein's destroyers survived the action by taking refuge for part of the morning at Durazzo, an Austrian-occupied port in northern Albania, before rejoining Horthy's cruisers to make it safely home. On the afternoon of May 15 a French destroyer sank after striking a mine laid by *UC 25* during the morning action, bringing the total Allied losses in the battle to two destroyers, three merchantmen, and fourteen drifters, against no losses for the attackers.[42]

The Battle of the Otranto Straits had the effect of opening the mouth of the Adriatic to U-boats for the following six weeks, during which time the Allies deployed drifters on the barrage line only

[42] See Paul G. Halpern, *The Battle of the Otranto Straits: Controlling the Gateway to the Adriatic in World War I* (Bloomington, IN: Indiana University Press, 2004).

during the daylight hours. The Austro-Hungarian victory, by a badly outnumbered force, caused further recriminations in the already tense relationship between the British, French, and Italians, especially after the Italian commander, the Duke of the Abruzzi, took the opportunity to once again request that the Allies contribute more resources to blockade the mouth of the Adriatic. The British sent just one additional light cruiser, but opened a seaplane station at Otranto, reinforcing Allied air superiority over the straits for the remainder of the war. The U-boat threat from the Adriatic necessitated a convoy system in the Mediterranean as well, including an American force based at Gibraltar and a significant Japanese contribution (one cruiser and fourteen destroyers) at Malta. Thus, Austria-Hungary, by maintaining a classic "fleet in being," continued to tie down an enemy force many times larger than its own. British frustration with the Italians and French, and the clear need for higher-profile British involvement, brought a series of command changes in August 1917 after Kerr was recalled home. The British Adriatic Squadron, downgraded to the "British Adriatic Force," remained under Abruzzi's overall authority (and, after a vacancy of a few months, directly under Commodore Sir Howard Kelly), while the British Eastern Mediterranean Squadron, after three years' existence, gave way to a restored Mediterranean Fleet command, with Admiral Sir Somerset Gough-Calthorpe at its head. As for the Otranto barrage, by the end of the war it had taken on a much more formidable character, but remained porous enough for a careful U-boat commander to get through. Niemöller, returning to the Adriatic for the first time in two years, in July 1918 captained *UC 67* through the straits, taking note of the "stout steel net... between the coast of Italy at Santa Maria di Leuca and the northern extremity of Corfu" that had not been there in 1916. To enable surface vessels to pass overhead, the top of the net was "a fathom" under water, while the bottom edge was "a good two hundred feet under water," certainly an inconvenience but hardly a barrier, as the straits were 2,600 feet (800 m) deep at their deepest point.[43]

Meanwhile, on the Dover barrage, Rear Admiral Bacon's plan to create a multilayered underwater "vertical wall of mines" was finally implemented after the resumption of unrestricted submarine warfare, and completed late in 1917.[44] The more formidable fixed barrage did

[43] Niemöller, *From U-Boat to Pulpit*, p. 88.
[44] Bacon, *The Dover Patrol*, vol. 1, p. 106.

not bring the end of drifter patrols; these continued to bring meager results, but on November 24 boats operating out of Ramsgate, 5 miles (7 km) east of Dover, caught *U 48* in their drag-nets.[45] Overall, the combination of fixed and dragged antisubmarine nets and mines claimed just six more U-boats during the remainder of the war, but several others were lost to minefields sown off the Dutch and Flemish coasts, or disappeared without a trace after leaving the Belgian ports of Ostend and Zeebrugge. German destroyers operating out of those bases had long posed a menace to vessels of the Auxiliary Patrol operating in the Straits of Dover, at much closer range than Cattaro to the Otranto Straits; indeed, Zeebrugge was just 80 miles (130 km) from Dover, Ostend slightly closer. During 1917 Bacon used coastal monitors to bombard both ports, with the heaviest shelling against Zeebrugge on the night of May 11/12 and Ostend on June 4–5, but the canals linking both ports to Bruges, 6 miles (10 km) inland, remained open to submarines and smaller German surface warships.[46]

During 1916 Bacon proposed the most ambitious antisubmarine barrage of all, the so-called Northern barrage, to close the "safe route" for U-boats around the north of Scotland into the open Atlantic. The Admiralty approved the project in September 1917, but work did not begin until the following March, after the stormy winter months had passed. By October 1918, the British and American navies had accomplished the monumental task of assembling nets and sowing 70,000 mines along the 325 miles (525 km) between the Orkney Islands and the coast of Norway, a line four times longer than the final iteration of the Otranto barrage. The results (six or seven U-boats sunk) hardly justified the massive effort and cost, estimated to have reached $40 million in 1918 dollars,[47] or equal to the price of the two newest US Navy dreadnoughts (the 32,000-ton *Mississippi* and *New Mexico*) combined.

In addition to depth charges, aerial bombing, Q-ships, and barrages, another potential weapon in the antisubmarine arsenal was the Allied superiority in capital ships, which the United States, from the time of its entry into the war, advocated using directly against submarine bases as the quickest way to end the U-boat threat. Given the belts of minefields and the natural obstacles protecting the U-boat bases of

---

[45] *Ibid.*, vol. 2, p. 71.   [46] *Ibid.*, vol. 1, pp. 138–144.
[47] Black, *The British Naval Staff*, p. 171.

the Central Powers in the North Sea and the Adriatic, the British considered such proposals fanciful, and no doubt found alarming the speech made by President Wilson on August 11, 1917, aboard the dreadnought *Pennsylvania* while on a visit to the Atlantic Fleet, in which he compared a submarine base to a hornet's nest, declaring that he was "willing to sacrifice half the fleet Great Britain and we together have to crush that nest, because if we crush it, the war is won."[48]

Wilson's remark may have been an indirect endorsement of a secret plan the Admiralty had shared with Lloyd George's war cabinet the previous month, under which the Allies would take advantage of their now overwhelming superiority in capital ships by refitting almost half of them for service in a special "Allied Inshore Fleet," while the rest constituted an "Allied Bluewater Fleet," assuming the role that Britain's Grand Fleet had served in the war thus far. The proposed Inshore Fleet, featuring hulls modified with bulges for protection against torpedoes and mines, would operate from a base established on one of Germany's coastal islands, either Sylt in the North Frisians, off the west coast of Schleswig, or Borkum in the East Frisians, near the German–Dutch border, the proximity of which allowed a "return to the old and definitely recognized policy of close and aggressive blockade," sufficient to seal all the enemy's ports and bases. As an alternative to seizing a German island – a costly venture, and one that might be easily overturned by a counterattack – the plan proposed the creation of an artificial harbor in the shallow waters of Horns Reef off the Danish coast, to be constructed by sinking caissons filled with concrete, the method eventually used in June 1944 to build the two "Mulberry" harbors at the Normandy beaches. The Inshore Fleet was to include twenty-four dreadnoughts (twelve British, eight US, and four French), backed by Britain's two most formidable pre-dreadnoughts, the *Lord Nelson* and *Agamemnon*, and the five surviving French pre-dreadnoughts of the *Danton* class. The Bluewater Fleet would include thirty dreadnoughts (twenty-one British, six US, and three French). The battle cruisers (all British) were not mentioned, but presumably free to operate either with the Bluewater Fleet or on assignments in the Mediterranean or elsewhere, while the sixteen largest British monitors, mounting a total of

---

[48] Quoted in Josephus Daniels, *Our Navy at War* (New York: George H. Dolan, 1922), p. 146.

thirty-two heavy guns, were to supplement the Inshore Fleet. The plan divided the most formidable ships, the British dreadnoughts with 15-inch (38-cm) guns, more or less equitably, assigning the five *Queen Elizabeth*s to the Bluewater Fleet and the four *Royal Sovereign*s to the Inshore Fleet, but, beyond that, the Bluewater Fleet included the newest dreadnoughts with the heaviest guns, among them the US Navy's six ships with 14-inch (35.6-cm) guns and the French navy's three with 14.2-inch (36-cm) guns, while the Inshore Fleet included the oldest dreadnoughts, with none mounting heavier than 12-inch guns. Because each of these fleets would enjoy roughly a 3:2 margin of superiority over the High Sea Fleet, the Admiralty considered each strong enough to take on the Germans without the help of the other.[49]

The plan reflected the Admiralty's frustration at "the policy of distant blockade," which "was not adopted from choice, but from necessity," because the unprecedented nature of the submarine and mine threats had precluded stationing a fleet closer to the enemy.[50] While Wilson's speech appeared to endorse the idea, his remarks may have been coincidental, for there remains no direct evidence that the British ever shared the plan with the Americans. In any event, nothing came of it, and on just one occasion thereafter did the British make aggressive use of capital ships in any way approaching what Wilson had advocated. On November 17, 1917, Beatty sent Vice Admiral T. W. D. Napier with the new battle cruisers *Courageous*, *Glorious*, and *Repulse*, eight light cruisers, and a number of destroyers into the Helgoland Bight to disrupt an otherwise routine German effort to clear paths for U-boats to sortie through the British minefields laid beyond the German mine perimeter. It was the only time that British capital ships ventured south of the 55°30′N "risk nothing" limit set in September 1916 by Jellicoe and Beatty, and the results were negligible. The British forces exchanged shots with the German warships covering that day's minesweeping operations, including the dreadnoughts *Kaiser* and *Kaiserin*, scoring five hits and sustaining seven before withdrawing. This inconclusive "Second Battle of Helgoland Bight," fought nearly a year before the Armistice, would be the war's last engagement involving British and German capital ships.

[49] Memorandum, "Naval War Policy," July 1917, TNA: PRO CAB24/19/99.
[50] Ibid., p. 3.

Foreshadowing the German submarine warfare capability of the Second World War, during the last year of the war two of the seven large "submarine cruisers" took advantage of their range to venture right up to North American coastal waters. Between May 24 and June 28, 1918, *U 151* (Captain Heinrich von Nostitz und Jänckendorff) sank twenty ships totaling 50,635 tons, including nine American vessels, among them the 5,093-ton passenger steamer *Carolina*, 125 miles (200 km) southeast of Sandy Hook on June 2, with the loss of thirteen lives. Nostitz's departure for home coincided with the arrival in American waters of *U 156* (*Kapitänleutnant* Richard Feldt), which between June 26 and August 26, 1918, sank thirty-six ships totaling 42,291 tons, among them fifteen American and twelve Canadian vessels. Feldt's victims included the 13,680-ton armored cruiser *San Diego*, the largest US Navy ship sunk in the war, which on July 19 struck a mine laid by *U 156* off Long Island. But not all the big U-boats enjoyed such success. The final cruise of *U 152* (*Kapitänleutnant* Adolf Franz) included an attack on an American convoy northwest of the Azores on September 29–30, resulting in damage to the 6,936-ton tanker *George G. Henry* and the sinking of the 5,130-ton freighter *Ticonderoga* (213 dead), but the latter was one of just two ships Franz managed to sink during the entire mission. A similar futility characterized the West African cruise of *U 153* (Captain Gernot Goetting) in the spring of 1918, which ventured as far south as Dakar, but sank just four ships (12,742 tons). One of the most successful U-boat captains, Max Valentiner, whose 144 confirmed sinkings (299,473 tons) placed him third among the war's German submariners, likewise had little luck commanding a "submarine cruiser." His *U 157* sank just seven ships (10,333 tons) on the war's longest sortie by a U-boat, a 139-day West African cruise (November 1917 to April 1918) all the way to the Gulf of Guinea, within 60 miles (96 km) of the Equator. While Valentiner valued the firepower of *U 157* he had nothing good to say about its handling. Owing to its "laughably weak" engines, on the surface it "ran more slowly than an ordinary steamer," while underwater it "was plump, not agile, and of course even slower than above water." Niemöller, second-in-command of *U 151* on a 114-day West African cruise (August to December 1917), had similar remarks about the handling of the design, blaming its 29-foot (8.9-m) beam, half as wide again as any other submarine of the Great War, for its tendency to rock fore-and-aft in heavy seas, conditions under which "seasickness claim[ed] many victims" even among veterans.[51]

The German navy started 1918 with 142 U-boats, and added sixty-nine more (including forty-seven *UB* boats) between New Year's Day and the Armistice. Another sixteen *UC* minelayers were completed but never activated. Against these additions, sixty-nine were sunk, five converted to training boats, and three interned in neutral countries. This left the Germans with 134 submarines available to sortie at the end of the war, almost exactly the strength of February 1917, when unrestricted submarine warfare resumed. Another 224 were under construction.[52] Unlike the Battle of the Atlantic in the Second World War, which featured a decisive shift of fortunes between March and May 1943 (from the Germans sinking Allied shipping faster than it could be replaced, to the Allies sinking German U-boats faster than they could be replaced), the action in the First World War featured no similar breaking point. After forty-three U-boats were sunk in the last five months of 1917, the monthly rate of loss actually eased during 1918, when sixty-nine were sunk in ten and a half months. At the same time, though, the amount of Allied tonnage sunk continued to fall, despite Germany maintaining a more or less constant number of submarines at sea, most of which were larger and more powerful than those deployed earlier in the war.

The monthly totals for 1918 included 295,630 tons in January, 335,200 tons in February, 368,750 tons in March, 300,070 tons in April, 296,560 tons in May, 268,505 tons in June, 280,820 tons in July, and 310,180 tons in August. Thereafter, the overall collapse of the German war effort brought a dramatic decline in the activity of U-boats. Thus, only their three best months of 1918 topped their worst month of 1917. In the end, the convoy system served as much to deter U-boat attacks as to actually protect merchantmen and troopships from them. Even though, by 1918, the training regime of the U-boat school at Eckernförde on the Baltic included stalking convoys of ships assembled for daily cruises in the bay,[53] on the high seas most U-boat captains avoided

---

[51] Valentiner, *Der Schrecken der Meere*, pp. 224–267, quoted at pp. 226–227; Niemöller, *From U-Boat to Pulpit*, pp. 54–82, quoted at p. 56. Other data from www.uboat.net.
[52] Grant, *U-Boats Destroyed*, p. 140.
[53] Valentiner, *Der Schrecken der Meere*, pp. 269–270.

**Figure 8.3** Captain Lothar von Arnauld de la Perière

the main convoy routes because the presence of so many escorting warships, armed with depth charges, made cruising in those waters too dangerous. That left the alternative of searching in less heavily traveled waters for significant targets steaming alone or unescorted, but there were precious few of those by the last months of the war, and the number of Q-ships among them made submariners wary of approaching the ones they did find. At the same time, the growing danger posed by land-based aircraft and harbor-based seaplanes kept U-boats away from the coastal waters where they had claimed most of their victims earlier in the war. Overall, with the improvements in detection and intelligence guiding the increasing arsenal of antisubmarine threats, the typical U-boat spent less of its time at sea in the role of hunter and more time as the hunted. These factors combined to result in a remarkable number of U-boat cruises during 1918 that met with little or no success.

Notwithstanding the ultimate failure of unrestricted submarine warfare, U-boat commanders numbered among the most celebrated war heroes on the German and Austro-Hungarian home fronts, and the esteem in which they were held only grew as the war dragged on and the Allied blockade caused more hardship. The leading commanders in terms of tonnage sunk were Germany's Lothar Arnauld de la Perière, whose submarines claimed 455,869 tons, including two gunboats, and for Austria-Hungary's much smaller effort, Georg von Trapp, who sank 60,294 tons, including an armored cruiser and a submarine. Arnauld's record appears all the more remarkable considering he did not become a U-boat commander until November 1915, after the first round of unrestricted submarine warfare had ended, and thus his entire total came in the last three years of the war.

## Conclusion

In the First World War, at sea as well as on land, offensive strategies brought significantly higher casualties for the attacker than for the defender. Undersea warfare was no exception. Germany lost over half of its operational U-boats, 178 of 335 (53 percent), and its junior partner in unrestricted submarine warfare, Austria-Hungary, lost 8 of 27 (30 percent). By comparison, Allied rates of submarine loss were much lower: 43 of 269 submarines (16 percent) for Britain, 13 of 72 (18 percent) for France, 9 of 61 (15 percent) for Russia, through December 1917, and 8 of 75 (11 percent) for Italy. A total of 4,474 German submariners lost their lives, a tiny fraction of the army's casualties but, of course, drawn from a much smaller pool of men. Aside from serving as a pilot (for any country), service aboard a German submarine carried with it the highest probability of death of any fighting role in the war. Yet among the commanders, Arnauld, Forstmann, and Valentiner not only led the way in enemy tonnage sunk, they also survived the war. Indeed, the six most successful U-boat captains all survived, as did fourteen of the top eighteen; Walther Schwieger, whose 185,212 tons sunk (including the *Lusitania*'s 30,400) placed him seventh on the list, was the most successful of those killed in action. Such figures, along with the relatively high loss rate of new U-boats on first cruises late in the war, suggest how important a talented, experienced commander could be to the survival of his crew. The German navy understood this and, even late in the war, with the situation becoming desperate, refused to send out submarines whose personnel had yet to log the requisite number of training hours. The 224 U-boats under construction at the Armistice included dozens that could have been commissioned had trained crews been available. Given the challenges of operating a smaller warship type under circumstances in which even the most routine moves could become hazardous or life-threatening, this dilemma had no solution. In the Second World War, the Germans would find, once again, that they could build U-boats faster than they could train competent crews to operate them.

Considered in light of the 178 U-boats and 4,474 submariners lost, the German navy of the Great War sank more enemy shipping (11.9 million tons) at a lower cost than either of history's other large-scale campaigns of submarine warfare. In 1939–45, Hitler's U-boats sank 14.6 million tons of Allied shipping, but lost a staggering 754 boats and 27,491 submariners, while in 1941–45, the US Navy's submarines sank 5.3 million tons of Japanese shipping at a cost of 52 boats and 3,506 American submariners. Yet the U-boats of the Great War failed miserably where it mattered most, defying the assumption that they would prevent significant numbers of American soldiers from being shipped to Europe – the key assumption in the German leadership's rationalization of the renewal of unrestricted submarine warfare. By the time of the Armistice, 2,079,880 US troops had made the crossing safely. U-boats sank just three troop transports and one escorting warship (a French armored cruiser) on the transatlantic route and, thanks to the rescue efforts of other ships in those convoys, only sixty-eight American soldiers were lost at sea. U-boats had no better luck against other Allied troopships, sinking just nine in 1917–18, all in the Mediterranean, with a net loss of life of less than 5,500 men. The war on land ended as it had begun, as a war of attrition in which sheer numbers of troops mattered more than anything else. Especially after the collapse of Russia and the victory of the Central Powers on the Eastern front, the Allies could not have forced the Germans to sue for peace without the manpower of the AEF weighing heavily in the balance. It took over a year for the American presence to be felt on the Western front, but at the Second Battle of the Marne (July 15–August 6, 1918), the high-water mark of Germany's last ditch offensive, its exhausted troops encountered fresh American divisions. Holtzendorff's conclusion, late in 1916, that unrestricted submarine warfare was "the right means to bring the war to a victorious end," and also "the only means to that end,"[54] was based on the assumption that, should the campaign fail, the result would be a continuation of the stalemate until a compromise peace, not defeat. But by bringing the United States into the war while also failing to stop the deployment of the AEF to France, the great gamble doomed Germany to lose the war.

[54] Holtzendorff to Hindenburg, December 22, 1916, text in Scheer, *Germany's High Sea Fleet*, pp. 248–252.

# 9 WAR AND REVOLUTION, 1917

In the autumn of 1914, with the war barely two months old, Tirpitz warned Admiral Hugo von Pohl, then chief of the *Admiralstab*, of the dire consequences if Germany's High Sea Fleet remained at anchor much longer: "morale is bound to be affected as the prospects of warlike activities become ever more remote."[1] After a year of relative idleness between the defeat at Dogger Bank and the appointment of Scheer, the German fleet's six sorties during 1916 dispelled such fears, but the renewed emphasis on submarine warfare once again placed the morale of the navy at risk by dooming so many of its sailors to inactivity. In sharp contrast to the average submarine of the Great War, whose two or three junior officers shared the hardships of their crew of two or three dozen men, the larger warships were social microcosms of the countries they represented. In the German navy, but even more so, in the Austro-Hungarian and Russian fleets, the routines aboard these vessels and even the physical configuration of shipboard space accentuated rather than ameliorated class differences. To make matters worse, because the most highly regarded junior officers were assigned to U-boats, or to the light cruisers and destroyers that remained the most active surface ships, less capable men were left to take their places aboard the battleships and larger cruisers. During the last two years of the war, this mediocre "middle management" aboard the big ships exacerbated the problem of the social gulf between officers and seamen, at a time when their inactivity made effective, enlightened command more

---

[1] Tirpitz to Pohl, October 11, 1914, text in Tirpitz, *My Memoirs*, vol. 2, p. 103.

important than ever. Men aboard ships anchored in home ports also had closer contact with the home front, leaving German sailors, and their Austro-Hungarian and Russian counterparts, more likely to see their own hardships in the context of the general social and political conditions affecting their countries, and to make common cause with those ashore who sought to change those conditions.

In August 1917, six months after the resumption of the undersea campaign, the first mutinies rocked the capital ships at Wilhelmshaven. By then, the Austro-Hungarian battle fleet at Pola, largely idle since its punitive bombardment of the enemy coast when Italy entered the war, had experienced mutiny as well. The Russian Black Sea Fleet, winning its war against the Ottoman navy, had seen more action and enjoyed better morale than the Russian Baltic Fleet, which experienced the most extensive unrest of all, coinciding with the fall of Nicholas II in the revolution of March 1917. The following month, Germany, keen to knock Russia out of the war before the weight of American intervention could be felt on the Western front, provided transport home from Switzerland for Vladimir Ilych Ulianov, known by the revolutionary alias Lenin, and the Bolshevik inner circle. Over the months that followed, the Bolsheviks were especially successful in gaining converts in the Russian navy, in particular in the Baltic Fleet. It was against this much weakened foe that the German navy, seeking action as an antidote to its own morale problems, launched a successful amphibious operation to secure the Gulf of Riga, incorporating lessons learned from its failure there two years earlier.

### The Russian navy, the March Revolution, and the Provisional Government

In the late summer of 1915, shortly after the initial failed German attempt to take Riga, Nicholas II went to the front to assume "personal command" of the Russian army. Because the tsar had no military expertise, the move did nothing for the army, while the cabal he left behind to run the government, including Empress Alexandra's favorite, Grigori Rasputin, only further discredited the tsarist regime on the home front. By the autumn of 1916, Nicholas II's critics among Russia's military leaders and the politicians in the Duma concluded that only decisive change could save the country, but they could agree on little other than that the murder of Rasputin, carried out by a group of young noblemen in December, was a positive step. By the beginning of 1917, the Russian army's front-line manpower was melting away. It had lost 2.7 million men killed or wounded, over 4 million were prisoners, and another 2.3 million were serving in the interior in garrisons, which were soon to join the country's relatively small number of overburdened factories to become hotbeds of revolution.

On January 22, the twelfth anniversary of the Bloody Sunday massacre of the Revolution of 1905, an upheaval Nicholas II had barely withstood, served as the catalyst for the largest demonstrations of the war thus far. Some 150,000 workers struck in Petrograd alone. Over the next six weeks the unrest continued to grow, until on March 8 a demonstration by 200,000 Petrograd workers called for an end to the tsarist regime and the war. At that point the tsar, still at the front, ordered the dissolution of the Duma and the use of force against the protesters. Two days later troops of the Petrograd garrison mutinied rather than fire on the crowds, and the revolution was underway. On March 12, the leaders of the Duma formed the Provisional Government, and the leaders of the street protests reestablished the Petrograd Soviet, the capital city's revolutionary council first formed during the Revolution of 1905.

Over the days that followed, the March Revolution accomplished the overthrow of the tsar with relatively little bloodshed, but of the 169 lives lost, over half were naval officers or petty officers killed at Kronstadt and Helsinki by the sailors serving under them. The main base of the Baltic Fleet at Kronstadt, on an island in the Gulf of Finland 19 miles (30 km) west of Petrograd, by 1917 was home to 30,000 naval personnel, men just as idle and restive as the soldiers of the Petrograd garrison. Vice Admiral Robert Nikolaevich Viren, a former Black Sea Fleet commander who had served as harbor admiral at Kronstadt since 1909, attempted to maintain strict discipline on the base in the midst of the growing unrest in the capital, and paid for it with his life. On the morning of March 14, mutineers surrounded him in Anchor Square and stabbed him to death with their bayonets, then went on to take control of the base, in the process killing another forty officers and a dozen petty officers. At the Baltic Fleet's forward base in Helsinki, Vice Admiral Adrian Nepenin, who had succeeded Vice Admiral Kanin as Baltic Fleet commander the previous September, managed to keep order that day and the next only by imposing an embargo on news from Petrograd and Kronstadt. On March 15, Nepenin and other admirals joined most Russian generals in calling for Nicholas II to abdicate; in the same message to Petrograd he remarked that "with enormous difficulty I control the fleet and retain the trust of the sailors."[2]

Shaken by the expression of no confidence from the leaders of his armed forces, Nicholas II abdicated on the evening of March 15, bypassing his sickly son, Aleksei, in favor of his brother, Grand Duke Michael. The next day Michael refused to accept the crown, instead calling on the Russian people to obey the Provisional Government. Naval leaders who expected the news of the tsar's overthrow to ease tensions in the fleet were surprised when the opposite happened. On the morning of March 16, as soon as Nepenin announced the abdication to the fleet, the crews of the pre-dreadnoughts *Andrei Pervozvanny* and *Imperator Pavel* mutinied and killed forty of their officers, including Vice Admiral Arkadii Nebolsin, commander of the squadron to which the ships belonged. Nepenin met with representatives of the mutineers and bought time by confirming his own allegiance to the Provisional Government, but the sailors rejected his demands for the release of imprisoned officers and the arrest of those who had murdered officers, and presented demands of their own, including the election of officers by their crews. The sailors soon asserted this right by electing a replacement for Nepenin, Vice Admiral Andrei Maksimov, the fleet's only senior officer with a "humane" reputation. Maksimov's peers had long distrusted him as an opportunist, a trait he displayed on March 17 when he appeared dockside of Nepenin's flagship in a motorcar festooned in red bunting, ready to take over the fleet. After Nepenin refused to relinquish command, citing the absence of orders from the Provisional Government, the mutineers shot and killed him. The Provisional Government defused the mutiny by quickly confirming Maksimov as Baltic Fleet commander, but he soon became a figurehead for Pavel Dybenko, chairman of the Baltic Fleet's central committee (*Tsentrobalt*), established in May 1917.[3]

As a revolutionary committee, *Tsentrobalt* took orders from the Petrograd Soviet, as did countless other soviets formed across the country by revolutionary workers, peasants, soldiers, and sailors. On March 14, the day before the tsar abdicated, the Petrograd Soviet had issued its famous Order Number One, sanctioning the creation of soviets within the armed forces and, in effect, ending traditional military discipline in Russia. The order affirmed that the soviets within each

---

[2] Leonard F. Guttridge, *Mutiny: A History of Naval Insurrection* (Annapolis, MD: Naval Institute Press, 2006), pp. 146–147; Nepenin quoted at p. 147.
[3] Guttridge, *Mutiny*, pp. 147–149.

**Figure 9.1** Pavel Dybenko

military unit, including the ships of the navy, were bound to obey the orders of the Provisional Government only if they did not conflict with the orders of the Petrograd Soviet. *Tsentrobalt* thus had veto power over all decisions taken by the leadership of the Baltic Fleet, making its chairman, Dybenko, a 28-year-old common sailor, the *de facto* fleet commander. The arrangement exemplified the chaotic weakness of the post-tsarist government. While, in theory, the Provisional Government inherited the full powers of the old regime and ran the country through the various ministries of the former tsarist bureaucracy, it had to accept a "dual power" arrangement with the Petrograd Soviet and its network of soviets. And because the Provisional Government made the fateful decision to keep Russia in the war, military and naval leaders faced the prospect of fighting while hamstrung by the requirement of the soviets that every officer ultimately had to justify every order to the soldiers or sailors serving under him. Aleksandr Kerensky, a leader of the Socialist Revolutionary Party (SRs), was the only member of both the Provisional Government and the Petrograd Soviet, and thus the central figure in the balancing act of "dual power." While he accumulated the titles of justice minister (March 1917), war minister, and navy minister (May), and retained the latter two when he became prime minister (July), Kerensky's peasant-based SRs and the Menshevik faction of Russian Marxists supported the Provisional Government's decision to keep Russia in the war, making Lenin's Bolsheviks distinctive as the leading antiwar party.

After the abdication of Nicholas II, revolutionary zeal manifested itself most visibly in the wholesale renaming of warships with distinctly tsarist names, such as the *Imperator Pavel* becoming the *Respublika*, but the real transformation came in personnel changes. By mid-summer *Tsentrobalt* had confirmed the elections of replacements for 306 officers, including two dozen admirals. In July, the central committee also accepted Kerensky's extraordinary promotion of Aleksandr Razvozov, a 38-year-old captain, to rear admiral and commander of the Baltic Fleet, replacing Maksimov.[4] Meanwhile, over the summer, Dybenko, a Bolshevik since 1907, played a central role in delivering the fleet to Lenin. During the so-called July Days (July 16–20), when the disastrous end of the Russian army's "Kerensky Offensive" against the Central Powers sparked a crisis within the Provisional Government and street demonstrations in Petrograd, *Tsentrobalt* mobilized support for a Bolshevik takeover and Dybenko personally led a naval contingent from Helsinki to the capital. At the time, the Bolsheviks were still a minority in both the Petrograd Soviet and the First All-Russian Congress of Soviets, which had convened the preceding month, and neither heeded Lenin's call to turn against the Provisional Government. After the collapse of the revolt, Lenin temporarily went into hiding in Finland; meanwhile, Kerensky had Dybenko arrested and attempted to purge *Tsentrobalt* of Bolsheviks.[5] As navy minister, Kerensky enjoyed the support of at least some sailors during the July Days, in particular a delegation from the Black Sea Fleet that participated in the storming of the Petrograd headquarters of the Bolsheviks, evidence that Lenin's followers did not yet have the entire navy on their side.[6]

If idleness predisposed sailors to mutiny, the Black Sea Fleet's frequent activity throughout the war, by units of all types, explains why it succumbed to serious morale problems later than the Baltic Fleet. Over the winter of 1916/17, Vice Admiral Kolchak attempted to recover from the demoralizing loss of the dreadnought *Imperatritsa Maria* to a magazine explosion (October 20, 1916) by preparing the Black Sea Fleet for a major assault on Constantinople. Four more

---

[4] D. G. Kirby, "A Navy in Revolution: The Russian Baltic Fleet in 1917," in Peter Karstens (ed.), *Motivating Soldiers: Morale or Mutiny* (London: Taylor & Francis, 1998), p. 205; Michael B. Barrett, *Operation Albion: The German Conquest of the Baltic Islands* (Bloomington, IN: Indiana University Press, 2008), p. 72.
[5] Kirby, "A Navy in Revolution," p. 207.
[6] Alexander Rabinowitch, *The Bolsheviks Come to Power: The Revolution of 1917 in Petrograd* (New York: W. W. Norton, 1978), p. 26.

seaplane tenders (converted from Romanian passenger liners) joined the existing tenders *Imperator Aleksandr I* and *Imperator Nikolai I*. These were deployed for raids against Sinope and several smaller northern Turkish coastal towns in the spring of 1917, none of which did much damage. After convoying a total of 53,000 troops from Sevastopol to the Caucasus front during 1916, the navy transported another 61,000 in the first four months of 1917 alone. As in the Baltic, in the Black Sea the revolution of March 1917 brought the wholesale renaming of warships and the organization of soviets aboard each of them, led by a Black Sea counterpart to *Tsentrobalt* known as *Tsentroflot*, though initially with far less Bolshevik influence. Kolchak took the dreadnought *Svobodnaya Rossiya* (ex-*Imperatritsa Ekaterina Velikaya*) to the Bosporus in late April and again in late May to cover preparatory minelaying operations, but by the end of spring the effects of Order Number One had caused enough of a deterioration in discipline that the larger warships could no longer be counted upon to operate effectively, and the planned attack on the Ottoman capital was never attempted. On June 5, when the soviets aboard his ships demanded that officers surrender all their weapons, an exasperated Kolchak assembled the crew of his flagship and, in a theatrical gesture, removed his sword and threw it into the sea. The following day he turned over command of the fleet to Rear Admiral V. K. Lukin and left his post, without first asking permission from the Provisional Government. Kerensky, who considered Kolchak a potential political rival, took advantage of the opportunity to reprimand him, then allowed him to leave Russia on a "technical mission" of naval officers to the United States. In August, *Tsentroflot* accepted Kerensky's extraordinary promotion of Aleksandr Nemits, a 38-year-old captain, to rear admiral and commander of the Black Sea Fleet, replacing Lukin. Meanwhile, on the Ottoman side of the Black Sea, Vice Admiral Souchon faced challenges of his own. The resumption of unrestricted submarine warfare brought the withdrawal of almost all German submarines from the Black Sea for use elsewhere, and a worsening coal shortage kept the flagship *Yavuz Sultan Selim* on a short leash operationally. On June 26, the *Svobodnaya Rossiya* appeared off the Bosporus for a third time, again to cover a mining operation, and exchanged fire with the light cruiser *Midilli*, returning to base from a mining operation of its own off the mouth of the Danube; in the war's last meeting between ships flying the Russian and Turkish flags, neither side managed to hit the other. On August 24, the *Svobodnaya Rossiya* covered a raid on the small northern Turkish port of Ordu by seaplane tenders and destroyers, supported by the auxiliary cruisers *Regele Carol I* and *Dacia*, former Romanian passenger ships armed by the Russians, but the operation was plagued by discipline problems and, in any event, failed to do much damage.[7]

The focus then shifted back to the Baltic, where Bolsheviks in *Tsentrobalt* and the Helsinki and Reval soviets played a crucial role in mobilizing naval personnel and local army garrisons against the late summer attempt by General Lavr Kornilov to march on Petrograd and suppress the revolution (September 9–13). Kerensky responded to the threat from the Right by appealing to the Left, releasing Bolsheviks imprisoned since the July Days, including Dybenko; this shrewd move paid immediate dividends when, on September 11, Kronstadt alone rushed 3,000 sailors to help to defend the capital. The role of the Bolsheviks in stopping the Kornilov coup strengthened their hand within the soviets, and further strengthened the soviets vis-à-vis Kerensky and the Provisional Government, who would not have survived without their support. The Kornilov affair also further radicalized the Baltic Fleet by leading suspicious sailors to question anew the political loyalties of their officers. For example, aboard the dreadnought *Petropavlovsk*, four junior officers were condemned to death by a vote of the crew and shot by a firing squad for the crime of refusing to affirm their support for "democratic organizations." Afterward, sailors of the Baltic Fleet joined soldiers and workers in electing an overwhelmingly Bolshevik leadership for a regional congress of soviets convening in Helsinki on September 22,[8] thus foreshadowing the Bolshevik triumphs in securing majorities in the soviets of Petrograd (October 5) and Moscow (October 15).

## The 1917 mutinies in Austria-Hungary and Germany

As the war approached its third anniversary, multinational Austria-Hungary ranked second only to Russia in the volatility of its internal situation. The sobering example of the fall of Nicholas II helped inspire

---

[7] Pavel N. Zyrianov, *Admiral Kolchak: verkhovnyi pravitel' Rossii*, 4th edn. (Moscow: Molodaia gvardiia, 2012), pp. 336–339 and *passim*; Peter Fleming, *The Fate of Admiral Kolchak* (New York: Harcourt, Brace & World, 1963), pp. 32–33; Langensiepen *et al.*, *Halbmond und Kaiseradler*, pp. 160–164, 166–167; René Greger, *The Russian Fleet, 1914–1917*, trans. Jill Gearing (London: Ian Allan, 1972), pp. 61–65.

[8] Rabinowitch, *The Bolsheviks Come to Power*, pp. 143–146, 168.

Emperor Charles, in May 1917, to reconvene the Austrian *Reichsrat* (which had last met in 1914) and promise future constitutional reforms that would facilitate "the free national and cultural development of equally privileged peoples." In June, Admiral Njegovan presided over the first imperial naval review since 1902, at which Charles was pleased to find the battle fleet in apparent good order despite two years of inactivity. But during the following month, sailors in Pola organized the first protests over a reduction in rations that had been introduced in January in the midst of the "turnip winter." The workers in the Pola Arsenal likewise were restive, on short rations of their own and, for those with families, separated from loved ones, as 64,400 civilians had been evacuated from the town. Because Austro-Hungarian airmen exchanged frequent (though not very destructive) raids with their Italian counterparts at Venice, the removal of civilians deemed non-essential to the war effort was touted as a safety measure. It also had political overtones, since ethnic Italians constituted a majority of Pola's population, and in other sensitive areas, such as along the Alpine front, Habsburg Italians had been relocated to camps in the interior of the empire amid concerns about their loyalty.[9]

Njegovan dealt leniently with the food protests of July, then faced a further decline in morale after introducing the rationing of clothing and shoes in August. When Charles visited the fleet again in October, crews assembled to greet him mixed the conventional cheers of "*Hurrah!*" with sarcastic shouts of "*Hunger!*," but with the emperor too far away to hear the difference. That same month, the Austro-Hungarian navy experienced its most serious breach of discipline of the war thus far when *Torpedoboot 11*, an older 115-ton vessel assigned to the small Dalmatian port of Sebenico, defected to Italy after a Slovene boatswain's mate and a Czech machinist led the crew in overpowering their two officers. The behavior of the mutineers that day – first sparing the lives of the officers, then destroying code books and other sensitive materials before reaching the Italian coast – indicates that war weariness rather than treason provided their motivation. But such details were not known to Njegovan and other navy leaders, or to their German counterparts, who actively feared a general mutiny of the Austro-Hungarian fleet.

---

[9] For this and the following paragraph, see Sondhaus, *The Naval Policy of Austria-Hungary*, pp. 308–312.

The Germans had good reason to question the reliability of the idle fleet of their allies, because by then their own navy had experienced its first mutiny. Vigilance against unrest in the German fleet dated from May Day, when naval authorities in Kiel had prohibited personnel from attending the local commemoration of the international workers' holiday, which included speeches by politicians of the Social Democratic Party (SPD) and its antiwar splinter, the Independent Social Democratic Party (USPD). Three weeks later, after sailors, stokers, and petty officers turned out for a rally in Kiel, which included a speech by an SPD Reichstag deputy critical of German war aims, the Baltic station command made all political meetings off limits. The following month, the North Sea station command at Wilhelmshaven warned the officers of the High Sea Fleet to be vigilant against the influence of the local USPD and imposed a ban on the circulation of its publications. These restrictions came at a time when overall inactivity caused the idle sailors and stokers to focus more on the hardships of their service. As the capital ships entered the summer of 1917 having not moved since the previous autumn, the crews chafed at their limited shore leave compared with that of the officers, many of whom kept private apartments in town, and at the poor quality and reduced quantity of their food supplies at a time when the typical officers' mess remained well stocked. Recognizing the food situation as a potential flashpoint for protests, on June 20 Admiral Eduard von Capelle, Tirpitz's successor as state secretary of the Imperial Navy Office, called for each ship to create a food commission (*Menagekommission*) representative of the crew, but most captains did not take the order seriously and thus missed an opportunity to defuse tensions.[10]

Aboard some of the ships where the commissions were created, the measure came too late to reconcile sailors and stokers with their officers. These included the dreadnought *Friedrich der Grosse*, where the food commission only provided the catalyst for much broader activism. The crew elected as head of its commission Seaman First Class Max Reichpietsch, a member of the USPD who had visited the party's headquarters in Berlin during a recent leave. Reichpietsch soon organized agitation for food commissions aboard ships whose captains had not

[10] Holger H. Herwig, *The German Naval Officer Corps, 1890–1918: A Social and Political History* (Oxford: Clarendon Press, 1973), pp. 199–202; Daniel Horn, *The German Naval Mutinies of World War I* (New Brunswick, NJ: Rutgers University Press, 1969), pp. 41–42, 65–66.

formed them. Along with shipmate Willi Sachse, a stoker, he also circulated USPD literature in the fleet, accompanied by a petition supporting the party's position at the peace conference of the Socialist International, then underway at Stockholm in neutral Sweden, calling for "peace without indemnities or annexations."[11] Within weeks, the Reichstag's Peace Resolution (July 19, 1917), passed by a coalition including the mainstream SPD, the Catholic Center Party, and progressive liberals, echoed the call for a just peace, in defiance of the annexationist policies embraced by Bethmann Hollweg, Hindenburg, and Ludendorff, thus contributing to a situation in which any spark was liable to enflame the fleet. The spark came on July 31, when an officer canceled a motion picture scheduled to be shown to the stokers of the dreadnought *Prinzregent Luitpold*. The following morning, Stoker Alban Köbis, an acquaintance of Reichpietsch and Sachse, joined another stoker in leading a brief strike by forty-five of their peers to protest the cancellation. A dozen of the strikers received two- and three-week jail terms, and even though these lenient sentences were suspended immediately, on August 2 around 600 of the *Prinzregent Luitpold*'s 700 sailors and stokers protested the punishments by going ashore and marching into Wilhelmshaven. After an officer cowed them into returning to their ship, their squadron commander, Vice Admiral Franz von Mauve, announced the dropping of all charges, but only as a ruse to pacify the crew and enable the *Prinzregent Luitpold* to be moved to the isolation of the roadstead, where formal charges were brought against Köbis and other leaders of the mutiny. The ensuing investigation led back to the *Friedrich der Grosse*, incriminating Reichpietsch and Sachse, and the latter, under leading questioning, made a confession that the USPD had sought to revolutionize the fleet. On August 26, these three were among five men sentenced to death by a naval court, but of the five only Köbis and Reichpietsch were executed, on Scheer's direct order. After the sentences were carried out, on September 5, Scheer boasted that "order was restored in the fleet," but other naval leaders, in particular Capelle, doubted that the exercise of making examples of two men had served its intended purpose.[12]

In any event, from August onward the captains of the High Sea Fleet sought to prevent further mutinies by identifying the malcontents

---

[11] Horn, *German Naval Mutinies*, pp. 112–113. For a brief synopsis of the Stockholm Conference, see Sondhaus, *World War I*, pp. 359–360.
[12] Horn, *German Naval Mutinies*, pp. 132–163, Scheer quoted at p. 163.

within their crews and sending them ashore. Over 150 were transferred during the trials of the mutineers and, during the autumn months, several hundred more followed, so many that the station command in Wilhelmshaven protested "the collection of all the worse elements... in the shore units" and finally ended the practice in December.[13] Scheer made up for the loss in manpower by deactivating the II Squadron, consisting of the newest pre-dreadnoughts, after its commander, Vice Admiral Hubert von Rebeur-Paschwitz, was sent to Constantinople in September to replace Souchon. The mutiny and the mass reassignments of personnel left the German navy particularly vulnerable, especially in light of intelligence reports indicating that the British had a fairly accurate picture of what had happened. Sir Eric Geddes, Carson's successor as First Lord of the Admiralty, reported on the mutiny to the war cabinet in early October, remarking that "there had been reports for some time that the state of affairs in German ships had been bad" and that "the Admiralty's view was that the trouble had been serious."[14] Nevertheless, aside from Napier's battle cruiser raid of November 17, which resulted in the inconclusive Second Battle of Helgoland Bight (see Chapter 8), the British at this stage made no attempt to test the fighting ability of the High Sea Fleet.

During the last months of 1917, the Germans pressured their Austro-Hungarian allies to follow their example and disarm more of their older warships not only to provide additional manpower to support the German U-boats at Pola and Cattaro, but also to have fewer idle men riding at anchor aboard ships not likely to see action again. A formal request to this effect came in November, after William II made a brief visit to Pola to inspect the Austro-Hungarian fleet and the German submarine base there. Njegovan agreed to decommission the oldest two classes of pre-dreadnoughts following the loss of one of them, the 5,600-ton coast defender *Wien*, torpedoed during a December nighttime raid on Trieste harbor by two Italian *motobarche antisommergibili* (MAS) boats, high-speed craft similar in design to the British CMB (coastal motor boat). He also retired the protected cruiser *Kaiser Franz Joseph I*, whose sister ship *Kaiserin Elisabeth* had been sunk by the Japanese at Tsingtao in 1914. As the war entered its last year, Njegovan ranked as the leading pessimist among the generals and

---

[13] Quoted in *Ibid.*, p. 190.
[14] "War Cabinet, 248," minutes of meeting of October 12, 1917, TNA: PRO CAB 23/4/22, p. 3.

admirals of the Central Powers. While the German navy feared a socialist upheaval on the Russian model, for the Austro-Hungarian navy the nationality problem caused greater concern, as every larger warship was a floating microcosm of the multinational empire. A Croatian loyal to the Habsburgs, Njegovan understood better than his peers the recent erosion of traditional Croatian fidelity to the Dual Monarchy, as well as the potential of the South Slav or Yugoslav ideal – the common cause of Croats and Slovenes with the Serbs – to be a disintegrating factor for Austria-Hungary as a whole and its navy in particular.[15]

## Second Riga, "Operation Albion," and the end of Russian naval operations

As early as May 1917, one month after the German High Command orchestrated the return of Lenin to Russia, Ludendorff pushed the navy to agree to a joint Baltic operation with the army in order to put further pressure on the Provisional Government. This endeavor would have the added benefit of providing a mission for the capital ships of the High Sea Fleet, breaking the monotony of life at anchor in Wilhelmshaven. Ludendorff's first choice of targets, the Aaland Islands, commanding the mouth of the Gulf of Bothnia between Sweden and Finland, was rejected out of hand by the navy as impractical, and planning failed to progress before the summer mutinies made joint operations, at least temporarily, out of the question. Rather than wait for the navy, the army proceeded with its own attack, targeting Riga, since August 1915 the northern terminus of the Eastern front.

In the two years since the front first came to Riga, the Russians had bolstered its defenses, headquartering their Twelfth Army there, but evacuated most of the city's workers to factories in other places out of harm's way. The families of the workers went with them, leaving barely half of Riga's prewar population of 475,000 still in the city when the Germans attacked again. Like the First Battle of Riga, the second battle began as an attempt by the army to secure its objectives without naval support. On September 1, 1917, the German Eighth Army (now under General Oskar von Hutier) attacked the city and quickly breached its western defenses. While this move forced the defenders to abandon Riga west of the Dvina, by September 3 a second, larger German

[15] Sondhaus, *The Naval Policy of Austria-Hungary*, pp. 313–316.

penetration through the southeastern defenses threatened to trap the Twelfth Army in the city. As the Russians began to retreat from Riga, Hutier's vigorous pursuit resulted in the capture of several thousand prisoners and 150 guns before the fighting subsided and the front stabilized near Wenden (Cēsis), 80 miles (130 km) to the northeast.[16] The three-day battle cost the Germans 4,200 casualties, the Russians 25,000, and left Riga in ruins, with the distinction of being one of the few eastern European cities to experience greater devastation in the First World War than in the Second. It would take until 1950 for Riga's population to recover to 1913 levels.

In contrast to August 1915, in September 1917 the defenders of Riga did not enjoy the same vigorous fire support from naval units deployed in the adjacent gulf, even though the Russian Baltic Fleet detachment there was actually larger than it had been two years earlier. The pre-dreadnought *Slava* and lighter vessels already on hand had been joined by a second battleship, the pre-dreadnought *Grazhdanin* (ex-*Tsesarevich*), as well as the armored cruisers *Bayan* and *Admiral Makarov*. Thanks to the dredging of Moon Sound, the Russians could now send ships as large as these (but not dreadnoughts) into the gulf from the north, directly from Helsinki, Kronstadt, and other bases on the Gulf of Finland, without risking them in the open Baltic, owing to their formidable minefields and the natural barrier formed by the islands of Ösel, Dagö, and Moon. In August, the naval command in the Gulf of Riga passed to Mikhail Bakhirev, now a vice admiral and, despite his monarchist sympathies, the navy's senior surviving officer. He was known as an aggressive commander, but Order Number One limited his efforts to use the forces at his disposal, and he could offer no help to the Twelfth Army during Hutier's attack. Thus, in 1917, unlike in 1915, the question for the Germans was not how to bring naval power to bear to take Riga itself, but how to use it to take control of the gulf after the city fell to the army.[17]

German army leaders now recognized that the occupation of Ösel, Dagö, and Moon was the key to securing the coastal flank of the army for a further advance from Riga toward Petrograd and, in particular, to securing the Gulf of Riga as an entrepôt for supplies to

[16] "Der Weltkrieg am 4. September 1917," *Amtliche Kriegs-Depeschen nach Berichten des Wolff'schen Telegr.-Bureaus*, vol. 7 (Berlin: Nationaler Verlag, 1918).
[17] Barrett, *Operation Albion*, pp. 28, 73, 84–85.

be shipped to the front directly from Germany. At the same time, in the aftermath of the Wilhelmshaven mutiny, their navy counterparts welcomed a major naval operation as an antidote to further unrest aboard the capital ships of the High Sea Fleet. On September 6, Admiral Holtzendorff and the army High Command staff resumed their earlier discussions about amphibious operations. The prevailing mood – the day after the executions of Köbis and Reichpietsch, and three days after Hutier's troops took the city of Riga – left all parties determined to act decisively. Holtzendorff informed the generals that the navy could move on just 25 days' notice, and with the onset of the Baltic winter fast approaching, there was little time to spare. Among the admirals only Prince Henry thought there was not enough time before the weather turned; Scheer, Hipper, and the others were keen to act. On September 11, planning began in earnest for the operation codenamed "Albion." Ten days later, William II signed the orders to proceed, confirming Vice Admiral Schmidt, veteran of the 1915 Riga campaign, as commander of the operation. The manpower for a landing on Ösel came from the 42nd (Alsatian) Division, part of Hutier's army in the Second Battle of Riga, which was pulled from the front northeast of the city and sent by rail to Libau, the assembly point for the operation. In its final form the plan called for the troops to take Ösel and Moon, linked by a causeway 2.2 miles (3.5 km) in length, while the navy destroyed the Russian warships defending the Gulf of Riga and Moon Sound. The success of these operations would isolate any Russians remaining on Dagö, deemed of secondary importance because it did not border the gulf. At the end of September *UC 58* reconnoitered the proposed landing site, at Tagga Bay (Tagalaht) near the northwest tip of Ösel, and returned to Libau reporting thin shore defenses and no mines. While the latter assessment, as it turned out, was overly optimistic, Tagga Bay's flat, sandy beaches made it the ideal place for an amphibious landing. As at Gallipoli, the troops would land on Ösel in longboats towed by steam launches, but in a step toward the future, the Germans adapted horse scows – boxy rectangular landing craft with drop-gate sterns – to enable field artillery and wagons, and the horses to pull them, to land directly on the beaches.[18]

---

[18] Bengelsdorf, *Der Seekrieg in der Ostsee*, pp. 112–113, 126, 131; Barrett, *Operation Albion*, pp. 1–3, 42–55. See also Erich von Tschischwitz, *The Army and Navy during the Conquest of the Baltic Islands in October 1917*, trans. Henry Hossfeld

Figure 9.2  Horse scow as landing craft

The only drawback of Tagga Bay was its relatively shallow water, insufficient to accommodate heavier warships or heavily laden transports; for this reason, the 20,000 men of the 42nd Division, along with 5,000 horses, 60 guns, and supplies, were dispersed among eighteen transport ships to ensure that none would ride low enough in the water to risk running aground. To escort them, Scheer sent nearly half the High Sea Fleet from Wilhelmshaven through the Kiel Canal to the Baltic, where they waited off Danzig to avoid contributing to the congestion at Libau. Schmidt's eleven capital ships included the lone battle cruiser *Moltke*, which he used as his flagship, ten dreadnoughts (among them the troubled *Prinzregent Luitpold* and *Friedrich der Grosse*), nine light cruisers, fifty-five destroyers and torpedo boats, six submarines, and a host of minesweepers. He had no shortage of talent among his subordinates. The two dreadnought squadrons were commanded by Vice Admiral Behncke, the most senior officer wounded at Jutland, and Vice Admiral Souchon, just returned from Constantinople; the two

(Fort Leavenworth, KS: Command and General Staff School Press, 1933), p. 26 and *passim*.

cruiser groups were commanded by Rear Admiral Hopman, a veteran of the Baltic theater, and Rear Admiral Ludwig von Reuter, who would command the High Sea Fleet during its postwar internment at Scapa Flow. Schmidt and his staff made the most of the short time at their disposal to prepare for the operation. On September 29, the day after *UC 58* scouted Tagga Bay, nearly 3,500 troops shipped aboard two of the transports to practice a beach landing in the outer harbor of Libau. Starting on October 1, German aircraft flew reconnaissance missions over Ösel, Dagö, and Moon whenever the weather permitted, taking 30,000 photographs. And during the first ten days of October, other airplanes and airships dropped 5,900 tons of bombs on the Russian defenses of the islands.[19]

The bombing raids focused on the weak shore batteries covering Tagga Bay, and on the much more formidable batteries added during 1916–17 in two key locations: at the southwest tip of Ösel, covering the western passage into the Gulf of Riga via the Irben Straits; and on Moon Island, covering the northern passage from the gulf into Moon Sound. The Russian garrison consisted of the 107th Division, theoretically equal in strength to the attacking Germans, but actually barely 10,000 men, three-quarters of whom garrisoned Ösel, the rest Dagö. These troops, like the sailors aboard Bakhirev's ships, had organized soviets, which cooperated with the civilian soviet at Arensburg (Kuressaare). Arensburg, a town of 5,000 located on the gulf side of Ösel, was also the island's only port. Few Russians lived on the islands, where, since the Middle Ages, Baltic German landlords had dominated Estonian peasants. The latter, constituting the overwhelming majority of the population, hated the Germans and the Russians more or less equally, and would remain passive bystanders to the battle raging around them.[20]

Given the degraded fighting ability of the Russian naval and military units in the area, the heavily mined waters around the islands posed the greatest threat to the attackers. Rough seas disrupted the German effort to clear mines until after October 6, when calmer weather enabled the requisite paths to be opened, with the loss of just two minesweepers. Schmidt's escort force arrived at Libau from Danzig on October 11, and by that evening the transports were all at sea, just as

[19] Bengelsdorf, *Der Seekrieg in der Ostsee*, pp. 113–114, 119–121.
[20] Barrett, *Operation Albion*, pp. 61–87 *passim*.

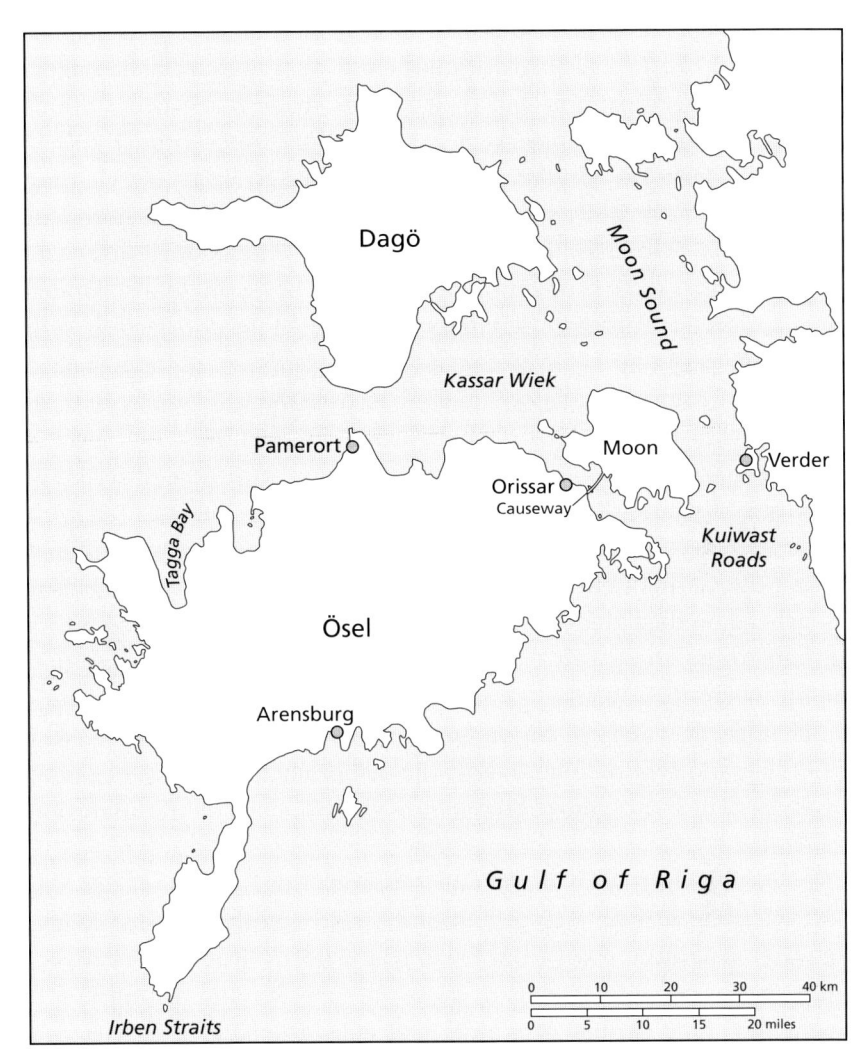

**Map 9.1** The Gulf of Riga

the weather turned again. The telltale bombing raids and minesweeping activity warned the Russians that an attack on the islands was imminent, but when it did not come, despite the good weather, on October 9, 10, or 11, the defenders assumed it must have been canceled. Thus, when the landings at Tagga Bay began at dawn on October 12, in rainy, foggy conditions, the Germans benefited from an element of surprise. At 05:10, one of the transports struck a mine in the bay, then was beached by its captain, but not before two torpedo boats rescued the 850 troops aboard; farther out to sea, the dreadnoughts *Bayern* and *Grosser Kurfürst* also struck mines, but were not fatally damaged. Otherwise, the transports and their escorts made it to their stations unscathed. The first troops went ashore before 06:00, under robust fire support from the *Moltke* and the dreadnoughts. By 10:00, German infantry had successfully stormed and taken all the Russian shore batteries, and by 11:00 the bay was deemed secure enough for horses and heavier supplies to be brought to the beaches. The Germans also landed a smaller force at Pamerort (Pammana), a point on the northern coast of Ösel 19 miles (30 km) east of Tagga Bay. While the main force pushed inland from Tagga Bay across the island to Arensburg, 17 miles (27 km) to the southeast, the Pamerort force, including a battalion on bicycles, raced to take Orrisar (Orissaare), 22 miles (35 km) east of its landing site, and secure the bridgehead at the causeway linking Ösel with Moon Island. Over the days that followed, the action on Ösel centered around the German efforts to take Arensburg and to hold the Orrisar bridgehead, in the latter case against increasingly desperate attempts by Russian troops to reopen their route of retreat to the safety of Moon Island, where they would be covered by the guns of Bakhirev's ships in the adjacent waters of Moon Sound. When the Germans succeeded in holding and reinforcing Orrisar, the demoralized Russians began to surrender. The last organized resistance on Ösel ended on the afternoon of October 15.[21]

Coinciding with the action on land, the Russians sought to block German attempts to get around Ösel by sea. In Kassar Wiek, the water separating Ösel from Dagö to the north, Russian destroyers skirmished with German destroyers on October 12 and again the following day. On October 13, Bakhirev decided to block larger German warships from moving eastward into Moon Sound by having a minefield laid between the two islands, but the crew of the minelayer *Pripyat* considered the mission too dangerous and voted not to obey the order, leaving the channel open. The following day an outraged Kerensky responded to this and lesser acts of insubordination with a front-page piece in *Izvestiia* holding the revolutionary sailors of the Baltic Fleet accountable for the German successes, alleging that "the Kronstadters have... succeeded in seeing to it that in this critical hour, not all of our

---

[21] Bengelsdorf, *Der Seekrieg in der Ostsee*, pp. 122–131; Barrett, *Operation Albion*, pp. 121–164 *passim*.

defenses are in place." The destroyer skirmishes in Kassar Wiek continued on October 14–15, while Bakhirev's attentions turned to the Irben Straits, separating Ösel from the Latvian mainland to the south. With the mainland coast in German hands since 1915, a heavy shore battery of 12-inch (30.5-cm) guns the Russians had installed on the southwest tip of the island became key to their quest to command the straits. After aerial bombing damaged the battery and demoralized its crew, on October 14 Bakhirev took the armored cruiser *Bayan* from Moon Sound across the Gulf of Riga to the straits to show his flag and boost the morale of the defenders. The ploy failed, and the following day, as the remaining troops on Ösel surrendered, he dispatched the battleship *Grazhdanin* via the same route to evacuate the battery's survivors. On October 16, the dreadnoughts *König* and *Kronprinz*, from Behncke's squadron, passed through the Irben Straits into the gulf and anchored at Arensburg. Thereafter Germans used the port at Arensburg, rather than Tagga Bay, to land the additional troops and supplies needed to secure their hold on Ösel.[22] After the Russian withdrawal the only Allied units active in the Gulf of Riga were three British submarines (C 26, C 27, and C 52), which targeted the German dreadnoughts but failed to torpedo them, hitting only the minesweeper tender *Indianola*, which was damaged but not sunk.[23] Things did not go as smoothly for the Germans on Dagö. Even though the initial plan called for the island to be bypassed on the assumption that its isolated garrison would surrender after Ösel and Moon fell, the Germans twice attempted to land troops on Dagö, on the morning of October 15 and again on the 16th. Both times they met with fierce resistance from the regiment of Russians garrisoning the island and withdrew rather than risk having their shaky beachhead overrun during the ensuing night.[24] The conquest of Dagö was postponed while the German focus shifted to Moon Island and the Russian squadron in Moon Sound.

With the only remaining formation of the Russian army's 107th Division defending Dagö, responsibility for Moon Island fell to the navy; indeed, the handful of survivors from the army who had fled Ösel to Moon before the causeway was blocked had no intention of fighting

---

[22] Bengelsdorf, *Der Seekrieg in der Ostsee*, pp. 132–139; Nekrasov, *Expendable Glory*, pp. 96–101. Kerensky quoted in Rabinowitch, *The Bolsheviks Come to Power*, p. 225, see also *ibid*. at p. 348 n. 5.

[23] Barrett, *Operation Albion*, p. 229.

[24] Bengelsdorf, *Der Seekrieg in der Ostsee*, p. 139.

on, wishing only to be transported from Moon to the mainland. After the German bicycle battalion made its surprise appearance at Orrisar, on October 13 Bakhirev deployed armed contingents from the crews of the *Slava*, *Grazhdanin*, and *Bayan* to prevent the enemy from advancing across the causeway. An appeal to the Baltic Fleet commander, Razvozov, for reinforcements met with enthusiastic support from Dybenko and *Tsentrobalt*, whose Bolshevik majority considered the German offensive a threat to their own goal of getting Lenin into power in Petrograd. Most of the relief troops, soldiers as well as sailors, came from Reval, the fortified base on the south shore of the Gulf of Finland, 80 miles (130 km) by rail from the ferry terminal at Verder (Virtsu) on Moon Sound. They trickled in, starting on October 14, but some refused to fight once they reached Moon Island, others would not board the ferries to cross Moon Sound once they reached Verder, and still others stopped their trains en route, refusing to go any farther. On October 16, a series of German attempts to force the causeway failed only because the defenders enjoyed support from Bakhirev's battleships and cruisers, firing across the island from Moon Sound. But the following morning Behncke's dreadnoughts *König* and *Kronprinz* arrived from Arensburg and appeared off Moon Island on its south (gulf) side, supported by two of Hopman's light cruisers, the *Kolberg* and *Strassburg*, forcing Bakhirev to shift his focus. As the Battle of Moon Sound began to the east of the island, a flotilla of small boats ferried German troops across the narrow channel dividing Ösel from the west side of Moon, outflanking the causeway. By the afternoon of October 17 the situation had become untenable for the Russians still fighting on Moon, but Bakhirev no longer controlled the sea between the island and the mainland, and ferries could not be used to evacuate them. Those who made it to safety crossed the sound in small boats under fire. When Moon fell on the afternoon of October 18, the Germans took some 5,000 prisoners.[25] The internal breakdown on the Russian side thus played no small part in the land phase of the campaign for the islands, but the Germans, to their credit, had done much to address the problems that had undermined the Allies at Gallipoli and their own earlier effort at Riga in 1915. Thanks to a translation of the interwar German account of the campaign, prepared by an American officer, the lessons learned by the Germans in the Gulf of Riga in 1917 helped to shape

[25] Barrett, *Operation Albion*, pp. 131, 168–179.

the approach that US Army and Marine Corps officers would take in preparing for their amphibious operations in the Second World War.[26]

The German plan for the naval phase of the campaign emphasized the economy of force. Facing battle in Moon Sound – a mine-infested, confined space, just 5.5 miles (8.5 km) wide at the ferry crossing – Schmidt allotted two of Behncke's dreadnoughts and two of Hopman's light cruisers to engage Bakhirev's two pre-dreadnoughts and two armored cruisers, counting on the German advantage in 12-inch (30.5-cm) guns, 20:8, plus discipline and morale to carry the day. Unaware of the extent of the disarray at Helsinki, Schmidt prepared for the contingency of a sortie by the Russian Baltic Fleet's four dreadnoughts and two remaining pre-dreadnoughts (*Andrei Pervozvanny* and *Imperator Pavel*) by keeping the flagship *Moltke* and the other eight dreadnoughts in reserve, posted around the islands. To initiate the battle, the *König* and *Kronprinz* were to move northward out of the Gulf of Riga and into the sound, providing covering fire for the minesweepers deployed to clear their way, while seaplanes bombed Bakhirev's ships, with the battle in the sound to follow once the mines had been swept. Bahkirev responded by deploying the *Bayan*, *Slava*, and *Grazhdanin* in a line-abreast V-formation, moving southward out of the sound and into the gulf, firing to disrupt the minesweeping effort. He detached his second armored cruiser, the *Admiral Makarov*, to support the Russian destroyers in Kassar Wiek, in the hope that German forces would not pass between Ösel and Dagö and into Moon Sound to fall upon him from the rear.

The battle began at 09:26 (Russian time) on the morning of October 17, when the squadron of German seaplanes attacked the Russian ships, but none of their bombs found its mark. Starting at 09:40, in the northeastern waters of the Gulf of Riga, the four battleships engaged in a sporadic, long-range artillery duel while the German minesweepers in between them continued their work; by 10:05 the *Slava* had closed

---

[26] Erich von Tschischwitz, *Armee und Marine bei der Eroberung der Baltischen Inseln im Oktober 1917* (Berlin: Eisenschmidt, 1931), translated by Colonel Henry Hossfeld as *The Army and Navy during the Conquest of the Baltic Islands in October 1917*, with the edition published by the Army Command and General Staff School, Fort Leavenworth, Kansas (1933) followed by another published by the Marine Corps Officers Training School, Quantico, Virginia (1936). See also Brian O'Sullivan, "Away All Boats: A Study of the Evolution and Development of Amphibious Warfare in the Pacific War," MA thesis, University of Canterbury, New Zealand, 2008, p. 50 and *passim*.

to within 22,000 yards (20,000 m) of the minesweepers and started to splash shells among them, forcing them to withdraw behind a smokescreen laid by destroyers. They resumed their work at 10:50, but again withdrew under cover of smoke after the *Grazhdanin* and *Bayan* – the latter with no guns heavier than 8 inches (20.3 cm) – joined the *Slava* in dropping shells among the minesweepers, sinking one of them. The duel between the larger warships continued, and after the *Slava* scored a hit on the *König* at 11:20, no doubt startling Behncke and his staff, the German dreadnoughts temporarily broke off the action and turned away. Around noon the battle entered an eerie intermission, with Bakhirev's ships stationary astride the southern approach to the sound, while the Germans regrouped farther south in the Gulf of Riga. The Germans resumed the attack shortly thereafter, pushing their minesweepers forward until, at 12:10, they again came under fire from the *Slava* and *Grazhdanin*, which sank two minesweepers along with a destroyer. As the minesweepers again retired behind a smokescreen, Behncke, confident that they had done their work, ordered the *König* and *Kronprinz* to reengage. After the German dreadnoughts steamed through the gap in the minefield, the three Russian ships retreated northward into Moon Sound, the range closing by the minute. Around 12:25, at a distance of 18,000 yards (16,500 m), the *König* landed a salvo on the *Slava*, scoring three hits simultaneously, while the *Kronprinz* hit the *Grazhdanin* once amidships. From then until 12:40, when they ceased firing, German gunners registered another four hits on the *Slava* and at least one (perhaps three) more on the *Grazhdanin*; of the seven shells that struck the *Slava*, at least three, and possibly five, inflicted damage below the waterline, causing the ship to take on a considerable amount of water. As the *Grazhdanin* and *Bayan* continued their withdrawal, the crippled *Slava* assumed the role of rear guard, taking fire from both the *Kronprinz* and the *König* and claiming one hit in return. German seaplanes reappeared to attack the *Slava*, but their bombs dropped harmlessly around the ship.[27]

    In an effort to save the *Slava* and also ensure that the *Grazhdanin* continued its escape, at this stage Bakhirev took his flagship *Bayan* closer to the enemy to draw fire away from the battered

[27] This and the following paragraphs are based on Nekrasov, *Expendable Glory*, pp. 103–108; Bengelsdorf, *Der Seekrieg in der Ostsee*, pp. 143–146; Barrett, *Operation Albion*, pp. 213–221; and Gary Staff, "Operation Albion: The Attack on the Baltic Islands," available at: www.gwpda.org/naval/albion.htm.

Figure 9.3 Wreck of the *Slava*, following the Battle of Moon Sound

battleships. The armored cruiser took one hit from the *König*, as luck would have it, in its forecastle mess, just as the ship's soviet was meeting there to formulate charges against Bakhirev for steaming into danger against a superior enemy. All but one of the committee was killed. The same shell blast also threatened the *Bayan*'s forward magazine, which had to be flooded as a precaution, slowing its subsequent withdrawal. The most dangerous time for the Russian warships came when they passed the narrowest point of the sound, the ferry crossing. The *Grazhdanin* and *Bayan* made it through, but by then the *Slava* was riding too low in the water to clear the shallows and had to be abandoned at 13:58. After the destroyers had rescued the *Slava*'s crew, scuttling charges rocked the ship, and for good measure one of the destroyers torpedoed it as well. Around 14:00 a reported sighting of a Russian submarine prompted the two German dreadnoughts to break off their pursuit of Bakhirev's remaining ships and undertake evasive maneuvers; they would have had to end the chase soon in any event, as the dredged channel leading out of Moon Sound to the north was too shallow for dreadnoughts to pass. Behncke's ships remained on alert for several hours before finally dropping anchor off Moon Island shortly after 19:00.

By then, Bakhirev's decision to leave behind the *Admiral Makarov* to protect his rear had paid off. Around 17:00, the light cruiser

*Emden* led a German destroyer flotilla out of Kassar Wiek, attempting to disrupt the Russian withdrawal northward through the sound, but the 8-inch (20.3-cm) guns of the Russian armored cruiser were more than a match for the *Emden*'s 5.9-inch (15-cm) guns, and the retreat continued unmolested. Meanwhile, Hopman's light cruisers *Kolberg* and *Strassburg* played no part in the Battle of Moon Sound. Around 13:25, Behncke had ordered them to leave the company of the dreadnoughts and to proceed into the narrow channel between Ösel and Moon Island, where they provided flanking fire against the Russian shore battery on Moon's southern coast. Around 17:45, with Russian resistance on the island collapsing, a landing party from the cruisers took the battery and held it until German troops arrived soon afterward. That evening, after the *Admiral Makarov* played its part in covering the Russian naval withdrawal, it joined the *Bayan* and *Grazhdanin* at the northern end of Moon Sound. From there, Bakhirev's ships retreated northward along the Estonian coast, scuttling four merchantmen to block the dredged channel behind them. Schmidt's last chance to crush the fleeing Russians would have been to intercept them when they emerged from the other end of the channel at the mouth of the Gulf of Finland, but Bakhirev foiled him by keeping his ships on the Estonian coast for two days before crossing the gulf under cover of darkness on the night of October 19/20. He reached Lapvik, the Finnish base used by Britain's Baltic submarine force, at dawn on the 20th.

The surrender of Ösel and Moon Island and the withdrawal of Bakhirev's squadron left the Russian regiment defending Dagö in a hopeless situation. On the evening of October 17, as the action on Moon Island and in Moon Sound came to an end, the Germans returned to Dagö with 3,600 men and 500 horses, a much larger force than those landed, unsuccessfully, on the previous two days. After standing their ground against the first and second landings, the Russian defenders collapsed in the face of the third landing, streaming to the northern side of the island on October 18. In full mutiny, the garrison demanded to be evacuated to the mainland, and by October 20 most of them were; of the 2,400 Russian troops on Dagö, only around 300 were killed or captured. After nine days (October 12–20) Operation Albion had come to an end, having cost Russia one battleship and one destroyer sunk, over 20,000 prisoners lost, and an unknown number killed and wounded. Equipment lost included 141 artillery pieces, 130 machine guns, and two armored cars, along with 2,000 horses. German losses included one destroyer, along with 16 minesweepers, trawlers, and smaller craft, 210 killed and 201 wounded; naval casualties accounted for roughly three-quarters of the dead and one-third of the wounded. The mined dreadnoughts *Bayern* and *Grosser Kurfürst* proved to be the costliest German losses, as the damage (especially to the *Bayern*) turned out to be greater than initially assumed and took several months to repair.[28]

The wartime operations of the Russian Baltic Fleet ended with Bakhirev's retreat to the Gulf of Finland, completed just eighteen days before the Bolshevik Revolution. The Black Sea Fleet remained active a bit longer, against an Ottoman navy now led by Rebeur-Paschwitz, who arrived at Constantinople on September 4 to take over from Souchon amid a wholesale exchange of command personnel from Germany. The last sortie of the Black Sea Fleet came on November 1, a week before the Bolshevik takeover. Rear Admiral Nemits left Sevastopol with the *Svobodnaya Rossiya*, the new dreadnought *Volya* (ex-*Imperator Aleksandr III*), three pre-dreadnoughts, four destroyers, and a seaplane tender for a raid against the Bosporus, but this formidable force had to turn back after the crew of Nemits' flagship mutinied.[29]

The success of Operation Albion put the German army in a position to be resupplied and reinforced through Riga, raising Russian fears that an offensive against Petrograd might be imminent. Ever since the failure of the "Kerensky Offensive" in July, the Russian army had practically ceased to exist south of the Pripet Marshes, allowing the Central Powers to march deep into Ukraine; now, the retreat from Riga raised doubts about the army's ability to hold the northern sector of the front, as well as the navy's competence to defend the Gulf of Finland. General Nikolai Dukhonin, appointed army commander after the Kornilov affair, remarked that in terms of sea power "we are in effect back to the age of Tsar Aleksei," father of Peter the Great, founder of the Russian navy.[30]

## The Russian navy and the Bolshevik Revolution

The condition of the Russian Baltic Fleet, now in complete disarray as a fighting force, had implications beyond just the security of Petrograd

---

[28] Barrett, *Operation Albion*, pp. 180–186, 229.
[29] Langensiepen *et al.*, *Halbmond und Kaiseradler*, pp. 164–166, 171; Halpern, *A Naval History of World War I*, p. 254.
[30] Quoted in Rabinowitch, *The Bolsheviks Come to Power*, p. 225.

and the survival of the Provisional Government, because of its role as a political asset of the Bolsheviks in the struggle within Russia. Indeed, on October 18, as the action in the Gulf of Riga drew to a close, Latvian Bolshevik Martin Latsis expressed concern that another attack by the German navy might destroy the Baltic Fleet before its sailors could help Lenin take power.[31] There is no record that Lenin shared his fears; indeed, after he returned to Petrograd on October 22 and, the next day, persuaded the Bolshevik inner circle to embrace his plan to overthrow the Provisional Government in a coup, his timeline remained purely political, requiring him to be in power by November 7 in order to present a *fait accompli* to the Second All-Russian Congress of Soviets, scheduled to convene in Petrograd that day.

With the Petrograd Soviet controlled by a Bolshevik majority, and the party, after October 23, committed to Lenin's plan to seize power, it fell to the newly formed Military Revolutionary Committee (MRC) to lay the groundwork for the coup. Acting, theoretically, to bolster the defenses of the capital against Germans and counterrevolutionaries, over the next two weeks the MRC placed its own commissars in the various regiments of the Petrograd garrison, and thereby placed the soviet's exercise of Order Number One firmly in the hands of the Bolsheviks. The MRC also extended its authority over the light cruiser *Aurora*, which had been sent to a Petrograd shipyard for repairs the previous autumn, and taken over by its crew in the March Revolution, when its commander was killed. Wary of the ship's pro-Bolshevik crew, on November 6, Kerensky's government ordered it to put to sea, only to have the MRC reject the order. The *Aurora* instead moved up the Neva River closer to the Winter Palace, seat of the Provisional Government.[32] To facilitate a Bolshevik takeover the following morning, before the Second All-Russian Congress of Soviets convened, on the evening of the 6th the MRC sent orders to Helsinki and Kronstadt for warships as well as sailors. Dybenko assured the MRC that "the cruisers will sail at dawn." As it turned out, no cruisers were among the ships that left for the capital on the morning of November 7. Dybenko managed to get five destroyers and a patrol boat to raise steam at Helsinki, while the motley flotilla leaving Kronstadt included two minelayers, an

---

[31] *Ibid.*, p. 200.
[32] John M. Thompson, *Revolutionary Russia, 1917*, 2nd edn. (New York: Macmillan, 1989), pp. 139, 148.

armed yacht, a training ship, and the old pre-dreadnought *Zaria Svobody* (ex-*Imperator Aleksandr II*), which had to be pushed and pulled along by tugboats. Most of these ships were not battle-ready, but merely transporting sailors to the capital; the minelayer *Amur*, for example, carried over a thousand men, more than three times its normal complement. Sailors who could not be fitted aboard these warships followed in a variety of commandeered civilian craft. Those traveling the much shorter distance from Kronstadt arrived first, and by early afternoon some 3,000 of them had joined the pro-Bolshevik forces already surrounding the Winter Palace. A Bolshevik petty officer, Ivan Sladkov, took control of the nearby Admiralty building and arrested the naval staff.[33]

The delay in the storming of the Winter Palace, from the afternoon of November 7 deep into the evening, resulted in part from last-minute negotiations by the MRC to bring uncommitted garrison regiments over to the side of the Bolsheviks, and in part because of the decision to wait for the arrival of Dybenko's flotilla and additional sailors coming from Helsinki by rail. Meanwhile, across town, Bolshevik delegates stalled the opening of the congress while Lenin fumed over the delays. He did not care about casualties, but lower-ranking Bolsheviks on the spot outside the Winter Palace hoped a show of force would cause the Provisional Government to surrender, thus avoiding unnecessary bloodshed. Unbeknown to them, the ministers inside no longer included Kerensky, who had slipped away in the morning in an effort to find loyal troops at the front. Among those left behind, Rear Admiral Dmitri Verderevsky, who had joined the cabinet after the Kornilov affair when Kerensky gave up the post of navy minister, ranked as the leading pessimist in the Provisional Government's last proceedings. His expertise came into play later that evening, when he confirmed that the fourteen 6-inch (15.2-cm) guns of the *Aurora*, anchored just down the Neva, represented more than enough firepower to reduce the Winter Palace to rubble. It remained to be seen if the cruiser's guns would be competently handled, or fired with intent to destroy. After the ministers chose to ignore an ultimatum to surrender by 17:10 or else face a shelling, the *Aurora*'s gunners waited nearly two and a half hours to fire their first round – a blank warning shot. Shortly

---

[33] Rabinowitch, *The Bolsheviks Come to Power*, pp. 262–263, 273–280, Dybenko quoted at p. 263.

thereafter, the ships of Dybenko's flotilla began to arrive in the Neva, having taken over 15 hours to steam the 200 miles (320 km) from Helsinki to Petrograd, but the sailors who made the trip by rail did not begin to detrain at Petrograd's Finland Station until the middle of the night, with the last of them arriving during the day on November 8, too late to participate in the coup. After 23:00 the *Aurora* finally opened fire on the Winter Palace, though during the subsequent bombardment only two shells actually struck the building; the rest, as one historian has noted, "exploded spectacularly but harmlessly over the Neva."[34] Some three hours later, with the Bolshevik ranks sufficiently reinforced and most of the garrison of the Winter Palace having melted away, the building was stormed and taken with little resistance.

Lenin had been unable to choreograph the desired *fait accompli* for the Second All-Russian Congress of Soviets, but before dawn on November 8 that body's Bolshevik and Left SR majority ratified the takeover. The congress thus became the *de facto* legislature of the new Soviet Russian government, which the following day approved Lenin's first cabinet (or Council of People's Commissars), including Dybenko, rewarded for his support with the portfolio of naval commissar. Razvozov and Nemits, the young admirals appointed by Kerensky (with the approval of the soviets) to command the Baltic and Black Sea fleets, remained in their posts. But Kolchak, en route home from his mission to the United States via the Pacific at the time the Bolsheviks seized power, wanted nothing to do with them; on December 6 he turned up at the British embassy in Tokyo, volunteering to continue to fight for the Allied cause in the service of Britain.

While the Allies still hoped to keep the Russians in the war, they feared the worst and for good reason. After declaring an end to all offensive operations at sea as well as on land, Soviet Russia opened peace negotiations with the Central Powers. A report submitted to the British cabinet on December 7 confirmed that "the Allies have decided that in the present state of affairs no further arrangements can be made for sending supplies to Russia."[35] Eight days later, Lenin's government concluded an armistice ending the First World War on the Eastern front, including the Baltic and Black Sea. The following month, with

---

[34] *Ibid.*, pp. 282–289.
[35] Memorandum, "Summary of Blockade Information," December 7, 1917, TNA: PRO CAB 24/34/101, p. 5.

German–Soviet negotiations for a permanent peace treaty underway at Brest-Litovsk, Lenin's government formally dissolved the Russian armed forces, creating in their place the "Worker-Peasant Red Army" (January 15, 1918) and "Worker-Peasant Red Navy" (January 30).

## Conclusion

At the onset of the war's last year, the Bolsheviks maintained a tenuous grip on power in Russia in the face of opposition across the political spectrum, ranging from their own rivals on the Left, the Mensheviks and SRs, to advocates of absolute monarchy on the extreme Right. The armistice neutralized the external threat, but the German victory at Riga left enemy troops and naval forces within striking distance of Petrograd. While a definitive peace treaty with the Central Powers remained to be signed, the new Red Navy in the Baltic and Black Sea, like the Red Army on land, was in no position to defend Russia should hostilities resume. Thus, the collapse of the Russian navy had considerable strategic significance, contributing not just to the rise of the Bolsheviks, but also to a deterioration in Russia's security that left little alternative to peace regardless of which party governed the country.

Beyond Russia, the mutiny and the central part played by sailors in the revolution sent a chill through the admiralties of Europe, but especially those of Germany and Austria-Hungary, whose navies shared similar overall circumstances. The mutinies experienced by the fleets of the Central Powers during 1917 paled in significance compared to the upheaval in the Russian navy, yet that they occurred at all had a sobering effect especially on the Germans. Indeed, for Austria-Hungary the morale of the navy had held up much better and for much longer than that of the army, which suffered mutinies of entire regiments as early as the spring of 1915, but for Germany, whose army, either victorious or holding its own on all fronts, had experienced no serious unrest thus far, the mutiny at Wilhelmshaven and its links to civilian war weariness and to the rise of German antiwar socialism caused considerable alarm. The leadership of the two navies responded very differently to the incidents of 1917. Njegovan, fearful of igniting the multinational tinderbox of men serving under him, chose to treat the defection to Italy of *Torpedoboot 11* as an isolated incident (wisely, since it turned out to be just that), and also dealt leniently with his navy's food protesters. Scheer, in contrast, chose to make examples of Köbis and Reichpietsch, confident that their executions would deter further unrest in the German navy. Neither Njegovan nor Scheer did much to alleviate the underlying tensions within their navies, though it is fair to say that, by the end of 1917, those tensions had reached a magnitude far greater than any commanding admiral could have dealt with on his own, as in each case the navy's afflictions were a microcosm of the broader tensions and unresolved issues within the country as a whole. For the Austro-Hungarian and German navies, the complete breakdown averted in 1917 would come in 1918, when both succumbed to mutiny and revolution.

# 10 FINAL OPERATIONS

"We entered this war because violations of right had occurred which touched us to the quick," observed President Wilson, harking back to his decision, in February 1917, to sever diplomatic relations with Germany over the resumption of unrestricted submarine warfare, and the declaration of war he had secured from Congress two months later. Now, on the afternoon of January 8, 1918, again addressing a joint session of Congress, he proceeded to unveil his Fourteen Points, a statement of American war aims and ideals that henceforth shaped the discourse about what peace might look like. Discounting the specific provisions for the Dardanelles and Bosporus to be "permanently opened," and for postwar Serbia and Poland each to have "free and secure access" to a port, only Wilson's second point, advocating "absolute freedom of navigation...alike in peace and in war" made any reference to the sea or the war's issues related to it. That same point, ironically, would be the only one that the Allied Supreme War Council never endorsed, because Britain viewed it not just as a condemnation of unrestricted submarine warfare, but of blockades such as the one it had imposed on Germany, which, ultimately, was so important to the Allied victory.[1]

Historians continue to debate the president's motives in promulgating such a list of aims, and especially his decision to do so without consulting the other Allied leaders. As a message to the Allied nations, the speech sought to assuage critics on the Left by recasting

---

[1] See Sondhaus, *World War I*, pp. 319–320, 436.

the war as a just cause being fought, at least in part, over universal principles. At the same time, it presented the Central Powers with the framework for a reasonable peace. The Bolshevik Revolution, exactly two months earlier, provided the backdrop for the speech, as Wilson's preamble made reference to the German–Soviet negotiations at Brest-Litovsk, and his sixth point, reaffirming Russian sovereignty and territorial integrity, reflected his hope that Lenin's government might yet keep Russia faithful to the Allies.[2] On that account the speech failed, but as a peace overture to the enemy – whose war-weary peoples, including soldiers and sailors, thereafter came to view the Allied leaders as more reasonable than their own – it succeeded brilliantly. Indeed, the first evidence of this victory came just twenty-six days after the speech, when a mutiny at Cattaro, Austria-Hungary's remote forward base of operations in the Adriatic, produced a list of demands that referred to the Fourteen Points, calling for a "sincere response to Wilson's note."[3]

The Austro-Hungarian navy would survive the Cattaro mutiny, but during 1918 the tottering Habsburg and Hohenzollern monarchies could offer nothing that fired the imagination like Wilson's vision for a liberal world order or Lenin's vision for a socialist one. Cattaro and Pola, along with Wilhelmshaven and Kiel, would reignite in rebellion in the war's last days, and until then the specter of the earlier mutinies, and the far bloodier example of what had happened in 1917 in the Russian Baltic and Black Sea fleets, haunted the navies of the Central Powers. Even though they acknowledged that the ultimate decision at sea hinged on the success or failure of their ongoing campaign of unrestricted submarine warfare, both continued to engage in surface operations in pursuit of their strategic goals, as did the Allies. From Finland on the Baltic to Georgia on the Black Sea, naval power facilitated German meddling in non-Russian territories seeking independence from Lenin's Russia. Meanwhile, in the North Sea, German naval forces in Flanders fended off British raids at Zeebrugge and Ostend. The High Sea Fleet sortied for the last time in April 1918, the Austro-Hungarian fleet in June, but neither engaged the enemy, and both experienced the ultimate

---

[2] John Milton Cooper, Jr., *Woodrow Wilson: A Biography* (New York: Alfred A. Knopf, 2009), pp. 420–424.

[3] "Was wir wollen," Cattaro, February 1, 1918, text in Richard Georg Plaschka, *Cattaro – Prag: Revolte und Revolution* (Graz: Verlag Hermann Böhlaus Nachf., 1963), p. 59.

demoralization of having capital ships damaged or sunk by torpedo attacks.

## The collapse of Austria-Hungary and the end of the war in the Adriatic

At the end of 1917, some six months after being seriously wounded in the Austro-Hungarian victory at the Battle of the Otranto Straits, Captain Miklós Horthy resumed active duty as commander of the dreadnought *Prinz Eugen* at Pola. "The battle fleet was not in good form," he later recalled. In contrast to his previous ship, the light cruiser *Novara*, and other smaller ships and submarines based at Cattaro, the big ships at the main base "had been largely inactive." As in the German navy, the combination of boredom and food rationing made the ships receptive to "the underground activities of the socialists," compounded in the case of Austria-Hungary by "the political agitation of Yugoslav, Czech, and Italian nationalists." By the time Horthy took command of the *Prinz Eugen*, the evening meal had become the catalyst for noisy breaches of discipline in which the crews would refuse to eat, then crowd the railings and ports of their ships to engage in what Horthy called "a craze for irrational cheering."[4] The shouts of "*Hurra*" would be answered from ship to ship, escalating into a sort of competitive noise-making involving thousands of men. These mass protests worsened in January 1918, following a further reduction in rations, prompting Admiral Njegovan to ban the *Hurra-Rufe* because "the crews of several ships have made it a cheer of protest."[5]

Njegovan and his officers soon faced a far more serious breach of discipline when the navy became swept up in a general strike organized by the Social Democrats of the various Habsburg nationalities, which by the end of January idled some 700,000 workers throughout the empire. On January 22, the 10,000 workers of the Pola Arsenal struck, led by Croatians mixing nationalism and socialism in calling for "a South Slav state of workers and peasants." They were supported by strikers of other nationalities, including ethnic Italians as well as skilled workers from Germany who were in Pola to provide technical support

---

[4] Miklós Horthy de Nagybánya, *Memoirs* (London: Hutchinson, 1956), pp. 87–88.
[5] Njegovan quoted in Richard Georg Plaschka, Horst Haselsteiner, and Arnold Suppan, *Innere Front: Militärassistenz, Widerstand und Umsturz in der Donaumonarchie 1918*, 2 vols. (Munich: Oldenbourg, 1974), vol. 1, p. 107.

for the U-boat campaign. On January 23, sailors of the fleet and soldiers of the Pola garrison joined the strikers in battling military police deployed to maintain order. Social Democratic leaders soon arrived to negotiate an end to the unrest, persuading the navy to increase the pay of arsenal workers, provide them with better clothing, and allow their families (evacuated earlier in the war) to return to the town. On January 28, the arsenal reopened and the sailors returned to their ships.[6]

Consistent with his approach to the unrest of 1917, Njegovan once again considered it sufficient that order had been restored in a difficult situation and imposed no punishments. He had barely recovered from the shock of the unrest at Pola when word arrived of a far more serious mutiny at the navy's second-largest base, Cattaro. Though the sailors stationed at this forward base had seen far more action than their peers at Pola, those serving in the larger ships there had shared a similar general idleness amid gradually worsening conditions, exacerbated by their remote location, in a fjord-like setting at the mountainous southern tip of Dalmatia. The situation was worst aboard the armored cruisers *Kaiser Karl VI* and *Sankt Georg*. The latter served as the flagship of Rear Admiral Alexander Hansa, head of the Cruiser Flotilla, who had spent most of the war at Cattaro and spared no expense in providing for his own comfort, including having his wife and children live with him aboard the *Sankt Georg*. Other senior officers enjoyed similar privileges, and lower-ranking officers with the means to do so kept apartments ashore for their wives or mistresses. While ordinary sailors endured repeated reductions in the quality and quantity of their food, the admiral maintained his own table close to prewar standards. As had been the case at Pola in January, and in the German and Austro-Hungarian mutinies of 1917, food served as a flashpoint for protest. On February 1, 1918, when the crew of the *Sankt Georg* assembled for the noon meal, the flagship erupted in mutiny. The ship was seized with no loss of life, but Hansa's flag captain, Egon Zipperer von Arbach, was shot in the head and ultimately barely survived his wound. Shouts of "*Hurra*," banned by Njegovan the previous month, thundered from the *Sankt Georg* and were echoed by the crews of the *Kaiser Karl VI* and other larger ships in the bay. Officers were confined to their quarters, but inexplicably the mutineers waited several hours to cut Hansa's communications with the outside world. His first telegram to Pola, sent

[6] *Ibid.*, vol. 1, pp. 61–76.

at 14:30, reported that all vessels within his sight except the submarines were flying red flags.[7]

That evening, committees elected by the mutinous crews presented Hansa with a list of demands reflecting a mixture of concerns. Practical points included appeals for more shore leave, a common mess for officers and sailors, more tobacco, an end to censorship of mail, and no future punishment for participants in the mutiny. The political points included immediate peace talks with the Allies, full political independence of Austria-Hungary "from other powers" (meaning Germany), support for the "Russian democratic proposal" for a peace without indemnities or annexations, a full demobilization and the creation of volunteer militias in place of armed forces, self-determination for all peoples, and an answer, in good faith, to Wilson's Fourteen Points.[8] Hansa, of course, could do nothing to address the broader political concerns, but he also dismissed most of the practical demands, offering only to consider more shore leave. His response only further inflamed the mutiny, and by the following morning almost all of the committees had ousted their moderates in favor of more radical leaders. Boatswain Franz Rasch of the *Sankt Georg*, a Moravian German, emerged as the dominant figure, but concluded that the rebellion must be led by an officer, ideally a Croatian with South Slav nationalist sympathies. After failing to find such an accomplice aboard any of the ships, he finally identified one at the Cattaro seaplane station: Reserve Ensign Antun Sešan, a young navy pilot whose desire to escape heavy gambling debts provided additional motivation to side with the mutineers. On the afternoon of February 2, Sešan arrived aboard the *Sankt Georg*, where he did little other than serve as a front man for Rasch and other radical ringleaders.

By the time Sešan boarded the flagship, the authorities ashore had already begun to move decisively to contain the mutiny. When the old harbor watch ship *Kronprinz Rudolf* defied the Cattaro garrison commander's order that no red-flagged vessel should move within the bay, a shore battery opened fire on the ship, killing one sailor and wounding several others. Sešan responded by directing the rest of the ships to clear for action but maintain their current positions.[9] Amid competing ultimata – the shore batteries threatening to shell ships that continued to fly the red flag, the *Sankt Georg* and *Kaiser Karl VI*

[7] Plaschka, *Cattaro – Prag*, p. 58   [8] Ibid., p. 59.   [9] Ibid., p. 125.

threatening to shell any that pulled down the red flag – the mutiny began to crumble aboard the smaller, more active ships that had not experienced the low morale and extreme social divisions prevailing aboard the larger units. Prince Liechtenstein, who had succeeded Horthy as captain of the light cruiser *Novara*, reasserted command of his ship, pulled down its red flag, and steamed for the inner harbor of Cattaro, away from the rest of the fleet. The light cruiser *Helgoland* (Captain Erich Heyssler) soon followed suit, along with most of the destroyers and torpedo boats. Shortly after dark on February 2, the mutineers of the *Kaiser Karl VI* struck their red flag, leaving the 7,400-ton *Sankt Georg* as the only formidable warship still in the hands of its crew. With Sešan too timid to appear before the captive Hansa, Rasch remained the strident voice of the mutiny and made it clear that he considered the point of no return to have passed. "Blood must flow in every revolution," he assured Hansa, "and it is all the same to me if I am hanged today or tomorrow. The entire navy stands by our side."[10]

But there was little evidence that the "entire navy" still supported the mutiny. In the early hours of February 3, the senior officer among those who had resumed command of their ships, Heyssler of the *Helgoland*, began to issue ultimata of his own, warning the *Sankt Georg* and other ships still flying red flags that they had until 10:00 that morning to surrender or be torpedoed. Well before the deadline, his hand was strengthened considerably by the three 10,600-ton pre-dreadnoughts of the *Erzherzog* class and an escort of fifteen smaller warships, dispatched from Pola by Njegovan to put down the uprising. Upon learning of the approach of these ships, Rasch and the remaining diehards convinced themselves that their comrades from Pola would appear off Cattaro under red flags, but when the *Ezherzog*s steamed into view flying their battle flags, the remaining mutineers capitulated. The *Sankt Georg* was the last to lower its red flag, at around 09:00, following a vote by the crew. In the final act of the two-day drama, Rasch went to Hansa's cabin, freed the admiral, then surrendered to him. By then Sešan, the only officer to join the uprising, had fled the flagship, returned to the seaplane station, then saved himself by flying across the Adriatic to Italy.[11]

In the immediate aftermath of the Cattaro mutiny, 800 sailors were deemed too unreliable to remain aboard their ships; following

---

[10] Quoted in *ibid.* at p. 155.   [11] *Ibid.*, pp. 169–180.

a formal inquiry, 392 were imprisoned. Croatians and Slovenes accounted for 43 percent of those remaining in custody, a somewhat larger share than the South Slav plurality within the navy as a whole, but the group included men of all nationalities, proof enough that war weariness and the overall conditions of service had mattered more than the anti-Habsburg forces of nationalism in inspiring the revolt. On February 10, one week after the mutiny ended, a military court sentenced four of its leaders to death, including Rasch and Jerko Šižgorić, the sailor who had shot Captain Zipperer of the *Sankt Georg*. They were executed the following morning. Most of the others facing charges spent the rest of the war in prison awaiting trial. In contrast to the publicity the Germans gave to their executions of Köbis and Reichpietsch at Wilhelmshaven five months earlier, Emperor Charles ordered news of the four Cattaro executions suppressed out of concern that the action would reignite mutiny in the fleet.[12]

Thus, even in eliminating the leaders of the mutiny, Austria-Hungary again moved much more cautiously than Germany had in addressing unrest within its navy. But when it came to dealing with the leadership issues that had contributed to the mutiny, Charles acted far more decisively than William II. Within a month, the twenty-eight highest-ranking Austro-Hungarian naval officers were forced to retire or to accept posts on land, paving the way for Horthy, newly promoted to rear admiral, to take over as fleet commander. The Hungarian captain's extraordinary advancement was reminiscent of Kerensky's elevation of Razvozov and Nemits in 1917, or the earlier promotion of Kolchak, but at forty-nine Horthy had roughly a decade more experience than his Russian counterparts, along with a war record that made him universally respected within the service. After taking charge in March 1918, he enjoyed a direct line to the emperor and *carte blanche* to reorganize the forces under his command. Horthy subsequently ordered wholesale reassignments of ships, officers, and thousands of sailors. At Cattaro, Heyssler replaced Hansa as commander of the Cruiser Flotilla, which became a cruiser force in name only, as the three pre-dreadnoughts of the *Ezherzog* class, commissioned 1906–7, remained there to replace the mutinous armored cruisers *Sankt Georg* and *Kaiser Karl VI*, both of which were disarmed. All other older battleships and cruisers were likewise deactivated. These changes, along with the earlier

---

[12] *Ibid.*, pp. 181–189.

decommissionings dictated by the manpower needs of the submarine campaign, left the Austro-Hungarian battle fleet, based at Pola under Horthy's direct command, with just its four dreadnoughts and the three pre-dreadnoughts of the 14,500-ton *Radetzky* class, commissioned in 1910–11. In addition to creating a more efficient fleet whose loyalty could be trusted, the downsizing had the practical effect of finally aligning the Austro-Hungarian navy with its coal supply, almost all of which had to be imported because so few mines in the Dual Monarchy produced coal of a quality suitable for warship use. During the prewar Balkan crisis the navy had stockpiled foreign coal, purchasing over 400,000 tons in 1913 alone, most of it from British sources, but by early 1918 the stock had dwindled to just 95,000 tons, or enough for the battle fleet to operate for 95 hours in its earlier, larger configuration.[13]

Allied inaction facilitated the ensuing quest to revive the Austro-Hungarian battle fleet. The month Horthy assumed command, a US Navy memorandum called the Adriatic "practically an Austrian lake, in which no Allied naval operations of importance are undertaken."[14] While this was an exaggeration, during the spring of 1918 Horthy took full advantage of the absence of pressure from the enemy, conducting maneuvers and gunnery practice on a scale the navy had not seen since before the war. Despite the shocking revelation in April of the "Sixtus Affair" and Emperor Charles' secret peace overtures to France, morale continued to improve. Exceptions to the rule received no quarter, as indicated in May when Horthy ordered the execution of two sailors (one Croatian, one Czech) found guilty of plotting a mutiny aboard one of the torpedo boats at Pola. In contrast to the official secrecy surrounding the Cattaro executions in February, on this occasion Horthy assembled contingents of twenty men from each of his ships to witness the work of the firing squad.[15]

By late spring Horthy deemed the fleet ready for action, a battle he hoped to provoke by repeating the previous year's successful raid on the Otranto barrage, only this time with a much larger force including the navy's four dreadnoughts. To avoid attracting attention prior to the attack on the barrage, set for the morning of June 11, Horthy ordered the dreadnoughts to proceed southward in pairs, under cover of the

---

[13] Sondhaus, *The Naval Policy of Austria-Hungary*, pp. 261, 330.
[14] Quoted in Halpern, *The Naval War in the Mediterranean*, p. 439.
[15] Sondhaus, *The Naval Policy of Austria-Hungary*, pp. 332, 334.

**Figure 10.1** Sinking of the *Szent István*

Dalmatian islands, through the deep waters along the coast rather than on the open sea. He left Pola on the evening of June 8 with the flagship *Viribus Unitis* and the *Prinz Eugen*; the *Tegetthoff* and *Szent István* followed late on the evening of the 9th. The first two dreadnoughts were halfway down the coast when the trailing pair, in the predawn hours of June 10, were attacked off Premuda Island, barely 40 miles (64 km) southeast of Pola, by two MAS boats, which the Italian navy had dispatched after receiving intelligence that Horthy's dreadnoughts had left Pola. While *MAS-21*'s two torpedoes buzzed harmlessly past the *Tegetthoff*, *MAS-15* (Captain Luigi Rizzo) scored hits on the *Szent István* with both of its shots. The attack occurred around 03:30, but the ship remained afloat until after 06:00, by which time daylight enabled the *Tegetthoff* to rescue all but eighty-nine of the *Szent István*'s crew of over 1,000. Even with three dreadnoughts, Horthy still had more than enough firepower to carry out his plan to raid the Otranto barrage, but the sinking confirmed that the element of surprise had been lost; had he proceeded, he ran the risk of being overwhelmed in a counterattack by a much larger Allied fleet, including Italian dreadnoughts from Taranto and French dreadnoughts from Corfu. His decision to cancel the operation and return to Pola, though prudent, was a crushing blow to the Austro-Hungarian navy. Facing a superior enemy on a heightened state of alert, Horthy saw no point in repeating the attempt. Meanwhile, the sinking of the *Szent István* made Rizzo (who had also commanded *MAS*-9 in the sinking of the *Wien* at Trieste the previous December) a national hero in Italy, and the threat posed by MAS boats gave Horthy another reason to keep his big ships in port. As late as August 1918 he continued to vouch for the battle-readiness of the fleet, but it never sortied again.[16]

In the last months of the war the navy focused on maintaining the supply line sustaining Austro-Hungarian troops on the western end of the Balkan front, which stretched across Albania and Macedonia eastward to the Greco-Bulgarian border. After the sudden collapse of Bulgaria compromised the entire front, naval vessels evacuated a number of troops via Durazzo, where, on October 2, elements of the Austro-Hungarian fleet saw action for the last time. That day, two destroyers, two submarines, and one torpedo boat fended off an attack on the port by three Italian armored cruisers, five British light cruisers, fourteen British and two Italian destroyers, Italian torpedo boats and MAS boats, American submarine chasers, submarines from the British, French, and Italian navies, and bombers from the British and Italian air services. The Austro-Hungarian *U 31* torpedoed but failed to sink a British cruiser, the only warship seriously damaged in the battle, which ended with the tiny force successfully shepherding two transports and a hospital ship safely to Cattaro. This lopsided final battle, in which a superior Allied force failed to crush its much smaller enemy, served as a fitting close to the Great War in the Adriatic, a theater in which the Central Powers had maintained control while compelling the Allies to deploy and maintain much larger naval forces than their own.[17]

## The Baltic and Black seas, and the end of the war in the east

After the German–Soviet armistice of December 15, 1917, Lenin favored the conclusion of a peace treaty as soon as possible, on whatever terms the Germans offered, to enable his new government to proceed with rebuilding and communizing Russia. Others in the Bolshevik inner

[16] *Ibid.*, pp. 334–336.    [17] *Ibid.*, pp. 340–341.

circle, envisaging a new communist world rising from the ashes of the Great War, advocated delay in the hope that the revolution would soon spread to the Central Powers, then to the rest of Europe and beyond, making treaties irrelevant. On January 11, the Soviet leadership empowered the commissar for foreign affairs, Leon Trotsky, to pursue the tactic of "no war, no peace," under which Soviet Russia would demobilize and unilaterally declare an end to the war without signing a peace agreement. The formal disbanding of the old armed forces and creation of the new Red Army and Red Navy later in the month also had the practical effect of enabling the Bolsheviks to release all officers with no further pay or pensions, on the grounds that the old Russian armed forces no longer existed, then call back to service only those considered ideologically reliable or useful enough to be worth the risk.

Frustrated by Trotsky's stonewalling, the Central Powers increased the pressure for a definitive settlement by concluding a separate peace treaty with Ukraine (February, 9, 1918), then sending their troops eastward, unopposed, all along the front. German troops occupied Minsk on February 18, prompting local nationalists to proclaim an independent Belarus. At that point the Soviet government asked for terms, only to have Ludendorff persuade Hindenburg to allow the offensive to continue, to occupy more territory for Ukraine, Belarus, and the other eastern vassal states the Germans now planned to create. The needs of the final German offensive on the Western front, due to begin the following month, finally caused an end to the march eastward. In the Treaty of Brest-Litovsk (March 3) the Soviet government recognized the independence of six new states created entirely from former Russian territory – Ukraine, Belarus, Finland, Estonia, Latvia, and Lithuania – of which all but Belarus had coastlines, thus dramatically reducing Russia's frontage on the Baltic and Black seas. The lost territories also included 34 percent of Russia's prewar population, 32 percent of its arable land, 54 percent of its industry, and 89 percent of its coal mines. A secret British assessment of the "no war, no peace" debacle summed it up best: "A barrage of words has so far proven in time of war to be an ineffective defence against an invading army."[18] Lenin took comfort in his belief that that the Germans would be defeated

---

[18] "Appreciation of the Attached Western and General Report No. 56," February 1918, TNA: PRO CAB 24/148/7, p. 1.

eventually anyway, making the concessions temporary. He could not have imagined that it would happen just eight months later.

In the meantime, Russian opponents of Lenin considered the Treaty of Brest-Litovsk proof that he had been a German agent all along. The settlement thus triggered a civil war that had been brewing ever since the Bolshevik Revolution, pitting the new Red Army and Red Navy against a disparate array of opponents collectively labeled as "Whites," including a Siberian army led by Kolchak. When he first turned up at the British embassy in Tokyo one month after Lenin seized power, the former Black Sea Fleet commander had placed himself "unconditionally and in whatever capacity at the disposal of His Majesty's Government."[19] Despite immediately recognizing Kolchak's usefulness as a pro-Allied, anti-Bolshevik Russian senior officer, they had difficulty deciding exactly what to do with him. They considered basing him in the Middle East before settling on Siberia, and persuading him to assume a leadership position with White Russian forces there. While Kolchak never considered serving under the Bolsheviks, veteran tsarist naval officers who did found it a harrowing experience. The contrasting fates of the initial fleet commanders, Razvozov and Nemits, served notice that there would be little rhyme or reason behind promotions or assignments, or who was purged and who survived; indeed, in this regard Lenin and Trotsky proved to be just as arbitrary in their decisions and paranoid in their motives as was Stalin later on. For example, between November 1917 and March 1918 the Soviet regime first confirmed that Razvozov would continue as head of the Baltic Fleet, then dismissed him, then reinstated him, before dismissing him a second time and placing him under arrest. Spared imprisonment, he was assigned to write a history of the Russian navy during the Great War and sent to the archives, where he remained for eighteen months until arrested a second time, for alleged collaboration with the Whites. He died in captivity in 1920, just before his forty-first birthday. Meanwhile, Nemits, commander of the Black Sea Fleet, fared much better even though his sympathies were far more suspect. After the Bolshevik Revolution, Nemits initially served under Ukrainian Bolshevik authorities, then continued as fleet commander after the Central Powers recognized an independent Ukraine, taking orders from a series of ever more right-wing governments in Kiev rather than the rival Ukrainian Soviet Republic. He even served in one of the governments, as navy

---

[19] Quoted in Fleming, *The Fate of Admiral Kolchak*, p. 32.

minister, before going back over to the Bolsheviks late in 1918. Nemitz went on to command the Red Navy from 1920 to 1924, survived the Stalin era, and finally died in 1967, at the age of eighty-eight.

The failure of Trotsky's "no war, no peace" strategy prior to the Treaty of Brest-Litovsk exposed the weakness of the new Red armed forces. To defend Petrograd against German armies advancing from the nearby Baltic states, Lenin appealed to Dybenko for sailors from the Baltic Fleet, but their intramural usefulness before and during the Bolshevik Revolution did not carry over into the field against combat-ready enemy troops. At Narva (February 25, 1918) the navy commissar's forces fled in panic before the Germans, leaving them in possession of all of Estonia, on a front just 75 miles (120 km) from Petrograd, close enough to prompt Lenin to move the capital to Moscow two weeks later. The German advance came with a number of Baltic Fleet warships still stationed at Reval, stranded by heavy ice in the Gulf of Finland. In this difficult situation, Captain Aleksei Shchastny emerged as the man of the hour, saving sixty-two ships of various types by leading them through the ice from Reval across the Gulf of Finland to the safety of Helsinki. After the Treaty of Brest-Litovsk required the Russians to evacuate Finland, Shchastny again emerged as the key figure in moving the same vessels and others previously stationed at the Finnish base; between March 12 and April 11 he guided some 200 Russian warships through the ice from Helsinki to Kronstadt, including the four Baltic dreadnoughts, saving them from capture. These exploits made Shchastny a hero and a celebrity, leading to his confirmation as Razvozov's successor in April 1918. But Shchastny proved to be too popular for his own good, and once Trotsky – now serving as commissar for war and navy – considered him a political threat, his days were numbered. In June 1918 he was arrested, tried for treason, and shot.[20] In a telling example of the capricious character of Soviet justice, the condemnation of the hero Shchastny coincided with the acquittal of Dybenko by a court martial. Within a year of the debacle at Narva, the former navy commissar returned to prominence as a general in the Red Army.

Shchastny's success in saving the Baltic Fleet, at a time of the year when ice would normally have immobilized it, was even more impressive because the winter cruises were undertaken under direct

---

[20] Alexander Rabinowitch, "The Shchastny File: Trotsky and the Case of the Hero of the Baltic Fleet," *Russian Review*, 58 (1999): 615–634.

pressure from the enemy. Just as the advance of German troops during "no war, no peace" forced the Red Navy's sudden evacuation of Reval, the subsequent evacuation of Helsinki was completed after Germany deployed a naval squadron and army division to Finland. The Red-versus-White conflict that gripped Russia from March 1918 was foreshadowed in Finland over the preceding months, as Finland's declaration of independence (December 6, 1917) brought to a head a power struggle between pro- and anti-Bolshevik Finns. While most Finnish workers remained pro-Bolshevik and, in Helsinki, were supported by the sailors of the naval base, during the autumn of 1917 Germany covertly sent munitions shipments to the White Finns, and further supported them by landing detachments of a Finnish rifle battalion that had been serving in the German army. On November 18, one such mission ended in the loss of *UC 57*, the last operational U-boat in the Baltic, to a Russian mine after it had successfully delivered eight Finnish soldiers and four tons of supplies from Libau.[21]

    Germany recognized the White Finnish government and, within the context of the renewed offensive during "no war, no peace," responded to its appeal for more substantial help by creating a special Baltic contingent (*Ostseeverband*), under the command of Rear Admiral Hugo Meurer, to convoy 10,000 German troops to Finland. Meurer's force included the dreadnoughts *Westfalen*, *Rheinland*, and *Posen*, the small coastal pre-dreadnought *Beowulf*, two light cruisers, a minelayer, and a host of destroyers, torpedo boats, and minesweepers. The troops embarked in Danzig aboard thirteen transports, most of which had been used for the Riga operation the previous October. Under Ludendorff's influence, the German plan called for the occupation of the Aaland Islands as a base of operations before landing troops on the Finnish mainland. Meurer's ships were underway when the Treaty of Brest-Litovsk was signed, but they proceeded as planned to the Aaland Islands, which they reached (with the help of icebreakers) on March 6. There, they found the 7,125-ton *Sverige* and two smaller pre-dreadnoughts of the Swedish navy, deployed to support an occupation of the ethnically Swedish islands after the declaration of Finnish independence. Negotiations between Berlin and Stockholm allowed the Germans to occupy some of the islands while the Swedes kept the rest. Meurer soon concluded what the navy had known all along, that the

---

[21] Bengelsdorf, *Der Seekrieg in der Ostsee*, pp. 158–159.

icebound islands were worthless as a base of operations against the Finnish mainland, and resolved to transport the division directly from Danzig to Hangö (Hanko) on the southwest coast of Finland, just under 100 miles (160 km) west of Helsinki. Meurer's contingent appeared off Hangö on April 3, surprising a small Red Navy detachment there, which scuttled four submarines rather than let them fall into German hands. The following day Soviet Russian negotiators arrived in Hangö to ensure that the Germans would not interfere with Shchastny's efforts to evacuate the rest of the Russian Baltic Fleet from Helsinki, as required under the Treaty of Brest-Litovsk. Meurer agreed, on the understanding that the Red Navy and Soviet Russians manning shore batteries at Helsinki would remain neutral while the Germans secured the capital for the White Finns. On April 11, while en route from Hangö to Helsinki, the *Rheinland* ran aground and suffered severe hull damage, leaving Meurer with just two dreadnoughts to lead the German contingent into Helsinki harbor the following evening, by which time the German division had marched along the coast from Hangö to within 6 miles (10 km) of the city. The neutrality of the Red Navy was not tested, as Shchastny had moved the last of its ships out of Helsinki the day before, but fighting between German troops and Red Finns lasted until April 14, when the Germans finally secured the city and turned it over to the local Whites. The naval contingent began to leave that day, but most of the troops stayed on until April 21, when the last remaining Soviet Russian troops surrendered the coastal fortifications of Helsinki to the White Finns. The dreadnoughts *Westfalen* and *Posen* left for home at the end of April, but the crippled *Rheinland* remained on the Finnish coast until July, when it was finally refloated, towed to Kiel, and subsequently removed from service, the only German dreadnought not sunk in action to leave the fleet before the Armistice. For the last several months of the war, German naval forces in the eastern Baltic consisted of one light cruiser and one minelayer.[22]

    Russia's definitive departure from the Great War also brought an end to the British navy's Baltic submarine campaign. The last seven operational boats, preserved for the contingency of torpedoing Russian warships to keep them out of German hands, were scuttled at Helsinki just before Meurer's force arrived, by which time it had become clear that the Red Navy was going to great lengths to accomplish the same

[22] *Ibid.*, pp. 161–169.

end. Thanks to the efforts to save the Russian Baltic Fleet, at least in theory, it remained a formidable force, including four dreadnoughts, four pre-dreadnoughts, five armored cruisers, and four protected cruisers. But by May 1918 two of the pre-dreadnoughts had been hulked and the rest of the fleet laid up, with the exception of three vessels: the dreadnought *Petropavlovsk*, the pre-dreadnought *Andrei Pervozvanny*, and the protected cruiser *Oleg*. Even this dramatically reduced fleet remained idle, as the civil war featured no action on the Baltic, but the deactivation of so many warships enabled the Bolshevik regime to assign the sailors to the Red Army, in which they performed loyally against the Whites on various fronts.

In the Black Sea, the end of hostilities between Germany and Russia proved to be far less clear-cut, and the existence of rival pro-German and pro-Soviet Ukrainian governments from February onward further confused the situation. While Brest-Litovsk had ended the eastward march of the Central Powers elsewhere along the Eastern front, in Ukraine the armies of Germany and Austria-Hungary continued to advance after March 3 to support the government they had recognized against its local Soviet rival and, more importantly, to secure the wheat fields for that year's harvest, which the hungry home fronts of the Central Powers so desperately needed. Germany's pre-1914 grain imports from the Russian Empire had come from Ukraine, but owing to the limitations of Russia's rail network most of this trade had been carried by sea, from Odessa around Europe to Hamburg and Bremen.[23] With the war having worsened the overland transport situation and Allied navies blocking the sea route, the Germans ultimately sought to ship the 1918 harvest from the Black Sea up the Danube and into Germany via Bavaria. Austria-Hungary eventually detached monitors and patrol boats from its Danube Flotilla to convoy these shipments, which it was supposed to share, but when harvest time came the two allies squabbled over the spoils until their exploitation became a moot point after the collapse of Bulgaria in early autumn closed the Danube route.[24]

In contrast to the Russian Baltic Fleet, the warships of the Black Sea Fleet were to remain a factor throughout the civil war, but their status in 1918 remained ambiguous. The Treaty of Brest-Litovsk required Russia to "either bring her warships into Russian ports and

[23] Offer, *The First World War: An Agrarian Interpretation*, p. 239.
[24] Sondhaus, *The Naval Policy of Austria-Hungary*, pp. 330–332, 340.

there detain them until the day of the conclusion of a general peace, or disarm them."[25] But the treaty concluded a month earlier between the Central Powers and Ukraine had made Sevastopol a Ukrainian port, and Ukraine then laid claim to the ships of the Black Sea Fleet. The occupation of Ukraine by the Central Powers further undercut the naval provisions of the Brest-Litovsk Treaty in that their advance along the coast threatened Russian naval assets supposedly neutralized until a comprehensive peace settlement, in particular the shipyard at Nikolaiev and the ships of the Black Sea Fleet at Sevastopol. Discounting Ukrainian claims, the Germans intended to seize the ships for their own use; indeed, Ludendorff and the High Command joined German naval leaders in hatching grandiose schemes for them, including adding the *Yavuz Sultan Selim* to the Russian units and taking the lot on a sortie through the Turkish straits and into the eastern Mediterranean, coordinated with a breakout of the Austro-Hungarian fleet from the Adriatic. Allied naval leaders, hampered by their own poor intelligence on the situation in the Black Sea, actively feared German–Soviet collusion and bolstered their own eastern Mediterranean forces accordingly.[26]

These fears were encouraged by the example set on January 20, 1918, by Vice Admiral Rebeur-Paschwitz, who took the *Yavuz Sultan Selim* through the Dardanelles into the Aegean, serving notice that the end of the Russian threat to Turkey had freed the ship for offensive action outside the Black Sea. The battle cruiser's big guns sank the British monitors *Lord Raglan* (127 dead) and *M 28* (11 dead) off Imbros, but within hours its escort, the *Midilli*, struck a mine off Mudros and sank (330 dead). While attempting to take the *Midilli* under tow, the *Yavuz Sultan Selim* struck a mine in the same field, but managed to limp back to the safety of the Dardanelles, only to blunder onto a sandbar after entering the straits. It remained stranded for five days, during which British aircraft from Mudros and the seaplane carrier *Ark Royal* repeatedly bombed it, but to little effect as none had the capacity to carry a bomb large enough to do much damage to a battle cruiser. The pre-dreadnought *Torgud Reis* finally led a successful effort to tow the big ship free.[27] Despite its less than glorious end, the sortie

---

[25] Treaty of Brest-Litovsk, March 3, 1918, Article 5, text in John W. Wheeler-Bennett, *Brest-Litovsk: The Forgotten Peace, March 1918* (New York: W. W. Norton, 1938, paperback edn., 1971), p. 406.
[26] Halpern, *The Naval War in the Mediterranean*, pp. 542–543.
[27] Langensiepen *et al.*, *Halbmond und Kaiseradler*, pp. 178–187.

was significant not only in prompting a renewed Allied appreciation for the threat posed by the *Yavuz Sultan Selim*, but also because the damage it sustained (which was more serious than the Allies ever suspected) could not be repaired at Constantinople, making it all the more important for the Germans to seize Sevastopol, which had a dry-dock large enough to accommodate a battle cruiser.

German troops occupied Odessa on March 13 and Nikolaiev four days later. As they continued to march toward the Crimea and Sevastopol, the Black Sea Fleet (by then flying the Ukrainian flag) split over the issue of whether to flee or remain at the base. Ultimately, Admiral Nemits' second-in-command, Vice Admiral Mikhail Sablin, heeded orders from Lenin's government to take the best ships to Novorossiysk, a Russian-controlled port some 210 miles (340 km) east of Sevastopol. The dreadnoughts *Svobodnaya Rossiya* and *Volya* and an escort of eighteen mostly newer destroyers went with Sablin, while the six pre-dreadnoughts and over twenty smaller warships, ranging in size from cruisers to submarines, remained behind under Admiral Nemits and fell into German hands. Sablin sortied on May 14, just as German troops entered Sevastopol, and his departure infuriated Ludendorff. After the Germans demanded that Sablin's ships return to Sevastopol, the soviets of the fleet voted to decide the matter, with each ship free to determine its own fate. On June 18, the *Volya* and three destroyers steamed back to Sevastopol, while the *Svobodnaya Rossiya* and the rest of the destroyers were scuttled at Novorossiysk. Meanwhile, Rebeur-Paschwitz brought the *Yavuz Sultan Selim* to Sevastopol for repairs which, when completed, would leave the Central Powers with two operational capital ships in the theater.[28]

On the diplomatic level, Germany's plans to take over the Black Sea Fleet were compromised not just by the Ukrainian claim to the ships but by the likelihood that the Turks would insist upon their share should the ships be treated as spoils of war. The Germans ultimately avoided both issues by concluding a separate treaty with Soviet Russia (August 27, 1918) formally borrowing the *Volya* and the other ships that had either remained at, or returned to, Sevastopol. The agreement clarified that "the warships seized will remain under German care until

---

[28] Halpern, *The Naval War in the Mediterranean*, pp. 543–546. Most Western historians confuse Mikhail (M. P.) Sablin with his brother and fellow-admiral Nikolai (N. P.) Sablin, an error apparently dating from British dispatches of the period.

the conclusion of the general peace."[29] A supplementary note specified that Germany would be allowed "the use for peaceful aims...of the men-of-war of the Black Sea Fleet," with the provision that "in case of war...they might also be used for military means." The Germans pledged to pay "full indemnity" for any Russian warships damaged or lost while in German service.[30] The separate treaty also added Georgia to the list of independent states carved out of former Russian territory. Germany had been meddling in the Caucasus since the preceding autumn, when *UB 42* twice crossed the Black Sea from Constantinople on special missions to transport Georgian nationalist leaders home, and during 1918 the Germans deployed 10,000 troops there. The treaty left Azerbaijan in the hands of the Russians, but on the condition that the Germans would receive one-quarter of Baku's oil output.[31]

As it turned out, it was impossible for the Germans to repair and man enough of the Black Sea Fleet to launch an Aegean sortie that would be anything other than suicidal. The Germans finally commissioned the *Volya* and a handful of former Russian destroyers and torpedo boats but not until October 15, by which time repairs on the *Yavuz Sultan Selim* still had not been completed. Meanwhile, to counter a breakout through the Dardanelles by the imagined German Black Sea force, in the summer of 1918 the Allies stationed their best pre-dreadnoughts, four French *Danton*s plus the British *Lord Nelson* and *Agamemnon*, close by in the Aegean. By autumn, the British added the dreadnoughts *Superb* and *Temeraire* to their revived Mediterranean Fleet, more in order to justify Admiral Gough-Calthorpe wresting local Allied command from the French than because the ships were really needed.[32] They were the first British dreadnoughts stationed in the Mediterranean theater since the withdrawal of the *Queen Elizabeth* in May 1915.

Understandably, the departure of the *Yavuz Sultan Selim* to Sevastopol for repairs, combined with the growth of Gough-Calthorpe's

---

[29] Supplementary Treaty, Berlin, August 27, 1918, Article 15, text in Wheeler-Bennett, *Brest-Litovsk*, pp. 433–434.
[30] Supplementary Note, Berlin, August 27, 1918, Point 10, text in Wheeler-Bennett, *Brest-Litovsk*, p. 437.
[31] Supplementary Treaty, Berlin, August 27, 1918, Articles 13 and 14, text in Wheeler-Bennett, *Brest-Litovsk*, p. 433; Langensiepen et al., *Halbmond und Kaiseradler*, pp. 171–172.
[32] Halpern, *The Naval War in the Mediterranean*, pp. 552–554, 559–560.

fleet at the mouth of the Dardanelles, prompted concerns in Constantinople that the straits could not be held against an Allied assault. In the war's last weeks the Turks appealed repeatedly for the Germans to send the *Volya* and some of the Russian pre-dreadnoughts to counter this threat. Meanwhile, Allied victories on land placed additional pressure on the Ottoman Empire. The collapse of Bulgaria in the second half of September left an Allied army bearing down on Constantinople from the west, while the success of the Arab revolt and British Imperial offensives in the Middle East cost the Turks the last of their Arab provinces. Damascus fell on October 1, followed by Aleppo on October 26, leaving an Allied army poised to invade Asia Minor from the south. At that point the Turks asked for terms. Gough-Calthorpe, rather than the Allied Mediterranean commander-in-chief, Admiral Gauchet, concluded the armistice with the Ottoman Empire, signed aboard the *Agamemnon* off Mudros on October 30. The *Yavuz Sultan Selim*, just returned to Constantinople, was left in Turkish hands three days later when Rebeur-Paschwitz and the German naval mission left for home.[33]

    Germany thus failed to parlay the end of its war against Russia into any sort of naval advantage against the Allies; efforts toward this end had an *ad hoc* character and, in any event, were never central to the German grand strategy, from early 1917 onward, to knock Russia out of the war first, then marshal resources for a defeat of the Western Allies. Even on land, the formal end of the war on the Eastern front did not have the desired decisive effect. Peace with Russia enabled Germany to redeploy thirty-three divisions to France, raising the German total there to 192 against 165 for the Allies as of March 1918, but another forty-three divisions were left in the east under various arrangements with the newly independent states, thus undercutting the very strategy that had caused the German High Command to send Lenin back to Russia in the first place.

## Tightening the blockade: North Sea surface operations, 1918

The German troops left in the east would be sorely missed in the final drive against Paris, especially since the overall headcount of German

[33] *Ibid.*, pp. 554, 564–565.

manpower on the Western front when the final offensive began (1.4 million men) revealed that the average division was operating with around 7,000 men. By then, the Allied blockade had helped to reduce the German army's daily ration to 2,500 calories per man, barely better than the average prewar civilian figure and significantly less than the enemy norm (for example, just over 3,000 calories in the Italian army, the least well fed of the Allied armies of 1918). Short rations contributed to a deterioration of discipline even on the attack; indeed, the spirit of the German army remained generally good up to the decisive Second Battle of the Marne (July 15–August 6), but too often hungry troops stopped to indulge in the food and wine found in the trenches they captured, slowing their progress. In order to maintain the army even on these reduced rations, the intake of the average German civilian fell below 1,000 calories per day, half of the minimum requirement for a moderately active adult, and in 1917–18 the average German adult lost 20 percent of their body weight.[34] By the last year of the war, the weekly per capita consumption of bread and flour in Germany stood at 63 percent of 1913 levels, fats at 27 percent, and meats at 22 percent; in comparison, for Britain, the figures for the same foods were 107 percent, 88 percent, and 62 percent, respectively.[35] The definitive study on the subject concludes that the statistical evidence does not support the labels of famine and starvation, but acknowledges that "getting hold of food became a matter of survival," and ultimately Germans purchased between 20 and 35 percent of their food on the black market.[36]

In the first days of their offensive in March 1918, the Germans almost succeeded in driving a wedge between the British and French sectors of the Western front. The near-disaster persuaded the Allies of the need for closer coordination of their efforts, and led to the appointment of France's Marshal Ferdinand Foch as Supreme Allied Commander. The Allied governments never created a joint command for their navies, but during the same month they empowered the Allied Blockade Commission (ABC) to coordinate the ongoing effort to stop food and supplies from reaching the Central Powers. Lloyd George, frustrated

[34] Alan Kramer, "Combatants and Noncombatants: Atrocities, Massacres, and War Crimes," in John Horne (ed.), *A Companion to World War I* (Chichester: Wiley-Blackwell, 2010), p. 195.
[35] Lance E. Davis and Stanley L. Engerman, *Naval Blockades in Peace and War: An Economic History since 1750* (Cambridge University Press, 2006), p. 209.
[36] Offer, *The First World War: An Agrarian Interpretation*, ch. 3, quoted at p. 54.

by what he considered to be a lack of vigor in the Allied effort in the North Sea, had agreed to create the ABC in December 1917, in one of a series of moves that included dismissing Jellicoe as First Sea Lord. Cecil chaired the ABC and half its members were British, but American, French, and Italian representatives were also at the table. Thereafter, the various organs of the Ministry of Blockade were subsumed by the ABC, diminishing the role of Cecil, who finally resigned his post in July. The commission provided a venue for the discussion of differences of opinion over policy, usually without resolving them, but like the Supreme Allied Command it set an important precedent for coordination that would be followed in the next world war. The blockade became more effective in 1918, but historians differ over how much of the improvement was attributable to the ABC and how much would have occurred in any event once the United States had left the ranks of the neutrals and joined the blockaders. Of the neutrals most under pressure by the actions of the ABC, Norway, Sweden, and Denmark all traded less with Germany in 1918 than in 1917, but still more than they had in 1913. Ultimately, the near-closing of German–Dutch trade ranked as the greatest achievement. Under relentless Allied pressure, Dutch exports to Germany fell from a value of just over £25 million in 1917 to just under £12 million in 1918, dramatically less than the £113 million registered for 1913. Overall, the total value of Germany's imports (not counting trade from its allies and occupied territories) fell to £66 million in 1918, down from £560 million in 1913, with most of the decline attributable to the blockade.[37]

In the operational realm, Jellicoe's successor, Admiral Sir Rosslyn Wemyss, sought to take a more active posture against the Germans in 1918, most visibly in supporting Beatty's request to move the entire Grand Fleet from Scapa Flow to the battle cruiser base at Rosyth, 250 miles (400 km) closer to Wilhelmshaven. The transfer of the ships, carried out in April 1918, reflected Beatty's new-found desire to seek another engagement with the High Sea Fleet before the war ended, a sharp departure from his earlier logic of "when you are winning, risk nothing" that he had shared with Jellicoe after Jutland.

Months before the relocation of the Grand Fleet, one of Wemyss' first actions as First Sea Lord was to appoint Churchill's friend Sir Roger Keyes, formerly de Robeck's chief of staff at the Dardanelles, to succeed Bacon as head of the Dover Patrol. Wemyss then supported

---

[37] Osborne, *Britain's Economic Blockade*, p. 180.

Keyes in his quest to revive his predecessor's earlier proposal for raids to close Zeebrugge and Ostend to the Germans. Keyes, by this time a vice admiral, refined Bacon's plan to block the mouth of the canal linking Bruges to Zeebrugge. Ultimately, he settled on a combination of commandos landed by the old light cruiser *Vindictive* to neutralize shore batteries, two old submarines packed with explosives to be sacrificed against key harbor installations, and three old cruisers filled with cement to be sunk as blockships across the canal. After being prepared under great secrecy, the operation was carried out on the night of April 22/23, 1918. From the start few things went right for the attackers. The *Vindictive* landed its commandos, but they suffered such high losses that they were unable to complete their mission. One of the submarines struck its target as planned, but the other broke its tow line en route to Zeebrugge and played no part in the raid. Finally, one blockship was sunk in the wrong place and the other two failed to completely close the canal mouth. Of the 1,700 men involved in the raid, 200 were killed and 300 wounded. The British initially hailed the attack as a great success, but the effort closed Zeebrugge for only a matter of days. A concurrent attack on Ostend, which, like Zeebrugge, was linked by canal to Bruges, also called for old cruisers to be sunk as blockships across the mouth of the canal. There, the attack failed completely thanks to the ingenuity of the local German harbor commander who, unbeknown to the British, routinely moved a landmark navigation buoy every evening to foil enemy attacks; on the night of April 22/23, the key buoy was 2,400 yards (2,200 m) from the mouth of the canal, and as a result the two cruisers sunk there were grounded harmlessly on sandbars. Plans for a second attack on Ostend, on the night of May 9/10, called for a preliminary bombing raid by the Royal Air Force (RAF) – formed one month earlier by the merger of the Royal Naval Air Service and the army's Royal Flying Corps – after which the *Vindictive*, heavily damaged in the Zeebrugge raid, and another old cruiser were to be sunk as blockships at the mouth of the canal. The operation ended with the wreck of the *Vindictive* in the desired location, but because Zeebrugge remained open, Bruges remained viable as a center of German naval activity until early October, when the final Allied offensive on the Western front forced its abandonment.[38]

[38] See Charles Sanford Terry, *Ostend and Zeebrugge, April 23–May 19, 1918: The Dispatches of Vice-Admiral Sir Roger Keyes and Other Narratives of the Operations* (London: Oxford University Press, 1919).

Meanwhile, in April 1918, coinciding with Beatty moving the Grand Fleet to Rosyth, the High Sea Fleet left Wilhelmshaven on its first North Sea sortie in nineteen months. After William II rejected his appeal for a blow against the southeast coast of England,[39] Scheer decided to repeat, in much greater force, a raid the light cruisers *Brummer* and *Bremse* had conducted in October 1917 against the Allied convoy route between Norway and Scotland. Striking shortly after the Neumünster cryptanalysts had broken the British convoy code, the two cruisers succeeded in sinking nine merchantmen in a convoy of twelve, along with two of their escorting destroyers.[40] The fleet sortie of April 23–24 came after Scheer learned that the British were using capital ships to escort convoys on the same Norway–Scotland route. Aside from the three older dreadnoughts assigned to Meurer's Finnish expedition, the operation involved every capital ship in the German navy. Departing Wilhelmshaven on the night of April 22/23, they headed north under cover of a heavy fog. Hipper and the five battle cruisers led the mission, followed some 60 miles (90 km) behind by Scheer with the flagship *Baden* and fifteen other dreadnoughts, a scouting group of light cruisers, and four flotillas of destroyers. The lack of reaction from the British (who, by coincidence, were preoccupied on April 22 and 23 with the Zeebrugge–Ostend operation) led Scheer to speculate that, for once, he enjoyed the element of surprise. But on the morning of April 24, as Hipper closed to within 40 miles (60 km) of the Norwegian coast off Stavanger, one of his ships, the *Moltke*, lost a propeller, touching off a chain of mechanical mishaps that left it with a damaged hull and flooded engine room. Undeterred, Scheer ordered Hipper to proceed to the convoy lane with the four remaining battle cruisers, while one of his dreadnoughts took the *Moltke* in tow. As luck would have it, the Germans missed by one day a westbound convoy whose escort included four British battle cruisers, and were too early to intercept the next eastbound convoy. Hipper carried the search to the latitude of 60°N, almost all the way to Bergen, before turning back. By noon on April 24, the Grand Fleet left Rosyth, alerted by the rise in German wireless traffic after the *Moltke*'s mishap, but Beatty sortied too late to intercept Scheer on his run home. By the morning of the 25th, with "the enemy...nowhere to be seen," Scheer ordered the

[39] Herwig, *German Naval Officer Corps*, p. 242.
[40] Headrick, *The Invisible Weapon*, pp. 164–166.

*Moltke*'s tow dropped, allowing the crippled battle cruiser, which had taken on 2,000 tons of water, to proceed the rest of the way home under its own power. The British almost made him regret the decision when, at 19:50 that evening, 40 miles (60 km) north of Helgoland, the British submarine *E 42* torpedoed the *Moltke*. Fortunately for Scheer, the blow struck "at a very acute angle," adding little to the considerable hull damage the ship had suffered in the propeller accident, and it was able to steam into Wilhelmshaven later that night. Had Scheer known that the Grand Fleet was at Rosyth, not Scapa Flow, he would never have ventured so far north. The High Sea Fleet's longest sortie of the war would also be its last.[41]

The near-loss of the *Moltke*, coming two weeks after the fatal stranding of the *Rheinland* on the Finnish coast, left a demoralized High Sea Fleet with twenty-two operational capital ships, against which the Grand Fleet had forty-three, not counting the dreadnoughts of the American division. As of March 1918, Beatty's striking power was further supplemented when the 19,500-ton *Furious*, laid down as a battle cruiser, joined the fleet as an aircraft carrier, widening Britain's lead in the emerging field of naval aviation. Starting with the *Ark Royal* off Gallipoli, the British had deployed seaplane tenders and primitive carriers in most operations conducted in coastal waters. In November 1915, they achieved the first successful wartime deck launch of a wheeled airplane, then, in September 1916, demonstrated that an airplane could land on a deck after hooking an arrestor cable. These breakthroughs led to the decision to build the 14,450-ton carrier *Argus* on the hull of an unfinished ocean liner and to complete the *Furious* as a carrier. While the *Argus* was built with a flush flight deck and no superstructure at all, the converted *Furious* initially featured distinct fore-and-aft takeoff and landing decks, separated by its original centerline superstructure and funnel. In this configuration, on July 19, 1918, it became the first carrier to launch and recover wheeled aircraft in a successful air raid, conducted by seven Sopwith Camels on the Tondern zeppelin sheds in Schleswig-Holstein. The difficulties for landing aircraft posed by the centerline obstacles led to their removal in a major reconstruction of the *Furious* undertaken after the war. Meanwhile, the *Argus* was commissioned in September 1918, too late to see action. By the time of the Armistice, Britain had begun work on the *Hermes*, the

---

[41] Scheer, *Germany's High Sea Fleet*, pp. 318–323.

**Figure 10.2** Aircraft carrier HMS *Argus*

first ship built from the keel up as an aircraft carrier, and was building a fourth carrier, the future *Eagle*, on the hull of a dreadnought originally laid down in Britain for the Chilean navy. In 1919, work began to convert the battle cruisers *Glorious* and *Courageous* to aircraft carriers as well.[42]

## The end of unrestricted submarine warfare

The High Sea Fleet returned to anchor after April 1918, with nothing left to accomplish in the Baltic after the Finnish expedition and no hope

[42] See Geoffrey Till, *Airpower and the Royal Navy, 1914–1945: A Historical Survey* (London: Jane's Publishing, 1979).

of achieving anything in the North Sea after Scheer's sortie. Meanwhile, as spring gave way to summer, "the gradual decline in the monthly sinkings accomplished by the U-boats" left Scheer and his colleagues "filled... with anxiety."[43] The navy's senior admirals appeared paralyzed by pessimism. The chief of the *Admiralstab*, Holtzendorff, had seen his optimistic calculations of early 1917 disproven by the success of Allied antisubmarine warfare, and he had no answer to the question of how to reverse the trend. Meanwhile, Capelle, state secretary of the Imperial Navy Office, had continued to fight a rear-guard action to save capital ship construction projects, defending the long-term primacy of the surface fleet over the submarine force even though he did not share Scheer's view (after the executions of Köbis and Reichpietsch) that its short-term reliability had been restored. In early August, Scheer finally persuaded William II that the officer corps had lost confidence in Holtzendorff and Capelle. The emperor then used Holtzendorff's age (sixty-five) and poor health as pretexts for changing the command structure. Scheer became chief of a new Naval High Command (*Seekriegsleitung*), inheriting most of Holtzendorff's powers but with direct operational oversight of the High Sea Fleet. Scheer's fleet command passed to Hipper, whose battle cruiser command went to Rear Admiral Reuter. Vice Admiral Behncke, commander of a dreadnought squadron for most of the war, succeeded Capelle at the Imperial Navy Office. As moves intended to revive the navy, the changes were far less dramatic than Horthy becoming commander of the Austro-Hungarian fleet or the elevation of Kolchak and other young captains to the rank of admiral in Russia in 1916–17. The new leaders, all in their early fifties, were a decade younger than the men they replaced, but Scheer, Hipper, and Behncke were hardly outsiders, and had little to offer in terms of new ideas or energy.

Once the changes were announced, Scheer and his staff relocated to Germany's Western front headquarters at Spa in Belgium to be in daily contact with the emperor and the generals. On August 12, Scheer met with Hindenburg and Ludendorff, whom he found deeply shaken by the recent Allied breakthrough at Amiens. "Both officers were much impressed with the gravity of the events which had occurred on August 8, and had placed our war on land definitely on the defensive." While it was not yet clear that the German army would never recover the initiative, Scheer later recalled "they both admitted that the main

---

[43] Scheer, *Germany's High Sea Fleet*, p. 328.

hope of a favorable end to the war lay in a successful offensive of the U-boats."[44] With nothing to offer against the convoy system and other Allied antisubmarine measures, the new naval leadership simply advocated more U-boats, as reflected in a construction program drafted by Behncke and announced on September 18. The Scheer Program, a naval complement to the Hindenburg Program of 1916, called for the monthly production of U-boats to triple by the end of 1919. Direct oversight of the program fell to Vice Admiral Ritter von Mann-Tiechler, former head of the U-boat department of the Imperial Navy Office, who soon succeeded Behncke as state secretary, but the grand design included no provisions for procuring the materials, assembling and feeding the workforce, or manning the submarines once they were built. Historians have been at a loss to explain the Scheer Program, the goals of which seem so divorced from the reality Germany faced in the autumn of 1918. Holger Herwig has concluded that it was little more than "a massive propaganda effort designed to have an effect at home and abroad."[45] Yet it was far from harmless rhetoric. Between August and October 1918, the Scheer Program, combined with the creation of the Naval High Command, had the negative consequence of being responsible, directly or indirectly, for the transfer of 48 percent of the fleet's warship commanders and 45 percent of first officers,[46] placing more of the best senior and mid-career men in posts on land at the same time that the U-boat campaign continued to take the best junior men for the submarine service. The effects would be seen in the final mutiny of the fleet, which found too many officers of lesser ability serving in unfamiliar circumstances.

For practical as well as political reasons, the failure of the German army to hold the Western front affected the continuation of unrestricted submarine warfare. The onset of the final Allied push all along the front (September 26–28) posed an immediate threat to the U-boat bases at Zeebrugge and Ostend. On September 29, in an emergency meeting at Spa, Ludendorff informed William II and German political leaders that "the condition of the army demands an immediate armistice in order to avoid a catastrophe."[47] Scheer ordered the abandonment of Ostend later that day, followed by Zeebrugge, 13 miles

[44] *Ibid.*, p. 333.   [45] Herwig, *"Luxury" Fleet*, p. 222.
[46] Horn, *German Naval Mutinies*, p. 215.
[47] Quoted in Hajo Holborn, *A History of Modern Germany, 1840–1945* (Princeton University Press, 1982), p. 502.

(21 km) to the east, on October 3, even though fighting continued in and around both towns into mid-October. The loss of the Flemish bases was a significant blow to the German effort at sea; despite having to brave the obstacles of the Dover barrage on their sorties, U-boats operating out of the two ports had been responsible for sinking 23 percent of the total Allied tonnage lost in the war. The decision not to evacuate Ostend and Zeebrugge earlier cost the German navy four submarines and thirteen destroyers and torpedo boats, all scuttled or abandoned with Allied troops approaching.[48] In the face of this setback, Scheer recalled that "General Ludendorff was in favor of keeping to the plan of strengthening the U-boat weapon" because "the threat it contained might be useful for securing the armistice desired by the army."[49] This required some wishful thinking, especially as the tonnage sunk by the existing U-boat force continued to drop, from 310,180 tons in August to just 171,970 tons in September, 116,240 tons in October, and 10,230 tons for the first eleven days of November.

Having lost the war, the High Command urged the emperor to proclaim a constitutional monarchy and turn the government over to the Reichstag parties that had supported the Peace Resolution of July 1917, reasoning that they would have better luck negotiating with the Allies. This strategy also enabled the generals to avoid responsibility for the defeat in the eyes of the public, by putting the politicians they liked the least in the position of having to conclude the unfavorable peace that was bound to follow. On October 2, Ludendorff sent his deputy, Major Baron Erich von der Bussche, to break the news to a shocked Reichstag that "we cannot win the war," and that the government would have to seek "the breaking-off of hostilities, so as to spare the German people and their allies further sacrifice."[50] The following day, the liberal Prince Max of Baden took over as chancellor, supported by a coalition including the SPD, the Catholic Center Party, and progressive liberals. On October 5, Prince Max informed Wilson of Germany's willingness to negotiate peace based on the Fourteen Points. In Austria-Hungary, Emperor Charles similarly sought to make his regime appear more

---

[48] Scheer, *Germany's High Sea Fleet*, pp. 340–341; *Conway, 1906–1921*, pp. 169, 172; see also at: www.uboat.net.
[49] Scheer, *Germany's High Sea Fleet*, p. 343.
[50] Major Freiherr von der Bussche's Address to the Reichstag of the Recommendations of the German High Command, October 2, 1918, text available at: firstworldwar.com/source/germancollapse_bussche.htm.

palatable to the Americans and to identify himself with the president's peace program. On October 16, he issued a proclamation promising a constitutional restructuring to provide autonomy to the various nationalities, as demanded in Wilson's tenth point, then, the following day, started to distance himself from the Germans by unilaterally ending the Austro-Hungarian navy's participation in unrestricted submarine warfare. In a series of meetings in Berlin beginning the same day, Scheer proposed offering Wilson "the cessation of the U-boat campaign...in exchange for the Armistice," but Prince Max informed him that Germany was "not in a position to make conditions."[51] The chancellor believed no serious negotiations would take place until after Germany ended unrestricted submarine warfare. William II soon came round to this view and, on October 21, ordered Scheer to call home all U-boats then at sea or stationed abroad.

Charles' autonomy proposal had the unintended consequence of prompting the leaders of the various nationalities to create their own provisional governments, accelerating the internal disintegration of Austria-Hungary and, with it, the German navy's timetable for closing down its submarine bases in the Adriatic. On October 24, the Italians turned up the pressure, launching a major offensive from the Alps to the Adriatic which met with little resistance all along the front; while the Italian navy did nothing to support the effort, the collapse of the Austro-Hungarian army soon left Trieste and Pola in danger of falling to the enemy from the land side. Desperate for an immediate end to the war, on October 26, Charles informed William II that their alliance had come to an end, but the hour had long passed for the Dual Monarchy to save itself by concluding a separate peace. In Pola, where his *UC 67* was based, Martin Niemöller was among the German submariners whose lives were suddenly turned upside down by the imminent end of the war. Niemöller later recalled orders received on October 27 "to get all seaworthy boats ready to return to Germany...in order to make them available for a last stand," with the stipulation "boats that could not be ready to sail within twenty-four hours were to be scuttled." The Germans sank ten U-boats judged unable to handle the month-long cruise home, then sent their crews, along with land-based staff and support personnel, back to Germany by rail. On October 28–29, Niemöller's *UC 67* and the remaining

---

[51] Scheer, *Germany's High Sea Fleet*, pp. 351, 353.

submarines from the Pola base began making their way down the Adriatic for a rendezvous with other U-boats coming out of Cattaro; in all, twelve German submarines made the voyage from the Adriatic to the Baltic via the Straits of Gibraltar, around the British Isles to the coast of Norway, then through the Skagerrak and Kattegat to Kiel. Under the orders of October 21 ending unrestricted submarine warfare, they were limited to attacking armed enemy ships, but only one was encountered en route: the pre-dreadnought *Britannia*, torpedoed by *UB 52* (Lieutenant Heinrich Kukat) off Gibraltar on November 9. The last casualty of the Great War at sea took two and a half hours to sink, enabling all but fifty of its crew to be saved. Three days later, while off Cape Finisterre, the U-boats received word of the Armistice via wireless. Several of them surfaced to enable their commanders to meet and discuss "whether we should continue the voyage home or seek internment in a Spanish port." The attitude of the crews, who wanted to go home, decided the issue, yet Niemöller recalled that "no trouble of any kind was experienced" and regarding discipline, "the crews were absolutely unaffected" by the news of the Armistice. They finally reached Kiel on November 25.[52] By then, all other U-boats deployed in the war's last weeks had returned home, and most had already been surrendered to the British under the terms of the Armistice.

## Germany and Austria-Hungary: the ultimate mutinies

The German preparations to depart Pola had an electrifying effect on the Austro-Hungarian fleet, making it impossible for Horthy to maintain discipline after October 27. That evening, the rebellious *Hurra-Rufe* echoed across the harbor for the first time since the unrest of January 1918, and by the following morning the captains of Horthy's battleships were unanimous in declaring their vessels unreliable for further operations. Recognizing that the disintegration of the empire left most sailors more anxious to return to their homes than to take over their ships, the admiral and his officers appealed for calm by promising "extensive furloughing... as soon as hostilities are ended."[53] But in making the

---

[52] Niemöller, *From U-Boat to Pulpit*, pp. 112–118.
[53] As authorized in *Armeekommando* to *Flottenkommando*, Baden, October 28, 1918, text in Sokol, *Österreich-Ungarns Seekrieg*, vol. 2, p. 719.

rounds of Pola during the day on October 28, Horthy found most ships already in the hands of their crews. Committees elected by the sailors presented him with lists of demands similar to those formulated by the Cattaro mutineers in February, including appeals to the Fourteen Points but also for a common mess and common conditions of service for officers and seamen alike. Several mentioned November 1 as a deadline, at which time they would abandon their ships and go home. Some officers found the situation unbearable. According to Niemöller, on the evening of the 28th "four young Austrian naval officers came aboard" his submarine just before it departed Pola, "asking for a passage to Germany."[54] Meanwhile, aboard the *Prinz Eugen*, Captain Alexander Milosević withdrew to his cabin and shot himself. On the night of October 28/29, a mob of local civilians waving Italian flags stormed the Officers' Club in Pola, and on the 29th, after the last of the Germans had left the base, gangs of mutineers looted their abandoned quarters. In their quest to maintain order, Horthy and his subordinates were hamstrung by a directive from Charles proscribing the use of deadly force, since under the circumstances the emperor considered all bloodshed senseless. Finally acknowledging the impending dismemberment of the Dual Monarchy, on October 30 Charles decided to turn the fleet over to the Yugoslav national council.

The political groundwork for this remarkable development had been falling into place for almost a month. On October 6, as soon as word arrived of the German peace overture to the United States, Croatian leaders in Zagreb formed a national council. Over the days that followed, they dispatched emissaries to Yugoslav émigré groups in the various Allied capitals. Finally, on the morning of October 29, they declared the end of Croatia's centuries-old dynastic tie to Hungary and called for a new union of Croatia and Dalmatia with Serbia. Slovenian and Bosnian groups also pledged their allegiance to the Yugoslav concept. Later that day, Hungarian officials turned over the port of Fiume to Croatians loyal to the national council. The imperial government appealed to Zagreb for help in restoring calm in the fleet, but the national council refused to act unless the navy was first placed under its authority. Faced with the alternatives of doing nothing or turning the fleet over to the Yugoslav national council, Charles opted for the latter course, instructing Horthy to work through South Slav officers to

---

[54] Niemöller, *From U-Boat to Pulpit*, p. 113.

make the transition as smooth as possible. A Slovenian officer, Captain Method Koch, who had been elected to a Yugoslav national committee in Pola on October 28, emerged as a central figure. At 13:00 on October 30, Charles cabled Horthy that a "dispatch concerning the release of crews and transfer of navy to Yugoslav national council will follow shortly."[55] Over the next seven hours, Charles and his political and military advisors drafted the terms under which the fleet would be transferred. All Austro-Hungarian officers, regardless of nationality, were granted permission to remain with the fleet in Yugoslav service, while all sailors not belonging to a South Slav nationality were to be furloughed. At 20:00, Horthy received his orders. He met with Koch aboard the flagship *Viribus Unitis* on the morning of October 31 to work out the details of the transfer. The formal ceremonies in Pola took place at 16:45 that afternoon. Horthy later recalled the emotional scene, and being "unable to begin my short farewell address to the men. As my flag was struck, all the flags on all the ships followed suit."[56] The red-white-red flag of Austria gave way to the red-white-blue Yugoslav flag, greeted by a thunderous twenty-one gun salute. The scene was repeated the following day at Cattaro. While Koch took over the administrative command in Pola, senior Croatian officers stepped forward to assume the higher positions of leadership. Captain Janko Vuković succeeded Horthy as commander of the fleet, and the Yugoslav national council brought Rear Admiral Dragutin Prica to Zagreb to serve as overall navy commander. The Austro-Hungarian navy, like the empire it served, ceased to exist.

    The collapse of Austria-Hungary, long feared by German leaders, preceded Imperial Germany's own collapse by barely a week, but for the navies, the ultimate mutinies came during the same days. In his capacity as head of the Naval High Command, Scheer acquiesced in the order to end the U-boat campaign, but was not willing to have his capital ships finish the war without a fight. Without consulting the emperor or the chancellor, he hatched a scheme to take the navy's remaining eighteen dreadnoughts and five battle cruisers on a final sortie, from Wilhelmshaven westward along the Dutch coast, then on a course to the west-southwest, straight to the Thames estuary, in the

---

[55] Sokol, *Österreich-Ungarns Seekrieg*, vol. 2, pp. 728–729; Plaschka *et al.*, *Innere Front*, vol. 2, pp. 233–234.
[56] Horthy, *Memoirs*, p. 92.

hope of drawing out the Grand Fleet for a final engagement. Known to history as Operations Plan 19, it was set it in motion via unwritten orders conveyed to Hipper on October 22, the day after the U-boats were recalled. Amid the preparations, on October 24, Wilson's response to Prince Max's latest peace overture – which had included Germany's unconditional abandonment of unrestricted submarine warfare – reached Berlin, and in Scheer's view "quite clearly demanded complete capitulation."[57] Indeed, Wilson questioned whether Prince Max's government was really in charge or the constitutional reforms promised by William II would actually take place, and concluded that if the United States "must deal with the military masters and the monarchical autocrats of Germany . . . it must demand not peace negotiations, but surrender."[58]

Hindenburg and Ludendorff responded by issuing a defiant order of the day to the army, while Scheer had Hipper promulgate the sortie order. Scheer then joined the generals in Berlin on October 25 to lobby the emperor and chancellor to reject Wilson's latest note, but their assurances of the fighting ability of an army that had retreated every day since August 8 and a fleet that had not sortied in six months rang hollow. Prince Max had little difficulty in persuading William II that further resistance would only lead to disaster. On October 26, the emperor accepted the resignation of Ludendorff, who went into exile in Sweden rather than risk his fate on an increasingly volatile home front; meanwhile, the chancellor issued a reassuring response to Wilson in order to keep the dialogue going. Scheer, with nothing to lose, had Hipper proceed with his plans, which by this time had evolved to include over two dozen recalled U-boats and, ironically, probably had better prospects tactically than any of Scheer's earlier sorties. The fleet was scheduled to raise steam on October 29, assemble in the roadstead off Wilhelmshaven during the night of the 29/30th, and head west for the final battle on the 31st. But during the day on October 27, the same day that Horthy lost control of the Austro-Hungarian fleet, Hipper's preliminary preparations tipped off the crews that a final sortie was imminent. Aware that Prince Max's government had requested an armistice, and having heard so many of their officers openly criticize

[57] Scheer, *Germany's High Sea Fleet*, p. 354.
[58] Third Wilson Reply, October 23, 1918, text in *Americanism: Woodrow Wilson's Speeches on the War*, ed. and comp. Oliver Marble Gale (Chicago, IL: The Baldwin Syndicate, 1918), pp. 143–144.

the chancellor and his government because of it, sailors and stokers were outraged not just that their lives would be risked once more in a war soon to be over, but that the naval leadership apparently wanted to sabotage the peace negotiations by actively seeking battle with the British. As the day progressed, four of the five battle cruisers reported active or passive resistance to orders. The final mutiny of the High Sea Fleet was underway.[59]

It has been suggested that the positions taken by Scheer and the generals on October 24–26 laid the groundwork for the German "counterrevolution" that followed the Armistice, in that they articulated positions in opposition to Prince Max's government that they and other conservative officers and politicians would later hark back to, in characterizing the peace settlement as a "stab in the back" by a liberal civilian leadership against a German army and navy still willing to carry on the fight.[60] Most scholars view Operations Plan 19 as a deliberate attempt by Scheer and his staff to undermine the chancellor and the armistice talks and sacrifice the fleet to satisfy their own archaic sense of honor.[61] But Hipper's biographer absolves him of complicity in this "admirals' rebellion," on the grounds that "it is difficult to ascertain beyond a reasonable doubt" that Hipper knew Scheer had not informed Prince Max about the proposed sortie. Rejecting the generally accepted view that Hipper was Scheer's accomplice in planning a suicide mission for the fleet, he argues that "the plan was feasible and offered the chance, at acceptable odds, for major military and political gain."[62] Of course, what mattered at the time, and to history, was what the crews of the High Sea Fleet thought, and as Scheer conceded, "the idea had taken root in their minds that they were to be uselessly sacrificed."[63] On October 28, the unrest from the battle cruisers to the dreadnoughts of the III Squadron, and took on such proportions that Hipper had to cancel the sortie order late on the 29th, by which time a heavy fog had made it impossible to proceed anyway. The following day, Hipper issued a strident, patriotic appeal to the fleet, in which he sought to

[59] Horn, *German Naval Mutinies*, pp. 218–222.
[60] Leonidas E. Hill, "Signal zur Konterrevolution? Der Plan zum letzten Vorstoß der deutschen Hochseeflotte am 30. Oktober 1918," *Vierteljahreshefte für Zeitgeschichte*, 36(1) (January 1988): 128.
[61] For example, Herwig, *German Naval Officer Corps*, p. 245.
[62] Philbin, *Admiral von Hipper*, pp. 159, 162.
[63] Scheer, *Germany's High Sea Fleet*, p. 355.

dispel "the rumor... that the officers of the navy desire a battle with a superior enemy such that the fleet would be shot to pieces and therefore not be surrendered with the armistice."[64] He then sought to reinstate the sortie order, ultimately just for the U-boats and the I Squadron, an inexplicable half-measure that served only to ignite rebellion aboard the dreadnoughts of that squadron. As late as midday on October 31, Hipper continued to try to get the I Squadron to move; on his orders a U-boat and two torpedo boats threatened to sink the *Thüringen*, compelling 200 mutineers aboard it to surrender, but this proved to be an isolated success against the forces of disorder. The IV Squadron likewise rose in rebellion on the night of October 30/31, leaving no part of the fleet unaffected.[65]

By the evening of October 31, Hipper had abandoned all hope of further operations and focused instead on restoring order, convincing himself that this could best be achieved by dispersing the dreadnoughts. The I Squadron was sent up the Elbe River, minus the worst of its mutinous ships, the *Thüringen* and *Helgoland*, which anchored at Wilhelmshaven along with the IV Squadron. Vice Admiral Hugo Kraft, who had succeeded Behncke as commander of the III Squadron in the reassignments of August 1918, persuaded Hipper to send his ships through the Kiel Canal to the Baltic. "I know my men," Kraft declared, with far too much confidence for someone who had spent all of ten weeks at his post. "They can be got back in hand if we go to Kiel."[66] The foolishness of Kraft's optimism was exposed as soon as the III Squadron arrived there. The crews reacted to his arrest of forty-seven ringleaders of the mutiny by rising again, and spreading the rebellion to the shore installations of the Baltic naval station, defying efforts by Souchon, recently appointed station chief, to maintain order. Under the dynamic leadership of stoker Karl Artelt, who had been an SPD activist in civilian life, the number of mutineers demonstrating ashore grew from 600 on November 2 to 3,000 the following day. At one point on November 3 a patrol dispatched by Souchon fired on the crowd, killing eight demonstrators, but the show of force only fueled the rebellion. On November 4, the rebels looted the arsenal

---

[64] "Appeal of Admiral Ritter von Hipper to the Enlisted Personnel of the High Sea Fleet," Wilhelmshaven, October 30, 1918, text in Philbin, *Admiral von Hipper*, pp. 165–166.
[65] Horn, *German Naval Mutinies*, pp. 222–226.
[66] Quoted in Philbin, *Admiral von Hipper*, p. 167.

to arm themselves, and were joined by troops from the garrison sent to stop them. They proceeded to elect a revolutionary council, on the Soviet Russian model, with Artelt as its head. Amid the chaos Souchon appealed to his last loyal seamen, the submariners, for support. U-boat ace Max Valentiner, who had put to sea on the morning of the 4th for training exercises, was recalled to Kiel along with other senior U-boat commanders and ordered to help quell the unrest ashore. Such efforts proved fruitless. By the morning of November 5 the number of armed men in the streets – mostly sailors – had reached 20,000, and by that afternoon the submarine base, too, was in the hands of the revolutionaries. Meanwhile, in the harbor, by the morning of the 5th every ship flew the red flag exccpt the dreadnought *König*, whose captain, Karl Weniger, continued to fly the battle flag, which he guarded himself, with the support of his first officer, Bruno Heinemann, and a young lieutenant, Wolfgang Zenker. At midday, the mutineers finally rushed the flagstaff, shot its three defenders, and replaced the battle flag with their red banner; Weniger survived his wounds, but Zenker and Heinemann were killed, the only two officers to lose their lives in the mutiny of the High Sea Fleet.[67] By the time of their deaths, SPD Reichstag deputy Gustav Noske was already emerging as the key figure in keeping the situation in Kiel from spinning out of control. Sent from Berlin by Prince Max at the navy's request, he arrived on the evening of November 4 and quickly gained the confidence of the sailors as well as their besieged officers; after two days as chair of the revolutionary council, he relinquished that post to inherit Souchon's powers as governor of Kiel. In his memoirs the arch-conservative Valentiner put politics aside in praising Noske for his personal bravery during those chaotic days, crediting him with reining in the revolution in Kiel and "leading it on a calmer path."[68]

Meanwhile, in Wilhelmshaven, open rebellion started much later and featured less intense confrontations. After anchoring there on November 1, the *Thüringen*, the *Helgoland*, and the dreadnoughts of the IV Squadron all put their least reliable men ashore, much to the dismay of the station chief, Admiral Günther von Krosigk, but by November 3 those remaining aboard had resorted to strikes to paralyze

---

[67] Valentiner, *Der Schrecken der Meere*, p. 277; Horn, *German Naval Mutinies*, pp. 235–245.
[68] Valentiner, *Der Schrecken der Meere*, p. 288.

the larger ships. The ultimate explosion came after news arrived, on November 5, that Kiel was in the hands of a revolutionary council. On the morning of the 6th, sailors abandoned their ships en masse to demonstrate in the streets of Wilhelmshaven. All detachments of marines and soldiers deployed to stop them joined the growing mob. After storming the prison to release their incarcerated comrades, they confronted Krosigk with a list of demands, then joined local workers in establishing a revolutionary council led by a stoker, Bernhard Kuhnt, who, like his counterpart Artelt in Kiel, had been an SPD activist before the war. Throughout the upheaval Hipper remained aboard the flagship *Baden*, which became a safe haven for officers and sailors seeking refuge from the mutiny. He made no attempt to help Krosigk, and late on the evening of November 6 informed Scheer that he was powerless to implement or enforce further orders. There was no equivalent to Noske in Kiel, and no need for one, as Kuhnt himself kept the more radical elements in check.[69]

The bravery of Zenker and Heinemann, who gave their lives defending the battle flag of the *König*, stood in sharp contrast to the indecision, if not cowardice, shown by most officers during the mutiny. Aside from the flag incident, no mutineers had used deadly force against their officers, and yet officers of all ranks, from Scheer and Hipper on down, used the words "Bolshevik" and "revolution" to refer to the events unfolding around them, and clearly feared the fate that had befallen so many officers in Russia in 1917. Even when nothing like a Bolshevik revolution actually occurred, many were convinced that it almost had; for example, in praising Noske for his role in defusing the revolution in Kiel, Valentiner asserted that "we officers have only him to thank that it did not turn out for us exactly as it had for our comrades in Russia."[70] Amid the fear and panic, in Kiel alone several hundred officers put on civilian clothing, walked away from their posts, and melted into the crowds, placing self-preservation above duty or honor. These included the emperor's brother, Admiral Prince Henry, titular Baltic Fleet commander, who escaped in disguise to Denmark with his wife and son. Being charitable to the prince, his panic was certainly understandable, as his wife was the sister of Empress Alexandra of Russia, murdered by the Bolsheviks along with the tsar and their

---

[69] Horn, *German Naval Mutinies*, pp. 261–264.
[70] Valentiner, *Der Schrecken der Meere*, p. 288.

children four months earlier, and their son, like the Tsarevich Aleksei, was a hemophiliac who required special care. In any case, even those officers who remained at their posts felt the need to compromise their dignity in doing so; Valentiner, for example, dressed in civilian clothes when walking the streets beyond the gates of naval installations.[71]

While the revolution sparked by the mutiny of the fleet was far less bloody than the previous year's upheavals in Russia, naval officers were not the only ones who actively feared it becoming so. On November 1, radical socialist leader Karl Liebknecht, released from prison just days earlier, alarmed his political rivals by issuing a stirring appeal for a German revolution. On November 5, after imperial authorities lost control of Kiel, sailors helped to spread the unrest to Hamburg and Bremen. At the same time, throughout the country, the number of strikers and demonstrators grew dramatically. On November 7, soviet-style revolutionary councils were established in Cologne, Hanover, and Frankfurt, while in Munich, USPD leader Kurt Eisner, like Liebknecht only recently released from prison, boldly proclaimed a Bavarian soviet republic. These developments sparked fears among Prince Max and his Reichstag supporters, as well as Allied leaders abroad, that the imperial government would give way to a revolutionary regime on the national level, and added a new sense of urgency to the peace process. On the morning of November 8, a German delegation headed by Center Party leader Matthias Erzberger, principal author of the July 1917 Peace Resolution, met a delegation headed by Marshal Ferdinand Foch near Allied headquarters at Compiègne. The Allied terms were harsher than the Germans expected, including the internment of the newest ships of the fleet and the surrender of all submarines. The army had to withdraw immediately to the country's 1914 borders, minus Alsace-Lorraine, to be ceded directly to France, and the rest of the west bank of the Rhine, to be occupied by Allied troops, then began demobilization. Meanwhile, the Allied armies were to remain intact. The Germans also had to return all Allied prisoners of war, but German POWs would remain in Allied hands until the signing of a definitive peace. Worst of all, the blockade would also remain in force until that time. Given seventy-two hours to sign the document, Erzberger sought further instructions, but by then Berlin was in chaos, as was the High Command's headquarters at Spa.

[71] Horn, *German Naval Mutinies*, pp. 234–235, 244–245, 254; Valentiner, *Der Schrecken der Meere*, p. 283.

Ludendorff's successor, General Wilhelm Groener, after ascertaining that retreating units could not be counted upon to defend the monarchy against the revolution, on November 9 informed William II that "the army... no longer stands behind Your Majesty."[72] Scheer urged the emperor not to abdicate on the grounds that it would leave the navy without a commander-in-chief, to which he replied "I no longer have a navy."[73]

On the afternoon of November 9, William II was still pondering abdication when word arrived from Berlin that Prince Max had already announced it, then resigned in favor of SPD leader Friedrich Ebert. Within an hour came word that the new chancellor's SPD colleague Philipp Scheidemann had proclaimed a republic, apparently to preempt Liebknecht's anticipated proclamation of a soviet republic. Later that day, the emperor left Spa for the Netherlands, where he would live in exile until his death in 1941. In the early hours of November 11, Erzberger and the German delegation returned to Compiègne where they signed the Armistice at 05:00 local time. Admiral Wemyss, Britain's First Sea Lord, joined Foch in signing for the Allies. The Great War ended six hours later, when the cease-fire went into effect at 11:00.

## Conclusion

In the wake of the Armistice, the former prime minister, Asquith, still grieving over a son killed at the Somme two years earlier, conceded that "with all deference to our soldiers, this war has been won with sea power."[74] Appropriately enough, long before any troops paraded home, the first tangible sign of victory came at sea. On the morning of November 21, the British light cruiser *Cardiff* led the High Sea Fleet, or at least most of it, from the Helgoland Bight across the North Sea to a rendezvous with the Grand Fleet around 40 miles (64 km) east of the mouth of the Firth of Forth. Beatty brought the fleet out of Rosyth, including the American division of five dreadnoughts and three cruisers representing the French navy. He formed his ships up in two long columns, between which the German column steamed. Ninety

---

[72] John W. Wheeler-Bennett, *Wooden Titan: Hindenburg in Twenty Years of German History, 1914–1934* (New York: William Morrow, 1936), pp. 197, 199.
[73] Scheer, *Germany's High Sea Fleet*, p. 358.
[74] Quoted in Davis and Engerman, *Naval Blockades*, p. 211.

minutes later, around 11:00, the multinational armada anchored in the Firth of Forth and, on Beatty's order, the German ships hauled down their battle flags. Denied their Trafalgar at Jutland, the British finally felt like victors, at least for the moment. The transfer of the interned ships to Scapa Flow followed on November 25–27. Germany's eleven newest dreadnoughts (five *Kaiser*s, four *König*s, and two *Bayern*s), all five battle cruisers, eight light cruisers, and fifty destroyers were to remain there until the Paris Peace Conference determined their fate, along with that of Germany as a whole. Because Hipper declined to remain at his post, it fell to Reuter, his successor as commander of the battle cruisers, to succeed him now as *de facto* commander of the fleet. After the ships reached Scapa Flow, the British quickly repatriated most of their crews to Germany; within three weeks, the 20,000 men aboard Reuter's ships had been reduced to skeleton crews totaling less than 5,000, who would endure the harsh winter at anchor in the Orkneys, and an uncertain spring beyond that. The submariners were spared a similar fate; in late November and early December, the German navy turned over 176 U-boats to the British at Harwich, including nearly two dozen too new to have seen action during the war, but their crews did not have to stay with them.

Meanwhile, in the Adriatic, Italy from the start rejected Austria-Hungary's transfer of the fleet to Yugoslav control, even though Yugoslavia, as the successor to Serbia, enjoyed the status of an Allied state. The morning after the ceremonies in Pola, two Italian navy saboteurs riding a small torpedo-like craft infiltrated the harbor and attached explosives to the hull of the flagship *Viribus Unitis*, which capsized and sank at 06:20, shortly after the charges were detonated. The 400 dead included Janko Vuković, Yugoslav fleet commander for less than a day. Italy's armistice with Austria-Hungary (November 4) allowed Italian warships into the naval harbor at Pola as well as the commercial ports of Trieste and Fiume. Yugoslav authorities in Pola soon relented and allowed the Italian flag to be raised aboard the ships there. During negotiations held on Corfu, the British were sympathetic to Yugoslav claims, but had no answer to the Italian question of how they would feel if the High Sea Fleet suddenly raised the Danish flag. The analogy may have been far-fetched, but the British promptly abandoned the Yugoslavs, who formally renounced their claim to the ships on November 10. While the internment of the High Sea Fleet gave the British an enviable moment of triumph definitively ending the war in the North Sea, the Italians were not destined to enjoy the same sort of closure in the Adriatic theater. They came closest four months later, on March 25, 1919, when the dreadnought *Tegetthoff*, one pre-dreadnought, eight cruisers and destroyers, and four submarines steamed into Venice under the Italian flag.[75]

The Allies completed their naval triumph by entering the Black Sea. After the Armistice, Admiral Gough-Calthorpe's flagship *Superb* led an Allied column through the Dardanelles, which anchored off Constantinople on November 13. Gough-Calthorpe proceeded to Sevastopol on November 26, to take possession of the Russian Black Sea warships that the Germans had seized in May 1918. The following spring the Allies scuttled fifteen Russian submarines during a Red Army offensive in the Crimea, and most of the surface warships were disarmed, their machinery removed or disabled to render them useless in case they fell into Bolshevik hands. Postwar Allied naval operations against the Bolsheviks in the Baltic and Black seas were made possible only by holding over war-weary sailors whose service terms had expired, and thus were unsustainable; mutinies during 1919 in both the British and French navies made this clear to anyone who doubted it. Later that year the Allies turned over the dreadnought *Volya* (renamed *General Alekseev*), three other Black Sea warships, and two submarines to the White Russian leader, General Baron Peter Wrangel, then withdrew. Ironically, the enemy capital ship that, throughout the war, attracted more attention than any other single naval vessel was the only one to remain beyond Allied control. The *Yavuz Sultan Selim* (ex-*Goeben*), left in Turkish hands on November 2 when Rebeur-Paschwitz and the German naval mission departed Constantinople, endured a precarious existence before emerging as flagship of the navy of the postwar Republic of Turkey, under the name *Yavuz*. It enjoyed the longest career of any of the capital ships that served in the Great War, before finally being decommissioned and sold for scrap in 1971.

At sea, as on land, in a losing effort the Central Powers inflicted more damage and casualties than they sustained. This was especially true in the largest classes of warships. Germany lost one battle cruiser and Austria-Hungary one dreadnought, against which Britain suffered losses of two dreadnoughts and three battle cruisers, while Italy, Japan, and Russia (before leaving the war in December 1917) lost

[75] Sondhaus, *The Naval Policy of Austria-Hungary*, pp. 356–359.

one dreadnought apiece. In pre-dreadnought battleships, Germany and Austria-Hungary each lost one, while Britain lost eleven, France four, Italy two, and Russia one. Thus, the British navy lost not just more of the most modern capital ships (dreadnoughts and battle cruisers) than the navies of the Central Powers, but as many as all other belligerents combined, and more pre-dreadnoughts than all the rest. Fortunately for Britain and for the Allies in general, the British victory in the prewar naval arms race provided such a wide margin of material superiority that such losses could be sustained without seriously jeopardizing the war effort. By the time the peace conference convened in Paris, the dismemberment of Austria-Hungary had reduced by one the ranks of the naval powers; it remained to be seen what peace would mean for the future of sea power in Germany or Russia, or, indeed, the victorious Allied powers.

# CONCLUSION: PEACE AND NAVAL DISARMAMENT

"This treaty ends, absolutely ends, the race in competition in naval armament," Charles Evans Hughes assured the assembled audience, presenting the final draft of the Washington Naval Treaty. "At the same time it leaves the relative security of the great naval powers unimpaired."[1] It was the crowning achievement in the career of one of the most talented American leaders never to serve as president, and a moment filled with irony. Hughes, former governor of New York and Supreme Court justice, had been the Republican nominee for president in 1916 and only narrowly lost to Woodrow Wilson. Now, in February 1922, as secretary of state in the isolationist administration of President Warren G. Harding, he had the honor of presenting the product of negotiations he had conducted over the previous three months in the spirit of the fourth of Wilson's Fourteen Points, which had called for disarmament "to the lowest point consistent with domestic safety." Coming after the reduction of the German navy by the Treaty of Versailles and the virtual destruction of the former tsarist fleet in the Russian civil war, the Washington conference of 1921–22 completed the cycle of naval disarmament, reducing by negotiation the fleets of the five remaining naval powers: Britain, the United States, Japan, France, and Italy.

The course of the Great War at sea had confirmed the deterrent capacity of capital ships, and that they did not have to be risked in combat in order to have strategic relevance. As a consequence, just ten

---

[1] Quoted in Merlo J. Pusey, *Charles Evans Hughes*, 2 vols. (New York: Macmillan, 1952), vol. 2, p. 488.

were sunk during the war, of which four were lost in port by accident or sabotage, joined by two more, one Russian and one Austro-Hungarian, sunk after those navies had stopped fighting. Thus, at war's end, 116 of the 128 capital ships commissioned by the eight largest belligerent navies since HMS *Dreadnought* in December 1906 remained afloat, far more than anyone could justify maintaining in peacetime. But as the peace conference opened at Paris, no one would have predicted that, just three years later, at Washington, a treaty would be signed imposing tonnage quotas that, as initially applied, allowed the five leading navies combined to maintain just sixty-three capital ships. Tirpitz's prewar navy laws reflected the general assumption that capital ships would have a twenty-five year service life, yet the wholesale scrapping of vessels under the postwar regime of international limits, much more than wartime losses, reduced the average service life for dreadnoughts and battle cruisers commissioned between 1906 and 1918 to just over thirteen years. Never before had so many ships that had cost so much money seen so little action during so few years in service.

## The Paris Peace Conference: the naval dimension

Notwithstanding the central role of the prewar German naval buildup in the tensions leading up to the war, and of German behavior on the high seas in bringing the United States into the conflict, naval matters attracted very little attention at the Paris Peace Conference. Nevertheless, the Treaty of Versailles, signed on June 28, 1919, by the Allied leaders and representatives of the new German republic, remains an important postscript to the Great War at sea in that it determined the fate of the world's second largest fleet and, independent of the subsequent Washington naval arms control regime, placed unique limits on the future German navy.

In its final form, the treaty included 440 articles, of which just seventeen concerned the German navy.[2] These "naval clauses," Articles 181–197, limited postwar Germany to six pre-dreadnought battleships, six light cruisers, twelve destroyers, and twelve torpedo boats. No submarines were allowed and, owing to the general ban on German

---

[2] "Peace Treaty of Versailles, Articles 159–213: Military, Naval and Air Clauses," available at: net.lib.byu.edu/~rdh7/wwi/versa/versa4.html.

military aviation, no aircraft carriers. All warships already interned were declared surrendered, and those in excess of the new quotas not already turned over to the Allies were to be surrendered within two months of the ratification of the treaty, most notably the eight older dreadnoughts of the *Nassau* and *Helgoland* classes, including the decommissioned *Rheinland*, none of which had been required to go to Scapa Flow in November 1918. All ships that had functioned as auxiliary cruisers were to be disarmed and returned to civilian use, and all surface warships and submarines under construction in German shipyards were to be scrapped, with the additional provision that machinery or other components of dismantled vessels could not "be sold or disposed of to foreign countries." Germany also had to surrender all "submarine salvage vessels and docks for submarines."

These provisions left Germany not just with a much smaller navy, but one that was obsolete even by prewar standards, including an armored tonnage roughly equal to that of Spain and not much greater than that of Sweden. The primary units were battleships from the 13,200-ton *Braunschweig* and *Deutschland* classes, and cruisers from the 2,650-ton *Gazelle* and 3,300-ton *Bremen* classes. Reflecting how old and relatively harmless these ships were, the Allies eventually allowed Germany to spare another two of its pre-dreadnoughts, two light cruisers, four destroyers, and four torpedo boats as reserve, training, or depot vessels. The battleships were not to be replaced until twenty-five years after their launching dates (1927 at the earliest), with shorter limits of twenty years for the cruisers and fifteen years for the destroyers and torpedo boats. The treaty limited newly constructed armored warships to 10,000 tons with 11-inch (28-cm) guns, cruisers to 6,000 tons, destroyers to 800 tons, and torpedo boats to 200 tons. The treaty also limited the manpower of the navy to an all-volunteer, long-service force of 15,000, including 1,500 officers. Reserves were not permitted, and merchant mariners were not allowed to receive any naval training. Ashore, naval fortifications on Helgoland and some of Germany's Baltic islands were to be demolished and no new works built. The last of the naval clauses, Article 197, temporarily restricted "the German high-power wireless telegraphy stations at Nauen, Hanover and Berlin" from making transmissions for the first three months after the treaty took effect, without specific permission from the Allies. It added the provision that "during the same period, Germany shall not build any more high-power wireless telegraphy stations in her own

Figure 11.1 Vice Admiral Ludwig von Reuter

territory or that of Austria, Hungary, Bulgaria or Turkey." The article's inclusion in the naval section recognized the centrality of wireless technology to the naval dimension of the Great War. These stipulations were made apparently because the Allies were concerned that wireless might be used to coordinate some sort of defiance or circumvention of the treaty.

## Defiance at Scapa Flow

Defiance indeed occurred, but wireless played no role in coordinating it. For seven months after their internment, the best ships of the High Sea Fleet remained isolated at Scapa Flow while the Allied powers deliberated the fate of Germany. During the first months of 1919, the crews were further reduced by periodic repatriations of sailors, the last of which, on June 18, left the fleet with a total of less than 2,000 men, roughly one-tenth the number needed to operate the ships at full strength. While there were no British guards posted aboard the ships, the Germans nonetheless were prisoners aboard the interned vessels, not allowed to go ashore and, aside from Reuter and his immediate staff, not allowed to visit from ship to ship. As a legacy of the revolutionary upheavals at Kiel and Wilhelmshaven, the ships had left Germany under the red flag, hoisting their battle flags while at sea.[3] Most had at least the remnants of sailors' committees aboard, and the degree of authority exercised by officers varied from one vessel to another. Overall, discipline was never very good, and almost no work was done to maintain or even clean the ships, which grew progressively dirtier as the months passed. The admiral fared no better than any other officer; the sailors' committee aboard the flagship *Friedrich der Grosse* made Reuter's life so miserable that in March 1919 he requested, and received, permission from the British to relocate his quarters to the light cruiser *Emden*. Meanwhile, officers and sailors alike suffered from hardships imposed by their captors. With their wireless sets confiscated, the Germans at Scapa Flow received very little news and only censored mail, and thus even Reuter remained largely ignorant of developments in the outside world, aside from what the local British commander, Vice Admiral Sir Sydney Fremantle, chose to share with him.[4]

Article 31 of the Armistice specified that "no destruction of ships or of materials [is] to be permitted before [their] evacuation, surrender, or restoration,"[5] yet even before the High Sea Fleet steamed into internment, the Naval High Command had discussed the possibility of scuttling the ships in the North Sea en route to Britain. Scheer and his staff decided at the time not to sink the fleet, fearing what the Allies would do in retaliation, yet by some accounts Reuter left for Britain with the understanding that, if or when the time came, the ships were to be destroyed rather than surrendered. But the Allies postponed this day of reckoning, because the Armistice, initially defined as a

---

[3] Friedrich Ruge, *Scapa Flow 1919: The End of the German Fleet*, trans. Derek Masters, ed. A. J. Watts (London: Ian Allan, 1973), pp. 50–51.

[4] *Ibid.*, pp. 61–82.

[5] "Allied Armistice Terms, November 11, 1918," text available at: www.firstworldwar.com/source/armisticeterms.htm.

one-month cease-fire, had to be extended repeatedly to accommodate the protracted negotiations at Paris. As early as January 1919 Reuter and his staff discussed scuttling the fleet. In May, he began laying plans to do so, after receiving news that the final peace terms were likely to require the surrender of all of the ships at Scapa Flow. Finally, acting on knowledge that the latest extension of the Armistice was due to expire on June 21, Reuter circulated orders for the individual ships to prepare to scuttle that day.[6] Fremantle neglected to inform him that the truce had been extended yet again to give the negotiators another seven days to put the finishing touches on the treaty; he even took his squadron out for exercises on the morning of the 21st, leaving only a handful of light vessels at Scapa Flow to guard the interned warships. Ironically, Fremantle, knowing that the German fleet would be surrendered under the treaty, had discussed with his superiors provisions for seizing the ships on the 21st to prevent Reuter from scuttling them, but owing to the further extension of the Armistice the British had made no plans to take action on that date.

At 11:20 on the morning of June 21, Reuter's *Emden* raised the signal to scuttle the fleet. Even with seacocks and watertight doors open, it took a while for the orders to have any noticeable effect, but by noon some of the dreadnoughts had begun to list, at which time Reuter had the ships raise their battle flags, last seen when Beatty ordered them hauled down seven months earlier, so that each could go under with its flag flying. At 12:20, upon receiving word that the scuttling was underway, Fremantle ordered his squadron back to Scapa Flow and, in the meantime, directed the vessels he had left behind to take measures to beach as many of the sinking ships as possible, but of the capital ships ultimately only the *Baden* was thus spared, and by the time Fremantle arrived on the scene at 14:30, nothing more could be done. Reuter's men abandoned their ships after raising their battle flags, but as they rowed ashore British guards fired on some of the lifeboats, killing nine men, including Captain Walter Schumann of the dreadnought *Markgraf*, and wounding another twenty-one.[7] When they finally returned to Germany in January 1920, the 1,860 survivors of the great scuttle were welcomed as heroes.

[6] Reuter, "Order to Scuttle," June 17, 1919, text in Ruge, *Scapa Flow 1919*, pp. 161–162.
[7] *Ibid.*, p. 163, includes a casualty list.

Once they recovered from the initial shock, the British were somewhat relieved that the High Sea Fleet had disposed of itself, for the ensuing negotiations over the distribution of the ships were bound to have been acrimonious. Admiral Wemyss went so far as to call the scuttling "a real blessing."[8] The French and Italians, who had coveted the German ships as reparations, afterward shifted their attention to the fate of the much smaller Austro-Hungarian navy. The surviving dreadnoughts, pre-dreadnoughts, armored cruisers, and older lighter vessels of the defunct Dual Monarchy all were eventually distributed among the victors and either scrapped or sunk in some form of target practice, but Italy commissioned two of the newer light cruisers and seven destroyers, while France commissioned one light cruiser, one destroyer, and the submarine *U 14* (ex-*Curie*), which reentered French service under its original name. Among the minor Allies, Yugoslavia was left to patrol its long Adriatic coast with just a dozen torpedo boats, while Greece received one Austro-Hungarian destroyer and split the remaining unclaimed torpedo boats with Romania and Portugal. The landlocked successor states of Austria and Hungary were limited to patrol boats on the Danube, a harsh reality that did not stop Admiral Horthy, Hungary's interwar leader, from taking considerable pride in his small riverine navy.[9] Meanwhile, from among the smaller vessels of the High Sea Fleet that were neither scuttled, scrapped, nor retained by the postwar German navy, France ultimately commissioned four light cruisers, nine destroyers, and ten submarines; Italy, three light cruisers and three destroyers; Belgium, fourteen torpedo boats; and Poland, six torpedo boats.[10]

## The Washington Naval Conference and the postwar naval balance

Wilson considered the signing of the Treaty of Versailles to be the high point of his public life, yet by June 1919 the seeds of his ultimate failure had already been sown. In midterm elections to Congress held in November 1918, just days before the Armistice, the American public

---

[8] Quoted in Stephen Roskill, *Naval Policy Between the Wars: The Period of Anglo-American Antagonism, 1919–1929* (London: Collins, 1968), p. 94.
[9] Sondhaus, *The Naval Policy of Austria-Hungary*, pp. 359–360.
[10] *Conway's All the World's Fighting Ships, 1922–1946* (London: Conway Maritime Press, 1985), pp. 257–258, 286–287, 348, 385.

returned a Republican majority whose leaders subsequently refused to ratify the treaty because they opposed the participation of the United States in the League of Nations, the fourteenth and, in Wilson's view, most important point in his vision for the postwar peace. In September 1919, during a speaking tour to build public support for the treaty, the president suffered a debilitating stroke, then spent most of the rest of his term in office in his bedroom at the White House. In the elections of November 1920, the Republican isolationist Harding won the presidency, and Republicans secured an overwhelming majority in Congress; later the same month, the League of Nations opened in Geneva without the United States participating. As far as the American government was concerned, the Versailles Treaty and the League became a dead letter. In July 1921, a joint resolution of Congress formally declared the state of war with Germany to have ended. But there was also the matter of disposing of Wilson's Naval Act of 1916, designed to give the United States a navy "second to none," with a battle fleet of thirty-five capital ships, including a dozen topping 40,000 tons displacement. In Wilson's last year in office, the Republican-dominated Congress had questioned whether the program served any purpose other than to incite a new naval arms race with Britain and Japan. The legislators slashed funding for the program, and upon taking office the Harding administration was keen to find a face-saving way to kill it.

It fell to Hughes, in his role as Harding's secretary of state, to plot a course out of the dilemma. Adding to the sense of urgency, in March 1921, shortly after Harding's inauguration, Lloyd George reaffirmed Britain's intention to maintain a navy at least as large as anyone else's, and also proposed the renewal of the Anglo-Japanese treaty of 1902, which the Americans had assumed would be allowed to lapse after the war. In this atmosphere Hughes seized upon the notion of offering up the American fleet plan as part of a general treaty of naval arms limits, and in August 1921 the United States issued invitations to a conference in Washington to discuss the matter. France and Italy promptly accepted, and Japan, though skeptical, agreed to participate out of fear of being left empty-handed in case the Anglo-Japanese alliance was not renewed. After first threatening not to attend, Britain ultimately sent a high-profile delegation including Arthur Balfour, the former prime minister and former First Lord of the Admiralty, along with Admiral Beatty, the postwar First Sea Lord (1919–27). Japan's delegation was led by Admiral Tomosaburo Kato, a former fleet commander who had served as navy minister since 1915, and included Vice Admiral Kanji Kato, head of the Naval Staff College. Premier Aristide Briand led the French delegation, while the Italian delegates included journalist and politician Luigi Albertini, future author of one of the most detailed and influential accounts of the outbreak of the war in 1914.

By the time the conference opened on November 12, 1921, economic realities had already forced Britain, France, and Italy into unilateral decisions to decommission and scrap large numbers of warships. Of the forty-five British dreadnoughts and battle cruisers in commission at the Armistice, three were slated for conversion to aircraft carriers, one (*Canada*, renamed *Almirante Latorre*) was delivered, albeit belatedly, to Chile in 1920, and another seventeen were stricken or sold for scrap, and broken up starting in 1921. The latter included HMS *Dreadnought* itself, sold in May 1921, obsolete after a service life of just fourteen and a half years. The thirty British pre-dreadnoughts still on hand at the end of the war were all disarmed, decommissioned, or scrapped between 1919 and 1922. France kept its seven dreadnoughts, but disarmed or decommissioned twelve of its sixteen remaining pre-dreadnoughts, scrapping most of them between 1920 and 1922. Italy likewise kept its five surviving dreadnoughts, but disarmed or decommissioned seven of its eleven remaining pre-dreadnoughts, which were scrapped between 1920 and 1923.

Because the destruction of the German fleet had left the British with no serious rivals in Europe, their delegation came to the conference seeking only to keep their navy equal to or larger than the American navy, and were heartened when Hughes, in a dynamic opening speech, called for all capital ships then under construction to be scrapped and none laid down for a period of ten years, and for the United States, Britain, and Japan to fix their capital ship tonnage at a ratio of 5:5:3. This bold proposal offered up the capital ships authorized in Wilson's Naval Act of 1916, of which fifteen were under construction but none yet completed, to which Hughes added the US Navy's two oldest dreadnoughts and thirteen newest pre-dreadnoughts, in all thirty battleships totaling nearly 850,000 tons, leaving the United States with roughly 500,000 tons in capital ships. Hughes proceeded to outline similar sacrifices the United States would expect, in return, from Britain and Japan, to get them down to their capital ship quotas of 500,000 tons and 300,000 tons, respectively. Entering the conference, the British wanted a 3:3:2 ratio of capital ships for the three leading naval powers and thus readily accepted 5:5:3; they also did not object to the tonnage quota because the sacrifice Hughes demanded of them, nearly 600,000 tons, included several ships the Admiralty was already scrapping or had decided to scrap.[11] Nevertheless, the magnitude of the proposal prompted the *Manchester Guardian* to observe that in a single speech, Hughes had sunk more British battleships than "all the admirals of the world had destroyed in a cycle of centuries."[12]

The Japanese, in contrast, had great difficulty with the American terms, which would require Japan to give up its long-term strategic goals of having a navy 70 percent as large as that of the United States, including an "eight-eight" fleet of battleships and battle cruisers. Having devised those goals himself in the prewar years, Tomosaburo Kato came to the conference prepared to argue for nothing less than a 10:10:7 standard, but that ratio, combined with a Japanese tonnage quota high enough to accommodate sixteen capital ships, would have fixed the capital ship quota for the United States and Britain at roughly 800,000 tons apiece, far more than they wanted or needed. Though taken aback at Hughes' opening speech, the elder Kato soon concluded that Japan had no realistic alternative but to accept the American proposal. His capitulation outraged Kanji Kato, who wanted absolute parity with Britain and the United States as a matter of principle, and considered 10:10:7 a generous compromise. Japan ultimately agreed to 5:5:3 in exchange for a ban on the United States or Britain building or upgrading any Pacific fortifications west of a line stretching from Alaska's Aleutian Islands to Hawaii to Panama.[13] But the Japanese also had to accept two other agreements negotiated during the Washington conference, both largely driven by everyone else's suspicion of Japan: the Four-Power Treaty, in which the United States and France joined Britain and Japan in pledging to maintain the status quo in the Pacific,

---

[11] Erik Goldstein, "The Evolution of British Diplomatic Strategy for the Washington Conference," in Erik Goldstein and John Maurer (eds.), *The Washington Conference, 1921–22: Naval Rivalry, East Asian Stability, and the Road to Pearl Harbor* (London: Frank Cass, 1994), pp. 14, 24; Thomas H. Buckley, "The Icarus Factor: The American Pursuit of Myth in Naval Arms Control, 1921–36," in Goldstein and Maurer (eds.), *The Washington Conference, 1921–22*, pp. 126, 130–131.

[12] Quoted in Pusey, *Charles Evans Hughes*, vol. 2, p. 471.

[13] Sadao Asada, "From Washington to London: The Imperial Japanese Navy and the Politics of Naval Limitation, 1921–30," in Erik Goldstein and John Maurer (eds.), *The Washington Conference, 1921–22: Naval Rivalry, East Asian Stability, and the Road to Pearl Harbor* (London: Frank Cass, 1994), pp. 152–153.

in exchange for the latter two allowing the Anglo-Japanese alliance to lapse, and the Nine-Power Treaty, including Italy along with China, Portugal, the Netherlands, and Belgium, affirming the sovereignty, independence, and territorial integrity of China.

France and Italy were not mentioned in Hughes' opening speech, and throughout the conference never exercised as much influence as the three leading naval powers. Their negotiating positions were simple enough: the French navy wanted to maintain its advantage over the Italian, while the Italian navy sought to gain on the French. Briand did not hesitate to disagree with Hughes even though France owed the United States $4 billion, exasperating the American statesman, who could not help but note that Balfour, whose country owed the United States much less, was far more circumspect even though the stakes for his country were far higher. Because the German example of unrestricted submarine warfare had reenergized a faction within their navy that promoted commerce raiding in the tradition of the *Jeune École*, the French also wanted no limits on units smaller than capital ships, to enable them to build a postwar fleet centered on cruisers, destroyers, and submarines. Italy entered the conference dreaming of Franco-Italian naval parity, but hoping for a quota 90 percent of France's strength and willing to accept 80 percent. Whereas France wanted Franco-Italian limits on numbers or tonnage of warships placed higher, to force Italy to build more in order to achieve parity, Italy wanted Franco-Italian limits to be placed as low as possible, so that it could have parity or near-parity without further short-term investment in naval construction. After considerable posturing, the French accepted parity with Italy, at the relatively low tonnage figure the Italians wanted on the condition that the ratios did not apply to cruisers, destroyers, or submarines. Their insistence that submarine construction should remain unregulated clashed with the British position that the outlawing of submarines should at least be discussed, but once the French got their way on submarines, the British joined them in insisting on no limits for cruisers, which Britain felt it needed more of, to defend its global interests, and destroyers, which everyone needed for antisubmarine warfare.[14]

---

[14] See Joel Blatt, "France and the Washington Conference," in Erik Goldstein and John Maurer (eds.), *The Washington Conference, 1921–22: Naval Rivalry, East Asian Stability, and the Road to Pearl Harbor* (London: Frank Cass, 1994),

The Washington Naval Treaty, signed on February 6, 1922, included capital ship tonnage quotas of 525,000 tons for Britain and the United States, 315,000 tons for Japan, and 175,000 tons for France and Italy. Based on the limit of 35,000 tons per new capital ship applying to replacement ships begun in 1931 and after, once the ten-year "naval holiday" expired, the quotas would have led to a naval balance by 1942 in which Britain and the United States each had fifteen capital ships (down from twenty-two and eighteen, respectively, in 1922), Japan nine (down from ten), and France and Italy five apiece, although the French and Italians specifically reserved the right to spend their 175,000 tons as they saw fit, on greater numbers of smaller battleships or battle cruisers. The treaty limited the primary armament of new capital ships to 16-inch (40.6-cm) guns. Special provisions in the treaty allowed Britain to lay down two battleships before 1931, the 33,300-ton *Nelson* and *Rodney* (built 1922–27), because its existing capital ships, on average, were several years older than their American or Japanese counterparts. France and Italy likewise each received permission to lay down a new battleship as early as 1927 for the same reason. A separate provision for aircraft carriers included tonnage limits of 135,000 tons for the United States and Britain, 81,000 tons for Japan, and 60,000 tons for France and Italy, with no restrictions on when new units could be built. Carriers were limited to 27,000 tons, but to facilitate the conversion of unfinished capital ship hulls to carriers, some 33,000-ton carriers were allowed (two apiece for the three leading navies, one apiece for France and Italy). As with existing capital ships, all hulls being converted to carriers were allowed an additional 3,000 tons for upgraded armor. The treaty defined a capital ship as "a vessel of war, not an aircraft carrier, whose displacement exceeds 10,000 tons... which carries a gun with a caliber exceeding 8 inches (203 mm)," thus leaving unregulated all warships of 10,000 tons or less, armed with 8-inch or lighter guns.[15]

At the Washington Conference, the United States abandoned the quest for a position of naval preeminence it could easily have achieved but had no desire, at this point in history, to assert. In this

pp. 192–219; Brian R. Sullivan, "Italian Naval Power and the Washington Disarmament Conference of 1921–22," in Goldstein and Maurer (eds.), *The Washington Conference, 1921–22*, pp. 220–248.

[15] See text of Washington Naval Treaty, with capital ship tables for each of the five navies, in Ichihashi Yamato, *The Washington Conference and After: A Historical Survey* (Palo Alto, CA: Stanford University Press, 1928), pp. 365–385.

respect the universal acclaim with which the American public and political leadership greeted the Washington Naval Treaty was consistent with the majority of Americans rejecting the Versailles Treaty, the League of Nations, and, in general, the mantle of world's leading power (military and naval as well as economic) that was there for the taking after the First World War. In the aftermath of the Second World War a far more assertive United States finally embraced Wilsonian internationalism, accepting its commitments and costs, but from the perspective of 1922 such a sacrifice seemed unnecessary. In presenting the final draft of the naval treaty to the conference, Hughes echoed the sentiments of virtually all his countrymen in asserting that "no more extraordinary or significant treaty has ever been made."[16]

Even though the treaty cost Britain its traditional status of leading naval power, a position it had fought so hard and spent so much to maintain as recently as the prewar naval race with Germany, the British public and political leadership greeted the agreement with an enthusiasm surpassed only by that of the Americans. Most recognized that Britain could no longer afford to maintain its traditional hegemony, and in any event the concession of parity had been made to a country it could not envisage fighting in the future. A clear majority shared the sentiments expressed by Lloyd George in the House of Commons when he called the treaty "one of the greatest achievements for peace that has ever been registered in the history of the world."[17] Briand fared much worse in presenting the treaty to the French public; indeed, his acceptance of capital ship parity with Italy toppled his government and delayed France's ratification of the treaty for over a year, until July 1923. Right-wing nationalists were especially hard on the treaty. Charles Maurras, leader of Action Française, went as far as to call it "Trafalgar II."[18] Meanwhile, for Italy, capital ship parity with France represented an exception to the general lack of respect it received from its fellow victors as a consequence of its poor showing during the war. Ultimately, neither the French nor the Italians took full advantage of their quotas under the treaty during the years in which it remained in effect. Neither navy exercised its right to lay down a new battleship

---

[16] Quoted in Pusey, *Charles Evans Hughes*, vol. 2, p. 488.
[17] Quoted in *ibid.*, vol. 2, p. 508.
[18] Blatt, "France and the Washington Conference," p. 206.

later in the 1920s, even though by then Italy had decommissioned one of its original dreadnoughts and France had lost one to shipwreck. The French built one aircraft carrier, but the Italians declined to match it, as the Fascist government of Benito Mussolini, coming to power eight months after the treaty was signed, focused its rearmament efforts on the Italian air force.

  The response to the treaty in Japan was far more negative than in France, and Japanese behavior afterward did not bode well for future peace in the Pacific. Whereas Briand's role in negotiating the treaty cost him the premiership in France (albeit only temporarily), in Japan the well-connected Tomosaburo Kato became prime minister as a reward for his statesmanship, but also on the reasoning that only by making a senior admiral the head of government would the government be able to compel the Japanese navy to comply with the treaty. After the elder Kato died of cancer in August 1923, the "treaty faction" within the navy, which considered it prudent for Japan to accept the new limits, lacked a strong leader, and as the years passed few Japanese politicians and fewer admirals remained faithful to the letter of the treaty, much less to its spirit. Reflecting the sensibilities of Kanji Kato and the "fleet faction," the Japanese were aggressive in doing whatever the rules allowed, and sometimes more, in contrast to the British and Americans, who, like the French and Italians, ultimately let their navies slip below the strength permitted under the limits. The Great Depression and subsequent London Naval Conference in 1930 resulted in the further extension of naval arms limits, but Kanji Kato outlived Tomosaburo Kato by sixteen years, long enough to lead the "fleet faction" within the Japanese naval officer corps into a political alliance with Japanese army leaders in charting the course to the Second World War, and to a conflict in the Pacific that would far surpass the Great War at sea in its size and scope of operations. By then, Britain's desire to avoid another war at all costs resulted in the Anglo-German Naval Treaty of 1935, in which the British unilaterally brought Nazi Germany into the interwar naval armaments regime by granting the Germans the right to a navy 35 percent the size of the British, or roughly equal to the existing treaty limits for France and Italy. The final nail in the coffin of the postwar regime of naval arms control came the following year, when Japan repudiated all the restrictions, making dead letters of the Washington and London treaties.

"As far as I am concerned, war with America starts now."[19] These alarming words were spoken by Kanji Kato not when Japan repudiated the naval arms limits in 1936, but fourteen years earlier, when his country agreed to sign the Washington Naval Treaty. Inasmuch as the dramatic reductions negotiated at Washington in 1921–22 reflected a goal articulated in Wilson's Fourteen Points and embraced by most of the victors, they were, for the world's navies, a direct extension of the peace process. Countless observers, at the time and ever since, have argued that the Great War accomplished little other than to sow the seeds of a much more destructive conflict a generation later. Kato died two years before his navy's surprise attack on Pearl Harbor brought Japan the war he had prophesied in 1922, yet he was among the first to see in the outcome of the First World War the inevitability of the Second.

## The Great War and naval warfare

A generation later, after another, greater naval war had been fought, critics of the Washington Conference pointed to its emphasis on regulating capital ships – dreadnoughts and battle cruisers – as being less than forward-looking, and yet, from the perspective of the time, the focus could not have been elsewhere. These ships had withstood the challenge of the submarine, and torpedo bulges would help to protect their hulls from more lethal torpedoes in the postwar era. In the interwar period the proliferation of synthetic systems of fire control, gradually replacing the analytic systems that had yielded such poor results in 1914–18, would make dreadnoughts and battle cruisers even more formidable against rivals on the surface. But where the submarine had failed to spark a revolution in naval warfare during the First World War, air power would succeed in doing so during the Second, demonstrating that surface superiority mattered little against an enemy that controlled the skies over the sea in question, either with land-based or carrier-based aircraft. Despite being fitted or retrofitted with scores of anti-aircraft guns, the capital ship would not measure up to the challenge from the air in the conflict of 1939–45.

---

[19] Quoted in Asada, "From Washington to London," p. 154.

From the perspective of the early 1920s, however, the main lesson of the conflict at sea was that a fleet-in-being of capital ships, even when at anchor most of the time, both deterred and determined the enemy's actions. Not only had the concentration of German capital ships in the High Sea Fleet compelled Britain to concentrate its forces in the Grand Fleet, but Austria-Hungary's four dreadnoughts in the Adriatic proved to be the determining factor in Allied actions well into the central Mediterranean. In the Baltic, the presence of Russia's four dreadnoughts dictated the size and scope of German movements, even though they very rarely left port. Most dramatically of all, the lone German battle cruiser *Goeben*, as the Turkish *Yavuz Sultan Selim*, had a disproportionate effect on Allied naval operations in the Black Sea and eastern Mediterranean, especially in the first half of the war but even into 1918. Within the context of the Great War, the deterrent capacity of capital ships meant that they did not have to be risked in combat in order to have strategic relevance.

The submarine earned pride of place as the emerging naval weapon of 1914–18, yet while unrestricted submarine warfare had made life miserable for the Allies, German U-boats did not come close to inflicting the sort of misery on the British home front that the British surface-ship blockade caused within Germany. Some antisubmarine measures pioneered in the First World War would be improved upon in the Second, in particular the use of depth charges, aircraft patrols, and of course the convoy system, while others, most notably the extensive antisubmarine barrages, were not, but one unmistakable lesson of the Great War had been that surface superiority trumped undersea superiority, just as decisively as air superiority, in the next world war, would trump surface superiority. The surface fleet advantage of the Allies in general, and of the British in particular, had been the key to the victory at sea. Even though the British navy lost as many dreadnoughts and battle cruisers as all other belligerents combined and, for pre-dreadnought battleships, more than the total lost by all other navies, Britain's victory in the prewar naval arms race provided such a wide margin of material superiority that such losses could be sustained without seriously jeopardizing the Allied war effort. The strategy of distant blockade, so frustrating for the blockaders, had worked not only in the North Sea against Germany, but in the Adriatic against Austria-Hungary as well, and in both cases it had been enforced with a preponderance of capital ships. With good reason, these ships emerged from the war with their strategic primacy intact, and their place in the postwar negotiation of arms limits reflected this reality.

In the postwar years, the centrality of the blockade in the Allied naval victory became obscured by international political considerations. The Allied (and especially British) narrative of the war at sea understandably emphasized the righteousness of the cause, building upon the rejection, by the general public in the Allied countries, of Germany's wartime attempt to equate the immorality of unrestricted submarine warfare with the immorality of the blockade. Documentation of, and reflection upon, the importance of the blockade, and especially the prewar planning behind it, would have undermined that narrative, especially since the U-boat campaign had emerged from the circumstances of the winter of 1914/15, when the last of Germany's cruisers were being swept from the seas, and was far less premeditated. Thus, through a variety of means, British authorities down to the 1960s suppressed or censored published materials related to the blockade, and strongly discouraged frank or detailed discussion of it in the memoirs of those most involved in its planning and execution.[20]

When Admiral Beatty, in his honorary capacity as Lord Rector of the University of Edinburgh, gave a speech at that institution in 1920 defending navies and their role in the world, he succumbed to just this sort of self-censorship. He couched his references to the strategy of blockade in the vaguest of terms, avoiding use of the word "blockade." Starting with the premise that "personal inconvenience is ... the factor that decides whether a struggle shall continue," he acknowledged that navies may cause such "inconvenience" to an enemy state "by cutting off those supplies from overseas upon which the nation is dependent," including "its food, its clothing, its manufacture, its commerce, and its munitions of war." Rather than associate this strategy directly with the recent Allied victory, he spent the rest of his speech detailing, from the Peloponnesian War to the Great War, the importance of a strong fleet in empowering a state to *avoid* being blockaded. Keeping faith with the concepts that had dominated the prewar discourse on sea power, Beatty invoked "the work of the American, Admiral Mahan," noting that "nowhere was its effect greater than in Germany." Indeed, in his emphasis on a strong fleet as the antidote to blockade, he used essentially the same Mahanian arguments that Tirpitz had employed to

---

[20] Lambert, *Planning Armageddon*, pp. 10–14.

justify German naval expansion before the war, only with a distinctive British twist. Emphasizing the role of the navy in the establishment and growth of the British Empire, the general tone followed his quoting of Sir Walter Raleigh: "Whosoever commands the sea commands the trade; whosoever commands the trade commands the riches of the world and, consequently, the world itself." But in a speech full of examples of navies entangled in the global struggle for wealth and power, Beatty concluded by drawing a thoughtful (though clearly partisan) distinction between the power of the state as reflected in navies compared with armies: "Sea power is ... essentially a power for peace; unaggressive itself, it is a shield against aggression. If wisely employed, it will not excite the odium of others, nor the suspicious jealousy that is the lot of those who pin their faith in armies. Hence there is no greater fallacy than to speak of 'navalism' as the sea counterpart of 'militarism.'"[21]

There was nothing unique about Beatty's conclusion, at least from the naval perspective; indeed, nearly a century later, the same logic underpinned a US Navy advertising campaign touting the American fleet as "a global force for good." Thus, there was no small irony in the postwar quest for international arms reduction focusing on the leading fleets, despite the contention that they did not endanger the peace as much as the most powerful standing armies or the emerging air forces. Because land and air forces (except for those of Germany) remained unregulated, the relative weight of navies in the universe of armed might available to a state declined. A bitter Anglo-American disagreement about whether and how to extend the Washington limits to cruisers, resolved in the London Naval Treaty of 1930 in a compromise that pleased no one, reflected second thoughts on the part of both Britain and the United States about their ability, post-Washington, to exploit the diplomatic value of naval power worldwide in anything approaching the traditional sense. From the days of wooden sailing ships down to the Great War, most international crises had involved some level of "gunboat diplomacy," ranging in weight from a single small warship to a squadron or entire fleet, depending upon the stakes involved. But the world in which every Great Power, even a near-landlocked Austria-Hungary, possessed a fleet respectable enough to play this game had

---

[21] "Lord Rector's Address at Edinburgh University, 28th October, 1920," text in W. S. Chalmers, *The Life and Letters of David, Earl Beatty* (London: Hodder & Stoughton, 1951), pp. 454–465.

now passed. The postwar regime of naval limits left just three true Great Power navies – the British, American, and Japanese – which the outcome of the next world war would reduce to just one, the American, eventually challenged worldwide during the Cold War by the Soviet fleet before again, by the dawn of the twenty-first century, being clearly in a class by itself. Seen in this light, the Great War at sea and its immediate aftermath represents a watershed in the history of navies in general, a giant step in the direction of a world in which Beatty's "power for peace" would rest not in the fleets maintained by most or all great powers, but in a single "global force for good," a formidable weapon in the arsenal of a lone superpower.

# BIBLIOGRAPHY

## Archival sources

Austria: Österreichisches Staatsarchiv, Haus- Hof- und Staatsarchiv, AR, F 44 – Marinewesen.
United Kingdom: National Archives, Public Record Office, Cabinet Papers (CAB).

## Memoirs and published primary sources

Ayres, Leonard P. *War with Germany: A Statistical Summary*. Washington, DC: US Government Printing Office, 1919.
Bacon, Reginald. *The Dover Patrol, 1915–1917*, 2 vols. New York: George H. Doran, 1919.
Bayly, Lewis. *Pull Together! The Memoirs of Admiral Sir Lewis Bayly*. London: George G. Harrap, 1939.
Beresford, Charles William de la Poer. *The Memoirs of Admiral Lord Charles Beresford*, 2 vols. Boston, MA: Little, Brown, 1914.
Brauer, Otto. *Die Kreuzerfahrten des "Prinz Eitel-Friedrich."* Berlin: August Scherl, 1918.
Campbell, Gordon. *My Mystery Ships*. Garden City, NY: Doubleday, Doran 1929.
Chatfield, Ernle. *The Navy and Defence: The Autobiography of Admiral of the Fleet Lord Chatfield*, 2 vols. London: Heinemann, 1942–47.
Churchill, Winston S. *The World Crisis*, 5 vols. New York: Charles Scribner's, 1923.
Corbett, Julian Stafford. *Some Principles of Naval Strategy*. London: Longmans, Green, 1911.

Crompton, Iwan. *Englands Verbrechen an U 41: Der zweite "Baralong"-Fall im Weltkrieg*, ed. Werner von Langsdorff. Gütersloh: C. Bertelsmann, 1941.
Daniels, Josephus. *Our Navy at War*. New York: George H. Dolan, 1922.
Fawcett, H. W. and G. W. W. Hooper (eds.). *The Fighting at Jutland: The Personal Experiences of Sixty Officers and Men of the British Fleet*. Annapolis, MD: Naval Institute Press, [1921] 2001.
Gale, Oliver Marble (ed./comp.). *Americanism: Woodrow Wilson's Speeches on the War*. Chicago, IL: The Baldwin Syndicate, 1918.
Hersing, Otto. *U 21 rettet die Dardanellen*. Leipzig: Amalthea-Verlag, 1932.
Horthy de Nagybánya, Miklós. *Memoirs*. London: Hutchinson, 1956.
Jellicoe, John Rushworth. *The Grand Fleet, 1914–1916: Its Creation, Development and Work*. New York: George H. Doran, 1919.
Keyes, Roger. *The Fight for Gallipoli: From the Naval Memoirs of Admiral of the Fleet Sir Roger Keyes*. London: Eyre & Spottiswoode, 1941.
Kirchhoff, Hermann (ed.). *Maximilian Graf von Spee, Der Sieger von Coronel: Das Lebensbild und die Erinnerungen eines deutschen Seemans*. Berlin: Marinedank-Verlag, 1915.
Kolchak, Aleksandr Vasiliyevich et al. *The Testimony of Kolchak and Other Siberian Materials*. Palo Alto, CA: Stanford University Press, 1935.
Lloyd George, David. *War Memoirs*, 6 vols. Boston, MA: Little, Brown, 1933–37.
Ludendorff, Erich. *Ludendorff's Own Story*, 2 vols. New York: Harper, 1919.
Niemöller, Martin. *From U-Boat to Pulpit*, trans. D. Hastie Smith. Chicago, IL: Willett, Clark, 1937.
Pochhammer, Hans. *Before Jutland: Admiral von Spee's Last Voyage*, trans. H. J. Stenning. London: Jarrolds, 1931.
 *Graf Spees letzter Fahrt: Erinnerungen an das Kreuzergeschwader*. Berlin: Täglichen Rundschau, 1918.
Ruge, Friedrich. *Scapa Flow 1919: The End of the German Fleet*, trans. Derek Masters, ed. A. J. Watts. London: Ian Allan, 1973.
Scheer, Reinhard. *Germany's High Sea Fleet in the World War*. London: Cassell, 1920.
Schneider, Heinrich. *Die letzte Fahrt des kleinen Kreuzers "Dresden."* Leipzig: K. F. Koehler, 1926.
Sims, William Snowden. *The Victory at Sea*, with Burton J. Hendrick. Garden City, NY: Doubleday, Page, 1920.
Terry, Charles Sanford. *Ostend and Zeebrugge, April 23–May 19, 1918: The Dispatches of Vice-Admiral Sir Roger Keyes and Other Narratives of the Operations*. London: Oxford University Press, 1919.
Tirpitz, Alfred von. *Erinnerungen*. Leipzig: Verlag von K. F. Koehler, 1920.
 *My Memoirs*, 2 vols. New York: Dodd, Mead, 1919.

Tschischwitz, Erich von. *Armee und Marine bei der Eroberung der Baltischen Inseln im Oktober 1917*, Berlin: Eisenschmidt, 1931, translated by Henry Hossfeld as *The Army and Navy during the Conquest of the Baltic Islands in October 1917*. Fort Leavenworth, KS: Command and General Staff School Press, 1933.

United States Congress, Senate, Committee on Commerce. *United States Shipping Board Emergency Fleet Corporation: Hearings Before the Committee on Commerce, United States Senate, Sixty-fifth Congress, Second [and Third] Session, on S.Res. 170*. Washington, DC: US Government Printing Office, 1918.

Valentiner, Max. *Der Schrecken der Meere: Meine U-Boot-Abenteuer*. Leipzig: Amalthea-Verlag, 1931.

Weddigen, Otto Eduard. *Otto Weddigen und seine Waffe: aus seinen Tagebüchern und nachgelassenen Papieren*. Berlin: Marinedank-verlag, 1915.

## Secondary sources

Abbatiello, John J. *Anti-Submarine Warfare in World War I: British Naval Aviation and the Defeat of the U-Boats*. London: Routledge, 2006.

Allen, Keith. "Food and the German Home Front: Evidence from Berlin," in Gail Braybon (ed.), *Evidence, History and the Great War: Historians and the Impact of 1914–18*. New York: Berghahn, 2003, pp. 172–197.

Asada, Sadao. "From Washington to London: The Imperial Japanese Navy and the Politics of Naval Limitation, 1921–30," in Goldstein and Maurer (eds.), *The Washington Conference, 1921–22*, pp. 147–191.

Baker, Duncan C. "Wireless Telegraphy during the Anglo-Boer War of 1899–1902," *Military History Journal*, 11(2) (December 1998).

Barrett, Michael B. *Operation Albion: The German Conquest of the Baltic Islands*. Bloomington, IN: Indiana University Press, 2008.

Beach, Edward L. *The United States Navy: 200 Years*. New York: Henry Holt, 1986.

Bengelsdorf, Lutz. *Der Seekrieg in der Ostsee 1914–1918*. Bremen: Hauschild, 2008.

Bennett, Geoffrey. *Coronel and the Falklands*. London: Batsford, 1962.

Berghahn, Volker R. *Der Tirpitz-Plan: Genesis und Verfall einer innenpolitischen Krisenstrategie unter Wilhelm II*. Düsseldorf: Droste, 1971.

Black, Nicholas. *The British Naval Staff in the First World War*. Woodbridge: Boydell Press, 2009.

Blatt, Joel. "France and the Washington Conference," in Goldstein and Maurer (eds.), *The Washington Conference, 1921–22*, pp. 192–219.

Boghardt, Thomas. *The Zimmermann Telegram: Intelligence, Diplomacy, and America's Entry into World War I*. Annapolis, MD: Naval Institute Press, 2012.

Brooks, John. "Dreadnought: Blunder or Stroke of Genius?" *War in History*, 14 (2007): 157–178.

*Dreadnought Gunnery and the Battle of Jutland: The Question of Fire Control*. London: Routledge, 2005.

Brown, D. K. *Warrior to Dreadnought: Warship Development, 1860–1905*. London: Chatham Publishing, 1997.

Buckley, Thomas H. "The Icarus Factor: The American Pursuit of Myth in Naval Arms Control, 1921–36," in Goldstein and Maurer (eds.), *The Washington Conference, 1921–22*, pp. 124–146.

Burns, Russell W. *Communications: An International History of the Formative Years*. London: Institution of Electrical Engineers, 2004.

Butler, Daniel Allen. *Distant Victory: The Battle of Jutland and the Allied Triumph in the First World War*. Westport, CT: Praeger Security International, 2006.

Campbell, N. J. M. *Jutland: An Analysis of the Fighting*. Annapolis, MD: Naval Institute Press, 1986.

Chalmers, W. S. *The Life and Letters of David, Earl Beatty*. London: Hodder & Stoughton, 1951.

Chatterton, E. Keble. *Q-Ships and their Story*. London: Sidgwick & Jackson, 1922.

Chickering, Roger. *Imperial Germany and the Great War, 1914–1918*. Cambridge University Press, 1998.

*Conway's All the World's Fighting Ships, 1906–1921*. London: Conway Maritime Press, 1985.

*Conway's All the World's Fighting Ships, 1922–1946*. London: Conway Maritime Press, 1985.

Cooper, John Milton, Jr. *Woodrow Wilson: A Biography*. New York: Alfred A. Knopf, 2009.

Corbett, Julian. *History of the Great War: Naval Operations*, 5 vols. London: Longmans, Green, 1920–31.

Davis, Lance E. and Stanley L. Engerman. *Naval Blockades in Peace and War: An Economic History since 1750*. Cambridge University Press, 2006.

Delany, Walter S. *Bayly's Navy*. Washington, DC: Naval Historical Foundation, 1980.

Doenecke, Justus D. *Nothing Less Than War: A New History of America's Entry into World War I*. Lexington, KT: University Press of Kentucky, 2011.

Epkenhans, Michael, Jörg Hillmann, and Frank Nägler. *Skagerrakschlacht: Vorgeschichte, Ereignis, Verarbeitung.* Munich: Oldenbourg, 2009.

Evans, David C. and Mark R. Peattie. *Kaigun: Strategy, Tactics, and Technology in the Imperial Japanese Navy, 1887–1941.* Annapolis, MD: Naval Institute Press, 1997.

Fairbanks, Charles H., Jr. "The Origins of the *Dreadnought* Revolution: A Historiographical Essay," *International History Review*, 13 (1991): 246–272.

Fleming, Peter. *The Fate of Admiral Kolchak.* New York: Harcourt, Brace & World, 1963.

Friedewald, Michael. "The Beginnings of Radio Communication in Germany, 1897–1918," *Journal of Radio Studies*, 7 (2000): 441–463.

Friedman, Norman. *British Carrier Aviation: The Evolution of the Ships and their Aircraft.* Annapolis, MD: Naval Institute Press, 1988.

*Naval Firepower: Battleship Guns and Gunnery in the Dreadnought Era.* Barnsley: Seaforth Publishing, 2008.

Goldstein, Erik. "The Evolution of British Diplomatic Strategy for the Washington Conference," in Goldstein and Maurer (eds.), *The Washington Conference, 1921–22*, pp. 4–34.

Goldstein, Erik and John Maurer (eds.). *The Washington Conference, 1921–22: Naval Rivalry, East Asian Stability, and the Road to Pearl Harbor.* London: Frank Cass, 1994.

Gordon, Andrew. *The Rules of the Game: Jutland and British Naval Command.* Annapolis, MD: Naval Institute Press, 1996.

Gottschall, Terrell D. *By Order of the Kaiser: Otto von Diederichs and the Rise of the Imperial German Navy, 1865–1902.* Annapolis, MD: Naval Institute Press, 2003.

Grant, Robert M. *U-boats Destroyed: The Effect of Anti-Submarine Warfare, 1914–1918.* London: Putnam, 1964.

Greger, René. *The Russian Fleet, 1914–1917*, trans. Jill Gearing. London: Ian Allan, 1972.

Gregory, Adrian. *The Last Great War: British Society and the First World War.* Cambridge University Press, 2008.

Grimes, Shawn T. *Strategy and War Planning in the British Navy, 1887–1918.* Woodbridge: Boydell Press, 2012.

Gromov, F. N. et al. *Tri Veka Rossiiskogo Flota*, 3 vols. St. Petersburg: Logos, 1996.

Gröner, Erich. *Die deutschen Kriegsschiffe, 1815–1945*, 8 vols. Coblenz: Bernard & Graefe, 1989.

Guttridge, Leonard F. *Mutiny: A History of Naval Insurrection.* Annapolis, MD: Naval Institute Press, 2006.

Halpern, Paul G. *A Naval History of World War I*. Annapolis, MD: Naval Institute Press, 1994.

*The Battle of the Otranto Straits: Controlling the Gateway to the Adriatic in World War I*. Bloomington, IN: Indiana University Press, 2004.

*The Mediterranean Naval Situation, 1908–1914*. Cambridge, MA: Harvard University Press, 1971.

*The Naval War in the Mediterranean*. Annapolis, MD: Naval Institute Press, 1987.

Hancock, H. E. *Wireless at Sea*. New York: Arno Press, [1950] 1974.

Hart, Peter. *Gallipoli*. Oxford University Press, 2011.

Headrick, Daniel R. *The Invisible Weapon: Telecommunications and International Politics, 1851–1945*. Oxford University Press, 1991.

Herwig, Holger H. *"Luxury" Fleet: The Imperial German Navy, 1888–1918*. London: Allen & Unwin, 1980 (paperback edn. Prometheus Books, 1987).

*The German Naval Officer Corps, 1890–1918: A Social and Political History*. Oxford: Clarendon Press, 1973.

Hill, Leonidas E. "Signal zur Konterrevolution? Der Plan zum letzten Vorstoß der deutschen Hochseeflotte am 30. Oktober 1918," *Vierteljahreshefte für Zeitgeschichte*, 36(1) (January 1988): 113–129.

Hobson, Rolf. *Imperialism at Sea: Naval Strategic Thought, the Ideology of Sea Power, and the Tirpitz Plan, 1875–1914*. Boston, MA: Brill, 2002.

Holborn, Hajo. *A History of Modern Germany, 1840–1945*. Princeton University Press, 1982.

Hong, Sungook. *Wireless: From Marconi's Black-Box to the Audion*. Cambridge, MA: MIT Press, 2001.

Horn, Daniel. *The German Naval Mutinies of World War I*. New Brunswick, NJ: Rutgers University Press, 1969.

Hughes, Thomas. "Learning to Fight: Bill Halsey and the Early American Destroyer Force," *Journal of Military History*, 77(1) (January 2013): 71–90.

Irving, John. *Coronel and the Falklands*. London: A. M. Philpot, 1927.

Jones, Jerry W. *U.S. Battleship Operations in World War I*. Annapolis, MD: Naval Institute Press, 1998.

Keegan, John. *Intelligence in War*. New York: Alfred A. Knopf, 2003.

Kelly, Patrick J. *Tirpitz and the Imperial German Navy*. Bloomington, IN: Indiana University Press, 2011.

Kemp, Paul. *U-boats Destroyed: German Submarine Losses in the Two World Wars*. Annapolis, MD: Naval Institute Press, 1997.

Kirby, D. G. "A Navy in Revolution: The Russian Baltic Fleet in 1917," in Peter Karstens (ed.), *Motivating Soldiers: Morale or Mutiny*, London: Taylor & Francis, 1998, pp. 199–212.

Kramer, Alan. "Combatants and Noncombatants: Atrocities, Massacres, and War Crimes," in John Horne (ed.), *A Companion to World War I*. Chichester: Wiley-Blackwell, 2010, pp. 188–201.

Kudlick, Walter. "Sealift for the AEF," available at: www.worldwar1.com/dbc/sealift.htm#a.

Lambert, Nicholas A. "Admiral Sir John Fisher and the Concept of Flotilla Defence, 1904–1909," *Journal of Military History*, 59 (1995): 639–660.

*Planning Armageddon: British Economic Warfare and the First World War*. Cambridge, MA: Harvard University Press, 2012.

*Sir John Fisher's Naval Revolution*. Columbia, SC: University of South Carolina Press, 1999.

Lambi, Ivo. *The Navy and German Power Politics, 1862–1914*. Boston, MA: Allen & Unwin, 1984.

Langensiepen, Bernd, Dirk Nottelmann, and Jochen Krüsmann. *Halbmond und Kaiseradler: Goeben und Breslau am Bosporus, 1914–1918*. Hamburg: Verlag E. S. Mittler, 1999.

Mäkelä, Matti E. *Souchon der Goebenadmiral greift in die Weltgeschichte ein*. Braunschweig: Friedrich Vieweg, 1936.

McKee, Fraser M. "An Explosive Story: The Rise and Fall of the Depth Charge," *Northern Mariner*, 3 (1993): 45–58.

McLaughlin, Stephen. "Russia: Rossiiskii imperatorskii flot," in Vincent P. O'Hara, W. David Dickson, and Richard Worth (eds.), *To Crown the Waves: The Great Navies of the First World War*. Annapolis, MD: Naval Institute Press, 2013, pp. 213–256.

Morison, Elting E. *Admiral Sims and the Modern American Navy*. Boston, MA: Houghton Mifflin, 1942.

Mücke, Hellmuth von. *The Emden–Ayesha Adventure: German Raiders in the South Seas and Beyond, 1914*. Annapolis, MD: Naval Institute Press, 2000.

Mueller, Michael. *Canaris: The Life and Death of Hitler's Spymaster*. London: Chatham, 2007.

Nekrasov, George M. *Expendable Glory: A Russian Battleship in the Baltic, 1915–1917*. Boulder, CO: East European Monographs, 2004.

Offer, Avner. *The First World War: An Agrarian Interpretation*. Oxford: Clarendon Press, 1989.

Osborne, Eric W. *Britain's Economic Blockade of Germany, 1914–1919*. London: Frank Cass, 2004.

O'Sullivan, Brian. "Away All Boats: A Study of the Evolution and Development of Amphibious Warfare in the Pacific War," MA thesis, University of Canterbury, New Zealand, 2008.

Paton, William A. *The Economic Position of the United Kingdom, 1912–1918*. Washington, DC: US Government Printing Office, 1919.

Peattie, Mark R. *Nan'yo: The Rise and Fall of the Japanese in Micronesia, 1885–1945*. Honolulu, HI: University of Hawaii Press, 1988.

Philbin, Tobias R., III. *Admiral von Hipper, The Inconvenient Hero*. Amsterdam: John Benjamins, 1982.

Plaschka, Richard Georg. *Cattaro – Prag: Revolte und Revolution*. Graz: Verlag Hermann Böhlaus Nachf., 1963.

Plaschka, Richard Georg, Horst Haselsteiner, and Arnold Suppan. *Innere Front: Militärassistenz, Widerstand und Umsturz in der Donaumonarchie 1918*, 2 vols. Munich: Oldenbourg, 1974.

Preston, Diana. *Lusitania: An Epic Tragedy*. New York: Walker Publishing, 2002.

Prior, Robin. *Gallipoli: The End of the Myth*. New Haven, CT: Yale University Press, 2009.

Pusey, Merlo J. *Charles Evans Hughes*, 2 vols. New York: Macmillan, 1952.

Rabinowitch, Alexander. *The Bolsheviks Come to Power: The Revolution of 1917 in Petrograd*. New York: W. W. Norton, 1978.

  "The Shchastny File: Trotsky and the Case of the Hero of the Baltic Fleet," *Russian Review*, 58 (1999): 615–634.

Roskill, Stephen. *Naval Policy Between the Wars: The Period of Anglo-American Antagonism, 1919–1929*. London: Collins, 1968.

Rudenno, Victor. *Gallipoli: Attack from the Sea*. New Haven, CT: Yale University Press, 2008.

Saxon, Timothy D. "Anglo-Japanese Naval Cooperation, 1914–1918," *Naval War College Review*, 53(1) (Winter 2000): 62–92.

Schmalenbach, Paul. *Die Geschichte der deutschen Schiffsartillerie*, 2nd edn. Herford: Koehlers Verlagsgesellschaft, 1968.

Seligmann, Matthew S. "New Weapons for New Targets: Sir John Fisher, the Threat from Germany, and the Building of HMS *Dreadnought* and HMS *Invincible*, 1902–1907," *International History Review*, 30 (2008): 303–331.

  *The Royal Navy and the German Threat 1901–1914: Admiralty Plans to Protect British Trade in a War Against Germany*. Oxford University Press, 2012.

Seton-Watson, Christopher. *Italy: From Liberalism to Fascism, 1870–1925*. London: Methuen, 1967.

Simons, R. W. "Guglielmo Marconi and Early Systems of Wireless Communication," *GEC Review*, 11 (1996): 37–55.

Sokol, Hans Hugo. *Österreich-Ungarns Seekrieg 1914–1918*, 2 vols. Graz: Akademische Druck- und Verlagsanstalt, [1933] 1967.

Sondhaus, Lawrence. *Preparing for Weltpolitik: German Sea Power before the Tirpitz Era*. Annapolis, MD: Naval Institute Press, 1997.
  *The Naval Policy of Austria-Hungary: Navalism, Industrial Development, and the Politics of Dualism, 1867–1918*. West Lafayette, IN: Purdue University Press, 1993.
  *World War I: The Global Revolution*. Cambridge University Press, 2011.
Staff, Gary. "Operation Albion: The Attack on the Baltic Islands," available at: www.gwpda.org/naval/albion.htm.
Steinberg, Jonathan. "The Copenhagen Complex," *Journal of Contemporary History*, 1(3) (1966): 23–46.
  *Yesterday's Deterrent: Tirpitz and the Birth of the German Battle Fleet*. New York: Macmillan, 1965.
Stevens, David. "1914–1918: World War I," in David Stevens (ed.), *The Royal Australian Navy*. Melbourne: Oxford University Press, 2001, pp. 29–54.
Stone, Norman. *The Eastern Front, 1914–1917*. New York: Charles Scribner's, 1975.
Sullivan, Brian R. "Italian Naval Power and the Washington Disarmament Conference of 1921–22," in Goldstein and Maurer (eds.), *The Washington Conference, 1921–22*, pp. 220–248.
Sumida, Jon Tetsuro. "A Matter of Timing: The Royal Navy and the Tactics of Decisive Battle, 1912–1916," *Journal of Military History*, 67 (2003): 85–136.
  *In Defence of Naval Supremacy: Finance, Technology, and British Naval Policy, 1889–1914*. London: Unwin Hyman, 1989.
  *Inventing Grand Strategy and Teaching Command: The Classic Works of Alfred Thayer Mahan Reconsidered*. Baltimore, MD: Johns Hopkins University Press, 1997.
  "The Quest for Reach: The Development of Long-Range Gunnery in the Royal Navy, 1901–1912," in Stephen D. Chiabotti (ed.), *Tooling for War: Military Transformation in the Industrial Age*, Chicago, IL: Imprint Publications, 1996, pp. 49–96.
Tarrant, V. E. *Jutland: The German Perspective*. Annapolis, MD: Naval Institute Press, 1995.
Thompson, John M. *Revolutionary Russia, 1917*, 2nd edn. New York: Macmillan, 1989.
Till, Geoffrey. "Adopting the Aircraft Carrier: The British, American, and Japanese Case Studies," in Williamson Murray and Allan R. Millett (eds.), *Military Innovation in the Interwar Period*. Cambridge University Press, 1996, pp. 191–226.
  *Airpower and the Royal Navy, 1914–1945: A Historical Survey*. London: Jane's Publishing, 1979.

Travers, Timothy H. E. "When Technology and Tactics Fail: Gallipoli 1915," in Stephen D. Chiabotti (ed.), *Tooling for War: Military Transformation in the Industrial Age*. Chicago, IL: Imprint Publications, 1996, pp. 97–122.

van der Vat, Dan. *The Ship that Changed the World: The Escape of the Goeben to the Dardanelles, 1914*. Bethesda, MD: Adler & Adler, 1986.

Walser, Ray. *France's Search for a Battle Fleet: Naval Policy and Naval Power, 1898–1914*. New York: Garland, 1992.

Wheeler-Bennett, John W. *Brest-Litovsk: The Forgotten Peace, March 1918*. New York: W. W. Norton, [1938] 1971.

*Wooden Titan: Hindenburg in Twenty Years of German History, 1914–1934*. New York: William Morrow, 1936.

Williamson, Samuel R., Jr. *The Politics of Grand Strategy: Britain and France Prepare for War, 1904–1914*. Cambridge, MA: Harvard University Press, 1969.

Wilson, Michael. "Early Submarines," in Robert Gardiner (ed.), *Steam, Steel, and Shellfire: The Steam Warship, 1815–1905*. Annapolis, MD: Naval Institute Press, 1992, pp. 147–157.

Yamato, Ichihashi. *The Washington Conference and After: A Historical Survey*. Palo Alto, CA: Stanford University Press, 1928.

Yates, Keith. *Flawed Victory: Jutland 1916*. Annapolis, MD: Naval Institute Press, 2000.

Zyrianov, Pavel N. *Admiral Kolchak: verkhovnyi pravitel' Rossii*, 4th edn. Moscow: Molodaia gvardiia, 2012.

# INDEX

Aaland Islands, 194, 290, 322
*Aboukir*, British armored cruiser, 118, 136
Abruzzi, Luigi of Savoy, Duke of the, Italian admiral, 59, 131, 132, 165, 268
  pictured, 166
Adalbert, Prince of Prussia, Admiral, 8
Aden, 87
*Admiral Makarov*, Russian armored cruiser, 194, 291, 299, 301, 302
Adriatic Sea, 22, 48, 54, 55, 58, 59, 95, 96, 98, 101, 102, 105, 119, 128, 129, 130, 131, 132, 139, 143, 144, 145, 146, 148, 165, 167, 168, 174, 184, 189, 235, 238, 241, 245, 249, 266, 267, 268, 270, 310, 314, 316, 318, 325, 338, 339, 349, 350, 358, 367
*AE 2*, Australian submarine, 178
Aegean Sea, 24, 103, 104, 105, 173, 178, 202, 234, 235, 325, 327
*Agamemnon*, British pre-dreadnought battleship, 41, 270, 327, 328
*Agincourt*, ex-*Sultan Osman-i Evvel*), British dreadnought, 104
Albania, 128, 166, 235, 266, 267, 318
*Albatross*, German minelayer, 194
Albertini, Luigi, Italian journalist and politician, 360
Aleksei, crown prince of Russia, 281, 347

Aleksei, tsar of Russia, 303
Aleutian Islands, 361
Alexandra, Russian empress, 279, 346
Algeria, 55, 97, 98
Allied Fleet
  First (Mediterranean), 131, 165
  Second (Mediterranean), 131
  Bluewater (North Sea), proposed, 270, 271
  Inshore (North Sea), proposed, 270, 271
Allied Supreme War Council, 309
*Almaz*, Russian seaplane tender, 189
*Almirante Latorre* (ex-*Canada*), Chilean dreadnought, 360
Alsace-Lorraine, 9, 20, 347
*Amalfi*, Italian armored cruiser, 146, 165
Amiens, Battle of (1918), 335
*Amiral Charner*, French armored cruiser, 181
*Amphion*, British light cruiser, 116
*Amur*, Russian minelayer, 305
Ancona, 132
*Ancona*, Italian passenger liner, 155, 156
*Andrei Pervozvanny*, Russian pre-dreadnought battleship, 281, 299, 324
Anglo-Boer War (1899–1902), 14, 32
Anglo-French naval conventions (1913–14), 53–54

382 / Index

Anglo-German Naval Treaty (1935), 365
Anglo-Japanese alliance (1902), 49, 62, 67, 359, 362
Antivari (Bar), 129, 130, 131
*Antwerp*, British Q-ship, 162
Anzac Cove, 179, 182, 184
Apia, 70
*Arabic*, British passenger liner, 153, 154, 157, 163, 249
*Arabis*, British sloop, 208
Arabs, and Arab Revolt (1916–18), 94, 328
Archangel, 225
Arensburg (Kuressaare), 294, 296, 297, 298
*Arethusa*, British light cruiser, 117, 208
Argentina, 25, 82, 88
Argo Company. *See* Pollen, Arthur Hungerford
*Argus*, British aircraft carrier, 333
  pictured, 334
*Ariadne*, German light cruiser, 117
*Arizona*, American dreadnought, 28
*Ark Royal*, British seaplane carrier, 47, 174, 181, 325, 333
armed merchantmen, 44
  German, 18, 89–90
armored cruisers. *See* cruisers, armored
Armstrong, British armaments manufacturer, 24
Arnauld de la Perière, Lothar von, German officer, 238, 248, 275
  pictured, 274
Artelt, Karl, German sailor, 344, 345
*Asama*, Japanese armored cruiser, 85
Ascension Island, 79
*Askold*, Russian light cruiser, 59
Asquith, Herbert Henry, British prime minister, 51, 52, 106, 160, 161, 174, 181, 246, 348
*Audacious*, British dreadnought, 118, 122
*Aurora*, Russian light cruiser, 304, 305, 306
Australia, 19, 67, 70, 72, 83, 84, 85, 87, 92, 121, 123, 174, 178, 184, 210, 261
*Australia*, British battle cruiser, 20, 57, 79, 84, 85, 122, 215

Australian navy, 57, 84
Austria-Hungary
  and prewar naval race with Italy, 22–24
  prewar relations of, with Germany, 22, 48
  prewar relations of, with Italy, 22, 48, 55, 58
  prewar relations of, with Russia, 22
  declares war on Serbia, 66, 96, 113
  and independent Ukraine, 324
  wartime relations of, with Germany, 134, 145, 313, 338
  wartime food shortages in, 138, 160, 286
  wartime instability in, 285, 290, 311
  ultimate disintegration of, 338
  signs armistice with Italy (1918), 349
Austro-Hungarian army, 55, 102, 131, 134, 338
Austro-Hungarian navy, 128
  influence of *Jeune École* in, 22
  and introduction of dreadnought design, 24
  prewar strength of, 58
  war plans of, 48
  in British war plans, 54, 98
  aircraft of, 47, 264
  Cruiser Flotilla of, 128, 129, 312, 315
  Danube Flotilla of, 324
  submarines of, 130, 145, 275
  and unrestricted submarine warfare, 143, 243, 246, 338
  bombards Italian coast (May 1915), 131–132
  espionage and sabotage campaigns of, in Italy, 132, 235
  mutinies of 1917 in, 286
  mutinies of 1918 in, 310, 311–315, 339–340
  capital ship losses of, 350
  downsizing of (1918), 316
  final sortie of, 318
  transferred to Yugoslav authorities, 340–341
  postwar dispersal of, 358
Azerbaijan, 327
Azores, 272

*B 11*, British submarine, 111
Bachmann, Gustav, German admiral, 128, 140, 141, 152, 154, 155
Bacon, Reginald, British admiral, viii, 46, 168, 268, 269, 330, 331
  pictured, 169
*Baden*, German dreadnought, 332, 339, 346, 357
Badger, Charles, American admiral, 60
Bakhirev, Mikhail, Russian admiral, 194, 291, 294, 296, 297, 298, 299, 300, 301, 302, 303
Baku, 327
Balfour, Arthur, British politician and statesman, 246, 359, 362
Balkan Wars (1912–13), 24, 53, 95, 101, 183
Baltic Sea, 48
*Baralong*, British Q-ship, 163
*Barbaros Hayreddin* (ex-*Kurfürst Friedrich Wilhelm*), Turkish pre-dreadnought battleship, 24, 108, 182
Barr and Stroud, manufacturer, 40
*Basileos Konstantinos*, Greek dreadnought project, 25
Battenberg, Prince Louis, British admiral, 43, 112, 113
battle cruisers
  introduction of, by British, 15, 42
  intended role of, 17
  design of, copied by Germans, 18
  design of, copied by Japanese, 27
battleships. *See also* dreadnoughts
  development of dreadnought type, 16, 42
  pre-dreadnought, defined, 17
Batum, 110
*Bayan*, Russian armored cruiser, 194, 291, 297, 298, 299, 300, 301, 302
*Bayern*, German dreadnought, 21, 229, 239, 240, 296, 303
Bayly, Sir Lewis, British admiral, 253, 254, 257, 259, 263
Beagle Channel, 78
Beatty, David, British admiral
  as battle cruiser commander, 116, 117, 118, 121, 124, 125, 127, 134, 139, 208, 211, 230, 231, 232
  at Jutland, 204, 215, 216, 217, 218, 219, 220, 221, 222, 223
  and naval intelligence, 214
  as Grand Fleet commander, 234, 255, 271, 330, 332, 333, 348, 349, 357
  serves as postwar First Sea Lord, 359, 368, 369, 370
  pictured, 105
Behncke, Paul, German admiral, 226, 293, 297, 298, 299, 300, 301, 302, 335, 336, 344
Behring, Ehler, German admiral, 190
Beitzen, Curt, German officer, 225
Belarus, 319
Belgium, 29, 51, 61, 98, 113, 119, 142, 147, 335, 358, 362
Belleville, manufacturer of boilers, 35
Below, Otto von, German general, 193
*Benedetto Brin*, Italian pre-dreadnought battleship, 132
*Beowulf*, German pre-dreadnought battleship, 194, 322
Berckheim, Baron Egewolf von, German officer, 190, 194
Berehaven, 257
Beresford, Sir Charles, British admiral, 52
Bergen, 232, 332
Bernstorff, Johann von, German diplomat, 154, 247, 248
Bethmann Hollweg, Theobald von, German chancellor, 20, 137, 139, 141, 151, 152, 154, 155, 157, 192, 242, 247, 288
Bismarck, Otto von, German chancellor, 9, 13, 22
*Bismarck*, German battleship, 37
Bismarck Archipelago, 64, 84
Bita Paka, 84
Bizerte (Binzart), 54, 58
Black, Nicholas, historian, 256
*Black Prince*, British armored cruiser, 223, 225
Black Sea, 26, 59, 95, 102, 104, 107, 108, 109, 110, 111, 146, 172, 173, 177, 186, 188, 189, 234, 235, 237, 245, 319, 324, 325, 350, 367
Blackwood, M. B. R., British officer, 265

blockade, Allied
 of Germany, 51, 53, 114, 115, 118,
  137, 151, 159, 160, 271, 309, 329,
  367
 of Austria-Hungary, 128, 160, 367
 and Allied Blockade Commission
  (ABC), 329, 330
*Blücher*, German armored cruiser, 19,
  120, 123, 124, 125, 126, 127, 190
Bolshevik party, 279, 282, 283, 284,
  285, 298, 303, 304, 305, 306, 318,
  319, 320, 321, 346
Bône (Annaba), 97, 98
Borkum, 147, 270
Bosporus, 94, 104, 107, 109, 110, 111,
  146, 173, 177, 178, 186, 284, 303,
  309
*Bouvet*, French pre-dreadnought
  battleship, 176
 pictured, 177
Boxer Rebellion (1900), 14, 48, 254
*Brandenburg*, German pre-dreadnought
  battleship, 10, 17, 24
Brauer, Otto, German officer, 90
Braun, Karl Ferdinand, German physicist,
  33, 34
*Braunschweig*, German pre-dreadnought
  battleship, 190, 191, 195, 196, 223,
  354
Brazil, 24, 25, 74, 250
Bremen, 66, 199, 324, 347
*Bremen*, German light cruiser, 354
*Bremse*, German light cruiser, 332
*Breslau*, German light cruiser, 94, 95,
  96, 98, 99, 101, 102, 104, 105
Brest, 54, 258, 259, 261
Brest-Litovsk, Treaty of (1918), 307,
  310, 319, 320, 321, 322, 324, 325
*Bretagne*, French dreadnought, 25
Briand, Aristide, French premier, 360,
  362, 364, 365
Brindisi, 59, 96, 101, 131, 132, 165,
  168, 266
*Bristol*, British light cruiser, 79, 82
Britain
 prewar relations of, with France, 13,
  25, 29
 prewar relations of, with Germany, 12,
  13, 15, 16, 17, 19, 20, 21, 29, 49

 prewar relations of, with Italy, 22
 prewar relations of, with Japan, 49, 67
 prewar relations of, with Russia, 13,
  26, 29, 67
 and prewar naval race with Germany,
  19–22
 builds battleships for Japan, 27
 builds warships for Chile, 122
 builds warships for Turks, 24, 101,
  104
 declares war on Austria-Hungary, 67
 declares war on Germany, 66, 67
 declares war on Ottoman Empire, 108
 industrial superiority of, 17
 merchant marine of, 158
 Middle East policies of, 94
 Ministry of Blockade in, 161, 246,
  330
 and Bolshevik Revolution, 306, 320
 wartime food shortages in, 329
 wartime policy of, toward Greece,
  184, 238
 wartime relations of, with Italy, 133,
  268
 wartime relations of, with United
  States, 160
*Britannia*, British pre-dreadnought
  battleship, 339
*Britannic*, British hospital ship, 234
British army
 British Expeditionary Force (BEF) of,
  116, 119, 261
 and Gallipoli, 179, 184
 Mediterranean Expeditionary Force
  (MEF) of, 176, 182
British navy
 and *Pax Britannica*, 13, 49
 and "two-power standard," 13, 19
 prewar exercises of, 42, 43
 and the *Jeune École*, 45
 and introduction of dreadnought
  design, 41
 war plans of, 50–52
 aircraft of, 47, 264
 Atlantic Fleet of, 49, 52, 53
 Auxiliary Patrol of, 164, 269
 Battle Cruiser Squadron of, 116
 Battle Cruiser Fleet of, 139, 204, 211,
  215, 216

capital ship losses of, 350, 367
Channel Fleet of, 49, 52, 53, 57, 74, 119, 120, 174, 181
China station of, 57
West African station of, 57
East Indies station of, 57
Eastern Mediterranean Squadron of, 171, 174, 268
Adriatic Squadron of, 165, 268
Fourth Cruiser Squadron of, 74, 87
Grand Fleet of, 30, 56, 57, 85, 95, 113, 116, 117, 118, 121, 123, 127, 139, 143, 148, 204, 205, 206, 207, 208, 209, 210, 211, 212, 213, 230, 231, 232, 234, 240, 252, 255, 270, 330, 332, 333, 342, 348, 367
Home Fleet of, 43, 49, 52, 53, 57, 112
Intelligence Division of (Room 40), 79, 121, 214, 249, 263
Mediterranean Fleet of, 49, 52, 53, 54, 57, 98, 99, 103, 106, 268, 327
North American and West Indian station of, 57
relations of, with United States Navy, 257
Royal Naval Division of, 178
submarines of, 46, 52, 184, 191, 275, 323
provides fire support for army in Flanders, 119, 165
deploys Q-ships, 162, 164
and Dardanelles operation, 174, 179, 184
at Jutland, 215, 216, 219, 223, 225, 227
and Washington Naval Treaty (1922), 363, 365
Brown–Curtis turbine engines, 27
Bruges, 147, 245, 269, 331
*Brummer*, German light cruiser, 332
Brusilov, Aleksei, Russian general, 237
Bryan, William Jennings, US secretary of state, 151, 152, 153, 158
Bulgaria, 104, 108, 166, 183, 187, 238, 250, 318, 324, 328, 355
Bülow, Bernhard von, German foreign secretary and chancellor, 13
*Bulwark*, British pre-dreadnought battleship, 226

Burián, Count István, Austro-Hungarian foreign minister, 156, 244
Burney, Sir Cecil, British admiral, 57
Bussche, Erich von der, German army officer, 337

C 26, British submarine, 297
C 27, British submarine, 297
C 52, British submarine, 297
*Caldwell*, American destroyer, 258
*Calvados*, French troopship, 146
Cameroon, 34, 86
Campbell, Gordon, British officer, 163, 164, 265
Canada, 72, 74, 261
*Canada* (ex-*Almirante Latorre*), British dreadnought, 122, 360
Çanakkale, 104, 111
Canaris, Wilhelm, German officer, 88
Canary Islands, 246
*Canopus*, British pre-dreadnought battleship, 74, 75, 76, 79, 80
Cape Finisterre, 339
Cape Hellas, 178, 184
Cape Horn, 69, 74, 78, 79, 82, 86
Cape Planka, 130
Cape Santa Maria di Leuca, 131, 168, 266, 268
Cape Verde Islands, 246
Capelle, Eduard von, German admiral, 287, 288, 335
Carden, Sir Sackville, British admiral, 106, 107, 171, 174, 175, 201
*Cardiff*, British light cruiser, 348
Caribbean Sea, 74, 87
*Carnarvon*, British armored cruiser, 79, 81
*Carolina*, American passenger steamer, 272
Carolines, the, 64, 72, 84, 85
Carson, Sir Edward, British politician, 246, 289
Cattaro (Kotor), 58, 102, 128, 129, 130, 131, 143, 144, 145, 165, 167, 168, 181, 244, 264, 266, 267, 269, 289, 310, 311, 312, 313, 314, 315, 316, 318, 339, 340, 341
Caucasus Mountains, 109, 110, 111, 173, 177, 235, 284, 327

*Cavour*, Italian dreadnought, 24, 96
Cecil, Robert, Lord, British politician, 118, 151, 161, 246, 330
Cemal Pasha, Turkish navy minister, 107
Center Party (Catholic), German, 288, 337, 347
Central Powers, 102, 104, 107, 146, 166, 172, 183, 187, 190, 191, 193, 198, 231, 233, 235, 237, 242, 244, 247, 249, 250, 270, 276, 283, 290, 303, 306, 310, 318, 319, 320, 324, 325, 326, 329, 350. *See also* Austria-Hungary; Bulgaria; Germany; Ottoman Empire
Cephalonia, 131, 144
Charles, emperor of Austria, king of Hungary, 243, 244, 286, 315, 316, 337, 338, 340, 341
Chatfield, Ernle, British officer, 204
Chatham, 52
Chile, 73, 74, 76, 77, 78, 85, 88, 90, 122, 159, 334, 360
China, 14, 49, 57, 62, 64, 86, 174, 254, 362
  and Chinese navy, 38, 39
  laborers from, to Europe, 261
Churchill, Winston S.
  as First Lord of the Admiralty, 20, 43, 47, 104, 109, 112, 113, 159, 160
  orders prewar redeployment of fleets, 53, 54
  and escape of the *Goeben*, 94, 98, 102
  and the *Lusitania*, 150
  and Dardanelles operation, 161, 171, 172, 173, 174, 175, 179, 181, 185, 201
  resigns from Admiralty, 181
Clausewitz, Karl von, Prussian officer and writer, 9, 10, 11
*Clemson*, American destroyer, 259
Cocos Islands, 87
*Cöln*, German light cruiser, 117
*Colossus*, British dreadnought, 222
*Conquest*, British cruiser, 210
Conrad von Hötzendorf, Franz, Austro-Hungarian general, 48
Constantine, king of Greece, 184, 238, 239

Constantinople, 88, 94, 95, 98, 100, 102, 103, 104, 107, 109, 110, 112, 171, 173, 177, 178, 186, 187, 188, 196, 236, 283, 289, 293, 303, 326, 327, 328, 350
Constanza, 237
convoys, Allied, 44, 55, 87, 98, 109, 110, 111, 131, 186, 236, 250, 255, 256, 257, 258, 259, 260, 261, 262, 263, 265, 266, 268, 272, 273, 274, 276, 322, 324, 332, 336, 367
Corbett, Sir Julian, British strategist, 47, 255
Corfu, 129, 166, 167, 168, 184, 238, 268, 317, 349
Cork Harbor, 57, 254, 257
*Cormoran* (ex-*Riasan*), German auxiliary cruiser, 66, 68, 69
*Cormoran*, German light cruiser, 65
Cornwall, 32, 142, 150, 163
*Cornwall*, British light cruiser, 79, 81
Coronel, Battle of (1914), 64, 74–76, 79, 80, 82, 90
*Courageous*, British battle cruiser, 191, 271
  converted to aircraft carrier, 334
*Courbet*, French dreadnought, 25, 53, 128
Cowles, Walter, American admiral, 60
Cradock, Sir Christopher, British admiral, 74, 75, 76, 79, 87
*Cressy*, British armored cruiser, 118, 136
Crete, 156
Crimea, 59, 110, 187, 326, 350
Croatia, and Croatians, 290, 311, 313, 315, 316, 340, 341
Cromarty, 113, 116, 121, 207, 226
cruisers
  and French *Jeune École*, 11
  eclipsed by battleships, 44
cruisers, armored, 17, 23, 26, 27, 38, 40, 45, 49, 53, 57
  hiatus in construction of, 17, 44
cruisers, light, 45
Cuba, 60, 250
Cunard Line, 148
Cuniberti, Vittorio, Italian naval architect, 41
*Curie*, French submarine, 145, 358

*Cushing*, American tanker, 150, 152, 153
Cuxhaven, 147
Czernin, Count Ottokar, Austro-Hungarian foreign minister, 244

*D 5*, British submarine, 120
*Dacia*, Russian auxiliary cruiser, 285
Dagö (Hiiumaa), 193, 197, 198, 199, 291, 292, 294, 296, 297, 299, 302
Dakar, 272
Dalmatia, 128, 312, 340
Damascus, 246, 328
*Dante Alighieri*, Italian dreadnought, 24
*Danton*, French pre-dreadnought battleship, 25, 53, 238, 249, 270
Danube River, 284, 324, 358
Danzig, 190, 191, 194, 293, 294, 322, 323
Dardanelles, 94, 100, 101, 104, 105, 106, 107, 111, 119, 128, 129, 144, 146, 161, 171, 172, 173, 174, 175, 177, 178, 179, 181, 182, 183, 184, 185, 187, 193, 196, 201, 238, 309, 325, 327, 328, 330, 350
  Allied naval strength at (1915), 202
Dartige du Fournet, Louis, French admiral, 166, 238
*Dartmouth*, British cruiser, 266
Darwinism, 9
de Robeck, John, British admiral, 175, 176, 181, 196, 330
*Defence*, British armored cruiser, 13, 128, 220, 221, 225, 226
*Defiance*, British torpedo depot ship, 30, 31
Denmark, 50, 204, 212, 216, 330, 346
depth charges, 164, 259, 263, 264, 269, 274, 367
*Derfflinger*, German battle cruiser, 20, 124, 125, 218, 219, 222, 223, 224
destroyers, 45
  introduction of, 15
*Deutschland*, German minelayer, 197
*Deutschland*, German pre-dreadnought battleship, 18, 191, 223, 354
Dodecanese Islands, 59
Doenitz, Karl, German officer, 187

Dogger Bank, 121, 139, 205, 207, 209, 212, 229, 231
  Battle of (1915), 123–127, 278
  Second Battle of (1916), 208
Dover, Straits of, 53, 57, 116, 226, 232, 269
  Allied barrage across, 164, 165, 167, 168, 268, 330, 337
Drake Passage, 78
*Dreadnought*, British all big-gun battleship, 16, 17, 18, 21, 23, 42, 52, 212, 215, 240, 360
  pictured, 16
*Dresden*, German light cruiser, 73, 74, 76, 78, 79, 81, 83, 88
Dreyer, Frederic, British officer and fire-control expert, 35, 36, 37, 40, 43
Duff, Alexander, British admiral, 256
Dukhonin, Nikolai, Russian general, 303
Dunkirk, 264
Durazzo (Durrës), 166, 267, 318
Dvina River, 192, 197, 198, 290
Dybenko, Pavel, Russian naval commissar, viii, 281, 282, 283, 285, 298, 304, 305, 306, 321
  pictured, 282

*E 1*, British submarine, 191, 197, 233
*E 9*, British submarine, 118, 191, 194
*E 11*, British submarine, 182
*E 15*, British submarine, 178
*E 31*, British submarine, 212
*E 42*, British submarine, 333
*Eagle*, British aircraft carrier, 334
East Indies, 57, 64, 69, 87, 90, 174
East Prussia, 190, 193
Easter Island, 73, 74, 88, 159
Ebergard, Andrei, Russian admiral, 59, 109, 110, 111, 177, 186, 187, 188, 189, 237
Ebert, Friedrich, German socialist leader, 348
Eckernförde, 273
Egypt, 156, 173, 174
  laborers from, to Europe, 261
Eichhorn, Hermann von, German general, 193

Eisner, Kurt, German socialist leader, 347
Elbe River, 114, 125, 195, 213, 344
*Elbing*, German light cruiser, 223
*Elsass*, German pre-dreadnought battleship, 196
*Emden*, German light cruiser, 65, 66, 67, 68, 69, 87, 88, 302, 356, 357
Ems River, 119
Emsmann, Hans Jochen, German officer, 241, 242
*Engadine*, British seaplane carrier, 212
Eniwetok Atoll, 84
Entente Cordiale (1904), 16, 25, 46, 49. See also Anglo-French naval conventions; Triple Entente
Enver Pasha, Turkish general and war minister, 101, 107, 109
  pictured, 188
*Erin* (ex-*Reşadiye*), British dreadnought, 104
Eritrea, 59
Erzberger, Matthias, German Center Party leader, 347, 348
Essen, Nikolai, Russian admiral, 59, 189, 190, 191, 194
Estonia, 192, 319, 321
Evan-Thomas, Hugh, British admiral, 216, 217, 218, 219, 220
*Evstafi*, Russian pre-dreadnought battleship, 108, 110, 187, 189

*Falaba*, British steamer, 150, 152, 153
Falkenhayn, Erich von, German general, 155, 156, 157, 191, 192, 193, 195
Falklands, Battle of the (1914), 62, 74, 78, 79–82, 83, 85, 86, 87, 88, 90, 121, 123, 124, 126, 174
*Falmouth*, British light cruiser, 230, 231
Fanning Island (Tabuaeran), 72, 92
*Fanning*, American destroyer, 259
*Farnborough* (ex-*Loderer*), British Q-ship, 163, 164, 265
*Fatih Sultan Mehmed*, Ottoman dreadnought project, 24, 25, 104
Feldkirchner, Johannes, German officer, 266
Feldt, Richard, German officer, 272
Feodosia, 107

Finland, 197, 199, 283, 290, 310, 319, 321, 322
Firth of Forth, 53, 118, 208, 211, 348, 349
Fisher, Sir John, British admiral
  early career of, 15, 46
  and battle cruisers, 15, 18, 42, 44, 79, 191
  and design of *Dreadnought*, 16, 41
  and destroyers, 15, 45
  and submarines, 47
  plans for war against Germany, 49–52
  redeploys prewar fleets, 49, 52
  retirement of, 18, 21, 35
  as wartime First Sea Lord, 30, 174, 191
  ultimate resignation of, 181
  pictured, 50
Fiume (Rijeka), 128, 340, 349
Flanders, 119, 140, 207, 208, 210, 232, 241, 248, 310
Fletcher, Frank, American officer, 259
Foch, Ferdinand, Marshal of France and Supreme Allied Commander, 329, 347, 348
*Formidable*, British pre-dreadnought battleship, 120
Forstmann, Walter, German officer, 248, 275
*Foucault*, French submarine, 264
Four-Power Treaty (1922), 361
Fox, Cecil, British officer, 118
France
  defeat of, in Franco-Prussian War (1870–71), 9
  prewar relations of, with Britain, 13, 15, 25
  prewar relations of, with Italy, 22, 48
  and prewar naval competition, 25
  declares war on Ottoman Empire, 108
  sub-Saharan colonies of, 261
  wartime relations of, with Italy, 133, 268
  wartime policy of, toward Greece, 184
Francis Ferdinand, archduke, heir to throne of Austria-Hungary, 23, 58, 64
Francis Joseph, emperor of Austria, king of Hungary, 23, 243

Francis, Ernest, British sailor, 218
Franco-Prussian War (1870–71), 8–9
Franco-Russian alliance, 13, 22, 48. *See also* Triple Entente
Franz, Adolf, German officer, 272
*Frauenlob*, German light cruiser, 223
Fremantle, Sir Sydney, British admiral, 356, 357
French army
  and Gallipoli, 184
French navy, 49, 53, 58, 120, 235, 271, 348
  in Franco-Prussian War (1870–71), 8
  and the *Jeune École*, 11, 15, 362
  prewar strength of, 13
  reputation of, for innovation, 17
  submarines of, 46, 184, 275
  torpedo boat program of, 46
  and aviation, 47
  prewar redeployment of, 53, 58
  Mediterranean Fleet of, 54, 58, 97, 102
  Northern Fleet of, 11
  wartime Channel forces of, 165
  abandons Adriatic (1915), 131
  and Dardanelles operation, 174, 184
  acquires German ships, postwar, 358
  and Washington Naval Treaty (1922), 362, 363, 365
Friedman, Norman, historian, 36, 37
*Friedrich Carl*, German armored cruiser, 190
*Friedrich der Grosse*, German dreadnought, viii, 208, 221, 225, 227, 287, 288, 293, 356
  pictured, 209
Frisian Islands, 147, 270
*Furious*, British battle cruiser, 191
  converted to aircraft carrier, 333
*Fuso*, Japanese dreadnought, 27

*Gäa*, Austro-Hungarian torpedo depot ship, 145
Gaba Tepe, 181
Galapagos Islands, 75
*Gallia*, French auxiliary cruiser, 238
Gallipoli, viii, ix, 3, 131, 144, 172, 173, 176, 178, 179, 181, 182, 184, 185, 186, 292, 298, 333

  total casualties (1915), 184
  landing, pictured, 180
*Gangut*, Russian dreadnought, 26, 189, 190, 195
*Garibaldi*, Italian armored cruiser, 165
Gauchet, Dominique-Marie, French admiral, 238, 328
*Gaulois*, French pre-dreadnought battleship, 175, 176, 235
*Gazelle*, German light cruiser, 354
*Geier*, German gunboat, 68, 69, 85, 96
*General Alekseev* (ex-*Volya*), White Russian dreadnought, 350
General Electric Company (AEG), German, 33
George V, king of Great Britain and Ireland, 112, 228
*George G. Henry*, American tanker, 272
*Georgi Pobiedonosets*, Russian pre-dreadnought battleship, 107, 109
Georgia, 310, 327
German army, 21, 29, 33, 134, 191, 241, 303
  Eighth Army of, 193, 198, 290
  Finns serving in, 322
  Niemen Army of, 193, 195
  rationing in, 329
  Tenth Army of, 193, 198
  defeat of (1918), 335, 336
German navy. *See also* submarine warfare, unrestricted
  in Franco-Prussian War (1870–71), 8
  initial growth of (1871–97), 9, 10
  becomes world's second strongest, 16
  fire-control systems of, 37
  prewar exercises of, 42
  war plans of, 48
  aircraft and airships of, 47, 147, 207, 208, 210, 211, 212, 213, 214, 224, 225, 229, 230, 333
  Baltic Fleet of, 58, 346
  Baltic contingent (*Ostseeverband*) of, 322
  deck officers (*Deckoffiziere*) in, 70
  East Asiatic Squadron of, 58, 62, 63–82, 83, 86

German navy (*cont.*)
  High Sea Fleet of, 52, 58, 113, 114, 115, 116, 117, 120, 121, 123, 124, 127, 139, 140, 154, 157, 189, 191, 195, 205, 206, 207, 208, 210, 211, 212, 227, 229, 230, 231, 232, 240, 271, 278, 287, 288, 289, 290, 293, 294, 310, 330, 332, 333, 334, 335, 343, 345, 348, 349, 367
  Mediterranean Division of, 55, 57, 95, 96, 107, 108, 111
  at Jutland, 213, 214, 216, 217, 219, 222, 225, 228
  capital ship losses of, 350
  abandons battleship construction (1917), 243
  mutinies of 1917 in, 287–288, 292
  mutinies of 1918 in, 336, 343–347
  and Operations Plan 19, 342, 343
  postwar internment of, at Scapa Flow, 355–357
  limited, under Versailles Treaty (1919), 353–355
  ships of, acquired by Allies, 358
  revival of, under Nazis, 365
  submarines of, 47, 141–142, 181, 242, 275, 276, 337, 349. *See also* submarine warfare, unrestricted
Germany
  unification of (1871), 9
  prewar growth of, 51
  prewar relations of, with Austria-Hungary, 22, 48
  prewar relations of, with Britain, 12, 13, 15, 16, 17, 19, 20, 21, 29, 49
  prewar relations of, with Italy, 22, 48
  claims colonial empire, 10
  and prewar naval race with Britain, 19–22
  war plans of, 48
  mobilizes against France, 66
  mobilizes against Russia, 66
  declares war on France, 97
  alliance of, with Ottoman Empire, 100, 101
  trade of, with United States, 160, 161, 245

  and Peace Resolution (1917), 288, 337, 347
  and independent Ukraine, 324
  wartime relations of, with Austria-Hungary, 134, 145, 313, 338
  wartime food shortages in, 138–139, 160, 246, 247, 251, 329
Gibraltar, 49, 53, 54, 97, 259, 268, 339
*Glasgow*, British light cruiser, 74, 75, 76, 79, 81, 88
*Glatton*, British monitor, 226
*Glitra*, British merchantman, 137
*Glorious*, British battle cruiser, 191, 271
  converted to aircraft carrier, 334
*Gloucester*, British light cruiser, 101, 102
*Gneisenau*, German armored cruiser, 58, 62, 63, 64, 65, 66, 67, 68, 69, 70, 72, 73, 75, 76, 77, 78, 79, 80, 81, 82, 126
*Goeben*, German battle cruiser, 20, 55, 57, 122, 128, 177, 350, 367. *See also Yavuz Sultan Selim*
  escapes Allies (1914), 94–104
  becomes *Yavuz Sultan Selim*, 105
Goetting, Gernot, German officer, 272
*Goliath*, British pre-dreadnought battleship, 181
*Good Hope*, British armored cruiser, 69, 74, 75
Gotland, and Gotland Raid (1915), 194, 199
Gough-Calthorpe, Sir Somerset, British admiral, 268, 327, 328, 350
*Grazhdanin* (ex-*Tsesarevich*), Russian pre-dreadnought battleship, 291, 297, 298, 299, 300, 301, 302
Great Yarmouth, 120, 209
Greece, 24, 27, 29, 45, 129, 184, 237, 358
  and prewar naval race with Ottoman Empire, 24–25
  neutrality of, 104
  joins Allies (1917), 238
Grenfell, F. H., British officer, 265
Grey, Sir Edward, British foreign secretary, 158, 159, 160, 246
Groener, Wilhelm, German general, 348

*Grosser Kurfürst*, German dreadnought, 222, 226, 229, 233, 296, 303
Guam, 64, 69, 85
Guantanamo Bay, 60
Guépratte, Emile-Paul, French admiral, 107, 111, 174, 175, 176
Gulf of Bothnia, 290
Gulf of Finland, 190, 191, 194, 195, 280, 291, 298, 302, 303, 321
Gulf of Guinea, 272
*Gulflight*, American tanker, 150, 152, 153
gunnery
  prewar evolution of, 35–43
*Gustave Zédé*, French submarine, 46
*Gymnote*, French submarine, 46

Haldane, Richard, Viscount, British war minister, 20, 21
Halsey, William "Bull," American officer, 259
Hamburg, 44, 101, 197, 261, 324, 347
Hamburg-Amerika Line, 44, 261
*Hamidiye*, Turkish light cruiser, 110, 111, 178, 187
Hamilton, Sir Ian, British general, 176, 179, 182, 184
*Hampshire*, British armored cruiser, 225
Hangö (Hanko), 323
Hankey, Maurice, British officer, 51, 61
Hansa, Alexander, Austro-Hungarian admiral, 312, 313, 314, 315
Harding, Warren G., US president, 352, 359
Hartlepool, 120, 211
Hartog, Johannes, German officer, 208
Harwich, 116, 118, 208, 210, 211, 230, 349
Haus, Anton, Austro-Hungarian admiral, 55, 58, 97, 99, 101, 102, 105, 112, 128, 129, 130, 131, 132, 243, 244
  pictured, 103
Hawaii, 60, 85, 361
*Hawke*, British cruiser, 118
Headrick, Daniel, historian, 214
Heimberg, Heino von, German officer, 146, 187
Heinemann, Bruno, German officer, 345, 346

*Hela*, German light cruiser, 118
Helgoland, 114, 118, 127, 147, 206, 209, 222, 314, 333, 348, 354
Helgoland Bight, First Battle of (1914), 116–117, 118
Helgoland Bight, Second Battle of (1917), 271, 289
*Helgoland*, German dreadnought, 15, 19, 344, 345, 354
Helsinki, 59, 195, 280, 283, 285, 291, 299, 304, 305, 321, 322, 323
Henderson, Reginald, British officer, 256, 257
Henry, Prince of Prussia, German admiral, 58, 172, 190, 195, 198, 292, 346
Herbert, Godfrey, British officer, 162, 163
*Hermes*, British aircraft carrier, 333
Hersing, Otto, German officer, 118, 144, 145, 181, 248
*Hertha*, German cruiser, 96
Hertz, Heinrich, German physicist, 32, 33
Herwig, Holger, historian, 336
Heyssler, Erich, Austro-Hungarian officer, 314, 315
*Hindenburg*, German battle cruiser, 21
Hindenburg, Paul von, German field marshal, 193, 199, 201, 231, 233, 242, 243, 288, 319, 335, 336
Hipper, Franz, German admiral
  as battle cruiser commander, 117, 120, 121, 123, 124, 125, 126, 127, 195, 196, 197, 198, 205, 208, 209, 210, 229, 230, 243, 292, 332
  pictured, 115
  at Jutland, 213, 214, 216, 217, 218, 219, 221, 222, 223
  as fleet commander, 335, 342
  and mutinies of 1918, 344, 346
  and final sortie, 343, 344
  abandons post at Armistice, 349
*Hizen*, Japanese pre-dreadnought, 85
*Hogue*, British armored cruiser, 118, 136
*Hohenzollern*, German imperial yacht, 56, 96
Holbrook, Norman, British officer, 111

Holland
   American submarine builder, 46
Holtzendorff, Henning von, German admiral, 154, 155, 156, 157, 242, 243, 244, 249, 254, 255, 260, 277, 292, 335
Hong Kong, 64
Honolulu, 66, 69, 72, 85
*Hood*, British battle cruiser, 37
Hood, Horace, British admiral, 37, 216, 219, 220, 221, 226
Hopman, Albert, German admiral, 194, 294, 298, 299, 302
Horns Reef, 206, 210, 212, 216, 232, 270
Horthy, Miklós, Austro-Hungarian admiral, 144, 266, 267, 311, 314, 315, 316, 317, 318, 335, 339, 340, 341, 358
House, Edward, advisor to President Wilson, 154
Howard, Thomas, American admiral, 60
Hughes, Charles Evans, US secretary of state, 352, 359, 360, 361, 362, 364
Humber, the, 57
Hutier, Oskar von, German general, 290, 291, 292

*Ibuki*, Japanese armored cruiser, 27, 87
*Imperator Aleksandr I*, Russian seaplane tender, 284
*Imperator Aleksandr III*, Russian dreadnought, 237
*Imperator Nikolai I*, Russian seaplane tender, 284
*Imperator Pavel*, Russian pre-dreadnought battleship, 281, 283, 299
*Imperatritsa Ekaterina Velikaya*, Russian dreadnought, 235, 237
*Imperatritsa Maria*, Russian dreadnought, 26, 109, 187, 189, 237, 283
*Indefatigable*, British battle cruiser, 98, 106, 174, 204, 218, 225, 226
Independent Social Democratic Party (USPD), German, 287, 288, 347
India, 87, 261

Indian Ocean, 69, 87, 88
*Indianola*, Russian minesweeper tender, 297
Indochina, French, 87
*Indomitable*, British battle cruiser, 98, 125
*Inflexible*, British battle cruiser, 79, 80, 81, 82, 85, 174, 176, 181, 202
   pictured, 83
Ingenohl, Friedrich von, German admiral, 58, 114, 121, 122, 123, 124, 125, 127, 140, 205
*Inverlyon*, British Q-ship, 163
*Invincible*, British battle cruiser, 16, 18, 42, 45, 57, 79, 80, 81, 82, 85, 204, 221, 225, 226
*Ioann Zlatoust*, Russian pre-dreadnought battleship, 108, 187, 189
Ionian Sea, 102
Irben (Irbe) Straits, 192, 193, 195, 196, 197, 198, 199, 201, 202, 294, 297
Ireland, 57, 118, 137, 140, 148, 153, 163, 164, 254, 257, 263, 264
Irish Sea, 232
*Iron Duke*, British dreadnought, 20, 225
*Irresistible*, British pre-dreadnought battleship, 176
Italian army, 132, 329
Italian navy, 24, 32, 41, 54, 132, 235, 338, 349
   influence of *Jeune École* in, 22
   and introduction of dreadnought design, 24
   war plans of, 48
   prewar strength of, 59
   submarines of, 275
   MAS boats of, 289, 317, 318
   capital ship losses of, 350
   acquires German ships, postwar, 358
   and Washington Naval Treaty (1922), 362, 363, 365
Italo-Turkish War (1911–12), 54
Italy
   prewar relations of, with Austria-Hungary, 22, 48, 55
   prewar relations of, with Britain, 22, 54
   prewar relations of, with France, 22, 48, 54

prewar relations of, with Germany, 22, 48
and prewar naval race with Austria-Hungary, 22–24
aircraft and airships of, 47
declares neutrality (1914), 96, 97
joins Entente (1915), 131, 132, 145
*Izumo*, Japanese armored cruiser, 85

*J 1*, British submarine, 233
Jackson, Sir Henry, British officer and wireless pioneer, 30, 31, 32
*Jacob Jones*, American destroyer, 259
Jade Bay, 114, 117
Jagow, Gottlieb von, German foreign secretary, 149, 152, 153
Jaluit, 84
Japan
 claims German Pacific colonies, 67, 83, 85, 251
 dreadnought program of, 25, 26
 industrial capability of, 27
 prewar relations of, with Britain, 49, 67
 rivalry of, with United States, 27
 wartime demands of, on China, 86
 wartime relations of, with United States, 86
Japanese navy, 38, 39
 victorious over Russians (1904–5), 16, 26, 33, 40–41, 49
 and introduction of dreadnought design, 41
 prewar strength of, 59
 First Fleet of, 59, 84
 Second Fleet of, 59, 67
 escorts Indian Ocean convoys, 87
 deploys ships in Mediterranean, 268
 capital ship losses of, 350
 and Washington Naval Treaty (1922), 361, 363, 365
Java, 64
*Jean Bart*, French dreadnought, 128, 130
Jellicoe, Sir John, British admiral, 30, 36, 43, 51, 228
 as Grand Fleet commander, 57, 113, 114, 116, 118, 121, 122, 125, 127, 139, 160, 204, 208, 209, 210, 211, 212, 229, 230, 231, 232, 330

 at Jutland, 215, 216, 217, 219, 220, 222, 223, 225, 226, 228
 and naval intelligence, 214, 230
 as First Sea Lord, 234, 253, 254, 255, 256, 260, 271
 dismissed, 330
 pictured, 215
Juan Fernandez Islands, 74, 88
July Crisis (1914), 54
Jutland, Battle of (1916), 204, 213–226
 fire control at, 36, 226–227

*Kaiser Franz Joseph I*, Austro-Hungarian cruiser, 289
*Kaiser Karl VI*, Austro-Hungarian armored cruiser, 312, 313, 314, 315
*Kaiser*, German dreadnought, 15, 20, 64, 84, 90, 207, 222, 271
*Kaiserin Elisabeth*, Austro-Hungarian cruiser, 58, 65, 289
*Kaiserin*, German dreadnought, 58, 65, 271
Kaiser-Wilhelmsland (New Guinea), 64, 84, 90
Kamimura, Hikonojo, Japanese admiral, 59, 67
Kanin, Viktor, Russian admiral, 194, 280
*Karlsruhe*, German light cruiser, 74, 87, 88
Kassar Wiek, 296, 299, 302
Kato, Kanji, Japanese admiral, 360, 361, 365, 366
Kato, Tomosaburo, Japanese admiral, 359, 361, 365
*Kawachi*, Japanese dreadnought, 85
Kelly, Sir Howard, British officer, 268
Kemal (Atatürk), Mustafa, Turkish general, 179, 185
*Kent*, British armored cruiser, 79, 81, 88, 211
Kerensky, Aleksandr, leader of Russian Provisional Government, 282, 283, 284, 285, 296, 303, 304, 305, 306, 315
Kerr, Mark, British admiral, 167, 168, 266, 268
Keyes, Sir Roger, British officer, 171, 176, 185, 330, 331

Kiaochow (Jiaozhou) Bay, 63, 67, 86
Kiel, 58, 113, 143, 189, 196, 197, 287, 293, 310, 323, 339, 344, 346, 347
Kiel Canal, 58, 113, 189, 196, 197, 293, 344
*Kilkis* (ex-*Mississippi*), Greek pre-dreadnought battleship, 25
*King Edward VII*, British pre-dreadnought battleship, 57, 209, 211, 212
Kitchener, Horatio Herbert, 1st Earl, British field marshal, 176, 179, 184, 225
Köbis, Alban, German sailor, 288, 292, 308, 315, 335
Koch, Method, Austro-Hungarian and Yugoslav officer, 341
*Kolberg*, German light cruiser, 124, 298, 302
Kolchak, Aleksandr, Russian admiral, viii, 199, 237, 283, 284, 306, 315, 320, 335
  pictured, 200
*Kongo*, Japanese battle cruiser, 27
*König*, German dreadnought, 8, 20, 21, 207, 222, 226, 229, 297, 298, 299, 300, 301, 345, 346
*König Albert*, German dreadnought, 213, 229
*König Wilhelm*, German armored frigate, 8
*Königin Luise*, German minelayer, 116
*Königsberg*, German light cruiser, 87, 88
Kornilov, Lavr, Russian general, 285, 303, 305
Kraft, Hugo, German admiral, 344
*Kronprinz Rudolf*, Austro-Hungarian pre-dreadnought battleship, 313
*Kronprinz*, German dreadnought, 89, 122, 233, 297, 298, 299, 300
*Kronprinz Wilhelm*, German auxiliary cruiser, 89
Kronstadt, 59, 190, 280, 285, 291, 304, 321
Krosigk, Günther von, German admiral, 345, 346
Krupp, German armaments manufacturer, 10, 27, 35
Kuhnt, Bernhard, German sailor, 346

Kuiwast Roads, 193
Kukat, Heinrich, German officer, 339
Kum Kale, 178
*Kurama*, Japanese armored cruiser, 84
Kure, 60
*Kurfürst Friedrich Wilhelm*, German pre-dreadnought battleship, 24

La Spezia, 32, 59
Lambert, Nicholas, historian, 51
*Landrail*, British destroyer, 264
Lans, Wilhelm von, German admiral, 127
Lansing, Robert, US secretary of state, 153, 154, 156, 163, 247
Lapeyrère, Augustin Boué de, French admiral, 58, 97, 105, 106, 128, 129, 130, 131, 144, 166
  pictured, 100
Lapvik, 191, 302
Latsis, Martin, Latvian Bolshevik leader, 304
Latvia, 148, 194, 198, 319
Lauenstein, Otto von, German general, 193
Laurence, Noel, British officer, 197, 233
Le Havre, 53
League of Nations, 359, 364
*Leipzig*, German light cruiser, 65, 66, 68, 73, 75, 76, 78, 79, 81, 82
Lemnos, 129, 174, 176, 184, 238
Lenin, Vladimir Ilych Ulianov, Bolshevik leader and Russian premier, 279, 282, 283, 290, 298, 304, 305, 306, 307, 310, 318, 319, 320, 321, 326, 328
*Léon Gambetta*, French armored cruiser, 131, 144
*Leonardo da Vinci*, Italian dreadnought, 235
Lesser Antilles, 87
*Leviathan* (ex-*Vaterland*), American troopship, 261
*Lexington*, American battle cruiser project, 252
Libau (Liepaja), 59, 147, 190, 191, 193, 194, 195, 196, 197, 198, 199, 292, 293, 294, 322
Libya, 22, 59

Liebknecht, Karl, German socialist leader, 347, 348
Liechtenstein, Prince Johannes von und zu, Austro-Hungarian officer, 266, 267, 314
Liman von Sanders, Otto, German general, 178
*Limnos* (ex-*Idaho*), Greek pre-dreadnought battleship, 25
*Lion*, British battle cruiser, 117, 124, 125, 126, 204, 217, 218, 219, 221
Lisbon, 235
Lissa, Battle of (1866), 38, 145
Lithuania, 189, 193, 198, 319
Liverpool, 148, 153, 207, 261
Lloyd George, David, British prime minister, 52, 246, 255, 256, 260, 270, 329, 359, 364
Loch Ewe, 57, 116, 118
Lodge, Henry Cabot, US senator, 159
London, Declaration of (1909), 51, 137, 141, 159, 246
London, Treaty of (1915), 131, 133
London financial market, 52
London Naval Treaty (1930), 365, 369
Long Island, 272
*Lord Nelson*, British pre-dreadnought battleship, 18, 41, 270, 327
*Lord Raglan*, British monitor, 325
Lorenz AG, German wireless telegraphy company, 34
Lough Swilly, 118
Lowestoft, 209, 211
Luckner, Count Felix von, German officer, 89
Lüdecke, Fritz, German officer, 88
Ludendorff, Erich, German general, 193, 199, 201, 231, 233, 241, 242, 288, 290, 319, 322, 325, 326, 335, 336, 337, 348
Lüderitz Bay, 86
Lukin, V. K., Russian admiral, 284
*Lusitania*, British passenger liner, 44, 148–154, 156, 158, 161, 162, 168, 233, 249, 265, 275
*Lützow*, German battle cruiser, 21, 122, 210, 217, 218, 219, 221, 222, 223, 224, 225, 226, 239

*M 28*, British monitor, 325
Maas, Leberecht, German admiral, 117
Macedonia, 148, 166, 238, 318
*Macedonia*, British armed merchant cruiser, 79, 82
Madang, 84
Madras, 87
*Magdeburg*, German light cruiser, 121, 123, 190
Mahan, Alfred Thayer, American officer and naval writer, 10, 11, 21, 28, 44, 97, 252, 368
*Mainz*, German light cruiser, 117
Maizuru, 60
*Majestic*, British pre-dreadnought battleship, 181
Maksimov, Andrei, Russian admiral, 281, 283
Malaya, 87
*Malaya*, British dreadnought, 219
Malta, 53, 54, 95, 98, 103, 106, 129, 130, 244, 265, 268
Manila, and Manila Bay, 60, 64 Battle of (1898), 39
Mann-Tiechler, Ritter von, German admiral, 336
*Marco Polo*, Italian armored cruiser, 59
Marconi, Guglielmo, inventor, 30–34 pictured, 33
Marconi International Marine Communication Company, 32
Marianas, 62, 64, 67, 68, 69, 72, 73, 84, 85
*Markgraf*, German dreadnought, 222, 226, 229, 357
*Marlborough*, British dreadnought, 221
Marmara, Sea of, 111, 173, 178, 182, 184, 186
Marne, First Battle of the (1914), 119, 130
Marne, Second Battle of the (1918), 276, 329
Marquesas Islands, 72, 73, 74
Marseilles, 265
*Marshal Ney*, British monitor, 119
*Marshal Soult*, British monitor, 119
Marshalls, the, 68, 69, 84, 85
Matapan, Cape, 102, 103
Matheson, C. G., British officer, 265

Matsumura, Tatsuro, Japanese admiral, 84
*Mauretania*, British passenger liner, 44
Maurras, Charles, French politician, 364
Mauve, Franz von, German admiral, 288
Max of Baden, Prince, German chancellor, 145, 194, 272, 287, 337, 338, 342, 343, 345, 347, 348
Mayo, Henry T., American admiral, 252
*Mecidiye*, Turkish light cruiser, 111
Mediterranean Sea, 48, 49, 53, 54, 55, 59, 325
  submarine warfare in, 143, 146, 168, 248, 276
Mehmed V
  Ottoman sultan, 108
Memel, 193
Menshevik party, 282
*Merkury*, Russian transport, 235
Messina, 55, 96, 97, 98, 99, 100, 101, 102, 104
*Mesudiye*, Turkish ironclad, 111
Metalanim (Nan Matol), 66
Meurer, Hugo, German admiral, 322, 323, 332
Mexico, 65, 66, 68, 85, 249
Meyer-Waldeck, Alfred, German officer, 67
Michael, grand duke of Russia, 281
Micronesia, 64, 84, 85
*Midilli* (ex-*Breslau*), Turkish light cruiser, 105, 106, 107, 108, 110, 111, 112, 178, 186, 187, 235, 236, 284, 325
*Mikasa*, Japanese pre-dreadnought battleship, 41
Milford Haven, 259
Milne, Sir Berkeley, British admiral, 57, 97, 98, 99, 101, 102, 103, 104, 106, 113
Milosević, Alexander, Austro-Hungarian officer, 340
mines and minefields, 26, 109, 110, 111, 114, 116, 119, 120, 131, 135, 147, 167, 168, 173, 175, 176, 178, 184, 186, 190, 194, 196, 197, 202, 207, 225, 245, 265, 268, 269, 270, 292, 294, 296, 299, 316, 325
*Minotaur*, British armored cruiser, 64, 72
*Mississippi*, American dreadnought, 269

*Moltke*, German battle cruiser, 19, 96, 126, 195, 197, 202, 218, 229, 233, 293, 296, 299, 332, 333
Moltke, Helmut von, the Younger, German general, 48
*Monarch*, Austro-Hungarian pre-dreadnought battleship, 58, 129
*Monmouth*, British armored cruiser, 64, 75
Monro, Sir Charles, British general, 182, 184
Montecuccoli, Count Rudolf, Austro-Hungarian admiral, 24, 55
Montenegro, 129, 131
Moon Sound, viii, 193, 195, 196, 291, 292, 294, 296, 298
  Battle of (1917), 299–302
Moraht, Robert, German officer, 249
Morgan, J. P., American financial services firm, 162
Morocco, 22
  and Moroccan crisis (1905), 16, 50
*Möwe*, German auxiliary cruiser, 89
Mücke, Hellmuth von, German officer, 87
Mudros, 174, 176, 178, 325, 328
Müller, Karl von, German officer, 69, 87
*München*, German light cruiser, 194
Mussolini, Benito, Italian prime minister, 365

Nagasaki, 64
Namibia (German Southwest Africa), 34, 86
Napier, T. W. D., British admiral, 271, 289
Naples, 99
Napoleonic Wars, 50, 79, 201
Narva, 321
*Narval*, French submarine, 46, 47
Nasmith, Martin, British officer, 182
*Nassau*, German dreadnought, 15, 18, 21, 197, 354
*Natal*, British cruiser, 226
Nauen, 354
Naval Defence Act (1889), 13
Naval War College, US, 253
Nebolsin, Arkadii, Russian admiral, 281
*Nelson*, British battleship, 363

Nemits, Aleksandr, Russian admiral, 284, 303, 306, 315, 320, 321, 326
Nepenin, Adrian, Russian admiral, 280, 281
*Neptune*, British dreadnought, 143
Netherlands, 51, 138, 140, 160, 234, 246, 251, 330, 348, 362
Neumünster, 147, 230, 332
Neva River, 304, 305, 306
*New Mexico*, American dreadnought, 269
New York, 148, 149, 153, 155, 161, 258, 261
*New York*, American dreadnought, 28
New Zealand, 19, 57, 67, 72, 83, 84, 87, 125, 174, 178, 184, 210, 261
*New Zealand*, British battle cruiser, 20, 57, 215, 217, 218, 223, 227
Newcastle, 231
Newfoundland, 32
Newport News, 89, 90, 169, 261
Nicholas II, tsar of Russia, 189, 192, 195, 250, 279, 280, 281, 283, 285
*Nicosian*, British freighter, 163
Niemöller, Martin, German officer, 145, 241, 242, 265, 268, 272, 338, 339, 340
*Nikolai I*, Russian seaplane tender, 189
Nikolaiev, 26, 109, 237, 325, 326
Nine-Power Treaty (1922), 362
Njegovan, Maximilian, Austro-Hungarian admiral, 244, 286, 289, 290, 307, 308, 311, 312, 314
*Nomad*, British destroyer, 219
Norfolk (UK), 120
Norfolk, Virginia, 60
*Normandie*, French dreadnought, 25
North German Lloyd, 44, 66, 68, 89
North Rona Island, 162
North Sea, 16, 22, 45, 48, 51, 52, 53, 57, 58, 85, 92, 93, 94, 95, 112, 113, 114, 116, 119, 121, 122, 123, 127, 128, 139, 140, 147, 164, 172, 174, 178, 181, 199, 206, 207, 208, 210, 212, 214, 216, 227, 230, 231, 251, 252, 270, 287, 310, 330, 332, 335, 348, 349, 367
  Northern Barrage laid across, 168, 269

Norway, 53, 113, 140, 164, 168, 217, 232, 269, 330, 332, 339
Noske, Gustav, German socialist leader, 345, 346
Nostitz und Jänckendorff, Heinrich von, German officer, 272
*Nottingham*, British light cruiser, 230, 231
*Novara*, Austro-Hungarian light cruiser, 144, 266, 311, 314
Novorossiysk, 107, 326
*Nürnberg*, German light cruiser, 65, 66, 67, 69, 72, 73, 75, 76, 79, 81, 82

Obry, Ludwig, Austro-Hungarian officer and inventor, 40
*Ocean*, British pre-dreadnought battleship, 176
Odenholm, 190
Odessa, 107, 111, 188, 192, 235, 324, 326
Offer, Avner, historian, 138
*Oldenburg*, German pre-dreadnought battleship, 10
*Oleg*, Russian cruiser, 324
Oran, 98, 146
Orkney Islands, 53, 113, 116, 269, 349
Ösel (Saaremaa), 192, 195, 196, 198, 199, 201, 291, 292, 294, 296, 297, 298, 299, 302
Ostend, 142, 202, 269, 310, 336
  raid on (1918), 331, 332
*Ostfriesland*, German dreadnought, 224
*Otranto*, British armed merchant cruiser, 75, 76, 79
Otranto, Straits of, 128, 131, 144, 269
  Allied barrage across, 164, 165, 167, 168, 266, 268, 269, 317
Otranto Straits, Battle of the (1917), 266–268, 311, 316
Ottoman army, 104, 109, 110, 174, 178, 179, 193, 235
Ottoman Empire, 2, 24, 60, 94, 100, 104, 106, 108, 171, 172, 250, 328
  and prewar naval race with Greece, 24–25
  alliance of, with Germany, 100, 101
  declares war on Triple Entente, 107
  signs armistice with Allies, 328

Ottoman navy, 24, 95, 104, 106, 107, 109, 111, 184, 189, 279, 303
  prewar British advisors of, 101, 106

Pachner, Paul, Austro-Hungarian officer, 129
Pacific Ocean, operations in, 10, 34, 58, 60, 62, 63, 64, 65, 67, 68, 69, 70, 74, 75, 79, 82, 83, 85, 86, 88, 90
Pacific Ocean, postwar balance in, 361, 365
Pagan, 62, 67, 68
Palestine, 94
*Pallada*, Russian armored cruiser, 190
Pamerort (Pammana), 296
*Pamiat Merkuria*, Russian cruiser, 186, 187, 189
Panama and Panama Canal, 75, 79, 85, 87, 361
Papeete, 71
*Pargust*, British Q-ship, 265
Parsons, turbine engine manufacturer, 35
*Pathfinder*, British light cruiser, 118
Pearl Harbor, 60
*Pegasus*, British cruiser, 87
Penang, 87
*Pennsylvania*, American dreadnought, 28, 270
*Penshurst*, British Q-ship, 265
Pentland Firth, 143
Pernau (Pärnu), 196
Pershing, John J., American general, 252, 257
*Persia*, British passenger liner, 156
Peter the Great, tsar of Russia, 303
Petragge, 199
Petrograd. *See* St. Petersburg; Petrograd Soviet
Petrograd Soviet, 55
  Military Revolutionary Committee (MRC) of, 58
*Petropavlovsk*, Russian dreadnought, 195, 285, 324
*Peyk*, Turkish gunboat, 110
Philippeville (Skikda), 97, 98
Philippines, 60, 85, 86
Picton Island, 78
Piraeus, 238, 239

Pochhammer, Hans, German officer, 62, 64, 66, 69, 72, 73, 76, 77, 78, 80, 81
Pohl, Hugo von, German admiral, 101, 127, 128, 136, 137, 139, 140, 141, 157, 195, 205, 278
Pola (Pula), 47, 58, 96, 99, 102, 128, 130, 131, 132, 143, 144, 145, 148, 165, 241, 243, 244, 246, 265, 279, 286, 289, 310, 311, 312, 314, 316, 317, 318, 338, 339, 340, 341, 349
Poland, 189, 192, 193, 195, 198, 309, 358
Pollen, Arthur Hungerford, British inventor, 35–37, 40, 43
*Pommern*, German pre-dreadnought battleship, 223, 224, 225
Ponape (Pohnpei), 65, 66, 68, 69, 72, 84
Port Arthur, 86
  siege of (1904–5), 26
Port Stanley, 74, 75, 79, 82
Portland, 113, 120
Portsmouth, 46
Portugal, 362
*Posen*, German dreadnought, 197, 223, 322, 323
Potenza River, 132
Premuda Island, 317
*President Lincoln*, American troopship, 258
Prica, Dragutin, Austro-Hungarian and Yugoslav admiral, 341
*Prince Charles*, British Q-ship, 162
*Princess Royal*, British battle cruiser, 79, 125, 127, 223
*Principe Umberto*, Italian troopship, 167
Pringle, Joel R. P., American officer, 259
*Prinz Adalbert*, German armored cruiser, 194, 199
*Prinz Eitel Friedrich*, German auxiliary cruiser, 66, 68, 69, 74, 76, 89, 90, 169
*Prinz Eugen*, Austro-Hungarian dreadnought, 311, 317, 340
*Prinz Heinrich*, German armored cruiser, 194, 196
*Prinzregent Luitpold*, German dreadnought, 288, 293

*Pripyat*, Russian minelayer, 296
*Privet*, British Q-ship, 265
*Provence*, French auxiliary cruiser, 238
*Provence*, French dreadnought, 238
Punta Arenas, 88

Q-ships, antisubmarine, 162, 163, 164, 259, 265, 269, 274
*Queen Elizabeth*, British dreadnought, 21, 122, 174, 176, 181, 211, 216, 217, 218, 219, 220, 271, 327
*Queen Mary*, British battle cruiser, 204, 218, 219, 225, 226
Queenstown (Cobh), 57, 254, 257, 258, 259

Rabaul, 84
*Radetzky*, Austro-Hungarian pre-dreadnought battleship, 23, 102, 129, 316
Raisp von Caliga, Erwin, Austro-Hungarian admiral, 102
Ramsgate, 269
Rasch, Franz, Austro-Hungarian sailor, 313, 314, 315
Rasputin, Grigori, 279
Razvozov, Aleksandr, Russian admiral, 283, 298, 306, 315, 320, 321
Rebeur-Paschwitz, Hubert von, German admiral, 289, 303, 325, 326, 328, 350
Red Army, Soviet Russian, 307, 319, 320, 321, 324, 350
Red Navy, Soviet Russian, 307, 319, 320, 321, 322, 323
*Redoubtable* (ex-*Revenge*), British pre-dreadnought battleship, 119
*Regele Carol I*, Russian auxiliary cruiser, 285
*Regina Elena*, Italian pre-dreadnought battleship, 59
*Regina Margherita*, Italian pre-dreadnought battleship, 235
Reichpietsch, Max, German sailor, 287, 288, 292, 308, 315, 335
Remy, Walter, German officer, 258
*Repulse*, British battle cruiser, 271
*Reşadiye*, Ottoman dreadnought, 24, 25, 104

*Respublika* (ex-*Imperator Pavel*), Russian pre-dreadnought battleship, 283
Reuter, Ludwig von, German admiral, viii, 294, 335, 349, 356, 357
pictured, 355
Reval (Tallinn), 59, 285, 298, 321, 322
*Rheinland*, German dreadnought, 323, 333, 354
Riga, 172, 190, 192, 303
and German attack of 1915, 193, 194, 195, 196, 197, 198, 199, 202, 233, 237, 298
and German attack of 1917, 279, 290, 291, 294, 297, 299, 304, 307, 322
Rimini, 132
*Rio de Janeiro*, Brazilian dreadnought project, 24
Rizzo, Luigi, Italian officer, 317, 318
*Rodney*, British battleship, 363
*Roland Morillot* (ex-*UB 26*), French submarine, 165
Romania, 104, 199, 233, 237, 358
*Roon*, German armored cruiser, 194, 196
Roosevelt, Theodore, US president, 151, 159
*Rostislav*, Russian pre-dreadnought battleship, 109, 186, 237
*Rostock*, German light cruiser, 224
Rosyth, 53, 113, 116, 118, 121, 124, 125, 207, 208, 215, 217, 229, 330, 332, 348
Rotterdam, 51, 160
Rouyer, Albert, French admiral, 58
Royal Air Force (RAF), British, 331
*Royal Edward*, British troopship, 146
Royal Naval College, UK, 254
*Royal Sovereign*, British dreadnought, 21, 122, 211
*Royal Sovereign*, British pre-dreadnought battleship, 10, 17
Rozhestvensky, Zinovy, Russian admiral, 40, 41
Rufiji River, 87
*Rumija*, Montenegrin royal yacht, 129, 131
*Rurik*, Russian armored cruiser, 194

Russia. *See also* Franco-Russian alliance
  Revolution of 1905 in, 280
  prewar relations of, with Britain, 13, 15, 26
  prewar trade of, with Germany, 138, 160
  declares war on Ottoman Empire, 108
  March Revolution (1917) in, 250, 279, 280, 304
  Provisional Government of, 280, 281, 282, 283, 284, 285, 290, 304, 305
  July Days (1917) in, 283, 285
  and First All-Russian Congress of Soviets, 283
  Bolshevik Revolution in, 303–306, 310, 320
  and Second All-Russian Congress of Soviets, 304, 306
  Soviet government established in, 306
  and peace settlement with Germany, 306, 307, 318, 319
Russian army, 195, 235, 237, 279, 280, 283, 297, 303
  Twelfth Army of, 290, 291
  replaced by Red Army, 307
Russian Civil War (1918–21), 320, 324, 352
Russian navy
  defeated by Japanese (1904–5), 16, 26, 33, 40–41, 59
  prewar strength of, 13
  Baltic Fleet of, 11, 26, 40, 59, 189, 190, 194, 195, 202, 279, 280, 281, 282, 283, 285, 291, 296, 298, 299, 303, 304, 306, 310, 320, 321, 323, 324
  Black Sea Fleet of, 26, 59, 108, 109, 112, 173, 177, 235, 237, 279, 280, 283, 284, 303, 306, 310, 320, 324, 325, 326, 327
  Siberian Flotilla of, 59
  and aviation, 48
  capital ship losses of, 350
  submarines of, 275
  mutinies of 1917 in, 281, 284
  impact of Soviet Order Number One in, 281, 284, 291, 304
  replaced by Red Navy, 307

Russo-Japanese War (1904–5), 16, 26, 33, 40–41, 42, 43, 49, 59

*S 116*, German destroyer, 118
Sablin, Mikhail, Russian admiral, 326
Sachse, Willi, German sailor, 288
*Sachsen*, German pre-dreadnought battleship, 15
Saipan, 64, 84
*Salamis*, Greek dreadnought project, 24, 25
Salonika (Thessaloniki), 166, 167, 184, 238, 244
Samoa, 63, 64, 70, 83, 84
*San Diego*, American armored cruiser, 272
San Francisco, 60, 64
*San Martino*, Italian armored cruiser, 32
Sandy Hook, 272
*Sankt Georg*, Austro-Hungarian armored cruiser, 312, 313, 314, 315
*Santee*, American Q-ship, 259
Santiago, Battle of (1898), 39
*Saphir*, French submarine, 178
Sardinia, 97, 249
Sari Bair, 182
Sasebo, 60
*Satsuma*, Japanese pre-dreadnought battleship, 27, 59, 84
Scapa Flow, 53, 57, 113, 114, 116, 118, 125, 129, 143, 207, 208, 211, 215, 216, 225, 226, 229, 241, 257, 294, 330, 333
  internment of German fleet at, 349, 354, 355–357
Scarborough, 120, 211
*Scharnhorst*, German armored cruiser, 58, 63, 64, 65, 66, 67, 69, 70, 73, 75, 76, 79, 80, 81, 82, 126
  pictured, 77
Scheer, Reinhard, German admiral
  as squadron commander, 114, 116, 117, 191, 192
  assesses Russian behavior, 189
  as fleet commander, 128, 157, 204, 205, 208, 209, 210, 211, 212, 213, 227, 228, 229, 230, 231, 232, 233, 234, 239, 278, 292, 293, 332, 333, 335

at Jutland, 205, 213, 214, 215, 217, 219, 221, 222, 223, 225, 226, 228
strategic vision of, 114, 115, 205, 206, 207, 208, 209, 210, 212, 213, 228, 229
supports unrestricted submarine warfare, 228, 242, 243, 335
and mutinies of 1917, 288, 289, 308, 335
and mutinies of 1918, 343, 346
heads Naval High Command, 335, 336, 337, 341
and Armistice negotiations, 338, 342, 356
recalls all submarines, 338
orders final sortie, 343
and abdication of William II, 348
pictured, 206
Scheidemann, Philipp, German socialist leader, 348
Schleswig-Holstein, 50, 333
*Schleswig-Holstein*, German pre-dreadnought battleship, 223
Schlieffen Plan, 48, 51, 55, 119
Schlosser, Friedrich, Austro-Hungarian officer, 167
Schmidt, Erhard, German admiral, 190, 191, 195, 196, 197, 198, 292, 293, 294, 299, 302
Schneider, Heinrich, German officer, 74, 78
Schumann, Walter, German officer, 357
Schwieger, Walther, German officer, 148, 233, 265, 275
Scilly Isles, 259
*Scourge*, British gunboat, 32
Sebenico, 286
*Seeadler*, German auxiliary cruiser, 89
Senigallia, 132
Serbia, 56, 66, 96, 99, 104, 112, 113, 166, 183, 238, 309, 340, 349
Serbian army, 167, 238
Sešan, Antun, Austro-Hungarian officer, 313, 314
*Settsu*, Japanese dreadnought, 27
Sevastopol, 59, 107, 109, 110, 187, 236, 237, 284, 303, 325, 326, 327, 350

*Seydlitz*, German battle cruiser, 124, 125, 126, 195, 210, 213, 219, 222, 223, 224
pictured, 224
Shanghai, 59, 66
Shantung (Shandong), 86
Shchastny, Aleksei, Russian officer, 321, 323
Sheerness, 52, 211, 212, 226, 230
Shetland Islands, 53
Sicily, 55, 97, 98, 102, 155
*Siegfried*, German pre-dreadnought battleship, 10, 14, 15, 57, 194
Siemens, German firm, 33, 38
Sims, William S., American admiral, 253, 254, 255, 256, 257, 259, 260
Singapore, 68
Sino-Japanese War (1894–95), 38
Sinope, 284
Sixtus, prince of Bourbon-Parma, and "Sixtus Affair," 244, 316
Šižgorić, Jerko, Austro-Hungarian sailor, 315
Skagerrak, 213, 222, 232, 339. *See* Jutland, Battle of
Slaby, Adolf, German wireless pioneer, 32, 33
Sladkov, Ivan, Russian petty officer, 305
*Slava*, Russian pre-dreadnought battleship, 195, 196, 197, 199, 291, 298, 299, 300, 301
pictured, 301
Slovenia, and Slovenes, 286, 315, 340
Sochi, 187
Social Democratic Party (SPD), German, 14, 29, 287, 288, 337, 344, 345, 346, 348
Socialist Revolutionary (SR) Party, Russian, 282, 306
Society Islands, 89
Souchon, Wilhelm, German and Turkish admiral
as commander of Mediterranean Division, 55, 96
and flight of *Goeben*, 96, 97, 104
enters Turkish service, 95, 105, 106
in Black Sea action, 107, 108, 109, 110, 111, 112, 173, 177, 178, 186, 187, 188, 189, 235, 236, 237, 284

Souchon, Wilhelm, German and Turkish admiral (cont.)
 recalled to Germany, 289, 303
 in Riga operation (1917), 293
 serves as Baltic station chief, 344, 345
 pictured, 236
South Africa, 261
*South Carolina*, American dreadnought, 27
*South Dakota*, American dreadnought project, 252
*Southampton*, British cruiser, 223
Spain, 25, 34, 159, 354
Spanish-American War (1898), 39
Spee, Count Maximilian von, German admiral, 62–67, 68–81, 82–87, 90–92, 94, 96, 121, 122, 123, 139, 159
 pictured, 65
Spee, Heinrich von, German officer, 69, 73
Spee, Otto von, German officer, 69
Spithead, 112
Spring-Rice, Sir Cecil, British diplomat, 151, 159
St. Nazaire, 261
 shipyard of, 25
St. Petersburg (Petrograd), 26, 48, 59, 189, 192, 199, 253, 280, 281, 283, 285, 291, 298, 303, 304, 306, 321
Stalin, Joseph, Bolshevik leader and Russian premier, 320
Stavanger, 332
Steinbrinck, Otto, German officer, 248
Stockholm
 socialist peace conference at, 288
*Stonecrop*, British Q-ship, 265
*Strassburg*, German light cruiser, 298, 302
Strasser, Peter, German officer, 213
Sturdee, Sir Doveton, British admiral, 79, 80, 82, 85
submarine warfare, unrestricted
 British prewar speculation about, 47
 German planning for (1914–15), 137
 German decision to begin (1915), 90, 139–141
 initial phase of (1915), 155, 160, 163, 165, 234, 242, 263
 Austro-Hungarian participation in, 143, 243, 338
 German plans to resume (1916–17), 157, 228, 231, 233, 234, 243, 277
 resumption of (1917), 156, 168, 234, 242, 244, 246, 247, 276, 284, 309
 second phase of (1917–18), 164, 241, 246, 254, 260, 262, 263, 266, 268, 273, 275, 310, 336
 end of (1918), 338, 339, 342
 postwar impact of, 362
 overall effect of, 367, 368
submarines
 introduction of, 17
 pioneered by French navy, 46
Suermene Bay, 235
Suez Canal, 87, 105, 174
Suffolk, 210
*Suffren*, French pre-dreadnought battleship, 176, 235
*Sultan Osman-i Evvel* (ex-*Rio de Janeiro*), Ottoman dreadnought, 24, 104
Sumatra, 87
Sumida, Jon, historian, 43
Sunderland, 213, 229, 230
*Superb*, British dreadnought, 327, 350
*Sussex*, French passenger ferry, 157, 248, 249
Suvla Bay, 179, 182, 184
*Sverige*, Swedish pre-dreadnought battleship, 322
*Svobodnaya Rossiya* (ex-*Imperatritsa Ekaterina Velikaya*), Russian dreadnought, 284, 303, 326
Swakopmund, 86
Sweden, 159, 288, 290, 330, 354
Swedish navy, 322
*Sydney*, Australian cruiser, 87
Sylt, 147, 270
*Szent István*, Austro-Hungarian dreadnought, viii, 317, 318
 pictured, 317

Tagga Bay (Tagalaht), 292, 293, 294, 295, 296, 297
Tahiti, 71, 72, 87
*Takachiyo*, Japanese cruiser, 68

Tamin, Yamaya, Japanese admiral, 59, 84
Tanzania (German East Africa), 34, 68, 86
Taranto, 59, 131, 132, 165, 168, 235, 317
Tarnów-Gorlice, Battle of (1915), 191, 193
*Tegetthoff*, Austro-Hungarian dreadnought, vii, 24, 317, 350
  pictured, 23
Tegetthoff, Wilhelm von, Austrian admiral, 145
Telefunken, German wireless telegraph company, 33, 34
telegraph cables, undersea, 34, 72, 87
telegraph, wireless. *See* wireless telegraphy
*Temeraire*, British dreadnought, 327
Terschelling, 206, 208, 210, 211
Texel Island, Battle of (1914), 118, 119, 121
Thames River, 119, 211, 341
Thiele, Georg, German officer, 119, 121
Thierry, Franz von, Austro-Hungarian officer, 130
*Thüringen*, German dreadnought, 344, 345
Thursby, Cecil, British admiral, 165, 167
*Ticonderoga*, American freighter, 272
Tientsin (Tianjin), 67
*Tiger*, British battle cruiser, 20, 124, 125, 126, 218, 223
*Tipperary*, British flotilla leader, 223
Tirpitz, Alfred von, German admiral
  early career of, 8, 9, 11
  and First Navy Law, 12, 13, 17
  and Second Navy Law, 14, 17
  and supplementary law of 1906, 14, 16
  and supplementary law of 1908, 19
  and supplementary law of 1912, 21
  "risk theory" of, 11, 114
  and prewar deployment of fleet, 52
  discourages preparation for blockade, 138
  and flight of *Goeben*, 101
  initial doubts of, regarding U-boats, 136
  advocates unrestricted submarine warfare, 136, 137, 139, 141, 154, 156, 245
  concerned about morale of fleet, 278
  criticizes fellow admirals, 122, 127
  loses influence, 154
  retirement of, 157
  pictured, 12
Togo, German colony, 34, 86
Togo, Heihachiro, Japanese admiral, 40, 41
Tondern, 147, 212, 333
*Torgud Reis* (ex-*Weißenburg*), Turkish pre-dreadnought battleship, 24, 108, 325
*Torpedoboot 11*, Austro-Hungarian torpedo boat, 286, 307
torpedoes
  range of, 40, 42
Toulon, 46, 48, 54, 58, 97, 99, 249
Trafalgar, Battle of (1805), 204, 227, 349, 364
Trans-Siberian Railway, 63
Trapp, Georg von, Austro-Hungarian officer, 131, 144, 275
Trebizond (Trabzon), 109, 110, 111, 177, 235
Trieste, 56, 96, 128, 289, 318, 338, 349
Triple Alliance, 22, 48, 54
Triple Alliance naval convention (1900), 22, 48, 49
Triple Alliance naval convention (1913), 54–56, 96, 97, 128
Triple Entente, 13, 26, 53, 54, 108, 192, 250
*Triumph*, British pre-dreadnought battleship, 67, 181
Trotsky, Russian commissar for foreign affairs and war, 319, 320, 321
Troubridge, Ernest, British admiral, 97, 98, 102, 103, 106
Truk, 64, 84
Trummler, Konrad, German admiral, 96
*Tsesarevich*, Russian pre-dreadnought battleship, 40
Tsingtao (Qingdao), 62, 63, 64, 65, 66, 67, 68, 72, 82, 86, 89, 289
*Tsukuba*, Japanese armored cruiser, 27
Tsushima, Battle of (1905), 26, 40, 41

Turkey, Republic of, 350
*Turquoise*, French submarine, 182
Tyrwhitt, Reginald, British officer, 116, 117, 208, 210, 211, 230

*U 1*, German submarine, 47
*U 4*, Austro-Hungarian submarine, 165
*U 5*, Austro-Hungarian submarine, 131, 144, 167
*U 6*, Austro-Hungarian submarine, 167, 266
*U 8*, German submarine, 165
*U 9*, German submarine, 118, 130, 136, 142
*U 10* (ex-*UB 1*), Austro-Hungarian submarine, 145
*U 11* (ex-*UB 15*), Austro-Hungarian submarine, 145, 146
*U 12*, Austro-Hungarian submarine, 130
*U 14* (ex-*Curie*), Austro-Hungarian submarine, 145, 358
*U 17*, German submarine, 137
*U 20*, German submarine, 148, 149, 232, 233, 265
*U 21*, German submarine, 118, 144, 145, 181, 248
*U 24*, German submarine, 120, 153, 163
*U 26*, German submarine, 190, 194
*U 27*, German submarine, 163
*U 28*, German submarine, 150
*U 29*, German submarine, 142, 143
*U 30*, German submarine, 150, 232, 233, 266
*U 31*, Austro-Hungarian submarine, 318
*U 32*, German submarine, 264
*U 34*, German submarine, 265
*U 35*, German submarine, 238, 248
*U 36*, German submarine, 162, 163
*U 38*, German submarine, 146, 155, 156
*U 39*, German submarine, 248
*U 41*, German submarine, 163
*U 48*, German submarine, 269
*U 52*, German submarine, 230, 235
*U 53*, German submarine, 259
  pictured, 144
*U 58*, German submarine, 259
*U 63*, German submarine, 230
*U 64*, German submarine, 249
*U 66*, German submarine, 230

*U 68*, German submarine, 164
*U 73*, German submarine, 234
*U 75*, German submarine, 225
*U 85*, German submarine, 265
*U 88*, German submarine, 265
*U 90*, German submarine, 258
*U 93*, German submarine, 245
*U 116*, German submarine, 241
*U 151*, German submarine, 244, 272
*U 152*, German submarine, 272
*U 153*, German submarine, 272
*U 156*, German submarine, 272
*U 157*, German submarine, 244, 272
*UB 1*, German submarine, 145, 146
*UB 3*, German submarine, 144, 145
*UB 7*, German submarine, 143, 144, 187
*UB 8*, German submarine, 143, 144, 145, 187
*UB 14*, German submarine, 146, 165, 187
*UB 15*, German submarine, 145, 146, 147
*UB 19*, German submarine, 265
*UB 26*, German submarine, 165
*UB 29*, German submarine, 157, 264
*UB 37*, German submarine, 265
*UB 42*, German submarine, 327
*UB 47*, German submarine, 235
*UB 52*, German submarine, 339
*UC 13*, German submarine, 187
*UC 15*, German submarine, 235
*UC 25*, German submarine, 266, 267
*UC 29*, German submarine, 265
*UC 57*, German submarine, 322
*UC 58*, German submarine, 292, 294
*UC 65*, German submarine, 248
*UC 67*, German submarine, 265, 268, 338
Ukraine, 303, 319, 320, 324, 325
*Undaunted*, British light cruiser, 118
United States
  dreadnought program of, 25, 26, 27–28
  sells pre-dreadnoughts to Greece, 25
  and wireless telegraphy, 34
  public opinion in, 137, 151, 158, 249
  opposes unrestricted submarine warfare, 140
  merchant marine of, 158

trade of, with Germany, 160, 161, 245
wartime relations of, with Britain, 160
wartime relations of, with Japan, 86
supplies Allies, 161
loans money to Allies, 161
declares war on Germany, 242, 250
joins Allies as "associated power," 250
declares war on Austria-Hungary, 250
Emergency Fleet Corporation of, 260
manpower of, in Europe (1918), 242, 276, 277

United States Army
American Expeditionary Force (AEF) of, 252, 261, 262, 276, 277

United States Navy
in Spanish-American War (1898), 39
and introduction of dreadnought design, 41
prewar strength of, 60
aircraft of, 47
submarines of, 259
expansion of (1916), 251, 258
Atlantic Fleet of, 60, 252
Pacific Fleet of, 60
Asiatic Fleet of, 60
contributes dreadnoughts to Grand Fleet, 257, 333, 348
deploys ships to Mediterranean, 268
destroyers of, and antisubmarine warfare, 257
and Washington Naval Treaty (1922), 363, 365

*Urbino*, British merchantman, 163

Valentiner, Max, German officer, 145, 146, 155, 156, 272, 275, 345, 346, 347
Valona (Vlorë), 166, 235, 266
Valparaiso, 73, 74, 76, 77, 78, 81
*Vanguard*, British dreadnought, 226
Varna, 108, 188, 237
Venice, 56, 59, 66, 96, 132, 146, 165, 286, 350
Venizelos, Eleftherios, Greek prime minister, 184, 238
Verder (Virtsu), 298
Verderevsky, Dmitri, Russian admiral, 305

Versailles, Treaty of (1919), 85, 352, 353, 358, 359, 364
Viazemsky, Sergei, Russian officer, 195, 196, 197, 199
Vickers, British shipbuilder, 24, 27, 46
*Vindex*, British seaplane carrier, 212
*Vindictive*, British light cruiser, 79, 331
*Vineta*, German cruiser, 96
*Viper*, British destroyer, 45
Viren, Robert Nikolaevich, Russian admiral, 280
*Viribus Unitis*, Austro-Hungarian dreadnought, 24, 317, 341, 349
Vitgeft, V. K., Russian admiral, 40
*Vittoria*, British Q-ship, 162
Vladivostok, 41, 59, 66, 87
*Volya* (ex-*Imperator Aleksandr III*), Russian dreadnought, 303, 326, 327, 328, 350
*Von der Tann*, German battle cruiser, 19, 124, 195, 196, 218, 219, 222, 229
Vuković, Janko, Austro-Hungarian and Yugoslav officer, 341, 349
Vulcan, German shipbuilder, 24, 25

*Wakamiya*, Japanese seaplane tender, 67
Wangenheim, Baron Hans von, German diplomat, 100, 104
Wardlaw, Mark, British officer, 162, 163
*Warrior*, British armored cruiser, 220, 221, 225
*Warspite*, British dreadnought, 219
Washington Naval Treaty (1922), 45, 352, 363, 364, 366
Weddigen, Otto, German officer, 118, 136, 142, 143
Wegener, Bernard, German officer, 163
*Weißenburg*, German pre-dreadnought battleship, 24
Wellington, New Zealand, 87
Wemyss, Sir Rosslyn, British admiral, 330, 348, 358
Wenden (Cēsis), 291
Weniger, Karl, German officer, 345
West Indies, 58
*Westfalen*, German dreadnought, 230, 322, 323
*Weymouth*, British light cruiser, 104
Whitby, 120, 211

White Star Line, 153
Whitehead, torpedo manufacturer, 35
Wiegand, Karl von, journalist, 137
*Wien*, Austro-Hungarian pre-dreadnought battleship, 289, 318
*Wiesbaden*, German light cruiser, 219, 220, 221, 223
Wight, Isle of, 53
Wilhelmshaven, 8, 52, 58, 64, 114, 117, 118, 120, 123, 129, 144, 189, 195, 205, 206, 208, 210, 211, 213, 217, 221, 223, 224, 227, 229, 230, 232, 233, 279, 287, 288, 289, 290, 292, 293, 307, 310, 315, 330, 332, 341, 344, 345
*Wilkes*, American destroyer, 259
William I, king of Prussia and German emperor, 8, 9
William II, king of Prussia and German emperor
  abdication of, 348
  and defeat of Germany, 336, 342, 348
  and dismissal of Bismarck, 13
  and prewar naval expansion, 11
  and Scheer, 205, 227, 228, 233, 332, 335, 348
  and submarine warfare, 139, 141, 151, 152, 154, 155, 157, 242, 338
  and Tirpitz, 14, 154
  and wartime fleet deployments, 95, 101, 117, 127, 128, 205, 292, 332
  pictured, 188
  promotes wireless technology, 33
  recognized as supreme allied commander, 231
  views of, concerning Britain, 10, 12
  visits of, to foreign ports and bases, 55, 96, 113, 289
Williamson, Samuel, historian, 54
Wilmot-Smith, A., British officer, 163
Wilson, Sir Arthur, British admiral, 35
Wilson, Woodrow, US president
  and submarine warfare, 140, 141, 149, 150, 151, 152, 153, 154, 157, 158, 159, 247, 248
  criticizes British policies, 158, 163
  and interned German shipping, 159, 160
  and loans to Allies, 161
  reelection of (1916), 247, 352
  breaks relations with Germany, 248
  asks Congress to declare war, 249, 250
  and Russian revolutions, 250, 310
  embargoes trade with Germany, 251
  and naval expansion, 251, 359, 360
  as wartime leader, 252, 253, 270, 271
  Fourteen Points of, 309, 310, 313, 337, 338, 352, 359, 366
  and Armistice talks, 342
  signs Versailles Treaty, 358
Windau (Ventspils), 195, 196, 198, 199
Windhoek, 34
Wireless Telegraph and Signal Company, 32
wireless telegraphy
  prewar development of, 30–34
  wartime use of, 62, 64, 71, 72, 73, 75, 78, 79, 83, 84, 86, 87, 97, 98, 100, 121, 123, 147, 180, 196, 214, 225, 232, 245, 246, 263, 332, 339, 354, 355
*Wittelsbach*, German pre-dreadnought battleship, 190, 195
Wrangel, Baron Peter, Russian general, 350
Wright brothers, American aviators, 47
*Wyandra* (ex-*Baralong*), British Q-ship, 163

Yalu, Battle of the (1894), 38, 39
Yap, 64, 72, 84
*Yavuz Sultan Selim* (ex-*Goeben*), Turkish battle cruiser, 95, 105, 106, 107, 108, 109, 110, 111, 112, 172, 173, 177, 178, 186, 187, 188, 235, 236, 284, 325, 326, 327, 328, 350, 367
Yellow Sea, Battle of the (1904), 40, 41
Yemen, 88
*Yenisei*, Russian minelayer, 194
Yokohama, 66
Yokosuka, 60
*Yorck*, German armored cruiser, 120
*Yorck*, German supply ship, 74
Young Turks ("Committee of Union and Progress"), 101

Yugoslav national council, 290, 311, 340, 341, 349

Zanzibar, 87
*Zaria Svobody* (ex-*Imperator Aleksandr II*), Russian pre-dreadnought battleship, 305
Zeebrugge, 165, 202, 232, 241, 269, 310, 336
  raid on (1918), 331, 332
Zeiss, German optics manufacturer, 38
*Zélée*, French gunboat, 71
Zenker, Wolfgang, German officer, 345, 346
*Zenta*, Austro-Hungarian light cruiser, 129
Zeppelin, Count Ferdinand, German airship pioneer, 47
*Zhemchug*, Russian light cruiser, 59, 87
Zimmermann, Arthur, German foreign secretary, 243
  telegram, 249, 250
Zionists, 94
Zipperer von Arbach, Austro-Hungarian officer, 312, 315
Zonguldak, 109, 111, 177, 186, 187, 237